Studies in Diplomacy and International Relations

General Editors: **Donna Lee**, Senior Lecturer in International Organisations and International Political Economy, University of Birmingham, UK and **Paul Sharp**, Professor of Political Science and Director of the Alworth Institute for International Studies at the University of Minnesota, Duluth, USA

The series was launched as Studies in Diplomacy in 1994 under the general editorship of G.R. Berridge. Its purpose is to encourage original scholarship on all aspects of the theory and practice of diplomacy. The new editors assumed their duties in 2003 with a mandate to maintain this focus while also publishing research which demonstrates the importance of diplomacy to contemporary international relations more broadly conceived.

Titles include:

G.R. Berridge (*editor*)
DIPLOMATIC CLASSICS
Selected Texts from Commynes to Vattel

G.R. Berridge, Maurice Keens-Soper and T.G. Otte
DIPLOMATIC THEORY FROM MACHIAVELLI TO KISSINGER

Herman J. Cohen
INTERVENING IN AFRICA
Superpower Peacemaking in a Troubled Continent

Andrew F. Cooper (*editor*)
NICHE DIPLOMACY
Middle Powers after the Cold War

Mai'a K. Davis Cross
THE EUROPEAN DIPLOMATIC CORPS
Diplomats and International Cooperation from Westphalia to Maastricht

David H. Dunn (*editor*)
DIPLOMACY AT THE HIGHEST LEVEL
The Evolution of International Summitry

Brian Hocking (*editor*)
FOREIGN MINISTRIES
Change and Adaptation

Brian Hocking and David Spence (*editors*)
FOREIGN MINISTRIES IN THE EUROPEAN UNION
Integrating Diplomats

Michael Hughes
DIPLOMACY BEFORE THE RUSSIAN REVOLUTION
Britain, Russia and the Old Diplomacy, 1894–1917

Gaynor Johnson
THE BERLIN EMBASSY OF LORD D'ABERNON, 1920–1926

Christer Jönsson and Martin Hall
ESSENCE OF DIPLOMACY

Donna Lee
MIDDLE POWERS AND COMMERCIAL DIPLOMACY
British Influence at the Kennedy Trade Round

Donna Lee, Ian Taylor and Paul D. Williams (*editors*)
THE NEW MULTILATERALISM IN SOUTH AFRICAN DIPLOMACY

Mario Liverani
INTERNATIONAL RELATIONS IN THE ANCIENT NEAR EAST, 1600–1100 BC

Jan Melissen (*editor*)
INNOVATION IN DIPLOMATIC PRACTICE
Soft Power in International Relations

THE NEW PUBLIC DIPLOMACY
Soft Power in International Relations

Peter Neville
APPEASING HITLER
The Diplomacy of Sir Nevile Henderson, 1937–39

M.J. Peterson
RECOGNITION OF GOVERNMENTS
Legal Doctrine and State Practice, 1815–1995

Gary D. Rawnsley
RADIO DIPLOMACY AND PROPAGANDA
The BBC and VOA in International Politics, 1956–64

TAIWAN'S INFORMAL DIPLOMACY AND PROPAGANDA

Ronald A. Walker
MULTILATERAL CONFERENCES
Purposeful International Negotiation

A. Nuri Yurdusev (*editor*)
OTTOMAN DIPLOMACY
Conventional or Unconventional?

Studies in Diplomacy and International Relations
Series Standing Order ISBN 0–333–71495–4
(*outside North America only*)

You can receive future titles in this series as they are published by placing a standing order. Please contact your bookseller or, in case of difficulty, write to us at the address below with your name and address, the title of the series and the ISBN quoted above.

Customer Services Department, Macmillan Distribution Ltd, Houndmills, Basingstoke, Hampshire RG21 6XS, England

The European Diplomatic Corps

Diplomats and International Cooperation from Westphalia to Maastricht

Mai'a K. Davis Cross
Assistant Professor of Political Science
Colgate University, USA

© Mai'a K. Davis Cross 2007

All rights reserved. No reproduction, copy or transmission of this publication may be made without written permission.

No paragraph of this publication may be reproduced, copied or transmitted save with written permission or in accordance with the provisions of the Copyright, Designs and Patents Act 1988, or under the terms of any licence permitting limited copying issued by the Copyright Licensing Agency, 90 Tottenham Court Road, London W1T 4LP.

Any person who does any unauthorised act in relation to this publication may be liable to criminal prosecution and civil claims for damages.

The author has asserted her right to be identified as the author of this work in accordance with the Copyright, Designs and Patents Act 1988.

First published 2007 by
PALGRAVE MACMILLAN
Houndmills, Basingstoke, Hampshire RG21 6XS and
175 Fifth Avenue, New York, N.Y. 10010
Companies and representatives throughout the world

PALGRAVE MACMILLAN is the global academic imprint of the Palgrave Macmillan division of St. Martin's Press, LLC and of Palgrave Macmillan Ltd. Macmillan® is a registered trademark in the United States, United Kingdom and other countries. Palgrave is a registered trademark in the European Union and other countries.

ISBN-13: 978–0–230–50075–4 hardback
ISBN-10: 0–230–50075–7 hardback

This book is printed on paper suitable for recycling and made from fully managed and sustained forest sources.

A catalogue record for this book is available from the British Library.

Library of Congress Cataloging-in-Publication Data
Cross, Mai'a K. Davis, 1977–
    The European diplomatic corps : diplomats and international cooperation from Westphalia to Maastricht / Mai'a K. Davis Cross.
        p. cm. — (Studies in diplomacy)
    Includes bibliographical references and index.
    ISBN 0–230–50075–7 (cloth)
    1. Diplomacy—History. 2. Diplomats—Europe—History. I. Title.
JZ1410.C76 2007
327.4—dc22   2006048313

10 9 8 7 6 5 4 3 2 1
16 15 14 13 12 11 10 09 08 07

Printed and bound in Great Britain by
Antony Rowe Ltd, Chippenham and Eastbourne

For my parents and Robert

Contents

List of Tables	ix
List of Figures	x
Acknowledgments	xi

1	**An Epistemic Community of Diplomats**	**1**
	Introduction	1
	Diplomacy and foreign policy	3
	The theoretical framework	5
	Methodology	8
2	**The Diplomatic Dialogue: Between Power and Cooperation**	**13**
	Alternative explanations for international cooperation	13
	Diplomats as an epistemic community	22
	Structural constraints on diplomats: Rules, norms, and organizations	28
	The case studies	31
3	**The Seventeenth Century and the Treaty of Westphalia**	**35**
	Climate of the times: The emergence of international society	35
	The European corps: Seventeenth century	36
	The lead-up to the Peace of Westphalia	45
	The Congress of Westphalia	48
	The epistemic community of diplomats	60
	Diplomatic agency	61
	The aftermath of Westphalia	65
4	**The Late Nineteenth Century and the Congress of Berlin**	**68**
	Climate of the times	68
	The society of diplomats	69
	The lead-up to the Congress of Berlin 1875–78	80
	The Congress of Berlin	82
	The negotiations	84
	The epistemic community of diplomats	97
	Diplomatic agency	100
	The aftermath of Berlin	103
5	**The Early Twentieth Century and the Treaty of Versailles**	**105**
	Climate of the times	105
	The society of diplomats	107

The lead-up to World War I 119
The negotiations 120
The epistemic community of diplomats: The commissions 134
Diplomatic agency 136
Conclusion 137

6 **The Late Twentieth Century and the Treaty on European Union** 139
Climate of the times 139
The society of diplomats 142
The lead-up to Maastricht: European Political Union 154
The negotiations 156
The Maastricht ratification process 174
Diplomatic agency 174
Conclusion 176

7 **The Twenty-first Century European Corps** 179
Climate of the times: Euro-skepticism 179
The diplomatic epistemic community: A cross-time comparison 180
Trends across time 186
Democracy or deception? 188
Toward a single voice: European diplomacy with the world 190

Notes 191

Bibliography 215

Index 232

List of Tables

3.1	Approximate size of armies in 1648	63
4.1	Alliances and treaties in effect at the Congress of Berlin regarding the Eastern Question	83
4.2	Plenipotentiaries and state leaders during the Congress of Berlin	86
5.1	Annual salary in 1914 according to rank for British diplomats	111
5.2	Major attendees at the Paris Peace Conference	121
6.1	Summary of the proposed changes to create CFSP, provided by the Spanish delegation	158
6.2	Summary: Diplomat delegations' initial negotiation stances founded on state preferences	159
6.3	Approximate order of negotiation stances from least federal to most federal	160
6.4	Note (8 November 1991) outlining the differences between the French–German and the English–Italian texts	168
6.5	Statesmen and diplomats involved in the Maastricht negotiations	177
7.1	Summary of results	181
7.2	Autonomy vs. agency	184
7.3	Examples of diplomatic agency against state instructions	185

List of Figures

1.1 Epistemic community as an independent variable for diplomatic agency in outcomes of international cooperation — 6
3.1 Europe after the treaties of Westphalia — 47
4.1 Europe after the Congress of Berlin 1878 — 84
6.1 Council of the European Union organizational chart — 144

Acknowledgments

I would like to acknowledge Ezra Suleiman, Kate McNamara, G. John Ikenberry, Andrew Moravcsik, Gary Bass, Aaron Friedberg, and Theodore Rabb for their guidance at Princeton. A special thanks to Ezra for sending me to Sciences Po and advising my dissertation from beginning to end. Thanks to the members of Coreper who gave me the opportunity to interview them. Also, Ejner Stendevad and Poul Christoffersen provided me with invaluable background information. I received special funding for this project from Princeton's Bradley Fellowship, Institute for International and Regional Studies, and the Program in Contemporary European Politics and Society, as well as the Research Council at Colgate University. For their work in the final preparation of the manuscript, I would like to thank John Morris and Jake Kawatski. Most importantly, my parents gave me the opportunity to pursue my studies (and everything else) in the first place, and Robert made it especially fun.

1
An Epistemic Community of Diplomats

Introduction

This book attempts to explain the significance of diplomats as agents of cooperation among states. It tells four different stories, each of a critical point in history, to illustrate how and why (or why not) diplomats in Western Europe have directly impacted the outcomes of international cooperation. Diplomats are defined as high-level government officials engaged in professional interaction as plenipotentiaries on the transnational level.[1] They represent their home states and are often called upon by state leaders to negotiate at international meetings and to write treaties. I argue that diplomats constitute an *epistemic community*, which, according to the definition offered by Peter Haas, is "a network of professionals with recognized expertise and competence in a particular domain and an authoritative claim to policy-relevant knowledge within that domain or issue area."[2] The concept of an epistemic community has thus far not been applied to diplomats, but I argue that this is an appropriate and useful expansion of the concept. Although diplomats start out as generalists, they quickly acquire specific expertise in their assigned region; from the start, they are professional experts at negotiation procedure, relationship building among nations, and the art of compromise. In the international system, they are the quintessential actors who resolve conditions of uncertainty in international cooperation and impact changes in the definition of state interests.

In a special issue of *International Organization* (1992), Peter Haas, Emanuel Adler, G. John Ikenberry, and others fully detail the importance of a research agenda based on epistemic communities.[3] They conclude, "We also offer a research program with which students of world politics can empirically study the role of ideas in international relations."[4] Since then, little work has gone into developing the concept of epistemic community in political science, both in midrange theorizing and in empirical research.[5] One way to bring the epistemic community literature closer to the forefront of political science theories is to focus on those actors central to the international decision-making process.

Thus far, the concept of epistemic community has been reserved for scientific or technical groups.[6] In the same issue of *IO*, Ethan Barnaby Kapstein writes about the policy convergence among central bankers from different countries during the crisis of the international payments system of the 1980s, but he declines to consider these central bankers as an epistemic community. The reason for this, he argues, is that they not only engaged in rigorous scientific investigation, but also made political decisions.[7] However, there is more potential in this concept than has been realized, and to tap into this potential, a reconceptualization is necessary. A new interpretation for epistemic community is offered here which includes consideration of nonscientific or technical groups, as well as those who directly impact political decision-making. In addition, an epistemic community is not simply considered to exist or not exist by virtue of a particular kind and level of knowledge, but is characterized by strength or weakness. Shared knowledge or expertise in a particular domain can be abundant or not, depending on the social background, selection, and training of the members. A strong epistemic community is defined as a cohesive group with strong professional norms, high status, and homogeneity, whereas a weak epistemic community has overall low status, weak norms, and heterogeneity among members. It is important to recognize that epistemic communities may range from nascent to fully established, and their strength may change over time depending on how often they hold meetings and interact to reinforce their cohesion. Most importantly, epistemic communities may actually be a part of the policy process, rather than just tangential to it. Under this interpretation, Kapstein's central bankers may be considered an epistemic community, although not technically strong at the time. The significant scholarly debate about the purpose, definition, and method pertaining to the concept of epistemic community will be addressed more fully in Chapter 2.

Are European diplomats agents of international cooperation or simply transmission belts for states? The argument that follows, in brief, is that the epistemic community's degree of cohesion in large part determines whether diplomats exercise agency during international meetings. When statesmen or national governments delegate authority to diplomats, this delegation is defined as autonomy. When diplomats act beyond this autonomy in ways that statesmen do not anticipate, they have exercised agency. Thus, if the epistemic community of diplomats is weak, diplomats tend to act within their delegated autonomy, and thus states themselves tend to dictate outcomes of international cooperation, using their diplomats as transmission belts.

Many scholars argue that diplomats exist simply to minimize transaction costs of negotiations among states, thus they facilitate accomplishment of the Pareto optimum.[8] Others argue that diplomats do not matter at all because outcomes of international relations simply reflect relative power. By contrast, I argue that diplomats can have an impact on international relations since processes of negotiation and persuasion often result in outcomes that do not conform to neorealist, neofunctionalist, or bargaining-theory explanations. In the next chapter, the theoretical debate about the role or nonrole of epistemic communities and diplomats will be fully addressed.

Diplomacy and foreign policy

First, to provide an overview of this book, I begin with a critical distinction first made by Harold Nicolson in 1939, and subsequently by Adam Watson some thirty years ago.[9] This distinction is between diplomacy as foreign policy and diplomacy as the *process* of negotiation and deliberation that promotes peace and cooperation among states.[10] Diplomacy as foreign policy is simply the expressed desire of states to use words before force. It is the default mode of operation for liberal states, and it is often the aim among nonliberal states to engage in diplomacy if they seek acceptance in international politics. However, diplomacy as foreign policy only captures a superficial element of the workings of international relations, and it encompasses a great number of international activities that do not include processes of cooperation. For example, states can engage in such unilateral contact as propaganda, espionage, and political or economic intervention. They can also engage in violent contact such as threat, deterrence, and economic war.[11]

Among early political scientists, the word "diplomacy" was used interchangeably with "international relations." Realists today use the word to describe how states receive information about relative power or threat before engaging in war. Liberals talk about diplomacy in terms of how interstate dialogue aids in differentiating the "other" or the nonliberal states from themselves. Neoliberal institutionalists speak of diplomacy in terms of its function. Their argument is that it promotes information exchange and reduces transaction costs for governments to produce the most efficient, interest-maximizing outcomes for states belonging to international institutions. These broad definitions of diplomacy are not only vastly different, but conceptually vague. With the ambiguity and inaccuracy inherent in arguments based on relative power, alternatives must be examined.

Following Harold Nicolson's definition of diplomacy as "management of international relations by negotiation,"[12] Adam Watson defines diplomacy as "the process of dialogue and negotiation by which states in a system conduct their relations and pursue their purposes by means short of war."[13] The definition of diplomacy as "the dialogue between independent states," must be made more specific. How do states have a dialogue, and does it matter that this dialogue takes place? Is diplomacy merely foreign policy of states or an ongoing process of dialogue among diplomats? Diplomacy as simply foreign policy, as an end in itself, does not exist in the real world. Diplomats are people with individual and collective agency who interact over time. Every diplomat is the product of a rich historical tradition of norms, negotiation, and representation. As can be observed in world politics today and in the past, whether the country is democratic, communist, or authoritarian, diplomacy is really a dialogue among people assigned to the job – the diplomats.

Watson rightly points out that it is important to distinguish between the power of the state and its ability to persuade through diplomatic means.[14] A definition of diplomacy as a dialogue among states may disguise the fact that there is this all-important disjuncture between power and cooperation. Relative power may play a role in determining whether or not state leaders decide to try to cooperate, but persuasion is, to a significant extent, out of the grasp of power. The ability to persuade is in the hands of the diplomats. This has most recently been evident in the mammoth efforts of Colin Powell to sell the Bush policies – often relying more on the perception of his own independence and public respect to bring some credibility to a policy that is otherwise resisted. This occurred perhaps most notably in the United Nations debates over the Iraq war, where some distancing by Powell lent his assurances credibility. Whether diplomats are successful in persuading depends in large part on whether they exercise agency. State instructions to diplomats rarely coincide with the situations that diplomats face at the negotiating table, and decisions need to be made on the spot taking full advantage of the relationships cultivated within the diplomatic epistemic community. Thus, diplomacy is defined here more narrowly as the operations of professional diplomats.

The cases in the following chapters capture precisely this process that occurs between the two points of power and cooperation. The main argument in this regard is that the time period during which persuasion occurs (primarily during meetings to conduct international negotiation) is just as important as the circumstances that lead up to the creation of the diplomatic corps. For example, who the diplomats are, whether they have interacted on prior occasions, what kind of training they have received, how they were selected, their skill level, and so on are all important. The lead-up to episodes of persuasion, even before the issues are known, can make or break the negotiations, even if everyone involved in devising the foreign policy has the full intention of cooperating. Naturally, the power and resources of each state has a bearing on the leverage diplomats have in negotiation, but outcomes still rest on the abilities of individual diplomats, and their dynamic as a collective. Perceptions of power, not actual power, are the key to any form of international relations whether in war or peace.[15] Diplomats may often contribute to such perceptions.

While political science has emphasized the success or failure of cooperation, the winners and losers, and the role of international organizations in creating efficient outcomes, very little study has gone into the actual processes of cooperation by the individuals, usually diplomats, who create and carry through the terms of international agreements.[16] This is the process of diplomacy, as opposed to diplomacy as foreign policy.

The theoretical framework

Are European diplomats agents of international cooperation or simply transmission belts for states?[17] What variables most contribute to successful diplomatic compromise? Diplomatic epistemic communities are also affected by structures, defined as the international rules or institutions that diplomats must abide by. What is the relationship between the structures constraining diplomats and their agency in making decisions? The nature of diplomatic agency and its impact on international cooperation are the main issues addressed in the empirical work of this book. Diplomatic agency can be seen at the level of the individual diplomat or at the level of the collective diplomatic corps, but the distinction is highly interrelated. It is difficult for an individual diplomat to exercise agency if no other diplomat will pay attention to him. Rather, the historical evidence shows that diplomats will individually exercise agency when they are strong as a collective.[18]

To understand the emergence and strength of the epistemic community during any given period of time, the primary independent variables that I consider to be contributing factors to the strength or weakness of the epistemic community of diplomats are meeting frequency among diplomats, social background (class- and education-based), training, and professional status.[19] Diplomats who meet more frequently prior to negotiations develop a rapport as well as working and personal relationships. Diplomats of similar social background are more easily able to share and appreciate each other's worldviews, and this facilitates action as a collective corps. Many diplomats, starting from the early twentieth century, attend the same universities and undergo a similar selection process, and these factors clearly contribute to maintaining a similar social background across the European diplomatic corps. Training for diplomats is a continuation of earlier education, but it also contributes strongly to a greater degree of professionalization and cohesion. Status affects recruitment and self-selection for the post, and is also indicative of the autonomy and trust state leaders are willing to grant to diplomats.

Shared professional norms allow diplomats to persuade each other, to reach consensus amongst themselves, and in large part to constitute the epistemic community of diplomats. Shared professional norms are defined as the protocol, procedure, and norms of consensus that diplomats share in common. They are distinguished from shared worldviews among diplomats, which refer to their substantive causal values about the operations of international relations. For example, European Union (EU) diplomats could share a worldview that more authority should be ceded from the member-state level to the supranational level of governance. However, in this project, norms do not include worldviews; they are confined to norms governing the professional interaction *within* the epistemic community. Depending on the strength of the epistemic community, diplomats will exercise agency at instances of major negotiations (Figure 1.1).

International meetings constitute critical points in time in which diplomats achieve cooperation on behalf of their states. Thus, episodes of international negotiation are the mechanism by which diplomats exercise agency.[20] The outcome of each meeting defines the extent to which diplomatic agency contributed to the treaty stipulations. A strong diplomatic epistemic community leads to agency and is reflected in the outcomes included in treaties.[21] Are the outcomes different from state instructions to diplomats? Was the process itself dictated by states or left in the hands of diplomats? To what extent did diplomatic agency result in outcomes unanticipated by statesmen? Ultimately, it is necessary to understand the processes leading up to and including the international meetings of diplomats to predict outcomes. The evidence in the following chapters shows why and to what degree diplomats impact outcomes of international cooperation through a cross-time comparison of diplomacy and international diplomatic meetings in Western Europe.

The existence of a cohesive transnational community of diplomats in Europe points to one major example of an explosion in the twentieth-century growth of epistemic communities, and it is an example that brings to light important international issues and policy choices. Many other epistemic communities – such as lawyers, judges, finance ministers, environmentalists, human rights activists, and bureaucrats – interact with the diplomatic epistemic community, particularly in today's global world.

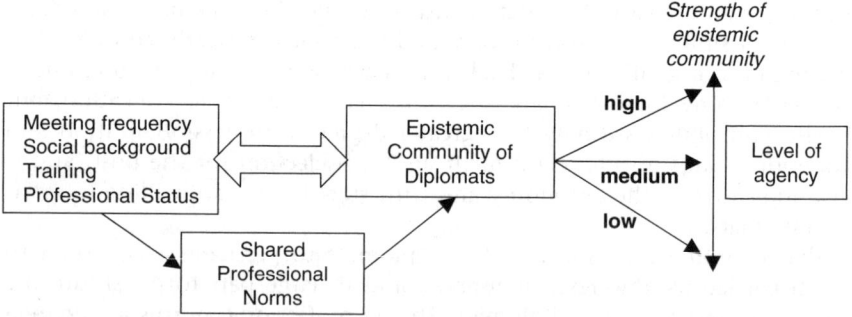

Figure 1.1 Epistemic community as an independent variable for diplomatic agency in outcomes of international cooperation (*Note*: Chapter 7 contains a summary chart of the four cases with the variables and outcomes labeled as high, medium, or low for each time period.)

They often possess the same qualities that define diplomatic epistemic communities and even share professional norms.[22]

Why is the study of epistemic communities in general, and of the diplomatic community in particular, so important? Europeanists tend to focus on smaller elements of EU epistemic communities, such as communication networks,[23] social networks based on symbolic interactionism,[24] or simply a shared solidarity (*esprit de corps*).[25] However, this narrow focus tends to leave out important factors that are part of the very genesis of a transnational network, such as professional status, meeting frequency, and social background (including the selection and training that go along with this). By including expertise and professionalism as important criteria, the concept of epistemic community goes beyond simple consideration of shared social, communication, or symbolic interactions to become a more dynamic theory.

In addition, the impact of diplomatic agency has major implications for modern theories that see outcomes of international relations as only the consequence of state actions and intent. This book questions the effectiveness of two competing and widely held viewpoints in the political science literature. First, and more broadly, the neorealist argument is that diplomats have no role in determining outcomes because states are the only actors in the international system and outcomes always reflect relative power and self-interest. While relative power considerations may occasionally determine the issues brought to the negotiation table, they do not determine international cooperation outcomes.

Second, bargaining theory predicts that diplomats are important to outcomes of international cooperation because they reduce transaction costs in negotiations among states and exercise delegated autonomy (as opposed to agency) to accomplish this.[26] Transaction costs consist of the expense and inefficiency that would be involved in international cooperation if the principals (statesmen), as nonexpert negotiators, were to conduct all foreign policy on their own. Rather than discounting the role of diplomats altogether, bargaining theory assumes that diplomats are useful and autonomous. Otherwise, why would they exist?

It is not necessarily true that bargaining theory never predicts outcomes. However, it is significantly inadequate to explain all outcomes, particularly when diplomats go beyond their delegated autonomy to exercise agency. As noted above, I define autonomy as the amount of decision-making space given to them by statesmen or international rules. Agency, however, is demonstrated when diplomats go beyond their space and take more decision-making into their own hands than they were given. In effect, autonomy is the reason they have jobs, but agency is what they do with the job that statesmen did not expect. Through the methodology of historical process tracing, it is possible to identify when diplomats go beyond their autonomy to exercise agency in ways not predicted by bargaining theory. However, this book is not primarily about bargaining theory, although it examines in part the related phenomenon of international decision-making. The focus here is explicitly on the dynamics of the European epistemic community of diplomats, the conditions that determine whether it is, overall, strong or weak, and the implications of this community. The reason for this departure from bargaining theory and rational choice is that they are largely overdeterministic and, as many scholars have argued, advance a snapshot view.[27] By ignoring factors such as relationships among negotiators, professional background, expertise, and shared normative frameworks many scholars pass up explanatory power.

I argue that diplomats are actors in their own right, and constitute a transnational community with shared norms and worldviews. The stronger the epistemic community of diplomats, the more likely it is that they will reach agreements, though not necessarily ones that may benefit the common good of all states.[28] Constructivism is the main perspective in political science that does advance specific, midrange theories that offer predictions about how processes and norms among transnational communities impact outcomes of international cooperation in concrete ways.[29] The focus of constructivist work has been on both governmental and nongovernmental actors. This perspective has elucidated the role of influential *norm entrepreneurs*[30] as well as a variety of international agents who are not simply extensions of the realist or functionalist power play among states. I argue that diplomats are not only norm entrepreneurs, but also at times key actors in their own right in the international arena.

The goal of this research is ultimately to explain the role of diplomacy in today's EU, predict its future importance for Europe and other regions, and pave the way for the development of effective international regimes and policies in other regions. For example, several multilateral organizations exist in the East Asian region, but they are mostly hollow with little power to implement multilateral initiatives. What explains this difference? Is the case of Europe necessarily exceptional? The prospects for future application of this project will be discussed more thoroughly in the conclusion.

Methodology

A powerful way of understanding the present is to take a historical, comparative approach to test the key determining variables for why diplomats have agency and to investigate to what degree and how this impacts cooperation. The research design is historical process tracing with case studies. While a cross-time comparison may not be useful in all political science topics, diplomacy is distinctive for its continuity over time alongside dramatic change. Thus, it is an ideal topic for a cross-time analysis; its fundamentals remain, while it adapts to the climate of the times. Because the degree of cohesion varies considerably over time, a historical approach provides a natural method of weighing the importance of the variables that contribute to a cohesive epistemic community of diplomats, as well as identifying possible trends.

The methodology combines historical sociology, interpretivism, and causal inference. Historical sociology is an important qualitative method among international-relations scholars that emphasizes history as a means of problematizing present-day phenomena. The aim of historical sociology is to rethink how we see the present, not by assuming that the past repeats itself, but by providing the context for today's world. Historical sociology uses historical process tracing to link events causally. The research in this project is based on semistructured ambassadorial interviews,[31] secondary research,[32] archival work,[33] and governmental documents.[34] Much political science research that deals with history has been criticized for lacking rigor, yet theories are greatly enhanced through a consideration of the past. As Clausewitz writes, "Historical examples clarify everything and also provide the best kind of proof in the empirical sciences."[35]

The second methodology employed here is interpretivism, which involves elements of descriptive inference or thick description. The focus on thick description enables consideration of multiple socially constructed realities.[36] In this project, the aim is to understand the complexity of diplomatic epistemic communities rather than to simplify them. The research is engaged in understanding the subjective view of the diplomats themselves, to understand their socially constructed reality. The interpretivist approach is the best method to understand the prior composition of the epistemic community of diplomats, which relies heavily on social construction and shared normative frameworks. The interviews conducted for this project were more conversational than close-ended. They are used as a source of insight for my hypotheses rather than for testing the hypotheses.[37]

The independent variables examined at both levels of the theory are structured as *family-resemblance* concepts as opposed to necessary and sufficient concepts.[38] That is, not all of the independent variables must have a high level of presence in order for the epistemic community of diplomats to be strong. There is naturally a sufficiency minimum, which I measure through descriptive inference in each case study. If all of the independent variables belonging to the family-resemblance group are present at high levels, then it is likely that the epistemic community will be strong. However, in cases when not all the variables are present at high levels, it is the overall combination of the presence and strength of the independent variables that indicate the strength of the epistemic community. At the same time, the epistemic community itself serves as an independent variable; it is mutually constitutive with status, training, social background, meeting frequency, and shared professional norms. In effect, the passing of time is an implicit variable in this project. Over time, diplomats have professionalized their own profession. Thus, as an epistemic community, they play a strong role in the formation of future diplomatic corps across Europe.

The third methodology is causal inference. Positivistic causality is an important aim of this study, although it is confined largely to the second part of the argument. Rather than using causal inference to understand the prior composition of the epistemic community of diplomats, which I argue is largely mutually constitutive, I engage in causal inference to understand how the strength or weakness of the epistemic community impacts outcomes of international cooperation during particular instances of negotiation. I still engage in process tracing, but I show a causal relationship between the strength of the epistemic community and outcomes. Simply looking at outcomes and comparing them to starting positions as snapshots does not elucidate motivations and causal mechanisms. The methodology of historical process tracing seeks to determine often-unobservable causal mechanisms by looking at the observable.[39] Although process tracing is less parsimonious than other forms of data analysis, it also tends to be less error prone than large-scale comparisons with broad generalizations.

The second part of the argument can also be part of a larger family-resemblance group. There may hypothetically be other reasons why diplomats exercise collective agency besides the strength of their epistemic community, though these would be rare cases. For example, another possible trigger for diplomatic agency could be a coincidence of preferences different from state interests that diplomats happen to share *despite* a weak epistemic community. Additionally, a strong epistemic community of diplomats may happen to agree entirely with state instructions and all state instructions from different countries may happen to be the same. Thus, it is possible to conceive of an epistemic community of diplomats (the independent variable) as a member of a larger family-resemblance group, but these other potential concepts are rare and beyond the scope of this book. This study considers the phenomenon of epistemic communities on a strength–weakness continuum rather than the dichotomous manner typical of necessary and sufficient concepts. A sufficiency minimum requires a cut-off point which dichotomizes the argument, but it is not necessary to define one here because a diplomatic epistemic community does not simply exist or not exist.[40] Thus, a family-resemblance methodological approach to the concepts examined here is the most suitable.

There are certain important scope conditions for consideration of the diplomats who constitute the epistemic community. They tend to be of the ambassadorial or deputy-ambassadorial rank as these diplomats are actually granted plenipotentiary power or autonomy by statesmen. Diplomats of lower rank are not generally granted any decision-making power and are not relevant to this study. The diplomats, for the most part, reside in Western Europe, but European diplomats in non-European countries are considered part of the overall epistemic community of diplomats if they correspond regularly with those engaged in major negotiations. However, they are tangential to the process of negotiation they do not attend. It is important to recognize the role of diplomats who contribute to negotiations from a distance. Naturally, some diplomats are more prone than others to foster transnational relationships, but it is the overall strength of the epistemic community that is critical to understanding outcomes.

Overall, the research design of this project is a cross-time study of the Western European region, tracing the changes in the diplomatic corps over time: (1) to observe the external impact of technology, regime change, and emergence of international organizations on the diplomatic epistemic community;[41] (2) to generalize about the potential impact of the variables contributing to the socialization and professionalization of diplomats; and (3) to suggest future trends. Not only is the whole project historically oriented, but each individual case study takes a longer-term historical approach rather than a snapshot, before–after approach.[42] However, it is important to note that this study is not path dependent, as this approach tends to discount human agency and the actors' ability to create unexpected paths of decision-making over time and to reverse their decision-making. Paul Pierson argues that once actors make a decision it is irreversible, and particular paths drop out of the realm of possibility. However, through the course of a single negotiation or in history more generally, diplomats often reverse their decisions or take a different path to a particular outcome.

Each case is designed to decipher the strength or weakness of the epistemic community and to deal with the counterfactual or alternative arguments provided by bargaining theory and neorealism. According to bargaining theory, supranational actors do not play a significant role in outcomes of international cooperation because national governments have interest-maximizing preferences that they rank according to the conditions of the negotiation and relative power. If they must compromise, national governments will only make concessions based on their rank-ordered preferences, thus it is possible to predict outcomes on the Pareto frontier.[43] This argument can be treated as counterfactual because it assumes the nonexistence of an epistemic community of diplomats. Bargaining theory will be explained more fully in the second chapter. The cases also deal more broadly with the neorealist alternative argument, which works from the null-hypothesis that diplomats do not matter at all. Neorealism can also be used to develop a counterfactual argument as it also assumes that outcomes can be predicted without consideration of the existence of an epistemic community of diplomats. Although some scholars now consider neorealism to be a straw-man argument, it is important to address this argument because it is still the dominant view of international relations.

The following research brings to light the ample evidence of diplomatic correspondence, meeting transcripts, governmental documents, state instructions, and historical context to decipher the causes of diplomatic processes and the outcomes of international cooperation. This book not only seeks to fill a gap in the literature about the processes of international cooperation, but also to offer some useful new insights about the role of transnational groups in international society. Are the international policy outcomes of these meetings or congresses of diplomats divergent from initial state preferences and instructions to diplomats? If deliberation among diplomats actually occurs, why is it or is it not successful? In the lead-up to the creation of the Treaty of Versailles, deliberation occurred but diplomatic status had fallen, making it impossible for diplomats to persuade recalcitrant state leaders. During other time periods, state leaders, Cabinet members, and kings believed in the effectiveness of diplomats as skillful, professional negotiators. These leaders, each sitting in his or her own seat of power, were often not acutely aware of the grander transnational network among their own diplomats and those of other states. However, entire archives of evidence show that its overarching presence, whether weak or strong, made the network bigger than its component parts, and many times an actor in its own right.

Many scholars, the media, and society in general tend to assume that diplomats, as professional negotiators, mediators, and coordinators, are decreasing in relevance because technology and globalization make the world a faster, smaller place. Why send a team of diplomats to meet with their counterparts in foreign countries when the leader of a country can simply pick up the phone and speak to the leader of another country? Many statesmen recognize that diplomacy is as necessary as ever, and to ignore the value of diplomacy is to take great risks with foreign relations. It is precisely because of globalization that there are many new issues on the table, powerful international organizations in place, and a multitude of transnational actors impacting political choices and policy decisions. Consequently, there is a general increase in the number of diplomats acting as envoys to international organizations. Alongside the renewal of the profession brought about by changes in global politics and the consolidation of international organizations, diplomats maintain many of the qualities, norms, protocols, and behavior that characterized them in the sixteenth and seventeenth centuries. It was popular in the 1950s and 1960s among historians to describe the somewhat surprising simultaneous evolution and stasis of the diplomatic role, but a new exploration of diplomacy with due regard to contemporary theories of political science is of the utmost importance.

2
The Diplomatic Dialogue: Between Power and Cooperation

Why is it important to investigate diplomats as an epistemic community? What does the concept of epistemic community explain that other theories of cooperation do not explain? If an epistemic community of diplomats does exist, what are the implications for our understanding of international cooperation? To answer these questions, it is important to first review the political science literature pertaining to international cooperation and negotiation more generally. Three broad categories of theories seek to explain these outcomes: neorealism, bargaining theory, and constructivism. This book builds upon the work of sociologists, organizational theorists, and constructivists as these approaches provide more explanatory power. Scholars from these fields have made substantial progress in the investigation of transnational networks, shared ideas, and shared causal beliefs, qualities critical to epistemic communities.

Although the neorealist school faces serious criticisms, it is necessary to fully engage this approach in investigating any theory of cooperation, as it provides the null hypothesis (diplomats do not matter at all). If it is true that power relationships are the exclusive determinants, then there is no role for diplomats. Bargaining theory also provides a critical alternative argument to the hypothesis that diplomats exercise collective agency and impact outcomes. This chapter provides a more in-depth look at the theoretical literature that attempts to explain outcomes of international cooperation, and draws upon sociology and constructivism to highlight the potential for the epistemic-community approach to better account for outcomes.

Alternative explanations for international cooperation

Realist diplomacy
Neorealist arguments that touch upon the topic of diplomacy tend to view it as synonymous with foreign policy. For some, diplomats constitute such

an insignificant backdrop to the international power play that they are not mentioned at all. For others, the existence of diplomats, and their clearly influential role in world politics, is a major point of contention that cannot be ignored. In the neorealist literature, diplomats are referred to both directly and as a part of the somewhat amorphous concept of "international society."

The general neorealist perception of the world is that relative power is the determining factor of international relations.[1] All states behave in a way to maximize self-interest, sovereignty, security, and influence in the world arena. Thus, diplomacy is simply the playing out of these competing state forces by individuals who are servants of the state. In other words, diplomats in a realist world are merely transmission belts of state preferences. A realist would assume that everything a diplomat says maximizes the power of his home state's position. At the same time, a realist would argue that what diplomats say to each other does not matter because outcomes of international relations will reflect the interests of the most powerful states in a chain down to the very smallest states who have no choice but to comply with the rules set by the bigger states. J.W. Burton argues, for example, that it is not necessary to distinguish between decision-makers and the diplomatic corps because diplomacy is based on power needs.[2] All foreign policy activity can thus be subsumed under one label of diplomacy. He writes,

> In contemporary conditions of highly developed permanent civil services and improved communications the term diplomacy is best used to include the whole process of managing relations with other States and international central office, assessment of immediate and longer-term interests, balancing of internal and external pressures, testing of likely responses to proposed policies, final implementation, and perception of the environment.[3]

Bundling all foreign relations into one package essentially dismisses any possibility that these complex processes *independently* impact outcomes of international relations. Diplomacy, in this view, is the playing out of competition among states that has a predetermined outcome based on relative power and the "billiard ball effect."[4]

Intergovernmentalism

In terms of today's EU, intergovernmentalists support the neorealist and neoliberal institutionalist argument that EU institutions merely aid in member-state decision-making by providing a set of rules for leaders to advance their states' preferences. Policies at the supranational level are simply a reflection and continuation of policies at the domestic level. Thus, according to the intergovernmentalists, expert national or supranational representatives such as the College of Commissioners or the Committee of Permanent Representatives (Coreper) have a negligible impact on integration or cooperation. Instead, the most powerful states act according to power-based interests, and the result is the adoption of *minimalist* measures in favor of the common good of EU member states. The intergovernmentalist approach only allows for the least common denominator to determine outcomes. It does, however, attempt to salvage structural realism by at least allowing that international institutions exist for a reason. However, it still claims that outcomes will conform to predictions based on power; they will just be obtained more efficiently.

Glarbo also tries to get around this problem by arguing either that the issue at hand has low salience, so it does not really matter that states choose to cooperate, or that there is an underlying material motive.[5] Andrew Moravcsik, though a prominent liberal, is a major proponent of *intergovernmental institutionalism*, arguing that states reach bargains to advance their interests in the EU, and that if the Commission were to overstep its bounds, the members would see that it is restrained.[6] He summarizes the main components of intergovernmental institutionalism: (1) intergovernmentalism is the continuation of domestic policy at the supranational level; (2) lowest-common-denominator bargaining is agreement based only on shared preferences among the largest states, unless exclusion forces agreement; and (3) strong limits to future sovereignty transfers is a unanimous agreement among states to adopt EC policies and preference for intergovernmental institutions such as the Council of Ministers, rather than the Parliament or Commission.[7]

As Moravcsik argues, intergovernmentalism is not unlike structural realism because supranational institutions and transnational phenomena are only permitted if they do not conflict with national preferences and power maximization. It places more of an emphasis on national leaders bargaining, but their preferences tend to coincide with the maximization of self-interest. Intergovernmentalism is different from pure realism in that it recognizes the value of international institutions as providing a common framework within which states bargain, and where transaction costs are minimized. Intergovernmental institutionalism is a more refined, EU-specific, version of intergovernmentalism that also accounts for changes in state preferences based on domestic factors, not just relative power.

The English School

In one respect, the realist school overlaps with the English School, a looser, quasi-constructivist variant of realism. Both agree that international cooperation is more likely with increased interaction over time among states. However, the causal *processes* advanced by the two approaches are different. Structural realism uses functionalism[8] to explain the emergence of international society, and points to the inevitability of growing compromise among states as they increasingly interact to solve problems.[9] The English

School also advances this temporal argument that over time, the development of international society is inevitable, but the process suggested is purposeful interaction. Hedley Bull and Adam Watson argue that international society exists when "states (or, more generally, a group of independent political communities) . . . have established by dialogue and consent common rules and institutions for the conduct of their relations, and recognize their common interest in maintaining these arrangements."[10] More specifically, in support of the English School approach, I argue that this dialogue is advanced through purposeful relationship building among diplomats. Diplomacy can be included under the umbrella of international society because it is one of the key transnational activities that allows states to cooperate and coexist within a power-based international system. At times, it is the only component of international society.[11]

The structural realist approach contrasts with the English School as it focuses on functionalism to the neglect of such English School concerns as shared norms, collective identity, and common worldviews. Buzan, a structuralist, argues, "Whether or not units share a common culture, at some point the regularity and intensity of their interactions will virtually force the development of a degree of recognition and accommodation among them. . . . International society could evolve functionally from the logic of anarchy without preexisting cultural bonds."[12]

Thus, structuralists argue that international society develops over time, through a *nonpurposeful* spillover effect.[13] The English School attributes more agency to diplomats, as it allows for diplomats to recognize common interest through dialogue, while the structuralists tend to discount apparent agency as purely coincidental. In sum, both approaches, by virtue of the world becoming a smaller place through globalization, communication technology, transportation, and international organizations, would agree that increased interaction among diplomats inevitably leads to mutual recognition among states. However, they disagree about the cause. For the structural realists, the interaction remains power-based, and simply conforms to functional efficiency because transaction costs are reduced when diplomats act upon knowledge acquired through increased interaction to make strategic decisions that benefit their home states.

The following arguments are intended simply to critique the realist approach through its own logic. First, the key factor missing from many realist approaches, as well as from that of the English School, is acknowledgement that international actors may find that their own power or even soft power[14] benefits from outcomes that maximize the interest of all states in the international system or the common good.[15] The development of international society and transnational identification can become an intentional goal of diplomats.

Second, there are ambiguous definitions of power and perceptions of power and there is a lag between changes in power and people's perceptions of it. For example, on several occasions in the seventeenth century, state officials drew up lists of what they believed to be an accurate ordering of states according to their relative levels of power.¹⁶ Not surprisingly, many of the lists were different. The desire to establish a visible pecking-order led to a constant dispute about precedence.¹⁷ A letter addressed to the Duc de Longueville at the beginning of the negotiations of Westphalia warned: "Of course after the ambassadors of the emperor, the first rank should belong to France. There will be contestations from the Swedish who will not want to cede to Spain or France."¹⁸ At the same time, the Swedish diplomats were instructed that *they* were to have precedence after the Emperor. Protocol was a major question for diplomats, and one that did not have an obvious answer. Even today, in a seemingly unipolar world, scholars who advance different definitions of power debate whether the EU may actually be a serious contender to US hegemony.¹⁹

Third, along these lines, competition to maximize power is not a zero-sum game. This is compounded by the fact that cooperation occurs over time; if a state defects from the general interest in the beginning, it sabotages all future deals. Diplomats, more specifically, may maximize their own power leverage by building up the agency of diplomats as a collective. Thus, the "go-it-alone" mentality, advocated by realists who view diplomats as simple transmission belts for states, may not be the best way to maximize gain during international negotiations.

Finally, the nature of the goals themselves can change with increased interaction among diplomats, thus causing everyone to shift their expectations based on discovering where the consensus point lies. Diplomats as individuals must have a degree of autonomy from their states in order to build independent and collective agency with other diplomats in the negotiation room.

In conclusion, the shortcut of realist logic, which collapses diplomacy under the concept of foreign policy, does not hold up under logical deduction. The empirical chapters of this book will provide evidence for this. To highlight one example, the main negotiations of the Treaty of Versailles consisted of state leaders conducting a kind of ad hoc summit known as the Group of Four. Despite their intention to cooperate and efforts to accomplish the best outcome for the winners of the Great War (Italy, France, England, Japan, and the United States) they were unable to produce a tenable treaty. The failure of this monumental diplomatic meeting was solely due to what occurred in the negotiation room. The leaders had already agreed to cooperate, but power reasoning alone does not automatically lead to the desired outcomes. As Checkel argues, realist arguments "define the universe of possible outcomes but do not explain why particular ones occur."²⁰

Two-level game diplomacy

The two-level game argument is a functional approach that states that diplomats enable efficient outcomes by reducing transaction costs. Thus, there exists a Pareto optimum for outcomes of international cooperation, and the results of diplomatic interaction will always lie somewhere on the Pareto frontier. According to this argument, the result *sets* are predetermined and it is only a matter of time for diplomats to discover the arena in which they may operate or the *win-set* of possible outcomes.

The notion of two-level games was first articulated by Robert Putnam[21] and is hailed by both international relations and comparative politics scholars for its emphasis on the domestic–international nexus. However, Putnam's theory builds on numerous precursors. James N. Rosenau writes about microdomestic factors and provides instances of foreign policies where domestic changes influence international affairs.[22] Nye and Keohane develop the notion of complex interdependence where international regimes are created and maintained through a system of interactions between states.[23] Katzenstein looks at the contribution of state strength and structural factors in the successful development of policies.[24] Finally, Katz argues that the main purpose of foreign economic policy is to make domestic policies compatible with the international political economy.[25]

Putnam synthesizes these precursors by operationalizing the international–domestic nexus. In his model of two-level games, Level I is the negotiation phase where diplomats bargain at the international table. Level II consists of the ratification stage in which there are separate discussions within each group of constituents about whether to ratify the agreement. The focus of this project is what happens on Level I. For Putnam, a win-set represents all the possible Level I agreements that would satisfy the Level II constituencies. The size of the win-set depends on the distribution of power, preferences, and possible coalitions among Level I constituents. The assumption is that the negotiator is faced with tradeoffs based on what will satisfy his or her Level II group, and this can be mapped with indifference curves. These indifference curves represent the various package deals that the negotiator finds to be of equal value. The combination of each negotiator's indifference curves and strategies with the strength of each state vis-à-vis domestic pressures determines the cooperative outcomes.

Putnam's model represents a clear improvement on previous *second-image* and *second-image reversed* theories that favor either domestic or international variables. However, looking specifically at the Level I group of negotiators, it is clear that a significant degree of elaboration is necessary to capture the complexities that routinely occur. First and foremost, outcomes rarely fall into the win-set category. Second, the interaction and processes among diplomats themselves are too simplified in the model. Putnam's model does not consider the impact of prior contact among diplomats in creating shared norms and worldviews or the ongoing processes of diplomatic identity, role, and norm construction engendered from the present diplomatic exchange. Third, the division between the domestic and international levels is not as clear-cut as Putnam presents it.

Delegation and principal–agent diplomacy

Classic principal–agent theory also provides an explanation for diplomatic behavior similarly building upon neofunctionalist assumptions. In this approach, the principals or statesmen delegate authority to the diplomats or agents to resolve issues of *contracting* in the international arena. Contracting refers to minimizing transaction costs by pursuing goals that would be too costly or difficult for the principal to perform himself. By virtue of being on location and having better access to information, the agent can exercise personal agency in his decision-making. Proponents of principal–agent theory assume that this agency is necessarily opportunistic behavior and thus disadvantages the principal. The assumption rests on neofunctionalism – that individual actors always maximize self-interest.[26] Opportunistic behavior is characterized as "shirking" or "slippage."

The second assumption follows from the first, and that is that the solution must be a perfect means to control the agent so that the principal's interests are always represented. Examination of such principal–agent scenarios and their solutions is commonly taken up by rational-choice theorists using the tools of microeconomics to understand processes and outcomes. Studies typically focus on the US Congress.

Principals continue to delegate authority, despite the risks that agents will exercise agency. First, according to the principal–agent approach, delegation occurs because agents may be more successful in resolving collective action problems with regard to long-term goals.[27] In other words, they may reduce transaction costs when *incomplete contracting* occurs, and only agents can clarify disputes since they were present at the original negotiation. Second, agents can take the blame for principals, or in this case elected officials, when unpopular decisions are made. The typical goal of principal–agent theorists is to understand how to control the potential unwieldiness involved in delegation.

Principal–agent theory is a popular approach among EU scholars, and can be an interesting approach to understanding the relationship between diplomats and statesmen. However, the assumption of opportunistic behavior is problematic empirically because of the countless examples of diplomats who assume personal risk for their love of country or desire for peace. Theoretically, these kinds of neofunctionalist arguments suffer the major drawback of only being able to assign preferences to actors after they act. If the assumption of opportunistic behavior is set aside, the theory is then reduced to information asymmetry and the realization that diplomats may exercise agency. It does not offer a comprehensive or causal means of understanding why, and ignores the possibility that agents may not be directly maximizing their own interest.

Bargaining theory

Bargaining theory is arguably the most relevant theory that is directly opposed to the notion that epistemic communities have a real impact on outcomes of international cooperation. Andrew Moravcsik and Kalypso Nicolaïdis address three prominent structural bargaining theories in their analysis of the Treaty of Amsterdam: garbage-can, geopolitical, and interdependence theories.[28] Garbage-can theory states that those negotiating do not have clear ideas of what their preferences are and thus form them during the process of negotiation. The geopolitical approach argues that governments' preferences are defined by their larger ideological stance, rather than the specific issues. That is, their preferences are defined by whether they are federalist or not. Interdependence theory, which Moravcsik and Nicolaïdis support, stipulates that preferences depend on economic and political–military interdependence. Empirically, they argue that national governments understood their preferences during the Amsterdam Treaty negotiations and ranked them accordingly. Although national representatives and supranational actors were involved in the negotiations, they did not generate outcomes any different from the rational weighing of national preferences. Thus, they claim that bargaining theory can predict outcomes by analyzing initial preferences of national governments.[29]

The major weakness of this approach, when specifically compared to the Berlin and Maastricht case studies of this book, is that the empirical evidence does not support it. State leaders did not spend much time negotiating the Treaty on European Union, nor did they maintain fixed preferences during the period of negotiation.[30] For the Maastricht Treaty, to the extent that statesmen or ministers did meet, diplomats provided all the documentation and draft treaties negotiated ahead of time for state leaders to use as a starting basis. It is only through historical process-tracing – examining the interdelegation memos, working papers, and secretariat summaries – that it is possible to observe the strong role diplomats played behind the scenes and the extent to which agreement would not have been possible had statesmen only bargained amongst themselves. Moreover, it is difficult, if not impossible, to determine what outcome statesmen would have reached had they performed the negotiations themselves unless one assumes that their preferences remain fixed. In this regard, preferences based on rational-choice theory tend to be similar to realist predictions. Before the circumstances of negotiation are known, state leaders' preferences typically support maximizing their own relative power in the international sphere.

Other examples of bargaining theory are the *Tit-for-Tat* strategy and *coercive* diplomacy.[31] In a Tit-for-Tat bargaining strategy, negotiations open with one side trying to be cooperative, and every subsequent move from each side reflects a balancing out of cooperative and confrontational negotiation stances.[32] Thomas Risse (formerly Risse-Kappen) argues that this theory is flawed as it does not consider the political context nor the possibility that negotiators are unable to always identify what is conciliatory and what is confrontational. The negotiators will continuously wonder whether they are being tricked and what the motivations behind a conciliatory gesture really are. Coercive diplomacy, on the other hand, involves only confrontational negotiations meaning that the other side has to back down or else war will ensue.[33] Coercive diplomacy is thus not really diplomacy at all, but a series of threats. Risse also outlines conditional reciprocity, which is a softer version of coercive diplomacy involving some points of compromise if the opponent agrees to the main stipulation of the negotiation. However, Risse argues that this approach is difficult to distinguish from coercive diplomacy because the main point is still to threaten war, which ultimately makes it difficult for the opponent to cooperate.

Theories of bargaining rest on the assumption that diplomats are instrumental; otherwise they would not exist and statesmen would not delegate authority to them. Kassim and Menon write that principals continue to delegate, despite the risks that agents will exercise agency.[34] They recognize the distinction between autonomy and agency and actually consider agency as a cost that principals must bear rather than the main point of delegation.[35] However, much bargaining-theory scholarship clumps autonomy together with agency, which I argue is a critical distinction in predicting outcomes of international cooperation. For example, using agency and autonomy interchangeably, Pollack writes, "I argue that the 'agency' or autonomy of a given supranational institution depends crucially on the efficacy and credibility of control mechanisms established by member-state principals, and that these vary from institution to institution leading to varying levels of supranational autonomy."[36]

Although bargaining theory may predict outcomes when diplomats are merely acting within their autonomy, when they act beyond their autonomy to exercise collective agency of their own, the results are not predicted by bargaining theory. Bargaining theory's methodology of comparing initial state preferences to final outcomes misses the critical processes that occur in between. There is evidently some "wiggle room" in which statesmen expect that diplomats may stretch the bounds of their autonomy and diplomats anticipate that statesmen will not overrule their actions. The area beyond this wiggle room is what is really interesting in an analysis of the processes of international cooperation. Diplomats deliberate and persuade each other as well as statesmen. Their ability to do this rests on their strength as an epistemic community. Much of bargaining theory examines the results after they have occurred, and defines initial state preferences in such a way that they explain outcomes.

Two-level game, principal–agent, and bargaining theories do not discount the role of diplomats. Instead, these theories treat them as part of the transmission belt for achieving Pareto-optimum results. Diplomats reduce transaction costs because they are professionals who have a greater understanding of rules and regulations, and because they have access to information. Thus,

Putnam sees diplomats as having an important role, yet denies the importance of human agency. Diplomats are agents of states, but with no ability to impact outcomes beyond choosing a predetermined win-set. However, international cooperation is more complicated than state power and preferences because it involves actors who are embedded in community, structures, and norms.[37] As Sverdrup argues, "The decision-making process needs to be situated in a distinct historical, institutional and contextual setting, revealing how actors are embedded in a web of structuring elements."[38] Indeed, Zito argues that epistemic communities influence actors' preferences themselves so they cannot only fall within a win-set.[39]

Diplomats as an epistemic community

There are several hypotheses advanced here that do not conform to the alternative theories of cooperation discussed above, but rather rely on an examination of microprocesses and internal group dynamics. By ignoring the subjective realities of the people who actually make decisions, explanations that fall under the rubric of neorealism and bargaining theory fail to explain outcomes in most cases. They take state and actor preferences as given (self-interest or power maximization) and unchangeable. By contrast, I argue that diplomats as influential, high-level actors do influence outcomes in significant ways and their ability to do so rests on the shared meanings and norms within their epistemic community. As stated in Chapter 1, the strength of the epistemic community of diplomats is mutually constitutive with their social background, professional status, training, meeting frequency, and shared professional norms. In other words, diplomats continuously redefine and perpetuate their own profession and epistemic community. Thus, I advance the following general hypotheses.

If the epistemic community of diplomats is strong, the diplomats are more likely to (1) exercise collective agency to reach a cooperative outcome, (2) change their preferences during the negotiation, (3) and successfully persuade their statesmen to support their collective decisions.

Thus, if the epistemic community of diplomats is strong, they hold a stronger norm of consensus, which encourages them to exercise agency.

If the epistemic community of diplomats is weak, they are *less* likely to (1) exercise collective agency to reach a cooperative outcome,[40] (2) advance different preferences from those expressed in their instructions, (3) and perform the negotiation without the heavy interference of statesmen.

Thus, if the epistemic community of diplomats is weak, they hold a weaker norm of consensus, which does not encourage them to exercise agency.

These hypotheses will be tested in the four cases to come. However, it is first necessary to explain the significance of epistemic communities and to detail the sociological and constructivist underpinnings that form the theoretical basis of this study.

Sociology and networks

Sociologists have contributed a great deal to our understanding of how professional networks arise, evolve, and influence outcomes. The study of sociology is based on the key notion that individuals behave according to their social roles, which are defined as scripts or collective conventions and individual (cognitive) schemas.[41] The focus is on microprocesses within groups or networks and on the dynamics of group members as they create social institutions and shared meanings. In addition, certain contexts are conducive to producing more general worldviews that are spread and shared outside of the network. The individual actor-driven model from sociology is particularly relevant to this study.

Frank Dobbin argues that institutions, cognition, power, and networks are the four main components that explain the creation of scripts and how they change.[42] According to Dobbin, *institutions* are conventions, traditions, and laws that provide individuals with behavioral scripts and causal meanings. They may confine behavior as well as provide roadmaps for new behavior. There is a substantial literature on institutional change.[43] *Cognition* is the psychological process in which each individual engages to understand his or her society's conventions. People with *power* influence customs and legal institutions through membership in certain professional networks. *Networks* not only provide individuals with an identity, but also provide prescriptive solutions based on shared causal meanings developed within the network. Importantly, networks house norm entrepreneurs or expert individuals who come up with critical new ideas that continuously redefine their subjective reality. Like institutions, networks have a dual role. They "may generate durable ties and practices through constitutive processes of social interaction or by shaping the opportunities and obstacles to exchange and cooperation."[44] Unlike institutions, networks emphasize the agency and culture of their members, and are less reliant on "punctuated equilibrium" or "exogenous shocks" for change.[45]

An understanding of the microprocesses within epistemic communities can be enhanced by identifying all four of these concepts. As will be observed in the four cases, diplomatic institutions are the rules of protocol and procedure, and professional norms that are inherited from one set of diplomats to another, and reshaped over time. These institutions can be enduring, so change is not recognized until after the fact, such as the gradual diminishing of the grand processions that would take place before a diplomatic negotiation during the seventeenth century. They can also be continuously redefined by the diplomats themselves, as when it is appropriate to allow the other diplomat to enter the room before you. Diplomats were increasingly given precedence for their *own* reputations rather than for the relative power of their home state. The process of institutionalization is "the spread and maintenance of sets of meanings."[46]

Cognition plays a critical role in allowing these changes in institutions to occur as well as in socializing new diplomats into the profession. Individual cognition enables each diplomat to realize his or her identity as a member of the epistemic community. Emile Durkheim's argument that social background or location impacts identity is a critical component to understanding European diplomats.[47] In support of Durkheim, a large part of the development of professional expertise and socialization among diplomats occurs prior to joining the epistemic community through social background, selection, and training. Upon joining the diplomatic corps, diplomats undergo a new phase of socialization within the *organizational field*.[48] Paul DiMaggio and Walter Powell argue, "In the initial stages of their life cycle, organizational fields display considerable diversity in approach and form. Once a field becomes well established, however, there is an inexorable push towards homogenization."[49] Through empirical investigation of the diplomatic epistemic community, it is possible to observe the cognitive- or identity-based origins of their organizational field.

Power is often a given for this particular type of epistemic community as long as they have high professional status. Power allows diplomats to influence people outside their epistemic community, in particular the statesmen who issued their instructions. As will be seen in three of the four cases (excepting the Versailles Treaty), power allows diplomats to persuade their statesmen. Power is particularly relevant in the literature on organizational fields, as it considers the influence of outside organizations on the organization being studied. Some sociologists have argued that organizations are externally controlled, and that there may be competing external pressures.[50] Diplomats, however, are in a unique position because power is vested in them as plenipotentiaries of states; thus, rather than being pulled in multiple directions, they have only two main loyalties: to their state and to each other. The study of organizational fields also addresses the creation of a single, stable organizational field, which is particularly relevant to diplomats, as they have historically professionalized their own profession. Fligstein argues that there are two problems with creating a stable organizational field: (1) the relationships within the field must be enforceable, and (2) governments must legitimize their agreements.[51] Again, diplomats are in the unique position of being protected from these concerns because (1) their job is treaty creation, which naturally enforces their relationships, and (2) governments grant them legitimacy from the start.

Finally, the concept of networks is the most closely associated with epistemic communities, as defined in the current political science literature, because it emphasizes elements of expertise, shared causal beliefs, and the importance of agency. The focus on networks of *agents* in sociology emerged in the late 1980s when DiMaggio and others moved away from examining only structures and institutions to bring in the role of *institutional entrepreneurs*.[52] I argue that the concept of networks in sociology corrects for the shortcomings of a purely institutional approach. Whereas institutions tend to embody path dependence, networks embody agency. Institutional arguments were not intended to leave out the possibility of idea generation and change, but they emphasized the ways in which institutions constrain by "structuring what is possible."[53] This analysis of an epistemic community of diplomats is intended to highlight the ways in which diplomats have pushed the boundaries of what is possible by continuously redefining preferences.

Constructivism and epistemic communities

Besides sociology, this study also draws upon constructivist theories to articulate the role of epistemic communities. Andreas Antoniades explicitly links the epistemic community concept to social constructivism.[54] Constructivist approaches to political science argue that reality is socially constructed, not an objective state of being. Thus, social interactions produce worldviews, norms, and ideas of what constitutes reality. Antoniades argues that the structures of international political life are social rather than material, and this is why epistemic communities are so important. Socially constructed beliefs about reality are particularly strong in epistemic communities, as shared causal beliefs are the main criteria that bring individuals together in an epistemic community. Clearly, there is close familiarity between constructivism in political science and network theory in sociology.

In contrast to how neorealist and bargaining theory treat international cooperation, I consider diplomats as an epistemic community in order to conceptualize their potential as actors in their own right. Ernst Haas, one of the chief proponents of the epistemic community concept, argues that interactions among elite transnational actors can result in outcomes that lie above or below the so-called Pareto frontier.[55] Furthermore, such a frontier representing optimal outcomes does not exist because the world never operates in such an idealized fashion with fixed national preferences.

According to Haas, results are not predetermined and can reflect worldviews and norms acquired during interaction leading to coalitions that cut across national boundaries.[56] Thus, during the course of negotiation, diplomats can change their preferences based on current factors. In the case of the EU, this is because diplomats know that they will continue to interact with each other. Issue linkage and forward linkage occur, locking participants into a transnational community. Consequently, they become quickly socialized in this environment and develop a loyalty to the transnational sphere, thus strengthening their epistemic community.[57] Glarbo articulates a similar constructivist position arguing that decisions about the Common Foreign and Security Policy[58] "emerge as social constructions, that is, as the results of national diplomacies intentionally and unintentionally communicating to themselves and to each other their intents and perceptions of political co-operation."[59]

Following the work of Ernst Haas, Peter Haas argues that the notion of epistemic communities provides a conceptual tool to understand conditions of uncertainty.[60] It is a means of understanding the value of ideas and collective meaning through a methodologically pluralistic program. Emanuel Adler and Peter Haas write,

> Between international structures and human volition lies interpretation. Before choices involving cooperation can be made, circumstances must be assessed and interests identified. In this regard, to study the ideas of epistemic communities and their impact on policy making is to immerse oneself in the inner world of international relations theory and to erase the artificial boundaries between international and domestic politics so that dynamic between structure and choice can be illuminated.[61]

This quote implicitly critiques Putnam's approach as creating a false dichotomy between the domestic and the international levels. Rather, they argue, the international system has strong transnational linkages.

There have also been a variety of critiques of the epistemic community literature. James Sebenius argues that the epistemic community concept is useful in that it is not necessarily confined to binary outcomes: either cooperation or defect.[62] Rather, it takes processes into consideration. Just as Robert Keohane and Robert Jervis point out, to understand outcomes of cooperation, it is necessary to pay attention to the unique blend of agreement and disagreement. Sebenius's criticism of the epistemic community approach is that it does not define the mechanism of cooperation, which he argues is negotiation. A study of diplomats, as professional negotiators, clearly overcomes this shortcoming.

Another critique, from Thomas Risse and Jeff Checkel, is that the epistemic community literature does not explain why members choose some ideas over others. Checkel writes, "How and under what conditions are [ideas] influential determinants of policy?"[63] Risse and Checkel support the notion that ideas, norms, and transnational networks are an indispensable part of understanding international relations. Structural theories such as realism and liberalism will never fully explain international outcomes unless they consider these factors. In particular, Risse argues that the end of the Cold War was largely due to the spread of ideas among transnational networks that advanced new understandings of Soviet security interests.[64] Western liberal internationalists formed ties with people from policy think tanks in the Soviet Union, including Mikhail Gorbachev, and their shared ideas had a causal impact on Soviet foreign policy. Risse seeks to correct for the shortcomings of the epistemic community approach by figuring out why "new thinkers" choose some ideas over others. In Risse's words, "Ideas do not float freely ... access to the political system, as well as the ability to build winning coalitions are determined by the *domestic structure* of the target state, that is, the nature of the political institutions, state–society relations, and the values and norms embedded in the political culture."[65]

In Risse's empirical analysis, he argues that three transnational networks during the Cold War held similar ideas, but had varying degrees of success. For him, this can be explained by the variation in domestic structure. Checkel concurs, criticizing constructivist approaches for being too weak to draw the connection between international norms and domestic agents.[66]

Risse's and Checkel's focus on domestic structure is an important part of the picture and is particularly relevant when examining single cases in which the goal of the research is to find out why certain ideas were favored over others in a certain context. In this regard, diplomats are unique as an epistemic community for two reasons. First, they are not subject to domestic pressures or public opinion, but receive their instructions from a single source. The impacts of "political institutions, state–society relations, and the values and norms embedded in the political culture" are largely transmitted through the instructions of democratically elected representatives to ambassadors. Moreover, they themselves are domestic actors so they can be said to embody certain kinds of domestic institutions. However, they do not reside in their home country so the broader diversity of domestic political culture and policy interests interfere less in their day-to-day lives. It is important to remember that domestic structures have not mattered greatly until relatively recently with the rise of democracy.

Second, the diplomatic epistemic community is unique because the diplomat's main goal is to reach agreement, not an easy task. The focus here is not so much on why some ideas are selected over others, but why diplomats *agree* on which ideas are selected. Moreover, to be able to generalize across time, rather than focusing on a single case, the actual content of the agreed-upon ideas is less important. Epistemic communities have an overarching norm of cooperation and consensus that can be strong or weak depending on the composition of the network. This norm of consensus determines the extent to which diplomats will be able to agree on certain ideas. When it comes to often-contentious negotiations where gridlock is a real possibility, reaching any agreement in the first place is a difficult proposition. This, in part, explains why in the past diplomats have reached negative outcomes reflecting ideas that do not benefit the common good.

Empirically, the literature on epistemic communities and transnational networks has addressed both governmental and nongovernmental actors. Adler, Haas, and others focus their empirical attention on the impact of nongovernmental epistemic communities. Their research is aimed at showing how and why epistemic communities impact state behavior and policy innovations, and how they evolve largely independently of government influence. Keck and Sikkink similarly look at nongovernmental epistemic communities or, as they label them, "transnational advocacy networks."[67] Kathleen McNamara and Anne-Marie Slaughter are among the scholars who have focused on governmental transnational communities. McNamara focuses on central bankers and treasury and finance officials in the EU who are close to the policy process. Anne-Marie Slaughter argues that it is no longer prime ministers, statesmen, and foreign ministers who drive international decision-making; it is now *government networks* comprised of judges, police investigators, financial regulators, and legislators.

This book supports the previous work of such scholars as McNamara, Risse, Checkel, Slaughter, and Sikkink who examine transnational linkages and bridge the gap between structural and ideational approaches. I seek to add to this growing body of literature by advancing the argument that ambassadors, as high-level diplomats in the political realm, also constitute a critical transnational group. Thus, while the term *diplomatic corps* is typically defined as all of the diplomats based in one capital city, I use the term more broadly to refer to the diplomats based in multiple European capitals, or the *transnational diplomatic corps*. This highlights the idea that diplomats may be involved in a transnational network distinct from purely "international" or "intergovernmental" interactions. As an epistemic community directly involved in various processes of official governmental interaction, the importance and uniqueness of diplomats cannot be ignored.

Structural constraints on diplomats: Rules, norms, and organizations

With the theoretical context laid out, it is important to return to the role of structure which does not determine everything but nevertheless plays an important role. On one side of the coin are diplomats as actors within an epistemic community; on the other side is the structure that constrains diplomatic processes. Sociology tends to emphasize the structures or constraints actors face in their behavior.[68] Structural constrains on behavior result from the institutionalization of previous conventions and customs and can be manifested as Adam Smith's "best practices" or Emile Durkheim's "myth and ritual." They also work to ensure that new practices or ideas conform in some way to the greater understanding of what is rational within the subjective reality of the diplomatic epistemic community.[69] Thus, structures such as rules, norms, and organizations allow autonomy of action within certain boundaries.

Here, I emphasize a critical distinction about the dual nature of structure in impacting the epistemic community of diplomats. I argue that diplomats simultaneously have autonomy from the state and exercise agency of their own. Autonomy is the room diplomats have to act within the structure that constrains them. It is mainly the explicit rules of the game, usually provided by states or institutions, specifying the context under which diplomats must operate.[70] Agency is defined as what diplomats *do* with their autonomy, and whether they go beyond it. In light of this distinction, I argue that previous work in the field of sociology is helpful in elucidating the nature of diplomatic agency. As sociologists contend, when new ideas are introduced by a network of professionals, these new ideas must in some way conform to an accepted form of rationality to be accepted as conventions. In other words, for diplomats to reach consensus on a particularly contentious issue, a successful outcome must be found among the options that implicitly fall within the shared meanings of all participants. Critically, these shared meanings can and do change during the course of interaction.

As mentioned, there is naturally a bit of wiggle room in the distinction between autonomy and agency. Diplomats may be able to anticipate what statesmen would allow them to agree to beyond what they stipulate in instructions. However, in some of the following cases, diplomats exercise agency even beyond this wiggle room to create outcomes that statesmen were initially against. Diplomats do not want to be overruled by statesmen, and they are skilled at determining when they could be overruled. This skill is derived from their collective professional expertise and ability to persuade statesmen using the cognitive tools derived within their network. Anticipation of being overruled is thus strongly related to the strength of the epistemic community. If the diplomatic epistemic community is strong, diplomats will anticipate that they can persuade statesmen.

The question of autonomy requires research of structure. One type of structure are the rules regulating the relationship between the diplomats and the state. During the Congress of Westphalia, diplomats were given full plenipotentiary powers so they could make on-the-spot decisions; however, they were also given orders to correspond regularly with the state, and sometimes they were sent specific instructions. Thus, their autonomy or structure was heavily regulated, but there was room for them to exercise agency, particularly in the short term. A remarkable finding in the case study of Westphalia is that the diplomats took liberties beyond their state-given autonomy to defy their state instructions in several instances. Events proceeded similarly during the Congress of Berlin.

A second type of structure faced by diplomats is less explicit and overlaps with agency. These are *norms*, defined as the unwritten codes of conduct that bind diplomats. It goes without saying that explicit rules are difficult for diplomats to change, but inexplicit norms can be just as binding for different reasons. For example, norms of protocol among diplomats express status and respect. There are cases in which lapses in following norms of protocol have had disastrous consequences for negotiations. Disregarding norms could seriously undermine a diplomat's attempt to reach reconciliation before the negotiations have even begun. Norms are strong forms of structure even though they are usually learned on the job and can change over time. Explicit rules tend to govern the relations between diplomats and the state, while implicit norms apply more to the relations within the international diplomatic community. This is why norms can both constrain and aid diplomatic interaction and the strength of the epistemic community, hence both serving as a source of agency and legitimizing that exercise of agency.

The normative school of thought arose in reaction against the argument that integration and regional institutionalization is functional or interest maximizing. Scholars such as Elster, Finnemore, Sikkink, and McNamara argue that it is necessary to incorporate the role of norms and ideas in looking at the emergence of institutions and regionalism. Ideas are related to norms in that they constitute the preinstitutionalized version of norms. Ideas here are defined as "shared causal beliefs."[71]

During the process of discourse and persuasion, certain ideas become institutionalized as norms. Jon Elster focuses on social norms as independent variables, arguing that norms hold emotional tonality that give them a grip on the mind.[72] Many ideas may be discarded in the process of negotiation and discourse before some gain a grip on the mind and attain the status of norms. Elster, however, chooses not to explain what he calls the "residual variable" that bridges the gap between preferences and opportunities. He argues that norms, like self-interest, are a natural human motivation, thus it is not possible for social scientists to fully understand how and why norms become more important than self-interest. In short, norms are at least partially shaped by self-interest, but not fully reducible.

Finnemore and Sikkink resolve the problem of the residual variable by setting out a dynamic norm life-cycle framework, arguing that norm emergence depends on norm entrepreneurs, organizational platforms, expertise, and transnational network resonance.[73] First, norm entrepreneurs trigger the emergence of a norm and try to spread the idea through persuasion. If enough people buy the idea, then it reaches a tipping point, and enters the second phase, the norm cascade. Finally, the norm is internalized in the third phase through socialization. The norm life-cycle framework provides a solution to the geopolitical school's reliance on systemic shocks, the neofunctionalists' assumption of interest maximization, and Elster's decision not to explain the residual variable. However, the norm life-cycle framework does not fully explain norm emergence because it skips one prior step in the timeline. What are the origins and motivations of the norm entrepreneurs themselves? I argue that diplomats are a strong example of norm entrepreneurs whose impact relies in part on the strength of their epistemic community. As mentioned, sociological studies of networks also provide a template for understanding the origins of norm entrepreneurs.

A third type of structure in autonomy is international organizations that serve as an umbrella for diplomatic interactions. The EU institutional structure is a major example of this. In Brussels, the Council provides common ground, literally, for diplomats to interact under the same roof both on a daily basis and for major intergovernmental meetings. As huge bureaucracies, international organizations provide the most structure for diplomats today. The hierarchy, decision-making procedures, and protocol are all highly institutionalized within each international organization. The supranational level mirrors the bureaucratic structures of national civil services and ministries of foreign affairs to a great extent. What does this leave for the role of diplomats today? This question is addressed in Chapter 6. Overall, it is critical to examine both sides of the coin, agency and structure.

The case studies

Scarcely a time exists since the development of the modern state that a scholar has not described the period as one of "new diplomacy." Mattingly attributes this to the seventeenth century; for Mangone, the late nineteenth century was a "new age of consultation"; Craig and Gilbert make reference to "new diplomacy" in their examination of the post-World War I period; and Hamilton and Langhorne label the post-World War II period as a new era of "total diplomacy." Interestingly, none really contradict the choices of others in deciding the timing of new diplomacy. I contend this is largely because no one is wrong. However, it would be inaccurate to completely distinguish one period of diplomacy from another and to describe diplomatic developments as sharp breaks from past traditions. The evolution of diplomacy is seamless, yet ever-changing. A diplomat from Renaissance Italy could slip into an embassy of today and recognize his profession.

Rather than trying to identify one major transition into an era of "new diplomacy" and embarking on the impossible task of justifying such a choice, I have selected four periods of new diplomacy. These time periods are more distinguishable than others as prime examples of changes in the diplomatic profession, though they are simply bigger targets along the continuum. For example, I did not choose the 1815 Congress of Vienna because even though the diplomatic conference itself was critical to international cooperation, the diplomatic profession at this time was not strikingly "new" compared to other times.[74] This chapter emphasizes the vast continuity in the practice of diplomacy, but the bulk of this book deals with change and development. Diplomats existed and worked toward goals of international cooperation long before particular issues were brought to the table, and remembered those issues long after outsiders to the profession forgot them. The diplomats ideally have a grander, loftier goal than any single negotiation or treaty, and that is to promote peace, cooperation, and the common good. Reaching toward a lofty goal is an intimate part of their identity as diplomats, but at the same time, one cannot neglect their self-interest. Diplomats typically have individual career aspirations as well as a collective goal to gain more power and authority for their profession. Many treaties created by diplomats in some way augment the power of the transnational diplomatic corps itself by attributing to them new powers in the form of monitoring or implementation of agreements. Additionally, individual diplomats will strive to please the statesmen who control their promotions. Thus, the lofty goal of the common good is only one part of diplomatic identity, though it represents the ideal. The diplomatic practice has admittedly fallen short of its stated purpose on occasion.[75]

The aim of this project is to understand the importance of diplomacy today and in the future. However, given the continuity of diplomacy over time, alongside its constant evolution, a historical analysis is necessary to understand the direction diplomacy is going, and to provide comparative examples. The four case studies are the mid-seventeenth, late nineteenth, early twentieth, and late twentieth centuries, and the corresponding negotiations are the Congresses and Treaties of Westphalia (1648), Berlin (1878), Versailles (1919), and Maastricht (1992).

In the sixteenth and seventeenth centuries, diplomats were accessories to war. They negotiated the conditions for beginning wars, conducting wars, and terminating wars. Members of the international system had no expectation that war could be prevented, but rather that war was a necessary way of life. After the 1648 Treaty of Westphalia, and the gradual international acceptance of a more formal, sovereign state system, the role of diplomats began to change. Diplomats were considered essential, not only for negotiating the conditions of going to war, but also the conditions for preventing war. Resident embassies, diplomats or ambassadors who remain in foreign countries to maintain state relationships, began to emerge first in the Italian states, then France, and finally in all of Europe. These diplomats were former ministers or secretaries of state, and had no formal education in diplomacy, as they would in future centuries. Anecdotally, the word *diplomacy* even originated from these resident embassies.[76] The ambassadors carried a *diploma* or a letter of credence certifying their power to negotiate and represent their sovereigns.

In the nineteenth century, diplomats were even more numerous, and maintained basically the same role they had developed since they were first professionalized in the seventeenth century. However, advances in communication technology, particularly the invention of the telegraph, brought the state closer to its diplomatic representatives. Interestingly, the telegraph did not restrict the autonomy of diplomats more than letters had previously. In addition, during this period diplomats underwent a more competitive selection and educational process, though most were still handpicked from the ranks of the privileged classes. Many changes in international relations, intellectual life, and worldviews had also occurred. The age of irreconcilable religious differences of the seventeenth century was replaced with an age of reason, scientific advancement, and relative peace in Europe. The only event akin to war, though more like a small battle, was the Crimean War. Nevertheless, territorial disputes remained a major source of international concern and diplomatic negotiation because the idea of state sovereignty was increasingly accepted as an international norm.

During the nineteenth century, not all conferences were to end war, but also to prevent war.[77] Mangone argues that this "new age of consultation" was marked by a willingness of states to negotiate and plead for cooperation as a *preventative* measure. The Congress of Berlin is just such an example, as it aimed to prevent war among the Great Powers to resolve Russia's unilateral action in the Balkans. In contrast to the seventeenth century, bureaucratization and professionalism made the nineteenth century seem like an era of new diplomacy. Yet, it is still described by many scholars in hindsight as the age of old diplomacy.[78] A stronger international society existed than in early modern times, but respect for international law and the establishment of international organizations and tribunals were still largely a distant dream.[79] It offered only the naissance of the idea of permanent international cooperation. In comparison to the twentieth century, nineteenth-century diplomacy was distinct for its lingering patronage and aristocratic ethos.

The post-World War I period experienced changes in the international system and a sharp break with past norms and worldviews. It was a time of new diplomacy because of these breaks with the past, but the newness was doomed to fail. The case of the Treaty of Versailles is distinct from the others as it is the only one in which a satisfactory cooperative solution to a Great War was not attained. Nevertheless, there is much to draw from the processes of diplomacy within the European corps during this era. It is an important case study in the evolution of diplomatic relationships and protocol because it points to the new direction toward summitry evident in the twentieth century.

In many ways, this period represents a low point in diplomatic agency. Efforts were articulated by statesmen to make the diplomatic process more transparent so that public opinion could have an impact as the negotiations went forward. Ultimately this was not accomplished, and much of the decision-making at the Paris Peace Conferences occurred behind closed doors with vague procedures and ad hoc protocol. Moreover, the major discussions to produce the Treaty of Versailles occurred in separate rooms creating a cleavage between the statesmen in attendance who were together in one room, and the professional diplomats in another. In this case, the statesmen did not grant autonomy to their diplomatic representatives to the detriment of outcomes of international cooperation. It is still revealing of diplomatic agency to look at what diplomats did accomplish in this highly constraining context, and as a counterfactual example of what happens when statesmen, rather than diplomats, largely determine outcomes.

Little more than a century after the Congress of Berlin, Europe is now organized under the supranational institution of the EU. The diplomats of today are the members of the Coreper. Communications technology, information sharing, and the ability to travel all mean that states could potentially carefully control their diplomats and maintain them as transmission belts of state power preferences. The strength of the diplomatic epistemic community, however, prevents this from happening. Diplomats are chosen under a meritocratic system of recruitment, education, and promotion. The general trend is that there are more and more European diplomatic representatives to international organizations, and a complex institutional apparatus with rules and regulations has developed alongside them. The intense bureaucratization of today's diplomats and an emphasis on technocracy is changing the way diplomacy is conducted, yet they still exercise agency, and informally determine 70–90 percent of EU decision-making.[80]

While many studies of international security in the modern era analyze why states fight wars in terms of state preferences or power interests, few have considered the decision-making process itself, and the role of modern diplomats in preventing international anarchy. This book does not contain an amelioration bias, the assumption that over time our ability to cooperate on the supranational level is always better now than it was in the past. Rather, by looking at past international negotiations, I argue that there are lessons to learn from past generalizations about diplomatic processes. Striking the right balance between the structural constraints of institutions and the space for diplomats to exercise agency will be of utmost importance to outcomes of international cooperation in the future EU and will help determine if it is perceived as democratic.

3
The Seventeenth Century and the Treaty of Westphalia

Climate of the times: The emergence of international society

The climate of international relations during the mid-seventeenth century was essentially absolutist and mercantilist. It was absolutist because monarchs vied for power over their territory, and tried to maximize this power in relation to other countries. It was mercantilist because merchants took the same attitude, believing that there was a limited amount of resources in the world. Just as kings aimed for a balance of power, merchants strove for a balance of trade. They engaged in ruthless economic competition for what they believed was a finite quantity of precious metals or bullion. International diplomacy and the emergence of a more codified system of international law were the only contenders against the prevalent climate of zero-sum gain, especially at the highest echelons of international society.

Westphalia was convened to find an end to the Thirty Years' War, the most intense and bloody struggle on a European scale until World War I. The challenges the peacemakers faced included religious and dynastic conflicts that had been tearing Europe apart for decades. During the lead-up to the Peace of Westphalia, there were fewer diplomats residing abroad than during the century before, but the quantity flourished greatly after 1648.[1] Their numbers were limited, but they were much more often representatives of states than of religious leaders, merchants, and large-scale land owners, as they often had been in the previous century. The quasi-diplomacy of the Middle Ages was gradually brushed aside[2] making room for the first important stages of diplomatic professionalization.[3]

The correspondence among diplomats and state leaders shows that diplomats often had different opinions from the state and, most significantly, acted upon them. They did this first of all because they had developed a greater, more-educated understanding of the position of other states through continued contact with other diplomats during and prior to negotiations at international meetings. Second, because they developed and maintained ties with other diplomats, both directly through face-to-face meetings and indirectly through mutual acquaintances. These were akin to the relationships among businessmen today, where a networking culture and a similar background and worldview often enables them to discover their common connections and shared knowledge relatively quickly. Without first establishing a common ground, it is difficult to reach reasoned compromises in daily meetings and negotiations.[4] Finally, diplomats acted upon their differing opinions because they were faced for the first time with the possibility of a conflict between duty to the prince and duty to peace or the common good.[5]

This chapter will first provide an overview of the mid-seventeenth-century diplomatic profession as a slowly modernizing, but rapidly spreading phenomenon in Western Europe, and of the historical significance of the Treaty of Westphalia. At this time, an epistemic community of diplomats was developed by virtue of shared status, similar social background, and meeting frequency, but diplomatic training was low as it was primarily received on the job. It is important to note that limited training does not preclude a professionalized diplomatic corps, although training can strengthen the cohesion and shared professional norms of the transnational diplomatic corps or epistemic community.[6] Because diplomats spent several years together negotiating the peace treaty, they developed relationships over time, even though they had spent little time together beforehand.

The second part of the chapter will focus on the process of decision-making at the Congress of Westphalia as a major diplomatic event. The analysis will consist of a detailed examination of the relationships between state leaders and diplomats and among diplomats themselves. To what extent did diplomats exercise collective agency and to what extent did they follow their instructions? To what extent did the strength of their epistemic community determine the outcomes at Westphalia?

The European corps: Seventeenth century

The 1648 Treaty of Westphalia was the first significant, large-scale multilateral meeting involving diplomats. The negotiations were more formal than the regular day-to-day meetings and had the express purpose of reaching an official, written agreement or treaty. Daily information sharing, by contrast, was an informal act conducted at the court of princes or with other ambassadors. It was basically a part of the "job description" of early resident ambassadors, but the style and manner with which it was carried out was open to interpretation. Minor understandings, concessions, or agreements could be reached through these regular communications, but they were often unwritten and subtle.

During this period, diplomacy was recognizable as a professional endeavor with standards of conduct, permanent embassies, and constant communication between the states and the diplomatic representatives. It is an interesting time to consider because the act of diplomacy by professionals contained elements of fifteenth- and sixteenth-century Italian Renaissance diplomacy, such as grand processions with great pomp, as well as qualities that continue to exist today, such as the emphasis on the order of proceedings and bureaucratic procedure. The special contribution of Venice to the diplomatic profession is significant. The excellence of their ambassadors set high standards from the start, and England had a permanent representative in Venice from the 1590s. The Swedish Chancellery (foreign ministry) created the practice of specialized *desks* in which experts were assigned to each particular state with which the Swedes dealt. Modernizing change occurred incrementally and, in the process, many of the customs and ceremonials of the past were recognized as inefficient and were gradually discarded.

Although there were numerous differences among countries and various levels of advancement in the field of diplomacy, there were certain characteristics – social background (who they were and why they were selected), status, and how often they met – which distinguished diplomats as a collective, and thus gave them a basis of shared norms, identity, and experiences. I argue that these shared qualities to some degree reinforced and created new bases of transnational ties. Alongside the more structural diplomatic professionalization, there existed a growing international society of diplomats that was based on agency and norms. The following subsections discuss how and why the variables of social background, meeting frequency, status, and shared professional norms contributed to a kind of diplomatic epistemic community in Western Europe.[7]

Qualities of a diplomat: Social background

In the early seventeenth century, ambassadors were chosen simply by virtue of being in the king's service. They were key figures in government, and were thus likely candidates for the king to send away as his representatives abroad. In the middle to late seventeenth century, diplomats continued to be selected through appointment, but they were often chosen for their ability to negotiate, engage in courtly manners, and maintain close ties to the crown.

There were, however, numerous disadvantages to pursuing a diplomatic assignment. As a result of the significant financial cost of taking on the position, many diplomats were wary of having to use up their own resources to carry out the job. Some even refused to become ambassadors because they were unwilling to spend their own money. At the time, it was often considered more prestigious to have a court appointment at home than to go abroad. Another disadvantage was that a long absence often severely limited the diplomat's chances of returning to a high level, well-paid job in the home state. After a while, people tended to regard them almost as foreigners, and hence with suspicion and uncertainty about their loyalties. There were also the physical discomforts and dangers of traveling long distances. With all these disadvantages, unqualified people were occasionally picked for jobs when those more qualified had refused. However, despite the hardships, some of history's most intelligent and able individuals, such as Hugo Grotius, the Count of Gondomar, and Peter Paul Rubens, became ambassadors at some point. A sense of serving their country and gaining membership in an elite international society drove many of them to ignore the costs. With the contributions of so many talented individuals, the diplomatic career professionalized rapidly, the assignments and rewards became more regularized, and a hierarchy was established.

Watson argues that, "Over the course of the seventeenth century, diplomacy became an art, a consciously and deliberately creative achievement in the European states system."[8] These professional diplomats were individuals authorized in the name of their country to conduct world politics on its behalf. Although they may have performed similar functions to soldiers, their domain was confined to peaceful means. One of the most famous original documents that reflect the qualities required of a diplomat in this era was François de Callières' manual, titled *On the Manner of Negotiating with Princes* and written in the 1690s.[9] Although this is somewhat later than the period considered here, the qualities and expectations of diplomats had not changed much from the mid-seventeenth century. Callières gives a detailed account of the attributes, talents, and appropriate behavior of diplomats. He stressed above all that to maintain the security of his state a diplomat should keep his master informed, make important friends, and take timely action. To accomplish this, a diplomat must have vast knowledge of the relative position of each state, all treaties in effect, territorial boundaries, and conflicting claims. Various sections of the European international system came together when previously they had had nothing to do with each other. Consequently, there was a virtually universal need to conduct continual negotiations, and disseminate information through permanent missions. Richelieu, in his *Testament Politique*, writes that the key to successful diplomacy is permanent negotiations, whether or not there is an important issue on the table.[10]

As Callières describes the profession, a diplomat needed to be a professional negotiator, primarily governed by rationality instead of passion.[11] Among other things, a diplomat should be intelligent, observant, handsome, possessing good judgment, of medium wealth (so as not to be distracted), and able to easily probe the minds of others. He was expected to have a gift for languages, courtly manners, sympathetic charm, and to be careful of flattery and bribery.[12] The goal was to avoid unnecessary misunderstandings, so a good diplomat used reason and persuasion to get princes to act on an accurate understanding of what their interests were. In conducting these meetings, diplomats constantly strove to find the potential for common ground rather than to prove that foreign sovereigns were wrong.

They were thus increasingly valued for honesty, and the ability to inspire confidence.[13] It was best if the corps was not drawn from high nobility, who were in many cases too proud to study foreign languages and cultures, but also not from people of low status who were considered incapable of conducting themselves elegantly. Unlike the beginning of the seventeenth century, they were not selected from a military or ecclesiastical background. Rather, they constituted a new professional class with a particular level and kind of education. Overall, the rise of a permanent diplomatic corps in each capital was accompanied by the creation of norms guiding the evolution of their international network.

It is important to remember that despite the long list of ideal qualities for a diplomat, few possessed them. The reason for this was largely the lack of training. Since diplomats were chosen for their connections, titles, or wealth, they typically had no experience at all.[14] As M.S. Anderson argues, "high social standing and systematic training do not mix."[15] The emphasis on proper training for diplomats was not really institutionalized until the nineteenth century, although some serious efforts were being made by the mid-eighteenth century.

Meeting frequency

Seventeenth-century diplomats in Western Europe not only interacted on an almost daily basis to maintain interstate relationships and deliver *démarches*,[16] they were also called upon to represent states at international meetings with full powers of decision-making, or as *plenipotentiaries*.[17] The diplomatic profession, although not fully bureaucratized, consisted of regular information sharing punctuated by major bilateral negotiations. As M.S. Anderson summarizes, "The most essential function of the diplomat . . . had always been the collecting and sending home of information."[18] They also sent frequent letters containing vital information to their counterparts in other countries.

The seventeenth century was marked by the widespread use of the resident diplomat in Western Europe. That is, diplomatic envoys could remain in their host countries for as long as there was an alliance with the home states. The rise of the resident diplomat created a kind of envoys club in each capital and a permanent transnational diplomatic corps. This enabled certain key norms of conduct and protocol to develop over time. Watson writes, "friendly personal relations among the envoys, even when their masters quarreled, helped to provide the oil which the institution needed in order to function smoothly."[19] To accomplish this, diplomats had to be able to meet with some frequency.

By the early seventeenth century, the Italian states, Spain, France, the Dutch republic (United Provinces of the Netherlands), and England all had permanent missions in other countries. Diplomatic envoys consisted of much more than the head ambassador. There would be translators, at least one secretary, a lawyer, sub-ambassadors, a cook, household staff, musicians, horses, and supplies. Extraordinary ambassadors were the most senior in rank, followed by ordinary ambassadors, agents, and envoys.[20] The size of the diplomatic staff was an indication of the status and power of the home state. Once an ambassador and his staff endured the long and treacherous journey to the host state, it was typical for them to reside there for an extended period – in some cases for over a decade – and to send a constant stream of messengers back home with the information they had gathered.

Even during this relatively early stage of professional diplomacy, certain standards of conduct and cultivation of shared worldviews provided a common ground for diplomats to draw upon. When the negotiators arrived in Westphalia, they may not have had occasion to meet before, yet they soon found they formed a kind of elite international society by virtue of their shared worldviews, their experiences and their status as colleagues at the congress. Each diplomat remained at the negotiations on average from four to six years, and, as a consequence, intensified their connections and shared understandings, building a basis for future interaction.

The diplomat at court: Professional status and norms

Diplomatic professional norms of behavior were perhaps the most visible element of diplomatic protocol. Including such things as diplomatic ceremonials, gift presentation, courtly manners, and proper placement of each country's representative based on state power, norms of protocol were a diplomat's major concern when traveling abroad. New ambassadors arriving in their host states were greeted with much pomp, and their procession of caravans and costumes were a source of public entertainment. Often times, programs were printed in advance to let spectators know the order, time, and place of the ambassadorial procession.[21]

Knowledge of protocol or ceremony was of utmost importance. In a letter shortly after the death of Louis XIII, the instructions for the Duke de Longueville, ambassador in Munster, stipulated: "The first difficulty that will be encountered in the peace treaty will concern the order of the meetings."[22] Understanding the implicit rules of protocol was as much the key to reaching compromise as skill at negotiation. Protocol was the way that ambassadors could show deference to each other as a reflection of the prestige of the countries they represented. It was based on a very complex and subtle knowledge of the intricacies of the history and relationships among states. During the course of the Congress of Westphalia, the diplomats increasingly learned to communicate, negotiate, and read each other's subtle tactics before finally signing off on the agreement.

Perhaps the most important component of protocol was precedence, or the order in which countries were ranked according to supremacy. The qualifications for precedence were seniority (defined as the age of the state), independence (the autonomous power of the sovereign), power (in terms of military strength), and custom (the traditional protocol of the past).[23] It was widely acknowledged that the Holy Roman Emperor had precedence in all matters. First, the Emperor's ancient lineage could be traced back to Charlemagne; second, he had a close relationship with the Catholic Church, which had a great deal of influence over the Empire; and third, the Emperor had influence over the member states.[24] The historical record shows that many sovereigns and diplomats believed that questions of precedence were a trivial matter, but the ceremony associated with it continued well into the eighteenth century making it a crucial symbolic norm.[25]

The reason protocol and precedence were so important was that status was one of the main preoccupations of the seventeenth-century diplomat. M.S. Anderson describes the age in general as "avidly status-conscious."[26] The manner in which the diplomat was received, where he sat at the table, the order in which diplomats spoke at meetings, all indicated the position of his country in the international arena. Any time a group of diplomats were assembled at one place, there was the potential that someone would be offended. Sometimes the ceremonial display of relative state status would lag behind the actual power positions, and this was one of the reasons diplomats became increasingly concerned with how these ceremonials played out.[27] As long as this norm persisted, status was a key factor in diplomacy, neglect of which resulted in grave insults and even revenge through duels. In the streets of London in 1661 almost fifty men were killed and wounded as a result of a protocol violation.[28] Interestingly, in the following century, status became more connected with the skills and reputation of the diplomat himself and not just the position of his country. This was an indication of diplomats' success at congresses and of their growing independence as agents of cooperation, not just transmission belts for states.[29]

The location of diplomatic meetings and negotiations was also an important diplomatic norm. Diplomats did not want to be seen as giving ground or being at a disadvantage before the negotiations even began, so it was important to find a neutral location agreeable to all parties. Sometimes this involved meeting in the middle of a bridge connecting two territories or picking a neutral host country. In 1659, for example, Cardinal Mazarin and Don Luis de Haro met in a small pavilion on the middle of a bridge on a small island between their two countries just so neither would walk on the other's territory and neither would appear inferior.[30] Neutral location is still an important factor that exists today. The institutions of the EU are carefully situated in Brussels, Luxembourg, and Strasbourg for politically strategic reasons.[31]

Finally, bribery was an important custom to be practiced with great care. Information was gathered either through payment or exchange of other information. Gift giving was necessary to avoid inadvertent insults and to maintain relationships, and it was considered a normal part of civilized behavior. A strategic bribe could result in big gains. It was up to the diplomat to decipher the rules of the game at each social gathering because certain key figures inevitably expected a gift. Diplomats, especially heads of missions, were rewarded upon their return. These gifts could be anything from gold chains to diamonds to albino falcons. In addition, successful diplomatic service also often led to greater rewards such as knighthood, nobility, or government positions.

Because of the custom of bribery and the necessary display of status, there was typically a shortage of money required to maintain the big diplomatic household. The life of a seventeenth-century diplomat was not an easy one. An ambassador was placed in a tough situation when resources ran out, and he had to continue to display his status, while duly respecting the status of others. Many state leaders were neglectful about providing for these ambassadors, and when they did, transporting the letters of credit or bills of exchange was a difficult proposition, encountering the same obstacles as diplomatic letters.

Rules of protocol and other norms evolved as a result of an increasingly status-conscious world in which diplomats were taking center stage. From today's perspective these norms may seem like relics of a quaint time, but they are really indicative of the strength of international society, and more specifically of an epistemic community that demonstrated due respect for transnational norms as a common platform to reach mutual understanding.

Communications: Before technology

Even before the advent of the telegraph and postal service, certain methods of communication with the home state were institutionalized in the diplomatic profession. The king, prince, regent, or minister expected information to be sent constantly, even though the journey between countries was often long and dangerous. An ambassador would initially leave with a formal set of instructions, including credentials and opening remarks, and then receive subsequent orders by mail. Couriers would deliver their messages with the risk of encountering wars, bandits, rough terrain, and foreign governments eager to steal information. Many of the letters were sent in code or cipher, and could occasionally arrive dangerously out of date. The lag in information often meant that the state could not participate in decision-making; by the time the state leader received the information it was too late to react. An ambassador abroad was clearly the expert on the information of the host state, and had to take initiative in decision-making based on his perceptions of what was in the best interest of his state. By the time he received word from his king, the pressing issues might already have been resolved out of necessity.

In addition, diplomats wrote to their colleagues at other courts sometimes as often as to their sovereign, enhancing their transnational community even across great distances. Considerable trust was placed in those diplomats representing state interests abroad. However, there was always the risk of disagreement between diplomats and the state, and even between diplomats themselves, since there were, as today, numerous conceptions of what constituted the state's best interests. Moreover, as shall be seen a little later on, the epistemic community of diplomats was not as strong as it would be in subsequent periods.

Diplomacy and international relations

How did diplomacy contribute to international order? On a microlevel, specific individuals interacted to create the diplomatic system while at the same time these interactions defined and institutionalized the profession. As they were increasingly sent abroad to conduct meetings with other diplomats, an entirely new collective identity based on membership emerged. Their constant correspondence and frequent meetings with one another helped enforce this. They were all bound by the transnational norms discussed in the previous sections. Violation of these norms would mean jeopardizing their membership in the transnational corps, which would in turn impair their ability to play an effective representative role for their state. Their motivations were different from other political actors because they were the only group to interact regularly, form ties, and develop standards of conduct. Even though merchants also interacted regularly through business transactions, they did not develop the same sorts of strong communal ties. The very nature of the mercantile profession was self-interest and economic maximization. Diplomats, on the other hand, were driven to perpetuate their emerging profession as a collective community because it greatly facilitated their end goals of communication and compromise. Subsequently, the socialization process led to increased professionalization.

The role of the diplomat was primarily to collect and deliver information for the state. However, many ambassadors did much more. During the first half of the seventeenth century, prior to the Peace of Westphalia, the states were still structurally quite weak. Most of this weakness was centered at the top as the fate of the state depended on the princes and many of them exercised bad judgment. In many cases, the increase in royal power had left the monarchs isolated and unaccountable to their subjects. To make up for the danger of power centered in the hands of one person, these "imperfect princes," as Garrett Mattingly describes them, consented to rely on a somewhat ad hoc group of administrators and servants to represent the state in international relations.[32] The princes, however, were often better served by these servants than they seemed to deserve.

These ambassadors and counselors were motivated to assume responsibility for the kings' mistakes, and could do so because of their growing relationships with other diplomats and their desire to maintain these relationships. As they increasingly viewed themselves as a collective, they began to cultivate beliefs about how the international system should operate. At first, they accomplished this in a disorganized fashion. There was a multiplication of offices, little coordination among officers, and poor record-keeping. Public offices typically came to be seen as personal property, and the system lacked an information hierarchy. Although these kings and princes relied on the duties performed by their servants, they still wanted to control them. One strategy often used was the attempt to divide them in order to rule them. It is thus puzzling that most historical evidence points to the fact that these early diplomats were not easily corruptible, even though the standards of honesty, according to our current sensibilities, were quite low. A major explanation for this is that the norms associated with their professionalization made self-interest a lesser goal than the desire for cooperation within their exclusive membership. Thus, an international society of shared status, norms, and identity developed and this contributed to the functioning of international relations. However, a negative side effect of the lack of bureaucracy and of less organized rule was that diplomats from the same country in many cases competed with each other, as will be observed in the Westphalia negotiations.

Diplomacy and other transnational ties

During the seventeenth century, many European states engaging in diplomacy had certain similarities such as religion, institutions, language, or economic relations.[33] Thus, a degree of contextual similarities consolidated in part by the international economic system also enabled diplomatic relations to work. In addition, international rules were necessary to protect these diplomats, and allow them to act with at least some degree of freedom. I argue that the early diplomats themselves defined and constituted their own profession, calling for norms of behavior, negotiation, and representation. They were also responsible for the codification and advent of international law, a legal basis for the protection of their roles in the international system. International law served to protect their actions and subsequently enhanced the depth of international society.

The legal mechanism that protected these international diplomatic networks was the concept of ambassadorial immunity, an issue that embodied an overlap in the sphere of international diplomacy and international law. Hugo Grotius, a diplomat himself, argued that the ambassador must have security in civil suits as well as criminal suits.[34] They should be treated the same as if they had never left their homeland. Grotius explained that although justice and equity should entail equal penalties for equal crimes, the law of nations must provide an exception for ambassadors. Their security as an international group enabled the maintenance of a network among states, and was thus more important to the welfare of the international system than their punishments as individuals. Moreover, the interests of the diplomat's home state were typically not the same as his host state's interests, so it would be difficult to insure a fair trial unaffected by ulterior motives. Ultimately, territorial rulers had to accept these tiny pockets of alien sovereignty within their territory.[35] The immunities from civil proceedings and exemptions from taxes helped overcome the hardships of a diplomatic career.

Overall, diplomacy became a distinctly collective endeavor with the development of personal ties and networks among envoys, and the need for efficiency in light of the constant quarreling of their royal masters. These actors not only enabled international cooperation by cultivating a norm of collegiality, but also served in defining their own profession. At this early stage of diplomatic professionalization, the variables of meeting frequency, (on-the-job) training, status, and social background indicate a relatively medium-strength diplomatic epistemic community.

The diplomatic epistemic community of the mid-seventeenth century does provide a strong case for the role of an epistemic community during a time in which other voices from international society were relatively nonexistent.[36] In that sense, seventeenth-century diplomats were remarkable for their uniqueness as the only major nonreligious epistemic community in the international arena that actually impacted outcomes, despite the relative weakness of the overall transnational dialogue. Despite the importance of its impact, the epistemic community of the mid-seventeenth century still must be described as no more than medium-strength in comparison to later periods. The best way to observe the operations of these diplomats in the climate of the times is to examine the crucial case of the Peace of Westphalia.

The lead-up to the Peace of Westphalia

The background to the Thirty Years' War, 1618–48, is significant as it highlights the power balances and alliances among states at the start of negotiations.[37] The following is only a brief summary of the history of the Thirty Years' War, as all the details and complexities would and have filled volumes. Three major factors led to the outbreak of all-out war. First, the Holy Roman Empire[38] had been plagued with political and religious tensions between the various Protestant and Catholic states for some time. Second, a conflict within the Empire emerged in 1618 over the imperial constitution of the kingdom of Bohemia. Because of the way these two factors were initially dealt with, a third issue developed concerning the Electors of the Holy Roman Empire. The Emperor Ferdinand (a devout Catholic) took the electorate away from the Protestant Palatinate and gave it to Catholic Bavaria as punishment for the Count Palatine Frederick's acceptance of the crown of Bohemia against the Emperor's wishes, and as a reward for the Duke of Bavaria's military support for the Emperor in this issue. The tenuous pre-1618 balance of power between Catholic and Protestant states had been thrown off, and the issue over Frederick's electoral status would play a continued role in keeping other Protestant states involved in the conflict. Protestants wanted the electorate restored to Frederick while Catholics were not willing to see it taken away from Bavaria. In this way, the relatively localized conflict in Bohemia brought to the fore the growing tensions between the rights of the Emperor and those of the estates who were represented in the Empire's *diet*, or assembly. Moreover, as a result of various dynastic and religious connections, countries outside of the Empire were soon drawn into the growing conflict as well.[39]

Coalitions grew among the states that fell within the boundaries of the Empire. The two major ones were the Protestant 'Union' formed in 1608 and the Catholic 'League' established in 1609. The coalitions were destabilized by cross-cutting cleavages, groups of people who supported some political issues and not others. At the same time, the Emperor used the support of his cousin, the king of Spain, to enhance his power and convert Protestant regions to Catholicism through war and, ultimately, the 1629 Edict of Restitution. The religious conflict between Protestants and Catholics and the tenuous power balances within the Empire were concerns for virtually every country in Europe, so many rulers felt they could intervene with legitimacy. Ultimately, this linked other European wars into a single big war.

The king of Spain, Philip IV, had many reasons for supporting the Holy Roman Emperor Ferdinand II and his son and successor Ferdinand III. Like Philip, both were Catholic descendents of his own great-grandfather Charles V. They were all members of the Habsburg family, whose Austrian and Spanish branches had remained closely tied through numerous intermarriages. Spain was simultaneously involved in an ongoing war with the Dutch, whom they considered to be rebels against Philip IV's rightful hereditary rule of the low countries, but the Dutch had been very successful in this war, and the Spanish needed support if they were to prevail. Thus, another motive for the Spanish king in helping the Emperor was to gain support in fighting the Dutch after the conflicts over religious differences and the imperial constitution were settled. The Spanish king's plans were not realized, however, as the Emperor was never able to fully subdue the rebellions in his own territory, and the states within the Empire had little interest in helping Spain in its conflict with the low countries.

Sweden, ruled by King Gustavus Adolphus, became involved in the Empire's conflict in 1630, but unlike Spain, opposed the Emperor for religious and, more importantly, political reasons. Swedish war aims were to limit the Emperor's authority, annex Pomerania, and secure an indemnity to pay off the mercenary soldiers it hired. As a Lutheran state, Sweden's ruler appealed to Protestant factions within the Empire. King Gustavus tried to expand his power in the Baltic Sea by conquering the northernmost Imperial territory, and by supporting the states of the Empire that were opposed to the Emperor.

Both the Swedes and the Dutch were allied with France in an anti-Habsburg coalition. Before 1635, France was not openly involved in the war, but worked behind the scenes to oppose the Habsburgs, their traditional enemy. Without directly attacking Spain, France intervened in any conflict against Spain, helping other countries (usually monetarily) in its defeat. Ultimately, the French king and his ministers chose realpolitik over their own Catholicism, and entered the war openly in 1635 on the side of the Protestant Swedes and Dutch. Thus, the United Provinces (the Dutch), Sweden, and France were allied in trying to defeat Spain and the Holy Roman Emperor.

The main division was thus between the two great Habsburg powers and their three opponents: France, the Dutch, and Sweden. As the Swedes became successful, the Emperor wanted to form a separate peace with them, in order to deal with his greatest foe, France. However, the strange alliance between Catholic France and pro-Protestant Sweden proved unbreakable despite an understandably large degree of distrust between the two. In order to oppose Spain's support of the Emperor, France had to support Sweden as well as the Protestant states within the Empire. These two countries signed the Treaty of Hamburg, thought of by many as a precursor to the Treaty of Westphalia (Figure 3.1), to insure their alliance until the end of the war.

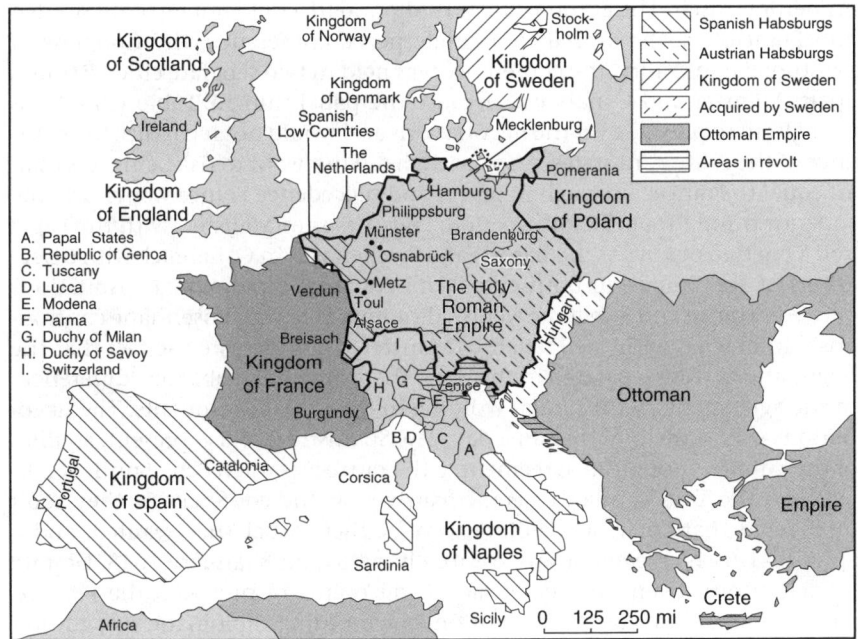

Figure 3.1 Europe after the treaties of Westphalia

The Congress of Westphalia

> You can act without any imaginable scruples.
>
> (A letter from Mazarin to French
> Ambassador the Duke de Longueville.)

Introduction

The second half of this chapter deals with the negotiations of the Congress of Westphalia as an example of diplomatic processes and agency. It will be argued here that diplomats exercised some degree of agency, but given their high degree of autonomy, the degree of demonstrated agency was only of medium strength. The lack of strong cohesion within the epistemic community also prevented strong examples of collective agency, but there were several episodes of individual agency. Until the lead-up to the negotiations, meetings among diplomats were largely bilateral at the courts of kings and princes, and except for informal, on-the-job learning, training was essentially nonexistent. These two factors contributed to a medium-strength epistemic community during the mid-seventeenth century.

The main representatives involved in the negotiations were those of France, Sweden, the various states within the Holy Roman Empire, and of the Emperor himself. The Empire, under Ferdinand III, could not separate Sweden and France,[40] so he agreed to a single peace conference, the Congress of Westphalia. In reality, the conference was held in two separate cities 30 miles apart, Münster and Osnabrück, because the papal nuncio, Fabio Chigi, was brought in to preside over the negotiations and would not recognize the existence of the Protestant states. Also, Sweden did not want to risk being less than an equal to France, although in power and precedence France was clearly the superior throughout this time period. France was in Münster (with the Papal and Venetian envoys as mediators) and Sweden was in Osnabrück with delegations of the Empire in both cities, and constant diplomatic consultations between France and Sweden. Swedish diplomat Schering Rosenhane continuously interacted with the French in Münster. Thus, despite the fact that the negotiations were separated in this way, there are remarkably few differences in the agreements, with similar wording in the actual documents. The negotiations even ended on the same day. The Spanish were also present, as allies of the Empire, though an agreement with France was not reached until 1659.

When the Dutch, allies of France, arrived at the conferences, they soon discovered that Spain was willing to offer them what they wanted, and a Spanish–Dutch agreement was eventually signed on 8 January 1648. Despite French efforts, even eventually sacrificing points of protocol, the Franco–Dutch alliance was lost.[41] In addition to conceding diplomatic recognition of their former rebels' sovereignty, the Spanish plenipotentiaries pleased the Dutch by treating them as equals. By agreeing to peace with the Emperor, however, the French still managed to isolate Spain. The Emperor strove to remain faithful to his Spanish cousin, Philip IV, but the states in the Empire were against continued fighting with Spain. Thus, the power of the combined states in the Empire over that of the Emperor himself contributed significantly to the Peace of Westphalia. All states within the Empire sent delegates, and their potential collective force was a great incentive to negotiate. Their presence at the negotiations was not originally expected, and not intended by the Emperor who initially sent some delegations away.[42] He never explicitly forbade them from participating and voting, but he also never made a move to insure their rights at the congress. However, the presence of the states within the Empire was just as important as that of the great powers.

The negotiations took approximately two years (1642–44) to get underway because of the need to settle preliminary administrative issues, and to exchange proxies. These proxies proved that the ambassadors had the authority to negotiate on behalf of their states. For example, the French proxy stated,

and generally we give more and absolute power to these same plenipotentiaries or to two of them, absent age, sickness or other obstacles of their colleague, to participate in the negotiation and to permit and to accord all that they judge is necessary to accomplish the general peace; all the way and with the same authority that we...would preserve the right to interrupt the proceedings and impose special execution, and the word of the King.[43]

The granting of absolute power in negotiations certainly represented a greater degree of delegated autonomy than in future time periods. However, the proxies can be somewhat misleading because the diplomats were always provided with thorough instructions. Around ten days after the French diplomats arrived, they received detailed instructions as well as several versions of possible peace treaties depending on the circumstances of the continuing war.[44]

Some delegations of diplomats completed their peace proposals on 4 December 1645, but the French and Swedes delayed since they wanted more representatives from the Empire to arrive to push for more universal acceptance of the legality of the treaty within the Empire.[45] During the delay, not only did representatives of other states within the Empire arrive, but other major powers as well. Every state of the continent participated, except for Russia, Poland/Lithuania, and England; all of whom, nevertheless, respected the treaty's validity.[46]

This brief summary of the arrival of diplomats and the preparation for negotiation paves the way for the bulk of this section, the negotiations themselves. The interactions within the international diplomatic community and between diplomats and sovereigns demonstrate the degree of agency diplomats had in promoting international cooperation alongside the considerable constraints brought about by competitiveness between diplomats of the same country. Moreover, the diplomats were not accustomed to such a large-scale multilateral meeting, as they would be in the nineteenth and twentieth centuries. More broadly, this was a difficult task because despite all of the efforts at state consolidation, through war and administrative centralization, many of the kingdoms still consisted of a hodgepodge of territories held together by the belief that one man was their common sovereign. War continued through the duration of the negotiations.

The negotiations

Konrad Repgen writes that there is "no precedent in European history for a process as tortuous as the peace conference in Westphalia."[47] The five great powers had been holding political peace talks long before the negotiations of Westphalia began, secret diplomacy had taken place between France and Spain, and the desire for a formal peace conference had been publicly discussed since 1634.[48] Without all of this preparation and discussion among the countries at war, the agreement, no matter how tortuous, might never have happened.

The two main issues on the table were the compensation to France and Sweden for their war efforts, and the grievances among the estates of the Empire. The first dominated the negotiations until 1647, and the rest were settled quickly afterwards. At the start of the meeting, all participants agreed that the main goal was peace, and no single country wanted to be the one to prevent this. At the same time, each diplomat was under pressure to secure the best possible deal for his own country, and to appease the preferences of his sovereign.[49] The main French minister, Cardinal Mazarin, wrote to Longueville in January, 1644, "The ambassadors must persuade the other creators of the treaty of the reasons for suggesting the sort of obligation that they face in order to repair these breaches in a unique way, and to make and maintain peace according to just conditions."[50]

An unprecedented number of some 109 envoys were present at the negotiations, in addition to 66 envoys of the Imperial estates, and 27 others representing various interests. 140 states within the Empire were actually represented because many envoys were asked by other Princes and independent entities to vote for them, having no diplomats of their own.[51] The congress took on its own dynamic over time and addressed problems that were not even on the original agenda, such as the independence of Switzerland.

The diplomats also defined the constitutional relationship between the Emperor and the member states. The settlement over religious differences accomplished more toleration than was expected. Each prince was allowed to choose the religion of the territory he ruled, but under a specific restriction: 1 January 1624 would be treated as a prewar status quo.[52] All those who had practiced a religion on this day were permitted to immigrate on favorable terms or continue to practice their religion even if their leader had changed his religion after that date.

The relationships were complex and it was not simply a matter of diplomats carrying out the policies of their sovereigns. State leaders gave diplomats autonomy to act and make decisions. For example, Mazarin wrote to them, "I have told you many things... not with the thought that you do them all, but so that in their diversity you can choose what you believe the most useful."[53] But they often took more than they were given. The diplomats wrote to Mazarin, in the name of their boy-king Louis XIV: "If we have violated our orders, Your Majesty will have enough goodness to pardon us for it."[54] Mazarin did not negotiate in writing over these differences with his diplomats, but he trusted them. No matter how absolute the state was, the diplomats could impact decision-making at the congress, and restrain state authority.

The following analysis will examine the relationship, first, between the French state (Cardinal Mazarin) and French diplomats (Longueville, d'Avaux, and Servien); second, between the Swedish state (Queen Kristina and Axel Oxenstierna) and Swedish diplomats (Johan Oxenstierna and Salvius); third, between the Emperor and the diplomats of the Empire (including the representatives of the Imperial member states); and fourth, the transnational relationships of the diplomats to each other.

France

Defining the French state: Mazarin

To understand the agency of diplomats, it is important to decipher their relationship with the state. Defining the state is a task that must be undertaken for each country and time period individually because of regime change and differences across time and between countries. As will be seen in the next case study, by the late nineteenth century the state was defined by a multitude of people and opinions because of emerging Cabinet governments and democratic principles. At the time of the negotiations at Westphalia, however, Cardinal Jules Mazarin was essentially the French state. His predecessor as first minister, Cardinal Richelieu, had a minor role at the beginning, and wrote the first main instructions to the diplomats, but died shortly after in 1642.

First, Minister Mazarin carried on Richelieu's policies. Louis XIV was still a child of four when Louis XIII died, so Anne of Austria, Louis's mother, was made Regent. However, she relied on Mazarin, and built a close relationship with him. Some historians describe Mazarin as Machiavellian because of his desire to gain more territory at any price. Nevertheless, Mazarin is also described as a moderate and an internationalist because he did not want to impose French power on the rest of Europe.[55] Andrew Lossky writes that Mazarin "regarded himself as a public servant of this Christian Commonwealth."[56] It is reasonable to conclude that he was at times a strict realist and at other times an internationalist, depending on the extent to which French interests were jeopardized.

There are three main reasons why Mazarin was, in essence, the definition of the French state. First, Anne of Austria followed his suggestions. Ruth Kleinman argues, "the established pattern of their collaboration" was simple: "he proposed and she followed."[57] Second, Mazarin had control over the secretaries of state, war, and foreign affairs. Third, the Council always ended up supporting Mazarin, even if it presented opposition at first. For example, Longueville and d'Avaux, the diplomats at the negotiations, were part of a six-person council or *Conseil d'en Haut* that exercised some decision-making authority during Louis' childhood. While they were sitting at Münster for the negotiations, Mazarin wrote to them complaining of the opposition he encountered from the Council in France. Two of the dissenters, Prince Gaston and Prince Condé, were eventually made to write letters to the plenipotentiaries indicating their support of the peace process and Mazarin's policies. Thus, even though the council existed, the members were made to agree with Mazarin.

He clearly represented the state on the home front, but restraints on his power did exist through the pressure of public opinion (of the nobility). As with his handling of the Council, he was tough about negotiating and bringing influential members of the nobility to his side. Croxton argues, "France's negotiating position was to a great extent, Mazarin's negotiating position."[58] He paid heed to others, but ultimately got his way. I argue that an important, overlooked restraint on Mazarin's power was not on the home front, but from abroad. The French diplomats received constant instruction from him, but they often defied his orders, and took liberties with their positions of power. As representatives of a rising, powerful state, the French delegates at the congress gained high ranking that facilitated their ability to get their own way.[59]

Mazarin was at base a realist and was concerned primarily with the welfare and territory of France. The war itself influenced the topic of the negotiations because fighting continued throughout the peace process. Clausewitz argues that military and diplomatic strategies have to be managed by the statesman alone; the leader is both a commander-in-chief and a statesman. In the seventeenth century, this role was merged in Mazarin, as the contending domestic powers were weak. It is in this role that Mazarin interacted with and instructed his diplomats.

The French delegation: Longueville, d'Avaux, and Servien

Anne of Austria personally chose d'Avaux while Mazarin chose Abel Servien. Mazarin at one point considered being a plenipotentiary himself in Westphalia, but eventually decided against it. D'Avaux and Servien were from the *noblesse de robe*. The Duke of Longueville was chosen to lead the delegation, and he was of royal blood. After Longueville, d'Avaux was ranked higher than Servien, but Servien had the greatest impact on the negotiations. Servien clearly stated where his priorities lay: "I have no other interest before my eyes than that of the State, of the service of the Queen, and that of His Eminence." D'Avaux, on the other hand, was more worried about the fate of Catholicism.

The two diplomats did not get along and started arguing before they even arrived in Münster. As the conference progressed, their disagreements became so strong that it interfered with the negotiations. It is likely that Servien was jealous of d'Avaux's higher status, and this precipitated the disagreements. The two competed to draft letters to the court, as they both sought the support of Mazarin for their differing stances on the negotiations. Mazarin always favored Servien, writing to him that, "If I were to send some special message to one of you without telling the others, it would be sooner to you, for all sorts of reasons, than to the others." However, d'Avaux retaliated against this, manipulated Mazarin's sympathies, by going so far as to tender his resignation if he was not going to get his way.

The foreign delegations, however, favored d'Avaux because he could speak German, was vocal in his support of Catholicism, and had a great knowledge of people. This foreign support, especially from the Swedes and Germans, upset Servien. D'Avaux faced the paradoxical situation of being supported internationally, but not domestically, an example of the importance of relationships among diplomats, even during this early period.

Longueville himself arrived in Münster on 30 June 1645, in large part to encourage Servien and d'Avaux to reach reconciliation. The French government expected that he would side with d'Avaux, but he decided to remain impartial so as not to tilt the balance against one or the other. His tactic of neutrality upset both subordinate diplomats. Longueville ended up serving as a go-between for the court and the rest of the delegation. He also became the tiebreaker; whichever side's policy he supported was usually approved. There were several other staff members of the delegation residing in both Münster and Osnabrück. Some were under the protection of d'Avaux and others answered to Servien. Despite the poor relationship between d'Avaux and Servien, whenever they did manage to agree, they inevitably got their demands, even if Mazarin was against the favored stance.

One factor that brought them together was their call for the precedence of the French state during the negotiations. After many years of its own domestic discord and of the European predominance of Spain, France was somewhat new to its position of power. Therefore, the diplomats and Mazarin were quick to take the opportunity to assert their priority. They created a visible display of the prestige of France by bringing an enormous staff and spending money extravagantly. Over 200 people attended to and resided with d'Avaux, and over 119 with Servien.[60] The staffs consisted of at least five secretaries each, pages, a priest, barbers, a doctor, cleaning women, horse assistants, and more. In addition to the staff, each ambassador had a group of nobles attending on them, eighteen for d'Avaux, and four for Servien. This massive staff represented the prestige of France, and was considered a necessity for people of their rank at the time. They received 100,000 livres per year for their job, but as this included living expenses, and bribes, they always required more money to be sent. A major topic of each letter from 1646 was the lack of funds to provide bribes and manage their large households.

Although the French diplomats were clearly entitled to a high rank in the international system, it sometimes got in the way of their goals for compromise. They wanted to promote the interests of the estates against the Empire, but they could not at the same time treat the estates with the same rank as themselves. When the Emperor insisted that the states within the Empire be given the same regard as the other major nations in attendance, the French diplomats faced a dilemma because they did not want to be seen as showing less regard toward these states than the Emperor himself.[61] Finally, the French delegates grudgingly conceded some points of protocol for the sake of the Peace, as ordered in a letter "written" by the six-year-old Louis XIV in 1645.[62]

What was the relationship between Mazarin and the diplomats at Westphalia? Mazarin gave them a degree of autonomy, but their initiative is what allowed them to impact the outcomes of the negotiations. After all, because they were in the field they had more extensive knowledge of news as it occurred, and developed relationships with the other diplomats as well as shared worldviews. The first minister was aware of this, and accepted the decisions made by the ambassadors as long as the diplomats believed it to be in the interest of France. Mazarin provided full and constant instruction to the diplomats, but they exercised their own agency to decide how to act. In general, the state provides the degree of structural autonomy for diplomats, but the manner in which they use this decision-making space is up to the diplomats. Mazarin wrote to them,

> When I gave you the liberty before the start of the campaign to do [what you wanted] more or less in many things, I considered very carefully into whose hands I committed this power, and that each of you had the zeal and the prudence necessary to know [whether] to hold firm or to diminish our demands, or even to increase them, according to whether the military campaign, which should set the negotiations in motion and regulate them, went well or poorly.[63]

Mazarin did have a means of controlling the actions of his diplomats through correspondences, but it was never perfect, especially because of the large delay in sending and receiving letters. By the time the diplomats received Mazarin's reactions to their decisions at the congress, the results of their actions had already been written up in the royal memo back in Paris.[64]

If the diplomats strayed too far from the instructions of the state, Mazarin could simply dismiss them, as he did with d'Avaux in 1648. The quarrels between the two diplomats also served as a check on one another. While Mazarin openly acknowledged that he was passing on a great deal of decision-making authority to them, at times he complained that the diplomats seemed to forget the contents of his letters. He wrote on one occasion, "the King does not want to reach the point of ruin."[65] For example, Mazarin disliked the first proposition submitted by France to the mediators in December 1644; as a consequence, he drafted his own second proposition at Court and sent it to his plenipotentiaries. This caused embarrassing delays on the French side as they continually communicated back to Mazarin on the decisions that they faced. Nevertheless, this close contact and checking of decisions with Mazarin was the exception and not the norm.

In several instances the diplomats went directly against Mazarin's orders. One example was over their demand for the possession of Philippsburg in May 1646, when Mazarin had instructed them to compromise as soon as possible. Another time was when the diplomats rallied against a truce with the Italian states, going against Mazarin's position. Not only did Mazarin accept the ways in which they altered his instructions or even went against them, he sought advice from them on how he should design his policy. Ideas from Münster were often reprinted in official memoranda in Paris shortly after they arrived in diplomatic correspondences. For example, the diplomats advised Mazarin that he was wrong in thinking that Bavaria was well disposed toward France. The one instance in which Mazarin ignored the advice of the plenipotentiaries was when he insisted on the exchange of Catalonia for the Spanish Low Countries. This demand was entirely unreasonable, and his intervention was, of course, unsuccessful.

Sweden

Defining the Swedish state: Queen Kristina and Axel Oxenstierna

Queen Kristina, daughter and heir of Gustavus Adolphus, and Chancellor Axel Oxenstierna were the primary decision-makers of the Swedish state. Axel Oxenstierna was regent for Kristina during the twelve years between her father's death and her eighteenth birthday on 18 December 1644. Even though Kristina officially took over the reins at this time, Oxenstierna's power and hold over the upper nobility continued. She disagreed with his policies, and had to fight to get her way. Conflict first arose between the two over whether and whom Kristina should marry; then the disagreements spread to policy decisions, in particular the outcome of the Peace of Westphalia.

The Council of State typically supervised and wrote diplomatic correspondences on behalf of Kristina, but she could bypass it whenever she wanted and did so on occasion. Once she reached her majority, she was adamant about bringing peace to Europe, and preventing Oxenstierna's camp from delaying it. She wanted the quickest possible peace on good terms for Sweden, and so instructed her diplomats to "bring the negotiation to a desirable conclusion, making [the terms to be obtained] as good as can be done without breaking the peace, and no longer dawdle with it as hitherto has been done."[66] She was implicating Axel in regard to the delay.

The Swedish state strove to gain equal footing with the French at the start of the negotiations, and this was one of the main reasons, besides religion, that the congress was held in two cities. The diplomatic instructions were to ensure that the Swedish delegation spoke directly after the Imperial delegation, and did not give a higher ranking to any other delegates. The aim of Kristina and Axel Oxenstierna in 1641 was "to preserve... the majesty and prestige of the realm and its equal status with other kingdoms."[67] When Swedish concerns were made public, the French retort was that they were clearly the most powerful state, and should have precedence. The disagreement over precedence put a strain on the alliance between France and Sweden, but ultimately it became clear that France would win out.

The Swedish delegation: Johan Oxenstierna and Salvius

The Swedish plenipotentiaries, Johan Adler Salvius and Johan Oxenstierna, Axel's son, were even more hostile toward each other than the French ambassadors, Servien and d'Avaux. Johan Oxenstierna was naturally bound to his father, and shared with him all the information he gathered, including the queen's direct correspondence with the diplomats. Although Salvius was at one point close to Axel Oxenstierna as well, he increasingly became more detached from the Chancellor's authority. He gained influence over the queen, and this enabled him to gain independent authority or autonomy at Westphalia. Kristina relied on Salvius to represent her demands for immediate peace during the final stages of the congress. Salvius, unlike Johan Oxenstierna, was not of the nobility or the ruling elite. Instead of a military approach, he was a businessman and was interested in the economics of international relations.[68] War hurt many forms of business, and he believed in the long run that Sweden's military was not as strong as it appeared and that it would not be able to protect its territory abroad. Salvius's goal was thus somewhat at odds with both Kristina's bid for a European peace, and Oxenstierna's adamancy about maximizing Sweden's territorial gains.

Chancellor Oxenstierna continued the policies of King Gustavus Adolphus who had been particularly concerned about the security of the long Swedish coastline. They both believed that the only way to protect this coast, rich with natural resources, was to control the opposite shores as well. The chancellor wrote to his son Johan that the other countries were jealous of them, so Sweden must do whatever was required to secure its lands. Salvius, on the other hand, was just as adamant that the results of the negotiation should be based on international consensus, and not Sweden's fear of its jealous neighbors. He argued correctly that the Swedish war was only possible financially with French money, and militarily with German soldiers. Sweden had all along benefited from international consensus, and by abandoning it, would lose its security and stability. The explicit instructions on 11 July 1643 to the diplomats from the Council of State were to pursue Swedish interests as discreetly as possible, all the while putting good diplomacy and maintaining alliances with other states as the first priority.[69] This stance was supported by Salvius, and privately backed by Johan Oxenstierna, even though at this point, both Queen Kristina and Axel Oxenstierna maintained Sweden's controversial occupation of Pomerania, an important region along the German Baltic coast that belonged to the Brandenburg elector, Frederick William, by treaty.

A strong example of the influence of diplomatic society was Johan Oxenstierna's somewhat privately held belief that Sweden should not lay claim to Pomerania because it meant losing friendships and alienating themselves at the negotiation. It was clearly not in his professional interest to disagree with his father and the Queen, but he did admit secretly to the Pomeranian diplomats that he did not support the Swedish state's claim (although at one point he had). Salvius, of course, was much more vociferous about rejecting his state's hard-line approach and embarked on a persuasion campaign to convince other diplomats of a compromise solution that would divide up Pomerania giving the eastern half to Frederick William and the western half to Sweden. Together, the two Swedish diplomats, despite personal differences, wrote letters to Stockholm dedicating much description to the strong opposition they faced over Sweden's occupation of Pomerania. The state eventually gave ground to their diplomats allowing that Salvius's partition idea could serve as a last resort during the negotiations. The Queen and Chancellor did not seem to grasp that they would be lucky to preserve the western half of Pomerania and still benefit from European consensus over the matter. It took seven months to negotiate.

At the same time, Imperial Ambassador Trauttmansdorff also displayed diplomatic agency of his own, criticizing Elector of Brandenburg Frederick William, and favoring to some extent the Swedish compromise solution. Earlier, Trauttmansdorff had warned Swedish Ambassador Rosenhane that Sweden would be highly inconsistent to act as though they supported the plight of the Protestant states while at the same time trying to seize their land. However, as the issue continued to sop up time at the congress, Trauttmansdorff altered his line, admonishing the elector of Brandenburg for making a big deal about territory he had never really controlled while the Emperor was ceding lands possessed by the Habsburgs for centuries.

Salvius shared policy goals with the French diplomat, d'Avaux, and was quite possibly friends with him. He chose to write letters directly to d'Avaux instead of to the French delegation in general. D'Avaux would sometimes follow his instructions verbatim.[70] Johan Oxenstierna had a closer bond with French ambassador Servien, but because of Oxenstierna's disagreeable temperament, Salvius was more popular with the French. They appreciated his refined disposition.

Both Swedish ambassadors were either weak in religious conviction or, as Salvius probably was, agnostic. Osiander writes that a basic consensus was reached at Westphalia in large part because of the decline of religious conviction as a mark of identity.[71] It was around this time that religious symbolism during treaty proceedings was beginning its slow decline.[72] It is important to note, however, that any decline in religious sentiments was largely among the diplomatic community as a distinct international society, and not in the European system as a whole. The Thirty Years' War was fought in large part over religion, and the Peace was made possible only by agreeing to disagree on the issue of religion.

The Empire

The Emperor and the princes

Ferdinand III, as Emperor, was the titular ruler of the Holy Roman Empire, but it was the Council of Electors that really represented power within the Empire. The Electors were seven of the most powerful and influential rulers amongst the many essentially sovereign states that made up the Empire, and each of the main religions, Catholic, Lutheran, and Reformed, was represented in their number. As their titles suggest, it fell to them to elect the new Emperor when the previous one died. In fact, Ferdinand III was not only Emperor, but as King of Bohemia, he was himself one of the seven electors. This is where his power base lay. In his capacity as Emperor, Ferdinand may have been the recognized sovereign by tradition and election, but his main role was symbolic and he had little real authority in the lands of the other electors. The Emperor symbolized the solidarity of the lands of the Empire and his people's loyalty to it, but he did not exercise true executive authority. Osiander argues that the sense of community, manifested through loyalty and structural inviolability, made consensus within the Empire more possible on issues that threatened stability, much more so than in the European system in general.[73]

Despite this common allegiance, the princes of the states within the Empire often conducted independent foreign policy with those outside of the Empire, most visibly during the Thirty Years' War. For this reason, it was expected that they would negotiate and act independently at Westphalia in much the same way as had the Italian princes in ages past.[74] They sent their own delegates and pursued their own ends, but unlike their Italian counterparts, they remained within the boundaries of the imperial constitution. They did not forget their common allegiance to the Empire, nor as Osiander puts it, "the inviolability of the structures or political framework by which the community was defined, and, on the other hand, loyalty to the community and its members and representatives."[75]

Thus, paradoxically, even though the Emperor had not gained the trust and true rule over the people, he had gained their indissoluble loyalty. Osiander argues that the loyalty principle also applied in a reciprocal manner from each state to other states in the Empire. Although the estates were not obedient or subservient to the Emperor as in the early Middle Ages, they wanted to maintain their autonomy alongside their coexistence within the Empire. These horizontal allegiances did not exist among European states outside of the Empire, as they did within the Holy Roman Empire, or as they do today in the EU. These strongly held norms cannot be predicted by a purely realist worldview, a fact that the French discovered during the course of the negotiations.

Diplomats of the empire

Johannes Krane, Trauttmansdorff, and Johann Maximilian Lamberg were the three ambassadors representing Ferdinand III at the congress. There were many others from the various member states of the Empire. For example, on the Protestant side, Brandenburg and Saxony were well represented, and a certain Dr Kaysar was responsible for the interests of the Mecklenburg ducal house. There was some conflict and confusion over protocol involving the Emperor and the states within the Empire. As usual, the Emperor's envoy received full precedence at the congress, and signed the treaties first. However, the Emperor had to accept the same title, "Holy Majesty," as the French and Swedish monarchs in the written treaty. This represented a slight demotion for the Emperor in matters of title and precedence.

Just as the Emperor's diplomats were accustomed to receiving precedence in all matters, the diplomats of the member states expected the same. When they encountered the Venetian ambassador and mediator Alvise Contarini in Münster, he declared that they were of lesser rank than those of Rome. Indeed, according to the general qualifications of precedence, this was true, and Contarini got his way in terms of the order of the proceedings. However, the French diplomats also asserted their claim to ranking in an unprecedented way by insisting on the same title for their sovereign as that held by the Emperor.

Diplomacy among the representatives of the member states was conducted alongside the larger diplomatic negotiations at Westphalia. The princes' diplomats sent letters to each other to find out who would support various proposals and who would not before they ever reached the table in Westphalia.

Overwhelmingly, decisions did not weaken the solidarity of the Empire as a whole. For example, in a meeting with d'Avaux, Dr Kaysar emphasized that the French intention to insure the liberty and rights of the Protestant states through an active presence in the Empire was not what the member states of the Empire wanted. Rather, the point of the negotiation was to find "ways of removing the foreign troops from the soil of the Empire; for in this consisted above all the freedom of the estates."⁷⁶ Thus, the representatives of the states within the Empire would prefer to give up some religious and political advantage rather than face the possible break-up of the Empire because of a foreign presence (i.e., the French).

As the congress progressed, the French learned the extent to which diplomats of the Empire would not compromise the solidarity of the Empire. Subsequently, they learned that this steadfastness applied not only to the Empire, but also among the Imperial diplomats themselves. Unlike the Italian princes, those of the Imperial states were not willing to have outside intervention. Longueville did not find the ambassadors from the states within the Empire very intelligent, and thought they were confused by some of the proceedings in the conference. He nevertheless found them friendly and frank, and the French delegation worked to accommodate their preferences for solidarity. This is another example of the shaping of the diplomatic community as a process over time as these basic preconditions had to be appreciated by all before compromises could be made. In addition, this information could not be included in state instructions because it was an unexpected discovery revealed through diplomatic interactions over time. The fact that the King of Spain was also the Duke of Burgundy complicated matters, because in this capacity he was a member of the Imperial Diet entitled to the military protection of the Empire. Only the diplomats could realize that any proposal they offered must not exacerbate the Empire's ties to Spain.

The epistemic community of diplomats

Now that the relationship of the diplomats to their states and the degree of agency they displayed has been established, the question remains: what about the relationship of the diplomats to each other? As mentioned above, diplomats had many informal occasions to meet, and often came to understandings around the dinner table. Another important method was through private letters sent from one diplomat to another, such as when Salvius was making an individual bid for the division of Pomerania. These methods were often just as effective as the formal negotiations, both directly as a means of persuasion and indirectly as a means of promoting a sense of collegiality among the transnational corps. Any kind of closer acquaintance or specific attention to each other's preferences oiled the machine of the negotiating process. In particular, informal methods of persuasion, combined with gift giving and flattery, produced results. In retrospect, however, it is clear that the level of cohesion of the diplomatic corps was not as great as it would be in future multilateral conferences.⁷⁷

The formal methods of negotiation at the congress followed strict procedural guidelines that often resulted in very little face-to-face persuasion. At the preliminary meeting in Hamburg in 1641 to determine the procedures of the congress, a triangle model was agreed upon.[78] According to the model, adversaries were not to speak directly to each other, but through an intermediary who would relay the position of each party back and forth. The French and Spanish thus never met at the same table, and France's interactions with the Emperor, except thrice, were through papal nuncio Chigi and Ambassador Contarini of Venice. At one period (from early autumn 1646 to spring of 1647), the Dutch served as mediators between France and Spain, turning the triangle model into a rectangular model with even less face-to-face interaction. Because the Swedes preferred not to have a mediator, they negotiated directly with the envoys of the Emperor and the Imperial member states. The meetings between the Spanish and the Dutch also did not follow the triangle model; these diplomats spoke directly to one another.

Diplomatic agency

There is ample evidence to suggest that the settlement of the Thirty Years' War and the Congress of Westphalia was not a result of purely power-based reasoning or efficiency. The examples of diplomatic influence in the preceding analysis are numerous. Collective, nonrealist goals were accomplished largely because of what occurred during the negotiations, and this was based largely on the role of the diplomats. First, the negotiations covered more than was originally necessary for the resolution of the war; they gradually took on a dynamic of their own. Second, diplomats were given autonomy to act, and occasionally exercised agency beyond this autonomy and went against state instructions. Third, the final treaty advanced the collective good as well as individual interests of the states involved. Many scholars point to the Peace of Westphalia as the first official document advancing the idea of international society. As Watson argues, "Diplomacy was becoming more collective."[79] Naturally, a sense of society among the diplomats resulted in a society among the states, albeit at an elite level.

The Treaty of Westphalia itself contains numerous examples of diplomatic initiative. While the majority of its articles deal with territorial claims and debts, several of them are about the collective welfare of the signatory states. One example is Article XLI in which the rule of law is upheld post facto. It states that the criminal sentences pronounced during the war about nonreligious matters were declared subject to review and judgment in a proper court. "The former judgments may be confirmed, amended, or quite erased, in case of Nullity."[80] Another example is Article XLIII, which declared that all nonroyalty who served in the war would be restored to honor without prejudice. "From the highest to the lowest, without any distinction or exception, with their Wives, Estates, shall be restored by all Partys in the State of Life, Honour, Renown, Liberty of Conscience." These are examples of provisions that went beyond the call of the states, and reflected a collective diplomatic interest in international society.

However, this period, more than any other studied in this work, was clearly dominated by realist concerns in an international environment of absolutism and zero-sum gain. There is considerable doubt as to whether statements made by sovereigns in favor of advancing the collective good were genuine rather than just posturing. Even Queen Kristina, the strongest advocate of European peace and cooperation, did not push strongly for the collective goal until she had managed to secure the territorial goals of Sweden. Sovereigns were clear in all their instructions and correspondence with the diplomats that they needed to maximize the interests of their state. Even Richelieu's idea for a cooperative system-wide security was surely not the real French goal. At the start of the negotiations, the French instructions referred to Christian princes instead of Christendom, stated that it was natural for these princes to have different interests, and justified war in the name of territorial interests or balance of power.[81] The flexibility and agency that diplomats took were not great compared to future congresses, but these levels increased throughout the course of the negotiation as they came to understand the positions of other states, and as they established a rapport with the other diplomats.

Realism as an alternative explanation

Was the result of the negotiation different from a realist prediction? The argument advanced here in light of the evidence is that diplomatic agency impacted the outcomes of international cooperation during the mid-seventeenth century, and in particular during the Congress of Westphalia. How does this argument hold up to the null hypothesis that diplomats are only transmission belts for states, and that states only seek to maximize power? Evan Luard, a scholar of the period, defines seventeenth-century power as the size of population, the organization of population, the size of army and navy, financial resources, military technology (but adapted by all quickly), generalship (leadership of military generals), and the ability of the state to mobilize forces for war.[82] He argues that, "Since warfare was the principal means by which the competition among states was conducted, the development of the state's military power was one of the principal ambitions of the rulers of the day."[83]

This definition of power specific to the seventeenth century is not so different from how realists define power for any period.[84] Neorealists define power as the ability of undifferentiated sovereign units to survive in a self-help world. This is a stricter definition of power that would not include such factors as the organization of population or generalship. Classical realists have a looser definition of power, and consider diplomacy and world government as an ideal, though unattainable, means of overcoming pure material competition.[85] Neoclassical realists consider perceptions of power as important as well.[86]

If power is defined in terms of Luard's qualifications, it is basically a form of base materialism that makes one state more powerful than another.[87] "A war-like environment encouraged the belief that a successful foreign policy could be conducted only by governments which could back it with effective armed power."[88] David J. Hill has also argued that the negotiators of the Peace of Westphalia were concerned only with maximizing national interest and ambition.[89] From the data in the Table 3.1, it is evident that France and Spain overwhelmingly had the largest armies. Yet, they were not ultimately set on continued warfare to maximize territorial and material gains.

A realist explanation of the outcome of the Congress of Westphalia is based on the relationship between a country's military power indicated here, and its gains made at the congress. According to the theory, (1) more powerful countries will gain while weaker countries lose, (2) states will try to balance against other powerful states, and (3) states will act as unitary actors. First, in terms of power-based outcomes the realist outcome is quite accurate for this time period compared to others (as will be seen in the following chapter). Second, balance of power occurred. Third, against realist predictions states were not unitary actors. The diplomats were not simply following state instructions, and this fact is very important because they, not the sovereigns, were present at the negotiations. By neglecting the process, realist theory misses the agency of diplomats, and the likelihood that cooperation would have failed without them. The following analysis explains these three factors further.

The first part of realist theory is the competition to maximize power or territory. The winners of territory were France and Sweden, and the losers were Spain and the Empire. France and Spain had the largest armies so a

Table 3.1 Approximate size of armies in 1648

Countries	1648
Austria	35,000
France	120,000
Great Britain	65,000
Prussia	8,000
Spain	150,000
Sweden	70,000
United Provinces	50,000

Note: The data includes mercenary and auxiliary forces. Also see: J. Childs, *Armies and Warfare in Europe, 1648–1789* and Paul Kennedy, *The Rise and Fall of the Great Powers*.
Source: Evan Luard, *The Balance of Power: The System of International Relations, 1648–1815*, London: Macmillan, 1992, p. 37.

realist explanation would find it in their best interest to continue fighting for more gains during the course of the negotiations. In fact, they did keep fighting until 1659. At the same time, their greater power should have enabled them to push for more territory through the negotiations. Indeed, France, by this point the most powerful country in Europe, gained the titles to the bishoprics of Metz, Toul, and Verdun, the city of Breisach, and ten Alsatian cities. Spain, although it had long been the greatest military power on the continent, had to recognize Dutch independence after eighty years of difficult fighting. Sweden was strengthened militarily by 1648 and became a great power in the eyes of others. The congress left Sweden in control of most of the Baltic, including even most of that sea's southernmost ports. Ferdinand III lost virtually all real political power in his capacity as Emperor, and the Empire itself lost territory to France and Sweden.

The second part of realist theory is that states will try to balance against other threatening powers. This explains why Sweden gained and Spain lost. States can find it in their best interest to ally with others for greater security as they did in the seventeenth century. As Callières writes, "There is indeed no prince so powerful that he can afford to neglect the assistance offered by a good alliance in resisting the forces of hostile power which are prompted by jealousy of his prosperity to unite in a hostile coalition."[90] No sovereign could risk allowing his enemy to have a stronger military through an alliance without himself striving to form an alliance. Thus, Mazarin and Kristina held steadfast to their "strange alliance" of Catholic and Protestant states, and Philip IV continued to support his Habsburg relative of the Empire. A power-based argument, however, is too simplistic in its stipulation that these alliances were built on immediate short-term self-interest.[91] As was observed from the proceedings at Westphalia, a great deal of effort on the part of diplomats went into the maintenance of these alliances. Self-interest alone does not immediately create alliances. Also, with so many conflicting allegiances, it is often difficult to calculate which alliances actually maximize self-interest.

Some of the material outcomes of the congress can be understood by the realist argument, especially during this period of strong absolutism and a zero-sum environment. However, the differences in outcomes from the realist prediction are crucial. The third part of realist theory, that states are unitary actors, is proven false in this case study. The biggest lapse in the realist argument is the neglect of the role of the diplomats who were alone responsible for the settlement itself. As the foregoing evidence makes abundantly clear, the diplomats were not simply transmission belts for their states. In fact, they did not always obey the instructions of their sovereigns, and they discovered entirely new collective initiatives that impacted outcomes. On many occasions, the fate of the outcomes rested on the talent, initiative, popularity, and independence of a particular diplomat. As the congress proceeded, the diplomats reached new understandings that were unexpected and unforeseen by the sovereigns. Cooperation would most likely not have been accomplished at all if not for the work of diplomats. Therefore, by ignoring this process, the realist null hypothesis fails to capture the beginning of an important trend in the role of diplomats as a community with agency distinct from the structure of the international system.

Bargaining theory as an alternative explanation

What about bargaining theory? Would it have predicted the outcomes at Westphalia? In this case, bargaining theory predicts the same outcomes as realist theory because the worldviews of the leaders involved were essentially absolutist. Each wanted to maximize the power of his or her own country, thus increasing self-interest. Mazarin was concerned with only France's welfare and territory. Similarly, Kristina's and Axel Oxenstierna's chief preference was "to preserve... the majesty and prestige of the realm and its equal status with other kingdoms."[92] Chancellor Oxenstierna's main priority was the security of the long Swedish coastline, and the need to control the opposite shores at the same time. They both also wanted to maintain Sweden's controversial occupation of Pomerania. Thus, they associated more power and land as the key to protecting Sweden's interests. While the treaty did not completely betray these initial preferences, numerous compromises among the diplomats meant that the leaders were not able to have all of their preferences fulfilled. However, Mazarin wanted an immediate compromise over Philippsburg, and the French diplomats persisted in demanding Philippsburg until they were successful. Axel Oxenstierna and Queen Kristina wanted control over Pomerania, and the diplomats supported a partition strategy, which they ultimately succeeded in advancing. These are just two examples from the preceding analysis that bargaining theory would predict. To the extent that diplomats exercise agency, it was because of the shared norms and professionalism that characterized their epistemic community at the time.

The aftermath of Westphalia

The Treaty of Westphalia launched an era that saw the growth of multilateral agreements and international congresses. Subsequent meetings referred back to the Westphalian model until it became institutionalized as a style of international negotiation. The mid-seventeenth century, culminating in the Treaty of Westphalia, provides a good window into the diplomatic role of early modern international relations. Prior to it, states typically made bilateral treaties that had no formal means of enforcement or revision. The treaty was eventually not sufficient to maintain peace and the integrity of all territorial boundaries, but a precedent was set for genuine efforts at multilateralism, continuity, and self-perpetuation of treaties of international cooperation.

The negotiations accomplished a greater degree of cooperation than had existed before. It brought an end to the war in the Holy Roman Empire fought because of long-lasting religious divisions, and created a new order in Europe with greater symbolic significance because of the unprecedented level of multinational cooperation. A version of Richelieu's idealistic scheme for a collective security arrangement, written before his death in 1642, was adopted in the final treaty. If any party's religion was infringed upon, and the matter could not be settled within three years, "each and any party to the present transaction [the Treaty of Westphalia] shall be obliged to join forces and counsel with the injured party and to take up arms to oppose the contravention."[93] The signatories of the treaty most likely had no intention of following through with such an arrangement either going into or coming out of the negotiations, but its significance as a great leap in ideas about cooperation lived on. The Peace of Westphalia became a standard for future diplomacy and negotiations, and international security alliances became commonplace.

The Thirty Years' War and its resolution played a strong role in unifying the territories of states and in concentrating the political power of their central institutions. After the Treaty of Westphalia, the office of Holy Roman Emperor was politically powerless.[94] Since individual rulers within and outside of the Empire could impose religious doctrine on their territory, the negotiations meant acceptance of autonomous power of sovereigns, even though in actuality territorial boundaries were very weak – at least until further centralization in the eighteenth century.[95] Within each kingdom, there were still many subterritories, and each had its own bureaucracy, system of estates, tradition, and sometimes even language and culture.[96]

Paradoxically, because the aggressive competition of the seventeenth century resulted in a degree of state consolidation, the eventual accomplishment of peace was facilitated as power was more clearly identifiable. The absolutist princes had a stronger hold than before on the collection of territories in their kingdoms through external war and internal bureaucratic centralization. They thus had the ability to grant plenipotentiary status to their diplomatic representatives. It would be difficult to give full plenipotentiary power away if rulers did not have it to give in the first place. This is a sharp break with the Middle Ages, as only sovereigns were able to send and receive diplomats starting from around the Treaty of Westphalia.[97]

As this process of state building continued, princes began to see themselves as "the personification of states," rather than as representatives of a ruling family.[98] Louis XIV declared himself actually to be the state. Personal status was only important if it was tied to the status, and thus visible power, of the state.[99] Thus, diplomats had a better concept of whom they represented, and this was more often states. However, as princes became more synonymous with the state, diplomats became increasingly recognized as individuals with status and prestige of *their own*. In the next century, diplomatic procedure and precedence demonstrated respect for the reputation and power of the diplomat himself, and not just the state he represented.

Although the Treaty of Westphalia was not to be the agreement to end all European wars, nor did it demonstrate the complete acceptance of the concept of territorial sovereignty, it did provide a good case study of the first professional diplomatic process. Ultimately, the collective security arrangement became simply an agreement to be good neighbors, to show goodwill whenever possible, and for the French and Swedes to guarantee the imperial constitution. Nevertheless, the process and production of the treaty shows that interaction and professionalization of diplomats over time was an important part of reaching agreement. Thus, power and state interests were not the only concerns. In fact, attention to diplomats is essential to understanding outcomes. Westphalia pushed diplomacy forward into the modern era, and toward the degree of professionalism that it was to accomplish in future centuries.

4
The Late Nineteenth Century and the Congress of Berlin

Climate of the times

The late nineteenth century was a time of relative peace, alliance building, and technological advancement. First, no wars had been fought among Western European powers since the Crimean War, which was settled by the 1856 Treaty of Paris; no wars were fought among the Great Powers[1] from the Franco-Prussian War in 1871 to World War I in 1914; and Germany and Italy had finally reached a unified stability.[2] Second, there was an urgent need for diplomats to continue supporting previously created alliances, as well as to build new ones.[3] Professional diplomats played a substantial role in giving governmental legitimacy to the creation of over 400 international nongovernmental organizations, and nearly 3000 international gatherings.[4] However, the massive growth in the number of international organizations from the 1860s had still not attained the status of mainstream diplomacy.[5] Third, advances in technology brought about new ways of communication such as the telegraph, telephone, newspaper, and radio, and faster ways of transportation such as the steamboat and railway.

Early democratization and growing nationalism also characterize the times. Some components of democracy, developed over the centuries for a variety of reasons, started to emerge in Western Europe, and later spread East and South. The nineteenth century witnessed the transition of power from royal courts to cabinets, especially in Britain and Germany.[6] Cabinet members commonly sought information from diplomats who were the most familiar with local politics in a region. The actions of diplomats and statesmen were occasionally checked by democratically elected parliaments and often differing opinions among the elite delayed policy decisions. In most countries, political and military power remained legally in the hands of sovereign rulers, but power was shared among other elites and statesmen. Many countries in Europe had adopted a nationalism based on imperialism, and borders were thus more strictly guarded. In Eastern Europe, Pan-Slavism, the idea that all Slavs should be united, encouraged a kind of nationalism in countries that had a large Orthodox Christian population. A side effect of nationalism was that it pushed governments toward creating a voice for the people. Popular participation was spreading and public opinion mattered more, even though foreign affairs were still governed by a small, elite few.

Despite the ability to communicate rapidly, and the increasingly rule-bound, bureaucratized nature of the profession, the diplomat's role was not diminished. The sheer quantity of telegraphs, typically around five per day, and long letters, several per week, meant that diplomats were not only constantly meeting with their colleagues and foreign sovereigns on a daily basis, they were also writing about it. The *Layard Papers* comprise the correspondences from the ambassador in Constantinople to the Foreign Secretary in London during the Eastern Crisis, and are an example of the sheer quantity and substance of the work of a single diplomat at the time.[7] More generally, diplomatic responsibility was supplemented in many areas in the increasingly complex world of popular opinion, party differences, territorial integrity, wide-flung empires, and trade. The role of sovereigns was decreasing with the rise of statesmen, so the definition of the state and its interests was even more open to interpretation.

A significant amount of the foreign policy dialogue in the late nineteenth century was focused on the fate of the Ottoman Empire, which was nearing its final demise. There were questions over how it would be divided up, who would exert influence, and where the boundaries would be. The future of the Turkish people was crucial in playing the Great Powers off one another, and adding an extra layer of turbulence. This chapter examines the Eastern Crisis, 1875–78, dealing with the relationship of the Great Powers to the Balkan Peninsula, and the final culmination of the crisis at the Congress of Berlin in 1878.

The first half of this chapter will discuss the qualities of the diplomatic profession and the extent to which diplomats formed an epistemic community with the ability to exercise collective agency. It will include a brief background of the relationships among states and the circumstances surrounding the Eastern Crisis. The second half of the chapter will look in detail at the Congress of Berlin as an actual example of how diplomats of the late nineteenth century contributed to international cooperation. Finally, some generalizations will be drawn about the transnational diplomatic corps of the time.

The society of diplomats

The centralized modern state had complex bureaucracies that impacted the structure of foreign services in Europe. Diplomats were governed by many more rules involving recruitment, training, wages, promotion, and retirement as a result of the general bureaucratization of the state. Much of the bureaucratization and professionalization that would overwhelmingly take over the diplomatic profession in the twentieth century had its origins much earlier. By the end of the eighteenth century, nearly every state in Europe had a special governmental division for the management of foreign policy and diplomacy. Alongside this, there also emerged a tension between the centralized governments and their foreign offices. The latter were granted decision-making authority to act on behalf of the states in foreign matters.

Yet, despite this newfound structure, there remained political space or structural autonomy for diplomats to act. Of all the state agencies, bureaucratization transformed the foreign service last, and had not yet reached the highest echelons of the diplomatic hierarchy. In Austria, for example, there was less red tape in the foreign office than in any other governmental department.[8] While residing abroad, ambassadors could take much of the decision-making into their own hands. With the decline of the absolute involvement of sovereigns, there was even some ambiguity about who in government was actually entitled to instruct and manage the foreign service. Some sovereigns preferred to instruct diplomats personally, while others trusted the authority of their statesmen or cabinet members. The trend was for this important responsibility to fall increasingly into the hands of the foreign secretary.

The late nineteenth century can be characterized as a time in which diplomats had structural autonomy from the state, high professionalism, and a growing but still weak diplomatic bureaucracy. Moreover, given this structural autonomy, diplomats exercised agency. For the first time, diplomats considered themselves more important than their instructions, and acted based on this commonly held norm that was in many ways unique to the period. As evidence of this, Lord Granville wrote to Mr Gladstone about the Constantinople conference, "I hear that Layard is to be sent... I think [he] will be faithful to instructions, if the latter are of the right sort."[9] In the seventeenth century, it was intended that diplomats were the conveyors of state instructions, though this did not always happen in practice; but in the late nineteenth century, many believed that a diplomat's expertise was worth more than his instructions. In most cases, diplomats acted first, sent a telegraph informing the foreign secretary of what had occurred, and then received a response of approval.[10] The use of the telegraph also meant that the instructions were short, and it was up to the ambassador to discover for himself the right course of action if circumstances should not go according to plan. In the mid-nineteenth century, British Foreign Secretary, Lord John Russell, stated that the invention of the telegraph meant that the ambassador had to supply a lot of his own instructions to supplement those of the foreign secretary.[11]

In the seventeenth century, diplomats exercised some agency with little bureaucracy; in the late nineteenth century, they exercised a great deal of agency despite growing bureaucracy. The bureaucratization provided the level of autonomy for diplomats in the late nineteenth century. By contrast, in the past, it was exclusively the sovereign who determined structural autonomy.

New structures: Bureaucratization, professionalization, and training

In the seventeenth century, diplomats were responsible for their own professionalization. In the late nineteenth century, diplomats benefited from a legacy of two centuries of professionalization when they began their careers in the foreign service. Nevertheless, further professionalization occurred rapidly throughout the nineteenth century, largely pushed forward by encroaching state bureaucratization. Compared to the fledgling states of the seventeenth century, the modern state was highly bureaucratized, complex, and centralized. Consequently, the foreign service was much more rule bound, hierarchical, and meritocratic. In a small handful of countries, the existing foreign service was pared down to diminish inflated staffs that were largely comprised of nobility and patronage appointments.[12] M.S. Anderson argues, "More and more governments now demanded diplomatic services systematically and even rigidly organized, in which efficiency carried more weight and merit could expect to be rewarded more effectively."[13] The selection and promotion procedures, however, were still highly subjective.

Much of the bureaucratic element was brought about by Napoleon, who was influenced by previous French kings and decided that the only way to control the state was through bureaucratization. In the early nineteenth century, Napoleon combined bureaucratization with personal control of foreign affairs, especially of diplomats. He did not trust his Foreign Minister, and ordered his diplomats to communicate with himself directly. He handpicked diplomats for appointments, preferred not to train professional diplomats, and double-checked their instructions before they were sent out.[14] Early on, Napoleon's attitude toward France's foreign affairs was similar to that of the absolutist monarchs and cardinals of the seventeenth century. Later, Napoleon initiated a system of meritocratic recruitment and training. While it was not really institutionalized as a working part of the system until the 1930s, 95 percent of the secretarial corps and two out of three diplomats were professionally trained by 1812.[15]

Napoleon's early nineteenth-century creation of a strongly hierarchical and bureaucratic diplomatic service became a legacy for the future. The hierarchy was based on prestige so that everyone strove for advancement. He created the *Légion d'Honneur* to encourage diplomats with financial compensation and prestige. As he said, "it is with baubles that men are led."[16] The hierarchy was arranged like a pyramid, positions were permanent, and families of diplomats were well cared for. Napoleon understood the benefits of stability and job security in promoting a collegial environment, where working relationships and shared culture promote greater functionality. Ultimately, he walked the middle ground between the Weberian ideal of separating administration from politics and monarchical favoritism. Comte de Walewski, France's foreign minister in the mid-nineteenth century, was critical in putting Napoleon's hierarchy into operation. After 1858, the Foreign Service was divided into three categories of secretaries with a salary and promotion scale to match. No one could be promoted without first serving as an unpaid attaché.[17]

Over the course of the nineteenth century, other countries followed and adopted the French model. The British Foreign Service underwent reforms in the 1860s and 1870s. As in France; competitive examinations were instituted to control entry into the civil service, bureaucratically led professionalization occurred, and there was increasing departmentalism in the Foreign Office.[18] In many European countries, recruits were required to have either a *licence en droit* or a university degree. Naturally, patronage remained, but more changes were to come, and it was eventually phased out, following France's lead. The British adopted the bureaucratic gradations instituted by Walewski, with corresponding pay and promotion. The gradual move toward the Weberian ideal experienced a lull during Salisbury's control of the Foreign Office beginning in April 1878. He insisted on doing a large portion of the dispatch writing himself and had the junior diplomats take care of the copying, ciphering, deciphering, and record keeping.[19] After 1898, when Salisbury's leadership of the Foreign Office came to an end, the diplomatic business became more efficient and modern in Britain. Secretaries increasingly used typewriters, and thus a thorough and legible record of diplomatic activity could be kept for future generations of diplomats. It took many years for Queen Victoria to accept typewritten documents and letters because "she wouldn't read print,"[20] an example of how much the use of a new technology can lag behind its creation. She finally agreed to receive typewritten copies, and "the circulation of dispatches in MS" came to an end. It was not really until the early twentieth century that typewriters became a visible element of the diplomatic profession. Even in today's EU, email is not ingrained as a mode of communication, although the use of the fax is more widespread.

Germany's foreign service was a step ahead with its reforms because of Napoleon's victories over Germany in the early nineteenth century. Before German unification, many of the small German states managed to maintain diplomatic envoys abroad, and some continued to maintain them even after unification. However, the main Foreign Ministry was set up in Berlin during the early nineteenth century and then moved to Wilhelmstrasse 76 in 1819. The Germans set up an examination system for entry into the Foreign Service. Those applying had to have at least three years of university, and had to have worked for their provincial governments for at least a year and a half.[21] Once the basic requirements were fulfilled, potential diplomats went through a year of unpaid work as an attaché, then several exams on history, law, commerce, and French.

Social background: Collegiality and a gilded lifestyle

In hindsight, the nineteenth century is labeled as "the golden age of the career diplomat."[22] Diplomats were selected from the competent and well-trained men of their countries. As always, the main task of the chosen few was to represent their countries abroad, and deal with rival interests. At the same time, they had a common heritage and unity as citizens of Europe. They had similar training, background, and worldviews. With increasing imperialism and the rapid technological, military, and economic development in Europe, they were even more prone to recognize their commonalities.

Despite the bureaucratization of state functions, diplomacy remained a bastion of nepotism, favoritism, and aristocracy in many ways. It had evolved into an exclusive occupation because only the higher social classes could meet the standards of education, the pay was low, the exam system was irregular, and the highest diplomatic posts were reserved for special appointments. Society, in turn, regarded the diplomatic corps with great respect, and commissioned many beautiful, regal buildings to reflect the prestige and status of the diplomats during this time. Society and government relied on the diplomats as experts in the field and in international relations. Many of the ideal qualities expressed by Callières and others in the seventeenth century were actualized in the nineteenth century. Most importantly, the people who possessed these qualities were more easily identified through a rigorous selection and training process. At a minimum, Western European governments created the infrastructure for meritocratic selection of diplomats.

Professional status

Diplomats had a "collective lofty cause" and exclusivity that contributed to identity formation as a transnational diplomatic corps.[23] They believed that they were entitled to respect and dignity within society, and special rights to protect the functions of their job. M.S. Anderson writes,

> A consciousness of belonging to a coherent professional group was both expressed and strengthened by the appearance, from the mid-nineteenth century onwards, of guides and yearbooks which for the first time listed the diplomats and foreign office officials in the serve of most of the European states. This also gave the general public for the first time some information, though in a summary and superficial way, about the men who carried out their country's foreign policy.[24]

However, as in the past, there was an element of distrust and suspicion because some members of society considered diplomats to be tainted by their overseas experiences, and not quite in touch with the culture and values of their home state. As a result of their foreign residence, diplomats often began to sympathize with circumstances in foreign countries and built relationships with the local sovereigns and leaders who were often charismatic and earnest when they met with foreign ambassadors. The Turkish Sultan invited A.H. Layard, British diplomat in Constantinople, to visit him whenever he felt like it, and Layard enjoyed many private dinners and walks through the Sultan's gardens, consequently developing a closer understanding of the sovereign's personal aims.

Although vestiges of suspicion remained, these diplomats deserved societal respect as they had more talent and skill than their predecessors and were much more willing to go out on a limb. Frequently, one diplomat would send out a circular to all the other diplomats or foreign ministers at once so that all could equally participate in the transnational dialogue. At the same time, it was equally common for secret diplomacy to occur between just two countries and for the other great powers to hear word of a private meeting after the negotiations were completed. Diplomatic method was a mixed bag, and the remaining degree of nonbureaucratization enabled diplomats to take initiative and to act quickly when they saw the opportunity.

There were benefits to the increasingly bureaucratic foreign service over the previous courtiers and royal favorites. They were less expensive, had a fixed salary, were trained experts, and were hired on a contractual basis. Diplomatic archives and libraries also became much more organized and thorough, thus serving as a resource and record of foreign activities.[25] Thus, diplomats were more constant and trustworthy. In turn, they viewed their status as a perk. Their shared notion of prestige led to the strengthening of norm formation, and contributed to the exclusivity of the transnational corps. For this reason, many aspiring diplomats competed for the chance to be an attaché, even without pay.[26]

Professional norms and meeting frequency

Shared norms, worldviews, and identity facilitated diplomatic agency. These norms governed the nature of the profession and bound the diplomats together. In other words, not only were there norms of protocol and precedence, but also norms of collegiality, which facilitated a cohesive corps that spanned state boundaries. Diplomats were more likely to take risks and initiative because they believed in their expertise and that of their colleagues. Paul Gordon Lauren argues that instead of selling their labor like a commodity, they believed themselves to be the embodiment of the state abroad. At the same time, they were distinct from the state through their unique training, background, and desire to exercise agency. New norms were supplemented and sometimes replaced old ones.

The concept of diplomatic corps extended transnationally to colleagues from other countries. Lauren argues, "At times, members of the corps diplomatique even considered themselves to be members of a cosmopolitan, culturally homogenous, European family."[27] Diplomats who resided in foreign cities for long periods felt indistinguishable from a transnational aristocratic class who regarded attention to national distinctions as plebeian. As evidence of this, it was typical for them to have foreign wives. Anderson writes, "The aristocracies which ruled so much of Europe could still see themselves even in 1914 as in some sense parts of a social order which transcended national boundaries."[28] One important contributing factor to this was that infighting, jealousies, and competition among diplomats from the same country decreased. This is in contrast to the mid-seventeenth century when French diplomats d'Avaux and Servien, and Swedish diplomats Oxenstierna and Salvius were competitive with each other and rarely got along at the Congress of Westphalia. Rather, during the late nineteenth century, cooperation among diplomats at home facilitated cooperation with their foreign counterparts. A second important factor is that the numbers of resident ambassadors grew, thus there was much more opportunity for building and maintaining relationships whether there was an immediate crisis or not.

Third, the emergence of an elite "European family" of diplomats can be attributed to a growing sense of shared culture, and the fact that the foreign ministries had independence from the general bureaucracy of the state, especially in France and Germany. For example, in France, visiting diplomats from other countries had a habit of leisurely socializing for hours in the Quai d'Orsay, what became known as *"le thé de cinq heures"* or the "five o'clock tea." The diplomats would not start working until midday and basically behaved like an aristocratic class. During their long teas, they would exchange information, and reinforce their "common spirit, doctrine, and manners."[29] The family of diplomats benefited from many luxuries, and thus no one was in a hurry to reform the system they had inherited. The remnants of patronage and the feeling that diplomats were the personal agents of monarchs persisted.

Besides the norms that bound diplomats together transnationally, norms of protocol and procedure continued to have importance when great issues were concerned. Before a congress was held, important choices were made about who the participants would be, where it would be held, what the issues would be, and who would mediate. As in the seventeenth century, diplomats carefully considered decisions about location. Throughout the nineteenth century, a norm emerged that the highest-ranking delegate of the host country would be the mediator. Thus, the negotiations to resolve the Eastern Crisis were held in Berlin and Chancellor Bismarck was the mediator. Many major cities such as Vienna, Berlin, and Paris had their chance to sponsor congresses, and each congress brought prestige to the country as well as risk. The diplomats' choice of Berlin as the location for the Congress of Berlin highlighted Germany's great significance to the balance of power in Europe; it also meant that Bismarck would be heavily responsible for the future of international security in Europe. Conferences in smaller towns kept distractions to a minimum, and allowed diplomats to spend more time getting to know each other.[30]

In preparation for congresses, diplomats also developed a propensity for reaching understandings with each other even before the first meeting. Naturally, no one wanted to leave the congress without a signed treaty, and this encouraged secret diplomacy ahead of time. As travel became easier, statesmen increasingly attended congresses alongside diplomats. However, it is clear that most of the work was left to the diplomats during this period. At the Congress of Berlin, it is notable that Bismarck, British Prime Minister Disraeli, and Chancellor Gorchakov were all advanced in years and in ill health.[31]

Diplomats were also subject to the more formal rules established at the 1815 Congress of Vienna. The purpose was to avoid the extensive debate over precedence that had occurred in the past and to facilitate the start of the real negotiations. First, the special committee at Vienna decided that there would be three classes of states, and diplomatic agents would be ranked according to the class of the state they represented. If there was a tie in the precedence of some diplomats, then rank would be determined based on the seniority of the resident ambassador in the capital where the conference would take place. Second, the Vienna committee decided upon official, universal categories for diplomatic rank. The highest ranks were ambassadors, nuncios, and legates; the middle ranks were envoys, ministers plenipotentiary, and agents of sovereigns; and the lowest ranks were the *charges d'affaires* of ministers or foreign secretaries.[32] In 1818, foreign ministries added a new category, *ministers resident*, ranked just after ministers plenipotentiary. The most senior resident ambassador received this title. By 1876, each great power had exchanged resident ambassadors with each of the others.

In terms of formal rules for conference procedure, the 1821 Congress of Aix-la-Chapelle produced the agreement that instead of producing multiple copies of treaties with different orders of signatures (*alternat*), the states would sign in alphabetical order based on the French spelling of the country's name.[33] The common language was still French, although Disraeli broke this precedent for the first time by speaking English during the Congress of Berlin. Bismarck had predicted the language problem prior to the congress, writing, "The tension would be increased by the use of the French language, in which Gorchakov and Decazes are undoubtedly superior to the English Minister and the others."[34] Diplomats and statesmen used French throughout the nineteenth century as the language of diplomacy, especially in multilateral settings. The British, however, increasingly broke the norm and spoke in English to assert their status. The growth of the United States and its increased interaction with European countries helped to push English into popularity in diplomatic circles until it was officially recognized at the Paris Peace Conferences.

As mentioned, new norms occasionally replaced or moderated old ones. The norm of gift giving or bribery experienced a decline, and British diplomats were actually forbidden from receiving presents from foreign governments starting from 1834.[35] The practice of the home state granting gifts to diplomats upon successful completion of a mission also diminished. Lavish dinners and entertainment continued to be an important part of diplomatic socializing, but hosting dinners was no longer considered an essential talent of diplomats.

Technology

Internationally, the advancement of science and technology had a major impact on the mode of diplomatic interactions, though it did not restrain them. First and foremost, the invention of the telegraph and the installation of underwater cables made it possible for states and diplomats to communicate as often as desired. In 1815, European leaders created the Universal Telegraph Union and in 1874 the General Postal Union emerged, transforming diplomats' day-to-day operations. Diplomats were in contact with each other and their home states much more than in the seventeenth century. Gladstone wrote to Granville once, "I had stupidly forgotten that you were in London or I should have reminded you that there are at least six fast trains a day each way between us with a good telegraph five minutes walk from our door."[36] Such was the ease of communications.

Because of this, it was possible for sovereigns to control diplomats more closely if they had the time and will to do so. With this increased ability of state leaders to communicate with their diplomatic representatives, did diplomats lose the agency they had in the past? Most unquestionably, the answer is no. Despite the technology, diplomats still managed to hold onto their ability to facilitate international outcomes through independent decision-making. Before, diplomats were more hesitant to take bold steps without some communication with their sovereign. Late nineteenth-century diplomats were freer to think in terms of creative possibilities because they could always send off a telegram at the last minute informing the state of their plans. Moreover, sovereigns and statesmen felt they could trust diplomats given their high status and abilities. During the Eastern Crisis, for example, most of the substantive communications were from the diplomats to the sovereigns or among diplomats in different locations.

Second, journalistic media advanced to the point where an event in the afternoon on one side of the world was reported to the other side of the world the morning of the same day.[37] Print was faster and cheaper, and censorship was gradually removed. This reduced one facet of diplomatic discourse, the rapid conveyance of general news. It also bolstered another facet, public opinion.

An important and necessary norm of the time was the etiquette of communication. Since diplomats could communicate through face-to-face contact, letters, and telegraphs, it was important for them to collectively discover which form of communication was appropriate given the circumstances. Colleagues would be gravely insulted if they received a telegraph when the import of the information required a personal, face-to-face meeting.

Diplomats used correspondence through the telegraph, but letter writing was still a major means of communication for less urgent and lengthy descriptions. It was the first time that the constant demand for information from sovereigns and state leaders *could* actually be supplied in a timely fashion by diplomats. However, there was a gap between the ability to supply the information and the quantity and quality of what the diplomats actually supplied. For example, British Ambassador at Constantinople, Lord Elliott, in his letters to Prime Minister Disraeli greatly underemphasized the degree of Bulgarian atrocities that were occurring, and this information led Disraeli to base his strong anti-Russian policy advocacy on false information.[38] Nevertheless, diplomats and foreign ministries used technology in unprecedented ways. When Austrian, Russian, and German diplomats sent out the Berlin Memorandum to the other Great Powers, they requested that the states respond by telegraph.[39] What would have taken weeks or even months in the past was settled in days. However, the abruptness and method of this request spurned Disraeli and the British administration, and they subsequently rejected it. The use of telegraph instead of a personal meeting added insult to injury.

Nineteenth-century diplomats and state leaders often sent telegraphs in code, and marked them "Secret" in case other countries intercepted the communications. For example, Queen Victoria sent a ciphered telegram to Disraeli saying, "Have the greatest suspicions of Russian proposals and trust nothing will be accepted which could divide us from Austria."[40] Overseas correspondences were also subject to some risk because during a war, telegraph lines could be closed down or closely controlled by anyone with access to them. During the Eastern Crisis, the ambassador in Constantinople had to get special permission to send out important telegrams, and all telegraphs were restricted in language.

In general, diplomats took full advantage of the telegraphic invention. It was secure, efficient, and enabled diplomats to communicate much more frequently, often four or five times per day. Indeed, leaders expected more out of their professionalized corps of diplomats, and often instructed them to send daily summaries of proceedings by letter. Waddington, the French diplomat at the Congress of Berlin, sent letters back virtually every day to one of the few important statesmen not at the congress, but only received a response from Monsieur Dufaure once or twice. The telegrams sent to Paris during the Congress of Berlin contained details of precedence, what each diplomat said and in what order, opinions on how France should act, and an extensive summary of the conclusion of the conference.

Diplomacy and international society

Hamilton and Langhorne argue that the professionalization and role of diplomats relied on the state system they served, and in particular whether or not governments and societies viewed themselves as part of the concert of Europe.[41] The tug of war between European identity and national identity meant that diplomats ultimately had to reconcile individual state interest for power with the common European interest for peace. The opposing pulls were stronger than in the seventeenth century. Recognition of the good of all states in international society was an established, idealistic worldview that had not existed so much in earlier times. Disraeli said to Parliament in his first speech as Britain's Prime Minister,

> That policy is a policy of peace – not peace at any price,[42] not a peace sought for the mere interest of England, but a policy of peace from the conviction that such a policy is for the general interests of the world. We don't believe that that policy is likely to be secured by a selfish isolation on the part of this country, but on the contrary, we believe it may be secured by sympathy with other countries, not merely in their prosperous fortunes, but even in their anxieties and troubles.[43]

Nearly all the European leaders at the time, including Turkey's, expressed the desire to protect the common good of international society. At the time of the Congress of Westphalia, the only form of effective international society was among the elite diplomats, and in this context only Queen Kristina openly spoke of the common good. In the late nineteenth century, by contrast, the idea of an international society of states had spread beyond the diplomats to the statesmen and to society in general.

There is usually, however, a discrepancy between rhetoric and action. Among statesmen and the public alike, there was much debate over whether to support "the general interests of the world" or to only consider the interests of one's own country. For example, despite the strategic and historic practice of supporting Turkey's independence, British popular opinion vociferously called for interference in Turkish affairs to stop the Bulgarian atrocities. The theoretical and practical import of the idea was often debated in Britain's House of Lords. On 3 June 1878, the Earl of Redesdale spoke about Russia's advance into Turkey, but not in terms of power and money. He said,

> Now, it appears to me that this is a matter of such intense importance, not merely in reference to the Treaty of San Stefano, but in regard to

International Law, and all former Treaties, and the demand is, in itself, so preposterous, that not this country only, but every civilized country in the world, ought to protest against it.[44]

He spoke of the importance of safeguarding international society through the protection and respect of international law. Without it, the state system would be no different from earlier periods of absolutism and zero-sum gain.

The spreading idea of international society meant that diplomats' goals were easier to accomplish. Diplomats had always existed to reach cooperation and understanding among states even when their sovereigns vehemently opposed one another and a solution seemed impossible. In the late nineteenth century, more people believed that there was always some possibility of compromise and that war should be regarded as a last resort. The belief gave diplomats more time and support in their endeavors.

The late nineteenth century provides ample evidence of growing international norms of cooperation, strong diplomatic discourse, and at the same time, a world still engaged in competition to maximize power. The two-and-a-half centuries that passed from the mid-seventeenth century to the late nineteenth century witnessed gradual and incremental changes in the practice of diplomacy. The Congress of Vienna, Congress of Paris, and conferences in London were the major diplomatic meetings to take place since Westphalia, and each contributed something vital to the advancement and modernization of the processes of negotiation, treaty agreement, and peace. However, it is important to remember that diplomacy by conference was still thought to be an unusual means of achieving international cooperation. Instead, constant streams of meetings, informal discussions, and letters were more popular. One of the major events of diplomatic and international relations at the time was the Eastern Crisis, which resulted in every form of diplomacy being concurrently exercised to avert a war among the Great Powers.

The lead-up to the Congress of Berlin 1875–78

The six great powers of Europe (Great Britain, Germany, Russia, Austria, France, and Italy) all had interests in the Balkan Peninsula. Access to the Dardanelles, the Aegean Sea, and the Black Sea were of utmost importance to trade and security. Prior to the congress, diplomats and statesmen laid much of its groundwork in smaller meetings.[45]

With the 1856 Treaty of Paris the Powers agreed that none would interfere with the integrity and independence of Turkey, and the Black Sea Clauses guaranteed neutrality of the sea. Alongside this, the Tripartite Treaty of Britain, France, and Austria stated that they would unite in the event of Russian revisionism. This "Crimean coalition" dissuaded Russian policy makers who did not want to come up against the force of three Great Powers at once. The hope was to safeguard the precarious balance on the Peninsula, and prevent any one power from gaining too much dominance, or a monopoly on the access to the seas.

The stipulations of the Treaty of Paris were short-lived and subject to numerous changes in the following years. However, the big breaking point that precipitated a true Eastern Crisis was when the Christian Serbs of Herzegovina, followed by those of Bosnia, revolted against the Muslim Turkish administration in 1875. They were tired of the maladministration and corruption of the government, and were held together by their distinct Pan-Slavic heritage, a mixture of western nationalism and Orthodox mysticism. They also felt that the Pan-Slavic Russians would come to their aid. This reality heightened tensions between Russia and Austria because if Russia gained more influence in the Balkans, Austria would no longer hold a balance with Russia. As citizens from Montenegro and Serbia rushed to support the uprising, the main diplomatic representative of Austria, Andrássy, wrote the famous *Andrássy Note* of December 1875, asking the Turkish government for reforms, and suggesting the means to accomplish this.

The Andrássy Note was written with the support of Germany's Bismarck who was trying mightily to suppress hostilities between Austria and Russia. All the Great Powers accepted the Andrássy Note, but the British were reluctant because they thought it violated the spirit of the Treaty of Paris – independence of Turkey. To the Turks, this reluctance meant that they could count on the British to support their autonomy in running internal affairs. Since ultimately Turkey did not heed the stipulations of the Andrássy Note, Gorchakov of Russia and Andrássy of Austria, with the backing of Bismarck, tried once more to encourage Turkey to reform, this time with the ineffective Berlin Memorandum of May 1876. However, the Turkish government could no longer really claim control over the situation in Herzegovina, Bosnia, and Bulgaria, even if they desired these reforms. British Prime Minister Disraeli and Foreign Minister Derby rejected it outright, and sent a fleet to Besika Bay as a show of support for Turkey. Once more, the British had been left out and felt they were being treated like a secondary power.

The British move to Besika Bay was to be undermined, however, when revolts broke out in Bulgaria. The Turks responded to this surprise revolt by unleashing the ferocious Bashi-bazouks on an almost totally unarmed Christian population, of which only the smallest fraction was implicated in the attempted insurrection. They tried to crush the revolt by murdering and abusing thousands of innocent people, many of them Christians. Some 15,000 Bulgarian men, women, and children were massacred, with all attendant circumstances of atrocity. Over seventy villages, two-hundred schools, and ten monasteries were destroyed.[46] The "Bulgarian atrocities" led public opinion in England to question their government's support of Turkey.

In December of 1876, the Constantinople Conference represented the final major attempt to reach a solution. All the Great Powers attended, but it adjourned the next month without reaching a clear compromise. Sultan Abdul Hamid agreed to a new constitution on 23 December, but nothing further, perhaps because of the perception that Britain would still protect Turkish autonomy from outside intervention. When no substantive changes were made in the Turkish administration, Russian ambassador Ignatiev, with the support of all the Great Powers, sent the London Protocol of March 1877 to the Sultan who rejected it immediately. Finally, Tsar Alexander declared war on Turkey on 24 April, claiming to act on behalf of Europe. Public opinion and nationalist sentiments of his Slavic population pushed him to this decision.

The end of the war left Russia triumphant, Turkey entirely at a loss, Austria uncertain whether to take a bribe from Russia or form an alliance with England, and Britain not wanting to make the slightest concession to its imperial interests. Austria and Russia were the main countries who sought to balance, but the turn of events made this difficult for the Austrians as Russia's 3 March 1878, Treaty of San Stefano created an entirely Slavic "Big Bulgaria" that effectively gave the Russian Tsar complete control over the Balkan area. Naturally, the British, French, Austrians, and Italians strongly objected to this revision to the earlier treaties because they could not afford to lose access to the seas for trade purposes. As the original signatories to the previous treaties, they could not stand for Russia running roughshod over international organization. Moreover, by this time all the countries involved had locked themselves into various secret alliances and treaties to protect their own interests and uphold the status quo balance of power.

The Congress of Berlin

> After all, known treaties are the least significant work of diplomatists. What is written down in them may some day be revealed; but secret agreements and tacit understandings made by the agents of Governments may be without end.
> (Francis Neilson, Member of Parliament 1910–15)

A.J.P. Taylor sums up the historical significance of the Congress of Berlin: "One of the few indisputable truths about the Eastern Question is that the Ottoman Empire could not be partitioned to the satisfaction of all the Great Powers involved."[47] Thus, it was a remarkable feat of diplomatic initiative. Because of many preexisting alliances, treaties, and secret obligations among states (Table 4.1), the circumstances surrounding the Congress of Berlin were complicated. Each diplomat or statesman had to remember the context in which he spoke, and make crucial decisions about which alliances to foster and which to sever. Ultimately, thirty-six years after the Congress of Berlin,

Table 4.1 Alliances and treaties in effect at the Congress of Berlin regarding the Eastern Question

Alliance/Treaty	Participating states	Date	Secret?[a]	Aim
Treaty of Paris	Six great powers	March 1856	No	Integrity of Turkey
Tripartite Agreement	Austria, France, Britain	April 1856	No	Combine efforts to stop potential Russian revisionism
Andrássy Note, Berlin Memorandum, London Protocol	Austria, Russia, Germany	1875–77	Yes	Trying to get Turkey to reform its administration
Reichstadt Agreement	Austria, Russia	8 July 1876	Yes	Nonintervention in connection with the Serbo-Turkish war
Budapest Conventions	Austria, Russia	18 March 1877	Yes	Austrian neutrality and right to occupy Bosnia and Herzegovina in the event of a Russo-Turkish war
Salisbury-Shuvalov Meeting	Britain, Russia	May 1878	No	Russian concessions on the Treaty of San Stefano
Cyprus Convention	Britain, Turkey	4 June 1878	Yes	Protection of British rights in the Balkans
Anglo-Austrian Treaty	Austria, Britain	6 June 1878	Yes	Mutual support for fate of Bosnia and Bulgaria

[a] A "secret" alliance or treaty means that it was negotiated among some Powers and not others. Austria, Russia, and Germany agreed to the Andrássy Note, Berlin Memorandum, and London Protocol before submitting them to Great Britain, Italy, and France for their approval. Some treaties were intentionally kept secret for a crucial period of time.

the breakdown of this diplomatic balancing act would result in World War I. The Congress of Berlin was a crucial turning point in international relations and the alliance system (Figure 4.1).

The *entente* founded in 1873 between the German, Russian, and Austrian Empires, basically a conservative "Holy Alliance," reinstated Austro-Russian diplomacy over the Turkish question and isolated France among other things.[48] The subsequent Andrássy Note, Berlin Memorandum, and London Protocol reflected efforts to uphold this *entente* and the Three Emperors' League. Andrássy and Gorchakov, the Austrian and Russian diplomats

Figure 4.1 Europe after the Congress of Berlin 1878 (*Source*: Based on Thomas Pearcy, W.W. Norton & Company. http://www.wwnorton.com/college/history/ralph/resource/32europe.htm.)

respectively, agreed to neither interfere in the domestic politics of Turkey nor help them to quell the rebellion, but to only be involved in gradual change in Balkan affairs.[49] Then, the same leaders met to conclude the Reichstadt Agreement in which Russia renounced any plans to occupy Constantinople, march troops into Serbia, form a "Big Bulgaria," or land on the right bank of the Danube. However, this alliance could not hold up to the counter-pressure of the Russian government's embarrassment from its many concessions, obligations to the Pan-Slavic people of the Ottoman Empire,[50] and a likely desire for more control on the Balkan peninsula. The alliance was destined to fail given the mutual, persistent ambitions of the Austro-Hungarian and Russian leaders in the Balkans.

The negotiations

Diplomacy at the Congress of Berlin carried on the traditions of centuries of negotiations, yet it was unique for its increased organization, professionalism, and presence of major political actors. From the start, Bismarck, the mediator at the congress, made clear the parameters and order of the issues to be discussed. The only questions permitted to be addressed related to the stipulations of the Treaty of San Stefano and the Treaty of Paris, and these would be discussed in order of importance. Thus, Bismarck ignored the British bid to force the Russian army out of the vicinity of Constantinople, and the first issue on the agenda was Bulgaria.

Originally, there was general agreement among the great powers in planning the negotiations that all countries would send diplomats as plenipotentiaries to Berlin. However, for one reason or another each country informed the others of their plans to send along their leading statesman as well, and before long the British, having the largest stake in the proceedings, designated both their Prime Minister and Foreign Secretary to attend. This decision prompted the Earl of Granville to argue in Parliament, "without the slightest disrespect to either of the noble Lords, I think that could be as well done by trained diplomatists of great experience as by two of the ablest men in England who have not the slightest experience in matters of the kind."[51] He tried to convince the others that Lord Derby, the recently resigned Foreign Secretary, believed that even though other countries had departed from their original intention to send diplomats, there was no reason for Britain to do the same.

After some debate, Granville's arguments were gracefully set aside, and Prime Minister Disraeli (Earl of Beaconsfield) decided he would let stand his decision to attend the congress as first plenipotentiary. In addition, Lord Salisbury, the new Foreign Secretary, would attend as second plenipotentiary. Thus, the Congress of Berlin was a meeting of statesmen, diplomats, and a few in between. "With Beaconsfield and Salisbury, Gorchakov and Shuvalov, Andrássy and Haymerle, Bismarck and Bülow, Waddington, and Corti all present at Berlin, there was practically no statesman of the first rank absent from the European council chamber, and their decisions would obviously bind Europe in a peculiarly solemn way."[52] In fact, many states were left without anyone of high authority to govern them at home during the negotiations of the Congress of Berlin. Table 4.2 presents the top dignitaries from each of the attending countries.

The main argument advanced here is that the diplomats were the real power behind the negotiations, demonstrating the value of autonomy, agency, and long-held diplomatic relationships to the outcome of cooperation. Resident Ambassadors in Berlin, Odo Russell, Sadoullah Bey, M.P. d'Oubril, Comte de Launay, Comte de Saint-Vallier, and Count Károlyi had already established a rapport with one another and the German diplomats and held solid relationships by virtue of residing in the German capital together for some time.

The statesmen in attendance were not only hindered by their "slightest experience in matters of the kind," they were also weakened by old age and ill health, and were uninformed of the details of the issues. Gorchakov was

Table 4.2 Plenipotentiaries and state leaders during the Congress of Berlin

Country	State monarchs	Plenipotentiaries (in order of rank)
Germany	King Wilhelm I	Otto von Bismarck (Chancellor) Prince Bismarck de Bülow (Foreign Secretary) Prince Hohenlohe-Schillingsfürst (ambassador in Paris)
Austria–Hungary	Emperor Francis Joseph	Count Andrássy (Foreign Secretary) Count Károlyi (ambassador in Berlin) Baron de Haymerle (ambassador in Rome)
France	President Mac-Mahon	M.W.H. Waddington (Foreign Secretary) Comte de Saint-Vallier (ambassador in Berlin) M.F.H. Desprez (political ambassador)
Britain	Queen Victoria	Disraeli, Earl of Beaconsfield (Prime Minister) Marquess of Salisbury (Foreign Secretary) Lord Odo Russell (ambassador in Berlin)
Italy	Benedetto Cairoli	Comte Corti (Foreign Secretary) Comte de Launay (ambassador in Berlin)
Russia	Tsar Alexander II	Prince Gorchakov (Foreign Secretary & Chancellor) Comte Shuvalov (ambassador in London) M.P. d'Oubril (ambassador in Berlin)
Turkey	Sultan Abdul Hamid	Carathéodory Pasha (Minister of Public Works) Mehemed Ali Pasha (Army Commander) Sadoullah Bey (ambassador in Berlin)

confined to a wheelchair; Bismarck was plagued by rheumatism, sleeplessness, and hearing loss; there was doubt over whether Disraeli could survive the journey to and from Berlin;[53] and Andrássy was coughing up blood.[54] Bismarck and Disraeli were ignorant of French, and Gorchakov could not follow the English language. When Disraeli used English at the congress, Gorchakov was at a loss. "Neither statesman was willing to give himself away, a series of comic misunderstandings ensued, glossed over by common consent."[55] These statesmen, however, did make a contribution, though in decidedly undiplomatic ways, as will be seen.

The following analysis is organized according to country (Germany, Britain, Austria-Hungary, Russia, and France), but the evidence throughout demonstrates the strong degree to which diplomats were primarily responsible for the outcomes, that they were each part of a shared transnational community, and that in many cases they did not adhere to their governments' beliefs about what defined the interests of the state. The first half of this chapter dealt with the general structural autonomy and make-up of the diplomatic corps, while this section provides the evidence for what diplomats actually accomplished with their diplomatic powers by looking at the specific example of the Congress of Berlin. After the country-by-country analysis, I will draw conclusions about the agency of the diplomatic epistemic community during the late nineteenth century and compare the empirical evidence to alternative explanations.

Germany

Germany was the host country for the Congress of Berlin and thus, according to protocol, provided mediation for the negotiations. Chancellor Otto von Bismarck, leading statesman and former diplomat, took the job, but not without a strong dose of skepticism and dread. He wrote in a letter, "Just because we are the only really disinterested Power... we should have to bear the responsibility for the almost certain failure of the Congress... every one of our decisions would bear the appearance of a deliberate choice between our more and less intimate friends."[56] It was an honor and a risk for a German to play the part of neutral arbiter. This role meant that the German state had grown in prestige and power in Europe, and if everything went well, would receive even more international acclaim. If the negotiations were a failure, as Bismarck at first expected, the heavy burden of blame would rest entirely on Germany's, or more appropriately, Bismarck's shoulders.

Although a statesman at the time, Bismarck was trained as a diplomat, and this explains much about his procedures, choices, and behavior at the congress. He had served as the representative for Prussia in both Russia and France for over a decade, and was well versed in the potential obstacles to reaching compromise beyond simply the issues themselves. Disraeli put it concisely when he described Bismarck's procedure as, "All questions are publicly introduced and privately settled."[57] Each point of negotiation had to be written in advance and distributed to the plenipotentiaries, then formally presented by the author before the others were permitted to respond. For the first time, the secretariat of a conference comprised more than one nationality, French and German, and from then on mixed secretariats became commonplace. As mentioned earlier, Bismarck was also responsible for the order of the proceedings, from most to least important issues, and the parameters of the discussion. Bismarck's choices as mediator were based on his knowledge of diplomatic procedure, potential obstacles to compromise, and desire for the congress to be a success. Indeed, by avoiding more controversial and tangential questions, and by following a strict procedure, Bismarck concluded the negotiations successfully after only one month.

While Bismarck's most important role was as "honest broker,"[58] it is critical to remember that he was also a representative of Germany. Because of the presence of Bismarck, Bülow, Hohenlohe, and their diplomatic staff, to an extent Germany was also participating in the negotiations. Bismarck, known as the "Iron Chancellor," was the center of power in Germany. Two decades before, Kaiser Wilhelm I had declared that Bismarck was more indispensable to Germany's future than he himself was. The sovereign's participation in the Congress of Berlin was curtailed by an assassination attempt a fortnight before the first meeting. Bismarck had long cultivated alliances of varying degrees with the other great powers, and however much he wanted to remain neutral, it was inevitable that there would be winners and losers at the congress, and he would play a role in determining this. In particular, the Three Emperors' League of Bismarck, Gorchakov, and Andrássy was of great importance to him, and it was this alliance that was the most threatened at the congress. Both the Russians and the Austrians had a lot at stake in terms of who would have more influence over the Balkan Peninsula, and by extension Germany's rank among European powers was contingent upon the outcome.

Bismarck inevitably tended to side more with Andrássy than with Gorchakov. However, it was not simply a matter of German self-interest. The three most important considerations for Bismarck at the congress were (1) a desire for cooperation among European powers, (2) his strong diplomatic relationships with Andrássy and Disraeli, and (3) the need to resolve the Russian Tsar's decision to act unilaterally and militarily in the Balkans. In terms of the first, Turkish diplomat Carathéodory Pasha wrote that Bismarck regarded the people of Turkey as "outside of the circle of civilized Europe, and that the consequences it could have on the relationships of the Great Powers of Europe must not be of interest in any eventuality."[59] Bismarck did not really care about the fate of the Bulgarians, but he was concerned with the relationships among the great powers and the common good of peace. Also, he wanted to be successful as a mediator.

For the second point, Bismarck had strong beliefs about who his friends were. While swearing to do anything in his power to support Andrássy and keep him in office, he called Gorchakov a senile imbecile lacking in tact.[60]

For the third point, in part because of the failed relationship between Bismarck and Gorchakov, and also because of Russia's military advance, Bismarck did not sympathize much with the Russian delegation. Joseph Fuller writes, "At the Congress of Berlin he saw to it that Austria received the compensation promised by Russia in advance – the tenure of Bosnia and Herzegovina – while allowing Russia's gains to be reduced to a minimum.... The 'honest broker' took a slight commission from one of his clients in advance."[61] The following sections will continue to emphasize the importance of Bismarck's influence and of his relationships at the congress.

Britain

The British state: Disraeli, the Cabinet, and public opinion

Britain provides the strongest example of a state in which power was spread uncertainly among the ruling elite, in large part as a result of the sovereign's declining role. Prime Minister Disraeli complained toward the end of 1877 that there were twelve members in the cabinet, and seven different viewpoints ranging from "peace at any price" to immediate aggression.[62] Queen Victoria, who became more vociferous and opinionated than previously in light of the growing crisis in the Balkans, held one of the most extreme viewpoints. Her letter-writing increased as she kept up a constant correspondence with those involved in the Eastern Question.[63] In particular, she wrote to Disraeli, supporting his actions and opinions, and to Foreign Secretary Lord Derby admonishing him for his *laissez-faire* approach to the East. In a letter to Derby she wrote,

> The Queen has never felt satisfied at *our inaction*, which has brought about, what the Queen *feels*, and so do many others, a *painful humiliation* for this country, which no action *now can remedy*; for it *ought* to have been taken *long ago* – and we *ought* to have acted up to our repeated declarations with regard to Constantinople.[64]

She took a strong stand, and supported an aggressive policy to stop the Russian army gaining control over Turkey because she did not want Britain to be seen as a weak state in the eyes of others. Yet, despite her legal claim to power, her actual control was declining. She held a close relationship with Disraeli and he persuaded her to support nearly everything he advocated.[65] Though sharing an aggressive, conservative stance with the Queen, Disraeli tended to tame her more extreme opinions. The Prime Minister firmly believed in the territorial integrity of Turkey, and that Britain should be neutral toward Turkey's behavior in the interest of supporting its autonomy, even if this meant eventually going to war to protect it.

Disraeli's stance was extreme in comparison to the Liberals, such as Granville, Derby, and Gladstone who wanted peace and compromise. Derby was eventually pushed into retirement in May 1878 for his policy line, but Granville and Gladstone (most notably) formed a strong opposition.[66] It was because of the lively debate among widely divergent voices that public opinion came to matter greatly in determining British foreign policy. Gladstone was instrumental in informing the British people of the atrocities in Bulgaria, and thus rallying public opinion against the Turkish government. This contrasted with the Queen and Disraeli's vehement anti-Russian stance. However, the Conservative delegation at Berlin had to pay attention to public opinion in light of the Bulgarian atrocities, and the fact that these atrocities had riled up public opinion against Disraeli's policies. The Conservative position of British neutrality and support for Turkish autonomy was thus heavily compromised. When Disraeli realized the weakness of his position, he looked for another conservative who could subtly push Britain's policy away from neutrality.

Salisbury

Lord Salisbury, a moderate conservative, was appointed to the office of Foreign Secretary at the end of May to replace Derby, and he was the diplomat who most impacted the outcomes at the Congress of Berlin. Although he officially held a political, as opposed to diplomatic, post at the time, he was new to it (just over two months) and he was a diplomat by training and experience. He had formerly served as the British plenipotentiary at the 1877 Constantinople Conference, and was thus highly qualified and informed on the Eastern Crisis. Upon his appointment, however, he had not established himself as Foreign Secretary, and there was some question about what stance he would take and whether he was the right man for the job. Salisbury immediately proved himself. On the night of his appointment, as reported by Lady Gwendolen Cecil (his daughter), Salisbury stayed up till three in the morning writing the famous April 1st Circular.[67] This was a great example of diplomatic initiative for he was not instructed, and it transformed Britain's reputation on the Eastern Question from a position of uncertainty to one of strength literally overnight.

Salisbury's April 1st Circular strongly rejected Russia's Treaty of San Stefano, advocated a compromise and cooperative solution among the great powers, and heavily influenced the Treaty of Berlin itself.[68] Although Salisbury, like Disraeli, was a Conservative, they held different opinions about Britain's foreign policy. Salisbury's main priorities were (1) a cooperative agreement among the great powers, (2) maintaining a close relationship with Bismarck, and (3) recognizing the relative weakness of Britain's land army. Britain's army had 100,000 troops, Russia's had 1.5 million, and Germany (all together) had over a million.[69] Disraeli's main priority, by contrast, was to demonstrate the power and firm resolve of Britain by enforcing his country's interests in the Balkans, which he believed rested on Turkish autonomy. In other words, he brought Britain dangerously close to war.

Salisbury espoused a realist worldview, but with a twist. He wrote, "Diplomacy which does not rest on force is the most feeble and futile of weapons, and except for bare self-defense, we have not the force."[70] The twist was that his actions and accomplishments did not reflect his statement. In the negotiations, he did not emphasize Britain's premier naval force, economic wealth, and social stability. A diplomat by profession, he could not abandon his diplomatic tools, and he followed the path of firm, patient diplomacy. Rather than power, he talked about compromise, and instead of Turkish autonomy, he supported Christian rights. His actions reflected his belief in diplomatic compromise, and his membership in the transnational corps. His diplomat colleagues would be let down if he abandoned the common goal he supported in Constantinople to advocate Disraeli's line of realpolitik.

Salisbury was of strategic necessity for Disraeli who knew that his policy of Turkish integrity was not going to work in light of British and international public opinion about the Bulgarian atrocities, and the cost of losing all ties to Russia. Disraeli relied on Salisbury's more moderate reputation to subtly change Britain's policy. He often said that it was Salisbury who "pulled the laboring oar,"[71] and indeed, Salisbury was able to negotiate and win practically all British demands at the congress. However, in the end, Salisbury's work did not reflect Disraeli's demands, but Gladstone's. As Seton-Watson argues, "where he differed from the Liberal statesman was not so much in opinion, as in emphasis, in mentality, in tactics, in sense of proportion, in his view of what should be said and what suppressed."[72] In sum, Salisbury held different priorities from Disraeli (much to the relief of his European colleagues), successfully acted upon them, and thus is largely responsible for the accomplishments at Berlin. Bismarck, although a great fan of Disraeli, expressed his joy at the arrival of Salisbury who would not lead Britain to war.

As a study in comparison, Disraeli, thoroughly not a diplomat, influenced the outcomes at Berlin from an entirely different approach. He can be credited with achieving the broad brushstrokes: mainly, making sure that Russia did not control access to the Mediterranean. At a banquet, he told Count Corti of Italy in confidence of his intention to withdraw if Russia did not back down from maintaining its "Big Bulgaria." Disraeli knew Corti would be the least likely to keep the information to himself, and before too long Bismarck found out. Bismarck immediately invited Disraeli to a private dinner saying, "Am I to understand it is an ultimatum?" Disraeli replied, "You are." The British Prime Minister had already asked his assistant to prepare a train for him that would leave the following morning if he did not get his way. Upon conclusion of his dinner with Bismarck, however, Disraeli sent a telegraph to the Queen stating that Russia was prepared to surrender.[73] Instead of encouraging compromise, Disraeli offered "all or nothing." It was then up to Salisbury to work out in what manner, and under what conditions this would occur.

Austria-Hungary

The state: The Emperor, Andrássy, and public opinion

There were fractures in the Austro-Hungarian government about what policy they should have in the Balkans, but the main divide was between the realpolitik camp and Andrássy's more idealistic worldview. Emperor Francis Joseph and other realists in the government believed that nationalism did not matter; their main aim was to acquire more land. Andrássy, a diplomat and statesman, was up against opposition in Vienna, but he *did* have the support of public opinion. Like Metternich in the past, he believed that Austria's stable position rested on the integrity of Turkey. Although this was the same policy as the Conservative British faction, Austrian interests were different. Andrássy advocated that Turkey needed to keep up the status quo, and put down extreme nationalism. If not, then the smaller Balkan states would combine forces with the support of Russia and leave Austria the "sick man" in Europe.[74] He supported a reasonable peace as much as he opposed a dangerous one,[75] and did not want to seek territorial aggrandizement for Austria unless it was a necessity to safeguard Austrian security. He was, however, more idealistic and optimistic than Bismarck, the embodiment of inflexible power tempered by intelligent reflection. Andrássy saw his fellow man as basically good, and liked to fight for the noble cause.

Francis Joseph had failed in the past, and was more open minded to Andrássy's more careful approach. The area in which the Emperor, the Austrian government, and Andrássy did concur was with regard to increased Austrian influence in the Balkans. Andrássy's motive was a little different. It was to simultaneously protect his own country's interests as well as the Serbians. Andrássy's son later writes, "This Congress did not create any opposition between Serbia and Austria-Hungary, but on the contrary, by increasing the power of Austria-Hungary in the vicinity of Serbia, it protected Serbian interests simultaneously."[76] Over time, Francis Joseph held loyalty and trust toward Andrássy, even when his policies ran against the Emperor's conservatism. As an expert negotiator, Andrássy got away with representing his own view, rather than the government's at the Congress of Berlin. His actions at the congress, however, pushed the boundaries of his room to maneuver, and the Emperor and his supporters made Andrássy retire after the Congress of Berlin.

Andrássy was also a controversial member of the Austrian leadership because of his political past. Even Gorchakov and Bismarck considered him a rebel because he had engaged in a war against his previous sovereign, and had even been sentenced to death by him.[77] As a politician-diplomat, he had no scruples about advocating opposing views from his government and sovereign. He first joined the service to support the Hungarian part of the hyphenated (Austro-Hungarian) Empire. Andrássy also stood apart from Gorchakov and Bismarck because he was a strong supporter of parliamentarism, while the other two were in favor of absolutism. Despite these differences, his skill as a diplomat enabled him to foster closer relationships with his two colleagues than they had with each other.

Andrássy: Politician and diplomat

Count Andrássy had a great role before, during, and after the Congress of Berlin. He was a Magyar aristocrat who headed the Ballhausplatz, the Austrian Foreign Ministry, from 1871 to 1879, and he was a soldier prior to this.[78] Like the Russian diplomat, Shuvalov, he was a charming and bright negotiator. He was lively and bold, though secretive, and many of his contemporaries found him to be somewhat exotic. He lived the life of Hungarian nobility, at least superficially, and he was a strong supporter of secret diplomacy.

Andrássy, like his Russian, British, and German counterparts, was very ill, but he was more able than his foreign counterparts. Importantly, he was supported by the most responsible, professional, and well-informed team at the congress. Count Károlyi, ambassador at Berlin, was an expert of seventeen years, and Baron Haymerle, ambassador in Rome, was very knowledgeable, though more bureaucratic. Károlyi had a close relationship with the British Ambassador Lord Odo Russell; the two diplomats and their spouses spent many evenings together enjoying the soirées at the Austrian embassy in Berlin.

Andrássy's goal was not to bring Russia humiliation nor did he want to conquer new lands for Austria, as many members of his government preferred.[79] Austria was already the home to five major national groups (12 million Germans, 10 million Magyars, 23 million Slavs, 3.5 million Rumanians, and 750,000 Italians[80]), so Andrássy believed that it would be difficult to control more foreign nationalities. His goal was to gain strong economic ties with the Balkan peoples, as well as to protect their right to sovereignty. The younger Count Andrássy writes of his father, "The leading principle of Andrássy's policy was that the [Austrian] Monarchy should use its powers for the protection of the liberty of the separate nations, and especially against the avarice or paternal attitude of the Czars, as well as the possibility of revenge on the part of the Sultan."[81] The Andrássy Note was of critical importance in the escalation of attention among the great powers to the events in the East. Unlike the Emperor, Andrássy recognized the importance of nationalism in the Balkans, and its power in instigating conflict and crisis.

As a diplomat, Andrássy was not very serious or interested in the protocol of foreign correspondence, preferring others to write for him, and even told jokes while reading important letters.[82] This was yet another reason for the Austrian government and his colleagues to be suspicious of his diplomatic ideas, further separating the politician-diplomat from the state. However, his close relationship with Bismarck more than made up for this. Andrássy wrote to Count Károlyi, already in Berlin, that he wished to arrive in the capital early to reach some preliminary understandings with Bismarck. Coincidentally, on that very day Bismarck also expressed the same desire to Andrássy.[83]

Bismarck and Andrássy

Bismarck had respect for Andrássy's straightforward, intelligent manner, which contrasted sharply with the Russian diplomat Gorchakov's petty, conceited, and gossipy personality. Gorchakov had a closer relationship with Andrássy because he was jealous of Bismarck and his glamorous diplomatic career. In fact, the tie between the Russian and the Austrian was so cozy that Bismarck considered forming an alliance with the English in 1878 to balance against the other two.[84]

Andrássy was fair, perfectly informed, and acutely aware of Bismarck's viewpoints. He attempted to incorporate Bismarck's interests as much as possible while dealing with the Eastern Question. The German Chancellor pledged the same in return saying that Germany needed to have a reliable and capable man to manage affairs in Vienna. While Gorchakov sent many irritating diplomatic notes and proposals, forcing Bismarck to decline on many occasions, Andrássy used his communication with Bismarck sparingly. Bismarck and Andrássy were also naturally inclined toward one another as they had similar personalities and worldviews.[85] They were guided by their consciences, upheld their convictions, were strongly patriotic, and took their duties seriously. They were not afraid to disagree with their colleagues or sovereigns, and readily faced unpopularity to stand up for their opinions. They were both unselfish, to the point where they would pursue peace over the fame of military victory. Above all, they were hardworking, thorough, and daring.

In sum, Andrássy was the plenipotentiary at the Congress of Berlin whose position most straddled the line between statesman and diplomat. He differed from his government's realist approach because of his belief in the importance of nationalism, the common good, and peace, and his desire to not seek territorial aggrandizement. As a statesman he stood apart from the mainstream views of his government and sovereign; as a diplomat, he was able to get away with this because of his negotiating talent and relationships to his colleagues in the diplomatic corps.

Russia

The state

Like Britain and Austria, the upper echelons of the Russian state were also plagued with ambiguity and uncertain division of power. The chief ministers were divided on policy, there was a climate of "ministerial anarchy," and there was internal competition for power. The Tsar officially held the reins of power, but he lacked information and advice because his chief ministers were so divided.[86] Consequently, he had to abandon his original desire to act as his own foreign minister in the issues of the Eastern Crisis. Much of this governmental instability can be attributed to Gorchakov's neglect and preoccupation with besting Shuvalov. The Tsar had little control over his divided government, but was persuaded by Ignatiev to support extreme Pan-Slavism, a policy that Austria could not live with. Gorchakov, like Andrássy, was also a politician-diplomat, though far less talented. He combined an odd mixture of diplomatic flourishes, courtly manners, and ignorance of details.

Gorchakov and Shuvalov

After the British delegates and Bismarck, the Russian delegates were naturally the center of attention at the Congress of Berlin because the primary goal of the congress was to reconcile Russia's stance with that of Britain and Austria and review the Treaty of San Stefano. At home, Ignatiev tended to get in the way of this as he was a strong supporter of Pan-Slav extremism, and had the loyalty of the Tsar.[87] In Berlin, Gorchakov was much more moderate in his stance, but could not take part in all of the meetings because of his failing health, old age, and his vision-clouding desire to end his career in personal glory.

The Russian delegates, Gorchakov and Shuvalov, were rivals and plagued by friction in their relationship to one another. The Tsar wanted Shuvalov to be the first plenipotentiary, but eventually gave the position to Gorchakov who was more experienced and the other's senior. Gorchakov was eighty at the time of the conference, and was the plenipotentiary chiefly involved in the Treaty of San Stefano. He reflected the old-school training of the eighteenth century, displaying courtly manners, elegance, and gracious, verbose phrasing during his speeches. He wanted to end his career with a big bang, and hoped to have enough glory to rival Bismarck. Like Disraeli to some extent, his vanity was much invested in the outcomes of the negotiations at Berlin.[88] His goals were to make Russia a winner in the negotiations and to gain the spotlight for himself at the expense of his colleagues, Shuvalov and Bismarck.[89] Like Andrássy, he strongly supported the alliance among the Three Emperors as a path to resolving the Eastern Crisis, but saw this as a route to his personal goals. Bismarck, unlike Andrássy and Gorchakov, viewed the Three Emperors League as a means of pushing the Eastern Question into the shadows.[90]

Gorchakov's usual eloquence was tainted by tactlessness toward Bismarck because of his personal jealousy, and this continually drove Bismarck closer to Andrássy. His policies and continued clumsiness toward Bismarck contributed greatly to the weakening of diplomatic ties between Germany and Russia.

Shuvalov, on the other hand, was far less of an obstacle for compromise during the negotiations. The other diplomats found him to be flexible and charming, hardworking and bright. He also had the support of the Tsar. The French plenipotentiary, Waddington, wrote in his correspondence to the French Foreign Office that Count Shuvalov had a personal rapport with the British plenipotentiaries, and spoke to them with familiarity.[91] Shuvalov was genuinely working for peace; he was well aware that Russia was not prepared to enter another war and that an alliance with Britain was beneficial and possible. He took risks with his career, but wanted to impress the Tsar and aimed to become Russian Chancellor someday.

The two Russian plenipotentiaries often and unnecessarily got in each other's way.[92] Andrássy's records indicate that at one of the meetings, he was taken aside first by Gorchakov and then by Shuvalov; each informed him that, though the other held the opposite stance, he would support Austria's occupation of Bosnia and Herzegovina.[93] The record of the Russian diplomats provides an example of how diplomatic relationships can encounter problems. Though Shuvalov participated effectively and intelligently, Gorchakov could neither gain entrance into the community of diplomats at Berlin nor get along with his own envoy. B.H. Sumner writes of Gorchakov,

> Like Disraeli, he left most of the real work to his second in command, was hazy as to particular points at issue, and was lamentable with maps. His experts soon found that he could not be trusted with anything secret.... he brought along an extremely confidential map showing the limits of the Russian concessions in Asia and spread it out before the curious eyes of Odo Russell, until Shuvalov succeeded in removing it.[94]

From then on, the secret maps were kept away from him. Even more threatening to the negotiations was that Gorchakov seemed to keep forgetting the concessions stipulated in the Anglo-Russian agreement. Naturally, this further encouraged the antagonism between the two primary Russian representatives, and at one point Shuvalov threatened to resign if Gorchakov was not replaced.

France

Except for Italy, France had the smallest role at the congress because of its domestic problems. Unlike the other European powers, the French did not send their top representative, but a novice. "[Disraeli] talked of Waddington as an able and moderate man, with great self-confidence, quite ignorant of Foreign Affairs, and likely to take unexpected steps."[95] France accepted the invitation to participate in the Congress of Berlin, but its role was far diminished compared to the last great conference, the Treaty of Paris in 1856. The French had just suffered defeat at the hands of the Germans and now, only a few years later, found themselves nervously attending a conference in Berlin. The French goal was to mediate since, like the Germans, they were relatively neutral and disinterested, being occupied with affairs at home. The chance at mediation could elevate France in the eyes of the other great powers despite a recent defeat in the Franco-Prussian war.

William Henry Waddington became Foreign Minister on 14 December 1877, he did not have training as a diplomat, and had not yet acquired a great deal of experience at the time he attended the congress. However, he prepared well for it, knew the issues at stake, and distinguished himself while in Berlin. He was of English birth and French education, but completed his university years in England.

The second plenipotentiary was M. de St. Vallier who was charming, hardworking, and well versed in diplomatic negotiation. He was a good friend and colleague of Waddington, and kept up his duties despite battling an incurable illness. St. Vallier was a well-planned choice on the part of the French because of his previous opposition to the Napoleonic war policy in 1870. He had also served as France's diplomatic representative during Germany's occupation. Because St. Vallier was the resident diplomat at Berlin, he was able to arrange for Waddington to meet with high government officials despite the fact that the latter was unknown in diplomatic and political circles. Waddington writes, "M. Minister and Dear President, I arrived in Berlin on the 10th of this month and since the day before yesterday, thanks to the work taken by Mr. the Count of St. Vallier, I immediately gained a rapport with the high personnel of the German government."[96] The third plenipotentiary, Desprez, was a standard French bureaucrat.

As a relatively objective participant in the congress and a first-time witness of diplomacy in action, Waddington noticed the way in which the unofficial meetings took on significant importance. In the interim after the first meeting, he wrote to the Quay d'Orsay that the plenipotentiaries were busy with more informal activities. Since many more arrived in Berlin late, and needed to be informed of what had occurred thus far, many reports and conversations were exchanged secondhand. Waddington reports that each diplomat tried to describe the negotiations that had occurred in a way most favorable to making allies of the newcomers.[97] He also notes that it was clear that each country's representative arrived with his own particular ideas, and he saw it as necessary for the French envoy to help the others realize their potential reconciliation. The French plenipotentiaries had the esteem and confidence of the other participants for their neutrality and eagerness to aid in achieving a European compromise. The period from 19 to 24 June 1878 was particularly difficult for those attending as they had reached deadlock, but when a through was finally made, it was attributed to the French.

The first letter of instruction that Waddington received from the Foreign Office was on 12 July 1878, nearly at the end of the congress, in which he was praised for upholding a double goal. This was the affirmation of France's rank in Europe as mediator over the difficult questions raised at the congress, and also the protection of the national interest.[98] The view of the French state was that the main importance of the congress was the durability of the transaction, and the support of the principles and values of France. Thus, Waddington's instructions consisted mostly of his general diplomatic duty and the honor of France, rather than explicit positions on the various issues. Despite its relatively small role, the French perspective provides evidence for the workings of the transnational corps, and the widely held support of the common good in Western Europe.

The epistemic community of diplomats

The transnational relationships and the wealth of diplomatic experience at the congress were strong and effective, mostly positive, and as important to the outcome as the issues themselves. What remains somewhat less evident in the official transcript of the meetings are the numerous occasions in which diplomats relied on their personal relationships and membership in their epistemic community. The fate of the congress rested as heavily (if not more heavily) on the internal dynamic of the epistemic community as it did on Bismarck's abilities as mediator.

The strict procedure instituted by Bismarck meant that few topics could be discussed outside of the immediate stipulations of the congress. He was quick to introduce topics, listen to speakers, and move on to the next issue, even at the protest of those present. When the British requested that the Russian troops be moved away from the vicinity of Constantinople because of the potential risk they presented to the Turks and the future of the congress, Bismarck declared that the issue was outside the agenda of the congress. Despite protests from the British, and from the Turkish plenipotentiaries who had the most to lose, Bismarck quickly stated, "the point is closed."[99] The requirement of distributing all motions in writing in advance also tended to constrain creative solutions at the official negotiation table. It is thus important to examine the unofficial discourse at Berlin, which reflects the strength and dynamism of the diplomatic epistemic community.

The Berlin corps

Dinners, lunches, and soirées were an important component of the congress. Notably, Salisbury was less in the limelight at the congress because he did most of his negotiating in private.[100] "The most appreciated feature of the congress was the sumptuous buffet, just off the conference hall. It was Radowitz's idea, originally frowned upon by Bismarck; and he justly plumed himself on it."[101] Four days went by between the first and second meetings so that the diplomats could get to know each other, attend many dinners, and engage in "secret" preliminary talks. In the first ten days, there were only three meetings to the disappointment of Bismarck, who wanted to get the negotiations over with as quickly as possible.

The buffet remained the center of many preliminary negotiations and much information gathering. The representatives of the Balkan states as well as others whose interests were affected anxiously loitered around the food to see if they might be able to sit in on some of the meetings that concerned their fate. Diplomats from Greece, Romania, Serbia, Montenegro, representatives of French holders of Ottoman bonds, English holders of Ottoman bonds, businessmen with strong railway interests at stake, journalists, a dozen representatives of Eastern churches, some Constantinople Greeks, and a Bosnian rebel leader all waited at the buffet outside the doors to the congress.[102] However, the interactions of most importance were those of the diplomats. They had already accomplished a great deal prior to the meeting, and they continued to make headway in the month that followed. The unofficial time outside of the meetings – at the buffet, during private dinners, and visits to each other's embassies – accomplished tacit understandings, and generated a lasting sense of community and common ties.

The greater importance of the success of this conference did not go unnoticed. The German Crown Princess wrote to Queen Victoria, "It has been a capital thing that the Foreign Ministers of different nations have made each other's acquaintance, it will make written communication a very different thing in future!"[103] The congress thus held a dual purpose, providing extended opportunities for diplomats, political diplomats, and statesmen to interact, and enabling compromise on the Eastern Question.

The wider corps

It is important to emphasize also that alongside the negotiations in Berlin, diplomats in other countries continued their correspondence, and were critical in the actual implementation and spread of information. The letters, telegraphs, and meetings continued in Constantinople and other major cities before, after, and even simultaneously with the Congress of Berlin. For Austria, Count Zichy, the Austrian Ambassador at Constantinople, and Count Beust, Austrian Ambassador in London contributed much.[104] Count Beust unilaterally offered to sign a Convention with Britain for common action. After much discussion in London, he was authorized to do so, and it was signed two months later on 6 June 1878.

The private papers of A.H. Layard demonstrate the crucial role played by a diplomat not invited to the congress. While in Constantinople, he acted in the interests of Britain and the Congress of Berlin. He maintained constant contact with the Foreign Office both under Derby and Salisbury, coordinated a whole host of British diplomats stationed all over the Ottoman Empire, and implemented the stipulations of the Treaty of Berlin. He writes to Salisbury just before the start of the negotiations,

> I have had a very satisfactory interview with the Sultan today. He begged me to thank you warmly for all that you and Lord Beaconsfield are doing for him, and to say that he attaches the greatest importance to Batoum not passing into the hands of the Russians, and trusts that you will be able to prevent it.[105]

During the congress, he writes,

> Porte complains that Congress has decided that Austria shall occupy and administer Bosnia and Herzegovina, without adding the reservation that, according to condition of Turkish Plenipotentiaries, it had been previously agreed that an understanding as to conditions should be come to between her and Turkey.[106]

Then, after the congress he writes,

> Representatives of the Great Powers met today at this Embassy, and appointed Commission to visit Rhodope and neighboring districts, in

pursuance of resolution of Congress. Commission will leave on Saturday for Philippopolis. I have named Consul-General, French and German Consuls, Austrian Military Attaché, Russian Second Secretary, and Italian Second Dragoman are the other members.[107]

The importance of the relationships he built and maintained in Turkey cannot be underscored enough. Each of the telegraphs quoted here show how this diplomatic network anticipated and prevented possible disaster, and possible reasons for the goals of the treaty to be undermined. As a resident ambassador, Layard had many secret, trustworthy sources, and knew the main governmental players personally. He met with the Sultan as a friend and colleague and had a permanent invitation to come to the palace whenever he felt like it or had information to pass on. He was clearly the British citizen with the most expertise on the affairs of Turkey because of his years of residence there. When Salisbury responded to Layard's communications, he often wrote something akin to, "You should remonstrate in the manner which seems to you likely to be most effectual."[108] Diplomats in the wider epistemic community exercised agency, and the information they provided from personal interviews was even more revealing than letters sent directly to and from sovereigns. Upon speaking with the Sultan about his problems with Russia, Layard writes to Lord Derby, "He spoke with such determination, but in a tone of sorrow and almost despair which was very touching."[109]

In sum, the epistemic community of diplomats at the Congress went beyond simply the relationships between each other. All of the diplomats present had met each other on previous occasions and operated based on acquired knowledge and respect. Particularly important were the unofficial meetings at the Congress of Berlin, which could have only been the result of a preexisting epistemic community. All of the terms discussed in Berlin, whether officially or unofficially, necessitated the follow-through work performed by the resident diplomats overseas.

Diplomatic agency

The case study of the Congress of Berlin, from the diplomats' perspective, provides an example of how the process of diplomacy was carried out and what impact diplomatic agency and community had on the outcomes. Although the bureaucratic structure of the diplomatic profession at the time was looser at the higher levels compared to the lower levels, encroaching bureaucratization is evident in the proceedings at Berlin. Whereas in the mid-seventeenth century, the main outlet of diplomatic agency was through individual initiative, during the late nineteenth century agency was accomplished more through collective action. Each diplomat found himself embedded in a wider diplomatic network held together by further interaction and strongly institutionalized norms and protocol.

As evidence of this, many sovereigns and statesmen held realist worldviews, yet the outcomes reflected the good of international society more generally. Although many countries were still largely monarchical, isolationist, and nationalist, the climate of the times was not so absolutist as the mid-seventeenth century. Sovereigns and statesmen are often quoted as saying that they wanted peace above all and the resolution of conflict in the interest of the common good of Europe. Layard writes to Derby, for example, "His Imperial Majesty answered, with great earnestness, that he was prepared to make every sacrifice in the interests of peace consistent with the dignity and independence of his country."[110] Disraeli, as mentioned before, shared the same opinion. Whether the state leaders genuinely believed what they so eloquently expressed or whether it was simply rhetoric can only be guessed, but the diplomats they employed and worked with in most cases did hold an actual belief in the European good. The worldview in support of the common good was much more prevalent than previously, and foretold its proper arrival as a collectively held international norm in today's environment.

Realism as an alternative explanation

Was the result of the negotiation different from a realist prediction? To maintain consistency with the seventeenth-century case study, the test variables for the realist prediction are: (1) more powerful countries will gain while weaker countries lose, (2) states will try to balance against other powerful states, and (3) states will act as unitary actors. A.J.P. Taylor, a realist in this regard, argues that the late nineteenth century was the height of anarchy among sovereign states, and that each sovereign leader believed that the best results for Europe would be accomplished if each acted in his own interest with complete liberty from the others. Taylor underplays the importance of the Congress of Berlin arguing that there was no solidarity or common belief among the Great Powers. In other words, states sought to balance, and this was not a difficult task, especially since France fell from predominance after the Franco-Prussian war.[111] However, Taylor's realist analysis neglects to examine the impact of the diplomatic processes examined in this chapter. The outcome was not simply a matter of relative power and states acting unilaterally.

To deal with the realist analysis on its own terms, I address the first variable of relative power. The winners, according to the theory, are the most powerful states. At the Congress of Berlin, Austria and Britain were the winners while Russia and Turkey were the losers. While the general division of winners and losers does reflect relative power, since Austria and Britain had the most powerful militaries, the outcomes were not a result of purely realpolitik reasoning. Moreover, the processes themselves also show that safeguarding power was not the Austrian and British diplomats' only concern; they also shared a genuine desire for the common good.

First, Andrássy remained faithful to his alliance with the German and Russian leaders throughout the Eastern Crisis, and did not threaten war to protect Austrian interests during Russia's advance toward Constantinople. Second, at the congress, he could have demanded territory for Austria, but he sought to strengthen economic and political ties, as well as to uphold the idea of sovereignty. Britain as the most powerful country in Europe at the time also could have entered into a war to secure British interests, particularly since British fleets were waiting for commands in the Marmara. The Turkish army was weak, and the Russian army exhausted by its war efforts for nearly a year. However, the Conservative British government was forced out of its foreign policy of isolation, and decided instead on a European compromise. Popular opinion pushed them, and diplomatic talent enabled them, to accomplish this compromise.

The second major realist prediction is that states will try to balance. This prediction does not hold up to scrutiny, particularly when diplomatic relationships are taken into consideration. First, Andrássy's diplomatic skills encouraged Bismarck to side with him instead of Gorchakov even though Austria was regarded as more militarily powerful than Russia. There is often more than one way for states to balance, and Bismarck could have favored either Austria or Russia. During the negotiations, however, the overwhelming goal was to insure European peace as well as Turkish sovereignty and independence, the appeasement of British popular opinion against the Bulgarian atrocities, and Russian support of Pan-Slavism. Thus, it was largely diplomatic relationships and a shared worldview that impacted the European position, not the desire to balance. Second, the European Great Powers had already reached a stable balance after the French defeat in the Franco-Prussian war, and the French did not seek revenge on Germany. Thus, despite changes in power and perceived threat, European statesmen and diplomats wanted to keep the status quo. The Eastern Crisis developed during this period of peace, but none of the Western European powers tried to balance against Russian encroachment in the Balkans even though Russia's actions would upset this balance. Rather, their diplomats engaged in negotiations and sought a solution that would benefit the common good of Europe.

In sum, the diplomatic collective, based on a shared worldview of the common European good, had an impact on outcomes. Closely related to this is the third realist variable that states will act unitarily. Balance of power was preserved, but not because each state worked for its own independent interest. Diplomatic relationships, procedure, protocol, and transnationalism were important in allowing this to happen.

Bargaining theory as an alternative explanation

This case study demonstrates the ways in which diplomats did not adhere to state preferences, but a short overview of the evidence is useful here. According to bargaining theory, national governments or states will determine outcomes of international cooperation based on ranked preferences that remain stable throughout the negotiations. Disraeli and Queen Victoria, representing the national interests of Britain, firmly believed in the territorial integrity of Turkey. Britain's first preference was to be neutral toward Turkey's behavior in the interest of supporting its autonomy. Its second preference was to go to war with Russia to preserve Turkey's autonomy. Britain was the most powerful, so bargaining theory would predict that one of Britain's top two preferences would be adopted. The outcome, however, was a cooperative agreement among great powers, with no possibility of war. Throughout the negotiation, Disraeli's preferences were forced to change as domestic and international public opinion expressed anti-Turkish instead of anti-Russian hatred and news spread of the Bulgarian atrocities. Disraeli tried to use Salisbury as a scapegoat to subtly change British preferences, but Salisbury exercised agency against Disraeli's preferences and in favor of the consensus in the diplomatic epistemic community and the Liberal faction at home.

From the Austro-Hungarian perspective, Emperor Francis Joseph and other realists in the government believed that nationalism and the territorial integrity of Turkey did not matter; their main preference was to acquire more land. By contrast, Andrássy's preference won out, and he favored the goal of keeping the status quo while putting down extreme nationalism in Turkey. The Russian Tsar's main preference, guided by Ignatiev, was to support extreme Pan-Slavism. This was not a policy that Austria could agree to, and ultimately Shuvalov, the Russian diplomat, impacted outcomes by siding with his colleagues in their quest for peace at any price. Unlike the Russian state, his preference was for creating an alliance with Britain, not striving for a Russian victory at the congress.

In comparison to the seventeenth century, diplomats had more collective agency. Outcomes of international cooperation were not simply the result of relative power or stable national preferences, but a widely shared worldview of the common European good backed up by a stronger epistemic community of diplomats.

The aftermath of Berlin

The Congress of Berlin enabled Austria, England, and Germany to confront Russia. All were aware of the danger that Russia would pursue a program of isolation, and this was great incentive for the congress to get underway.[112] Russian troops had been positioned in the neighborhood of Constantinople for three months. There were twenty meetings total over the course of one month, 13 June to 13 July 1878, though most of the negotiations actually took place beforehand. The results of the congress were the aversion of large-scale war, the creation of Bulgaria, redrawing of the boundaries in the Balkans, and Austria's increased power. Turkey was clearly the loser in all of this.

Besides the actual events, the Congress of Berlin, like that of Westphalia, created important precedence for future diplomatic negotiations. As Mangone writes, "At Berlin in 1878 the chief states of Europe solidified the conference system by respecting precedents, improving procedure, and solving international problems by collective negotiation."[113] Lacking at this meeting, however, was the creation of an international organization that could provide channels through which the "energy for change could be fueled, controlled, and spent."[114] The historical scholarship is divided on whether the Congress of Berlin actually accomplished anything or not. It was the eventual breaking of the diplomatic understandings accomplished at Berlin that precipitated the lead-up to World War I. Relations were particularly strained between Germany and Russia after the congress because of Bismarck's decision to side with the Austrians against his longtime ally. It was only in hindsight, however, that the Russians blamed Bismarck for not supporting them, even though at the time they did not question his role as the "honest broker."

Overall, diplomacy of the late nineteenth century had evolved into a much tighter network than in the seventeenth century. Increased bureaucratization enhanced professionalism, and the growing widespread belief in international norms and the common good further increased the cohesion of the diplomatic epistemic community. In action, these diplomats were markedly different from their statesman and sovereign counterparts. At the same time, the line between diplomat and statesman became fuzzy as more and more of the latter tried their hand at diplomacy, albeit as amateurs. Membership in the epistemic community still provided a distinguishing line. Diplomats had much autonomy from the state, but they acted beyond this, and were successful in reaching cooperative outcomes because of their shared relationships and worldviews. It is highly doubtful that a resolution would have been accomplished had the Congress of Berlin been only a summit meeting amongst state leaders. The diplomats, both in and outside of Berlin, made cooperation possible.

5
The Early Twentieth Century and the Treaty of Versailles

Climate of the times

Before the outbreak of war in 1914, Europeans felt confident about their position in the world. They were at the center of scientific and technological progress, trade, and industry. There was a widespread worldview that peace and prosperity went hand in hand with liberalism and European culture, but that war was a legitimate means of accomplishing foreign policy if peaceful means were impossible. Thus, leaders of European states built up their modern military arsenal with the belief that defensive peace and modern weapons would prevent a long war from occurring. They took for granted that wars would be quick, strong, and effective.

With the eventual breakdown of the diplomatic compromises reached at the Congress of Berlin, the countries of Europe – and eventually the United States – entered the Great War of 1914. Prior to the outbreak of war, institutional modernization and professionalization of diplomats continued, but out of necessity these efforts were put aside from 1914 to 1918 in favor of more pressing war matters. As war spread across Europe, diplomats were greatly occupied with helping travelers who relied on their embassies abroad for assistance. By the end of the war, diplomats expected to emerge from the sidelines and resume their old role of international mediation, and they were more prepared for this than ever before. To their surprise, this was not to be; the power gained by statesmen during the war in the realm of foreign policy remained largely in their hands.

The Supreme War Council, which was comprised of the Allied leaders, continued its existence during the postwar negotiations in another guise, the Supreme Peace Council or Council of Ten. This chapter will show that diplomatic professionalization continued, but autonomy did not grow, and that the status of diplomats fell to its lowest point since their emergence as plenipotentiaries of kings. The result was that the strength of the diplomatic epistemic community reached a low point. As a consequence, their agency as individuals and as a collective was relatively weak.

It was in the aftermath of World War I that European statesmen and society in general perceived *old diplomacy* – referring to the gilded age of the late nineteenth century – as no longer effective, and believed major changes were necessary to prevent future outbreaks on the scale of the Great War of 1914.[1] As a result of this perceived failure and pointed blame, diplomacy after the war was labeled *new diplomacy*, and all of European society hoped that this newness would prevent such a war from ever happening again. At the time, new diplomacy was intended to refer to a transition from secret to open diplomacy, or the ability for the public to more closely scrutinize the actions taken by plenipotentiaries behind closed doors. In practice, new diplomacy meant that the statesmen took over the role of professional diplomats. Assigning a label, new diplomacy, is distinct from actually following through with reforms. In reference to this period, Hamilton and Langhorne write,

> The political leaders of the inter-war years too often confused the execution with the making of foreign policy, espoused the principles of the new diplomacy while adopting its techniques to pursue objectives worthy of the old, and through an excess of zeal and want of foresight plunged the world into a war which completed the destruction of the European states system.[2]

When the statesmen took over diplomatic functions, they could not best the work of professional diplomats. Instead of new diplomacy as open diplomacy, new diplomacy meant summitry, defined as direct conferences of statesmen or political leaders, as opposed to negotiation by professional diplomats. Secret diplomacy persisted except the processes of negotiation and cooperation were now in the hands of amateurs.

New means of transportation by rail and steamboat had allowed statesmen and foreign ministers to participate in international conferences on an ad hoc basis since the nineteenth century, but summitry really took off during World War I. Politicians ignored the lessons of history: direct negotiations by state leaders are rarely successful, and involve a great deal of risk.[3] Nevertheless, at this time statesmen and foreign ministers had legitimacy because of a widespread societal belief that the outbreak of war was evidence itself that international relations by diplomats did not work.[4] The status of diplomats had fallen. Europeans believed that the primary holders of power, the statesmen, had to meet face to face to ensure outcomes of international cooperation in a democratic and open fashion.

Despite the drawbacks of summitry and amateur diplomacy, face-to-face meetings were easier to organize because of the distinct emergence of a small group of great powers with the relegation of smaller powers to a position of noninfluence in international relations. For example, Sweden, which was a European super-power from the seventeenth to the nineteenth century, became a smaller power that preferred not to participate in international disputes. In effect, summitry meant the coordination of only four or five individuals participating in important international decisions.

The World War I period is an important case in the evolution of diplomatic relationships and protocol because it highlights this new direction toward summitry evident in the early twentieth century. In many ways, it represents a low point in diplomatic agency, and it certainly was a low point in the level of autonomy and status for the diplomatic corps. The fact that the major European countries were more often democracies than in the past shows that democracy is less important as an indicator of whether diplomats have agency. During this period of *increased* levels of democracy in Europe, diplomats had even *less* autonomy. Another unexpected conclusion, alluded to in the previous chapter, is that the level of technology is also not a significant indicator of whether diplomats have agency. Rather, technology, such as the telegraph or telephone, simply changes the *means* with which diplomacy is practiced, but does not impact the substance. If anything, the telegraph gave diplomats more autonomy to act as instructions were dramatically shortened. Thus, the two variables that stand out in this case are status and, by association, autonomy. The low presence of these factors means that diplomats, and as an epistemic community, were restricted by the rules of the game. The story of the negotiations leading to the Treaty of Versailles and the predominant role of statesmen show the failure and ineffectiveness of a process in which the diplomatic corps largely observed from the sidelines.

The next section provides evidence that the diplomatic epistemic community during the early twentieth century was strong by virtue of social background, training, and meeting frequency, and by extension their shared norms and identity. However, this evidence also shows that their status and autonomy were severely curtailed and, as a result, diplomatic agency was almost nonexistent. This analysis is followed by a brief discussion of the lead-up to World War I and the alliance system going into the Paris Peace Conference. The second half of the chapter is dedicated to the negotiations that produced the 1919 Treaty of Versailles, particularly focusing on the division between statesmen and diplomats and the conference's lack of procedural organization. I argue here that neorealist and bargaining theories cannot predict why cooperation failed, but by considering this case as a counter-factual example of diplomatic agency, it is clear why state leaders could not succeed in the way that diplomats had at Westphalia in 1648 and Berlin in 1878.

The society of diplomats

European statesmen, led by the guiding principles of US President Woodrow Wilson, emphasized the need for new openness in diplomatic processes and national self-determination instead of balance of power. European diplomats, by contrast, continued to focus on the selection, composition, and training of a professional corps that would work effectively and efficiently to conduct international relations through organizational procedure, negotiation, and compromise. The idea of the "professional diplomat" had become such an institution in Europe that government officials emphasized less its emerging role, and more the ways that it could be ameliorated through reform. In all Western European countries, efforts were made to rethink the diplomatic bureaucracy and propose reforms to the selection process, pay structure, and promotion decisions of the foreign service to make it more meritocratic and reflective of society.

However, simultaneous with the professionalization and reforms of the foreign service was the great loss in status and heavy restrictions on autonomy, factors that were largely exogenously driven at this time. Gordon A. Craig writes of the British Foreign Service:

> In the sphere of diplomacy proper, functions formerly reserved to the professional diplomats were farmed out to other departments of the government, while important tasks of negotiation were taken over by political leaders whose newfound enthusiasm for foreign affairs was generally unguided either by training or experience. In consequence, postwar British diplomacy came to be characterized by dangerous defects of coordination, as well as by a high degree of amateurishness, imprecision, and feckless opportunism. These faults of technique were directly related to the inadequacies of British policy in the interbellum period, a period which, it need hardly be added, is in little danger of being regarded by future historians as one in which British statesmanship distinguished itself.[5]

Craig's distrust of politicians echoes the sentiments of many before, most prominently, Philippe de Commynes, a professional diplomat of the Middle Ages, who warned that direct negotiation among monarchs always made any situation worse, and enhanced bitterness between the parties where friendship may have persisted.[6] The figurative suffocation of the diplomatic corps was coupled with an attitude among some diplomats that they actually *should* step aside during times of war to let exigencies of grand strategy take precedence. When increasingly nondiplomatic representatives began to take over their role during World War I, for the most part they did not protest. However, after the war, during the negotiations of the Treaty of Versailles diplomats expected to resume their traditional role of mediation and negotiation, the role they had worked hard to acquire up to 1914 through their own professionalization.

The postwar period was also in many ways a continuation of prewar diplomacy, particularly in terms of the development of a transnational diplomatic corps. M.S. Anderson argues, "The nineteenth and twentieth centuries saw the continuation of trends already clearly visible – a consolidation of the network of diplomatic links between the European states and a further growth and elaboration of foreign offices."[7] In addition, there was a definite move toward involvement of nondiplomatic actors in traditional diplomatic roles ever since the Congress of Berlin. The emerging phenomenon of the politician–diplomat, observed at the Berlin Congress, was precipitated during World War I. Indeed, many elite decision-makers heralded the end of the gilded age of the career diplomat. The glamorous, high-powered lifestyle diplomats were known for in the past was now referred to as laziness.

What these profits of doom failed to recognize, however, is that the diplomats' demise lay only in their treatment by statesmen and society and not through any failing in the profession itself. In fact, the inklings of professionalism and transnationalism observed in the seventeenth century and partially achieved by the nineteenth century had nearly reached fruition in the early twentieth century. After three centuries of gradual evolution, many diplomats were selected and promoted based on merit, received extensive education prior to selection, underwent additional on-the-job training, had a regularized system of pay, and were increasingly specialized. The statesmen who sought to phase out the professional diplomat were incomparably less prepared for the tasks than those they sought to replace. Alongside greater bureaucratization and standardization, norms of ceremony and precedence experienced a decline. The time expended on pomp and processions, and the anxiety associated with these practices decreased, but did not disappear from major events.

To what extent was professional diplomacy in the early twentieth century a meritocratic ideal? Did the qualities of a diplomat expressed by Callières in the seventeenth century still hold weight? How widespread were the transnational professional norms of protocol and precedence and how did they change? Addressing these questions alongside the issue of state encroachment on diplomatic autonomy will help establish the strength of the epistemic community in the early twentieth century.

Bureaucratization and professionalization

Bismarck was one of the most powerful leaders of the foreign service and, despite having established a more professionalized and bureaucratic system, preferred to keep the reins of control in his own hands. With the fall of Bismarck in 1890 and the rise of Wilhelm II to power in Germany, German diplomats gained greater independence. They followed Bismarck's instructions in the late nineteenth century, but only occasionally followed Wilhelm's instructions who would rule sporadically. Lamar Cecil argues that under Bismarck, diplomats were obedient because of their respect and admiration for him, but under Wilhelm II, they were obedient as servants of the state.[8]

Bismarck was not unlike Napoleon in terms of his relationship with the foreign service, and his role in its professionalization. With a weak leadership, and loosening of the procedural and structural safeguards created earlier, there was a decline in professionalization. It was so noticeable that people outside of the government apparatus criticized the changes in the corps. Professionalization, however, does not go hand in hand with autonomy. After 1890, the foreign service reverted to a style of operation similar to that of 1871, but throughout this rise and fall of professionalization, diplomats lacked autonomy. As Cecil describes it,

> Those who serve the state as bureaucrats possess an influence on policy only when the circumstances in which they hold their offices enable them to express their opinions freely and to have some measure of independence on acting on those ideas.... From 1871 to 1914, the German diplomatic service did not function under such conditions, for throughout the period its members both in Berlin and in the field were, with few exceptions, not trusted lieutenants but rather orderlies of superior figures who allowed them little independence and who often dismissed their opinions as irrelevant or useless.[9]

Professionalization had opposing impacts on diplomats. It held diplomats to stricter rules to follow thereby decreasing their autonomy, but also gave them more legitimacy as an important governmental arm, which tended to increase their role abroad.

There were two major changes to the bureaucracy of the foreign services in Europe. First, reforms were introduced and seriously pursued as a means of making the foreign service more meritocratic and open to a wider circle of potential applicants. Second, and somewhat as a consequence of this, the foreign office, as the home base for diplomats, started to more firmly assert a separation from the mainstream civil service. While bureaucratization in the early to mid-nineteenth century gave more power to the foreign office as the foreign policy arm of the state, bureaucratization in the late nineteenth and twentieth centuries increasingly separated the foreign office from the state and state bureaucracy bringing it closer to the diplomatic service. Thus, in contrast to the late nineteenth century, the foreign office during the early twentieth century was less a part of the definition of the state, and more a part of the foreign or diplomatic service. This meant that diplomats had a stronger bureaucratic apparatus at home to support their work abroad.

The foreign services in Europe, for the most part, increased only slightly in size during the turn of the century. There was a marked acceleration in this increase starting from around 1904. For example in France, there were 70 diplomats in 1814, 90 in 1870, and 170 by 1914.[10] In Britain, there were still fewer than 150 career diplomats by 1914. Some countries, like Holland, Denmark, and Sweden and the Swiss cantons did not want to participate in international conflicts, and had decreasing numbers of diplomats. There were only 20 Danish diplomats in 1914.[11] In comparison to today, foreign services were very small except for the notable exception of a growth in overseas missions, especially in Asia and Africa. At the same time, there was massive growth in other sectors of the bureaucratic structure of the state, so the foreign service was relatively small among government institutions. International business, competition, and alliances meant that the realm of foreign policy was greater, so despite the small size of the corps, diplomats had more work to do. As women were allowed to enter the work force as secretaries, diplomats of lower ranks were free to do more of the substantive work and many more of them had decision-making authority to deal with new issues. The leisure of the five o'clock tea was no longer a part of the office culture.

Naturally, bureaucratization and professionalization progressed at slightly different paces across countries. In Britain in the early twentieth century, diplomats were still paid less than was necessary to support their lifestyles. Until 1908, diplomats from Great Britain, Austria-Hungary, Germany, Russia, and Italy were required to have a personal income to support their lives as diplomats. After 1908, the requirement was abolished in Germany (although this reform was ultimately ignored), but everywhere, diplomats still needed to supply a portion of their funds. In fact, German diplomats were paid more than other bureaucrats, but less than their counterparts in foreign countries. Table 5.1 shows the various gradations in salary according to rank in Britain. It is interesting to note that only the British Ambassador in Berlin could live entirely off his government paycheck as the events of World War I approached.[12]

The early twentieth century is distinguished from the late nineteenth century for the much more focused efforts at bureaucratic reform. The diplomatic profession was regarded as fully formulized, and it was now possible to turn a critical eye to its practices. Reformers suggested that the elite *corps*

Table 5.1 Annual salary in 1914 according to rank for British diplomats

Attachés (two years)	£0
Third Secretaries	£150
Second Secretaries	£200
First Secretaries	£300
Counselors	£500–£1000
Paris Embassy	£11,500
Berlin Embassy	£8,000
Rome Embassy	£7,000

Source: Zara Steiner, *The Foreign Office and Foreign Policy, 1898–1914*, London: Ashfield Press, 1969.

should be more open to those talented individuals below the upper echelons of society. In 1905–06, reforms were passed in the British diplomatic service stipulating that there would be a new division of labor between intellectual and mechanical types of work, and more of the responsibility of the Permanent Under-Secretary would be shared with junior clerks.[13] Another important effort for reform was the abolishment of the property qualification. Of course, in a roundabout way this rule would eventually lead to the requirement that diplomats earn higher salaries so that they could survive on government support alone.

On 29 September 1916, the British Foreign Office submitted a plan to the Treasury for improving salaries.[14] However, the two British bureaucracies had opposing goals. The leaders of the Foreign Office strove to maintain their degree of independence from the central bureaucracy, while the Treasury, along with the British government, sought to encourage further integration of the Foreign Office with the Civil Service. The Treasury department rejected the reform proposal. It would have to be convinced of the need to augment all Civil Service salaries, and not simply those of diplomats. Thus, in the early twentieth century, one observes the continuing competitive relationship between the diplomats and the foreign office, as well as a newer phenomenon of competition of the foreign office with the rest of the British bureaucracy. The foreign office had developed a degree of specialization in foreign affairs that distinguished it from the main civil service. The diplomats, however, needed to be paid even more than the members of the foreign office to sustain a more costly life abroad, and the necessary entertaining that went along with it.

Many other reforms were submitted and debated. In Britain, there were reforms of the lower ranks, promotion procedures, the role of secretaries, the grading of archivists, general reorganization, and the relationship between the Foreign Office and the Foreign Service. These reforms were aimed at creating a more meritocratic system and dealing with the rapidly increasing workload while still operating within a constricted budget. The MacDonnell Commission was particularly important in terms of reforms in the immediate prewar period. This Commission was one of several, and it impacted recruiting procedures through a detailed statistical analysis of the education and social background of applicants. The conclusion was that an open examination was insufficient to test applicants; a better plan would be to make the diplomatic service a subdivision of the civil service, putting it under the same testing system. In addition, it recommended that officers from various offices should be allowed interchangeability, the flexibility to transfer to other offices. The commission again recommended the abolishment of the property qualification along with the system of unpaid attachés, thus allowing potential diplomats who were not independently wealthy to have a chance at the Foreign Service. As Raymond A. Jones argues, "What was envisaged was a future with wider opportunities for fewer but more able diplomats."[15] Soon the war overtook these plans for reforms, and the suggestions of the MacDonnell Commission were left aside until after the war.

The French government introduced many of its reforms *after* the Paris Peace Conference. The French had more of an opportunity to improve their foreign service at this later time because the status of diplomats had not declined as much as it had in other European countries. There was far less suspicion of diplomatic activities particularly because the events at the Paris Peace Conference convinced the French of the importance of maintaining the Entente alliance through a more professional Quai d'Orsay. After 1919, there were practically no bureaucratic reforms pursued in France, but, according to a 1920 Chamber of Deputies report, there was an expressed desire to strengthen the role of diplomats and to continue to improve their quality and training.[16] There was a clear need for concrete reform in terms of diplomatic salaries as the declining value of the Franc meant that efforts at meritocratic recruiting were still hampered by the wealth prerequisite. Substantial efforts at reform did not occur in France until 1932.

There was one exception, the creation of the permanent post of Secretary General, occupied by Philippe Berthelot, whose role it was to coordinate all levels of diplomacy and operations within the Quai d'Orsay. Besides the obviously centralizing nature of this new post, the aim was to make the foreign service less susceptible to changes in political leadership, and to maintain the traditions of diplomacy. Thus, like in Britain, the French Diplomatic Service and Quai d'Orsay had a greater degree of separation from politics, bringing the foreign office and foreign service closer together. The authority of the new Secretary General would balance the power of the Premier who typically held the post of Minister of Foreign Affairs.[17] Despite the closer definition of the foreign office with the diplomats, the autonomy of French diplomats during the negotiations themselves was just as severely curtailed as diplomats from other European countries. Even before the outbreak of war, the autonomy of diplomats was decreasing while alongside this, professionalization continued. Thus, the early twentieth century marks a separation of the twin trajectories of professionalization and autonomy.

Social background and training

Diplomats were increasingly drawn from the commoners while the number of those from the aristocracy experienced a decline. In Britain from 1860 to 1914, the percentage of aristocrats fell from 52 to 38 percent, and the percentage of commoners rose from 48 to 62 percent.[18] The principle of democratic representation in the political elite meant that the composition of the corps more closely reflected the composition of the general population. However, in all Western European countries, the level of democratic selection and promotion within the foreign service tended to reflect the level of democracy in each country, which was not very high compared to today's standards.¹⁹ Many children of diplomats were drawn to the profession as children of parents in the military were drawn to political sectors. In Germany, where there was a large aristocratic class; 10 percent more of the diplomatic service was drawn from the nobility than in Britain.²⁰ Only Third Republic France had fewer aristocratic diplomats than in Britain. Around 45 percent of French diplomats were nobles between 1870 and 1914.

It is thus clear that the diplomatic service was still largely drawn from wealthier classes. Ironically, as a diplomat became successful, he depleted his own wealth more quickly as it became increasingly necessary to provide entertainment and maintain a lifestyle comparable to his position. Cecil argues, "The burden of entertainment worsened after the turn of the century, and Foreign Office officials noted that the mounting taste for luxury of the *belle époque* as well as the increased cost of living in metropolitan centers was out-pricing the means of even wealthy diplomats."²¹ In a kind of copycat effect, the more one country's diplomat displayed a luxurious lifestyle, the more the other countries' diplomats had to follow suit.

Education was also a good indicator of social status among early twentieth-century British diplomats. The great majority of diplomats attended Eton, and around 57 percent of diplomats received a university education. Most went to Oxford or Cambridge, just as their American counterparts were largely drawn from Harvard University, and French diplomats were from the *École Libre des Sciences Politiques*. Of the 192 new French diplomats between 1907 and 1927, 153 were educated at *École Libre*.²² The propensity to select diplomats from the same university led to a natural collegiality in the transnational diplomatic corps. However, a university education was still not a requirement for the entrance examinations, which focused on foreign language fluency. Prospective diplomats would travel to Germany and France for a year or two to acquire their language skills. Upon their return, instead of attending university, British diplomats would take an examination preparation course at Scoone's crammer.²³

Across Europe, these qualifying exams had age restrictions, usually somewhere between 18 and 25, and covered numerous subjects and skills. For example, dictation, translation, and oral and written exams in foreign languages, as well as geography, history, orthography, and précis writing were commonly tested in Britain for a position as an unpaid attaché. A further exam was required for promotion to a paid attaché position. The second exam tested the language, religion, and culture of the country where the new attaché would serve, the commercial and political foreign policy of that country, and general international law.²⁴ In fact, the exam was so difficult that applicant scores were exceptionally poor. In Germany as well, diplomats had to pass numerous requirements for entrance and promotion in the diplomatic service. To begin, they had to be at least 25 years of age and a German citizen. Connections were still a useful factor, as well as a legacy of family members in the corps. From 1871 to 1914, in Germany, there were

24 diplomat fathers with 29 diplomat sons, and some families boasted three generations in the corps.[25] Lamar Cecil concludes, "As a result, the imperial diplomatic corps was an assemblage of men of real ability in some cases, of little other than luminous lineage in others."[26]

Despite the wealth requirement, in Britain, the selection process was more open than in the late nineteenth century. Eventually, in 1905, Lord Lansdowne decided to make diplomats and members of the Foreign Office take the Class I examination of the civil service. By doing this, the university requirement became necessary and the emphasis on foreign languages was lowered. Before 1907, 60 percent of the entering diplomats were not university educated, and after 1907 this was true for only 15 percent.[27] A Board of Selection, also Lansdowne's suggestion in 1905, was established in 1907. Candidates were permitted to take an entrance exam when they were between the ages of 22 and 25 as long as they had an official nomination.[28] Subsequently, the private secretary had the power to promote and transfer diplomats. Eventually, there arose in Britain a reform effort to standardize the diplomatic exam system with that of the general civil service. This idea met with much resistance because diplomats recognizably had a different set of tasks to deal with than domestic bureaucrats.

In Germany, a university education was standard, and from 1871 to 1914 just under one-third of the 548 diplomats had a Doctor Juris degree.[29] The first exam for an aspiring German diplomat tested legal knowledge. Besides the grueling eight-hour oral exam, covering such topics as European history since 1648, domestic and international constitutional law, international economy, political geography, and finance, candidates were closely judged for their social skills. This high degree of common knowledge and skills among the corps contributed to their sense of common identity. Bismarck left behind a tradition of diplomats who possessed social graces, good appearance, the ability to hold alcohol, and excellent conversation skills. Prince Karl Max von Lichnowsky, who was chancellor from 1899 to 1904, was also concerned that candidates be able to fit in with a shared "social culture" and possess a comfort with *usage du monde*.

Qualifying exams were an important part of selection, and a source of great anxiety and preparation. However, diplomats were still often appointed to positions. Before, appointments were based exclusively on patronage and political connections, but in the early twentieth century, merit and career accomplishments increasingly had to be taken into consideration.[30]

In France, most of the major posts abroad were filled with professional diplomats, but the Foreign Minister would, on rare occasion, make ambassadorial appointments. The French tended to value professionalism much more than in other democratic countries. There were fewer appointments, a greater recruitment of nonaristocrats, and even the advisory staff of the Minister of Foreign Affairs was a selected group of professional diplomats.

However, in the postwar years, like in other countries, diplomats abroad were given less and less autonomy to make on-the-spot decisions.[31] They continued to send policy suggestions back to Paris based on their specific knowledge and opinions, but they were consistently ignored. With Hitler's eventual rise to power, this disregard for the opinions and autonomy of professional diplomats had dire consequences.

Meeting frequency and technology

Meeting frequency had not changed much since the late nineteenth century. Diplomats from the same country met together often, but meetings with their foreign counterparts were less common. Bilateral meetings in major capitals took place, but multilateral meetings were reserved primarily for treaty negotiations, such as the Paris Peace Conference. The quality of meetings was affected by the somewhat shorter time periods that a diplomat would remain in one place, the lower professional status, and external criticism of the corps. Thus, cultivated relationships in one locale were of a shorter duration and dealt with less significant matters.

Appointments to an embassy were much shorter than in the late nineteenth century, with the average time around four years and ten months.[32] In the past, these appointments were often ten to twenty years. Odo Russell, for example, served for thirteen years in one place. One reason for this was the greater flexibility to make lateral transfers between the foreign office and the foreign service, particularly in Britain and France. Also, the heads of embassies were younger. Between 1900 and 1914, the average age of the nine appointed ambassadors was fifty-four. In France, the highest positions in the Quai d'Orsay were reserved only for diplomats who had served abroad and returned to Paris with a distinguished record of representing France.[33] Despite the continued small size of the diplomatic corps, the epistemic community expanded in membership by virtue of the more meritocratic selection processes and job interchangeability within the governmental apparatus.

The telephone was the telegraph of the early twentieth century, but just like the telegraph, and Internet today, widespread use did not fundamentally change the nature of the diplomatic profession. Hamilton and Langhorne argue, "The statesman–diplomat had of course long been a feature of international politics. Yet there was during the inter-war years a quickening in the pace and tempo of ministerial diplomacy.... None of this can be explained simply by reference to improved and faster methods of communication."[34]

Hamilton and Langhorne agree with M.S. Anderson, who argues that the telegraph did not tilt the balance in favor of inflexible orders, but meant that instructions were short and required individual initiative on the part of the diplomats. In France, diplomats scorned the use of the telephone, telegraph, and typewriter as if the technologies still had not proven their utility.[35] Face-to-face meetings were still highly valued and a part of the professional protocol of diplomatic negotiation. Statesmen and diplomats typically traveled by train or steamship to attend multilateral conferences, at the same time demonstrating their respect for the status of other diplomats and for the tradition of face-to-face diplomatic negotiation.

Status

As mentioned earlier, status declined significantly during this period. The supposed failure of diplomacy to prevent the Great War was a big factor. There was also the ongoing negative image associated with secret diplomacy and foreignness. Practically since the emergence of the profession, diplomats were regarded with suspicion or were thought to be spies because of the long periods of time spent overseas; the Great War reinforced this perception. To a certain extent, in the early twentieth century, status also experienced a decline because of democratization, which worked against the previously aristocratic tendency of the foreign service.

Status within the foreign service community was weighted toward the political division. In Germany, an officer of the Political Division was known to interact with the highest officials in the Wilhelmstrasse directly. Lamar Cecil writes, "So great was the repute of the division that a counselor with long service there regarded being appointed minister to a minor German state as a demotion, while an envoy reassigned to Berlin considered being placed in any section other than the Political Division a similarly deplorable fate."[36] The political division was not required to share information with the other divisions, and served as the direct liaison with the diplomats. In Germany, diplomats were required to spend some time serving in the political division before receiving their assignments abroad. According to Bismarck, this enabled the domestic and foreign branches of the foreign service to become more compatible. In Germany, each newly hired diplomat would be assigned to a Foreign office political officer who would orientate him to the Wilhelmstrasse. Upon receiving his post abroad, the new diplomat would then be assigned to the particular political officer in charge of the same geographical region. This counselor would be an important domestic contact, and would monitor the diplomat's assignments, quality of work, and behavior.[37]

Nevertheless, the political officers of the foreign office had a slightly lower status than the diplomats, who were required to have a more in-depth knowledge of foreign languages and political systems. The foreign office, in turn, had a higher status than other divisions of the civil service. In sum, the overall status of diplomats had fallen, but political diplomats still had a higher status compared to other governmental divisions, and this gave the transnational European corps a sense of shared identity and prestige.

Another European norm shared among diplomats was that they all tended to have transnational worldviews and a clear sense of belonging to international society. M.S. Anderson argues,

High and assured social status helped to keep diplomats, especially high-ranking ones, as in the past distinctly cosmopolitan in outlook. The aristocracies which ruled so much of Europe could still see themselves even in 1914 as in some sense parts of a social order which transcended national boundaries. They were united across these dividing-lines by fundamental similarities of outlook and often of education.[38]

Thus, growing professionalization and meritocracy did not detract from transnational ties, norms, and shared identity. Since most European foreign services engaged in reforms around the same time, the diplomats in the field still found that they had much in common. They were all subject to new entrance exams, education requirements, and training. They all experienced a gradual loosening of aristocratic and wealth requirements. Although they spent a smaller number of years in any given location abroad, they did this together and were more likely to see someone they worked with in one country again in another country. High status of diplomats within the bureaucracy meant that they were together regarded as the governmental elite, despite falling status in the outside world.

Paradiplomacy and amateur diplomats

Inter-Allied conferences of diplomats were numerous during the war. At the same time, nondiplomatic representatives practicing "paradiplomacy," defined as nonprofessionalized diplomacy, were in some cases considered more effective than traditional ambassadors. For the first time since before the Treaty of Westphalia, quasi-diplomacy reached a new popularity and government called upon individuals with specific expertise to perform the job of diplomats. At the Paris Peace Conference, for example, the British Treasury, not the Foreign Office, sent representatives to attend the reparation commission. The attitude was that if old-school diplomats could not deliver, leaders would not hesitate to rely on less traditional representatives.[39]

Reforms in the British Foreign Service introduced the principle of interchangeability, which contributed in a significant way to the employment of amateurs in overseas missions. Interchangeability meant that those who worked in the Foreign Office could become diplomats and vice versa. The result was that the overall quality and expertise of diplomats fell as nonexperts were allowed to go out into the field with no prior knowledge of the diplomatic role overseas.

Defining the state: Propaganda, publicity, and public opinion

Besides a lack of skill at professional negotiation, public opinion hampered politicians who were constantly striving to gain its support. Because the world was divided into two blocs, it was easy to identify who the "other" was and portray this group as the enemy. Public opinion was clearly more significant to foreign offices than in the past, and it was one of the prime factors driving governments to limit the autonomy of professional diplomats.[40] Many created information *bureaux* within the foreign office like the Ministry of Information and Political Intelligence Unit, and some foreign offices employed Press Attachés. These various offices kept track of how newspapers reported events domestically and abroad, disseminated reports to diplomats, and sometimes attempted to spin the news themselves to impact public opinion. Increasingly, statesmen cared about how their policies and political stances were regarded abroad. Pressuring other countries' domestic opinion was a means of indirectly impacting their foreign policies.

The role of public opinion was not really significant until the very end of the nineteenth century, and was still not a great concern in the early twentieth century, particularly compared to the late twentieth century. During the Great War, leaders were increasingly concerned with public opinion and tried to use propaganda through film and cinema to tilt it in their favor. When ideas of Wilsonianism and *open diplomacy* were spread among the European populace, it became more of an important consideration for statesmen working on foreign policy. While public opinion impacted the climate of the times and the processes of governmental decision-making, it only indirectly impacted diplomatic processes. In essence, public opinion became part of the definition of the state. So it was encompassed in instructions to diplomats, and provided a tight cage from which statesmen had to operate.

The lead-up to World War I

At the start of World War I, France, Great Britain, and Russia were allies in the Triple Entente, and Germany, Austria-Hungary, and Italy were allies in the Triple Alliance. The members of the two blocs tried to maintain an equilibrium or balance of power, and they were willing to engage in military action to do so. Around the time when Otto von Bismarck retired from his Chancellorship in 1890, the balance began to fall apart. A second, then third, Balkan crisis posed a threat to the precarious balance. In particular, the statesmen of the Austro-Hungarian Empire were looking for an excuse to go to war with Serbia, as they were concerned about increasing anti–Austro-Hungarian sentiment. In 1914, Serbian teenager Gavrilo Princip assassinated the Austro-Hungarian heir, Francis Ferdinand, and his consort, which led to a domino effect of international conflict.

The war between Austria and Serbia grew to an all out world war in large part because of the alliance system. Each had to come to the other's aid and they were all bound by treaties to do so. Austrian leaders blamed the assassination on a Serbian conspiracy, and issued an ultimatum that could not be met without a complete loss of Serbian independence. This was the excuse they needed to attack Serbia. Austrian leaders declared war on Serbia on 28 July 1914, and Russia mobilized its forces two days later. In response to Russia's actions, German leaders mobilized their troops and declared war first on Russia (1 August 1914) and then on France (3 August 1914). France was an ally of Russia, and the German Plan was to march through Belgium, violating Belgian neutrality, to get to France, and then to turn around and engage Russia. Great Britain entered the war a few days later declaring war on Germany as its army entered Belgian territory.

The freedom of the United States was born out of European rivalries, chiefly that of France and Britain. In addition, Britain had controlled the oceans ever since 1815. The United States entered the war in large part because the defeat of the European Allies would mean that the Atlantic shores would be controlled by German domination.[41] In addition, Germany's indiscriminate attacks on ships caused many American merchant vessels to suffer attacks as well. In the summer of 1918, it became apparent to the leaders of Germany and Austria-Hungary that they could not win the war. On 8 January 1918, US President Woodrow Wilson made his Fourteen Points speech to Congress, and on 3 October Prince Max Von Baden, the German Chancellor, contacted Wilson to request an armistice based on the Fourteen Points.

The negotiations

From 12 January through June, 1919, well over 1040 delegates and 70 plenipotentiaries from 32 countries met in Paris to try to reach a compromise on the conditions of peace in Europe.[42] Each of the Great Powers had five plenipotentiaries, and the smaller powers had between one and three depending on size and stake in the war. The negotiations continued for some time after these crucial six months, but the Treaty of Versailles, signed on 28 June 1919, contained the most important decisions regarding Germany. The primary participants were statesmen representing the victors of the war. These were Premier Georges Clemenceau of France, Prime Minister David Lloyd George of Great Britain, Prime Minister Vittorio Emanuele Orlando of Italy, President Woodrow Wilson of the United States, and occasionally Makino of Japan. They each brought with them to Paris their foreign secretaries (Pichon of France, Balfour of Great Britain, Lansing of the United States, Sonnino of Italy, and Chinda of Japan), hundreds of technical experts, and professional diplomats. Many other European and non-European states who were less involved in the war were also present at the negotiations, but the Allies excluded the defeated powers of Germany, Austria-Hungary, the Ottoman Empire, and Soviet Russia from the negotiations. Table 5.2 lists the major attendees of the Paris Peace Conference.

The Council of Ten (aka Supreme Peace Council) was the original primary decision-making body at Paris, and it was an outgrowth and continuation

Table 5.2 Major attendees at the Paris Peace Conference

Country	Politicians	Foreign secretaries	Diplomats
France	Georges Clemenceau (PM)	Pichon	Jules Cambon André Tardieu Philippe Berthelot
Great Britain	David Lloyd George (PM) Philip Kerr (personal secretary)	A.J. Balfour	Lord Charles Hardinge Sir Eyre Crowe James Headlam-Morley William Tyrrell
United States	Woodrow Wilson (President) Colonel Edward M. House (personal aid)	Lansing	Dr Sidney E. Mezes Christian A. Herter Charles Seymour
Italy	Orlando	Sonnino	
Japan	Makino	Chinda	
Nonattendee: Germany	Matthias Erzberger	Brockdorff-Rantzau	Kurt von Lersner

of the Supreme War Council, which had been holding inter-Allied meetings during the course of the war. The development of the Supreme War Council, largely attended by premiers, later provided the framework for the armistice and peace negotiations. F.S. Marston argues, "By the autumn of 1918, therefore, there had developed practices of consultation that were greatly to influence the form of the peace negotiations, and in the background was an elaborate organization of executive control."[43] The four major allies were members of the Supreme War Council, and gradually the United States began to take part so that there was no question that the United States would continue to be involved in the peace negotiations. Following the wartime framework, the Council of Ten included the five premiers and their foreign secretaries.

Also in the room were their advisors, experts, and secretaries, and occasionally representatives of other countries would be invited to join in, bringing the daily total attendance of the Council of Ten to over thirty individuals. The main disadvantages resulting from this setup were inefficiency of progress and daily leaks to the press. It was inefficient because of the emphasis on holding informal "conversations" on irrelevant issues instead of formal negotiations, and ad hoc decision-making instead of following an agenda. The lack of secrecy meant that there could be political repercussions for each opinion expressed by the plenipotentiaries. The system of circulation of printed copies of meeting minutes and decisions no doubt added to the lack of secrecy.[44] On 25 March 1919, it was informally announced in the press that the Big Four (Wilson, Lloyd George, Clemenceau, and Orlando) would from then on meet privately in a Council of Four, with the Foreign Ministers forming a separate Council of Five. The secretariat of the Council of Ten, consisting of Paul Dutasta as Principal Secretary-General along with Mr Grew, Count Aldrovandi, Sadao Saburi (who was essentially defunct), and Sir Maurice Hankey (who was informally appointed as the Secretary to the Council of Four). The system of printing and circulating the meeting minutes was abandoned at first and then severely limited.[45] Thus, pressure from public opinion and the press subsided for a while, until it was unleashed in full force with the eventual dissemination of the draft treaty.

Many scholars focus on the role of the Big Four (or Three as Orlando was in a subordinate position and at times withdrew) to the neglect of the diplomats who were also present in great numbers behind the scenes. This neglect is somewhat justified as the status and autonomy of diplomats had fallen dramatically. Although many diplomats were present at the negotiations there was a divide between diplomats and nondiplomats, and this division was a great theme throughout the conference. Lovin argues,

> This created an undercurrent of competitive activity at the conference between those who believed in traditional diplomacy and wanted to save its traditions and strengthen its position, and those who believed diplomatic decisions had to be responsive to the public will and that the foreign service needed to be altered to include nondiplomatic types.[46]

There are many scholarly works expounding upon the mistakes made at the Paris conference, and how the statesmen fell short of accomplishing their goals. Another way of looking at these failures is to realize the ways in which the statesmen fell short of accomplishing what professional diplomats might have produced in their stead. The case study of the Versailles negotiations represents an empirical counter-factual to the other cases examined in this book.

There are numerous reasons for the Treaty of Versailles' failure, but several stand out more than others. First and foremost, no one followed a preliminary plan or organization for the conference. Second, once the negotiators met in Paris, they did not know whether they were negotiating a final or preliminary treaty. Third, they did not know whether Germany would participate in the congress or sign an imposed treaty. Finally, the negotiators as statesmen were oppressively hampered by the expected reaction of public opinion.[47] All of these issues are connected to a fundamental lack of process and procedure, and all could have been eliminated had diplomats presided at the negotiations. The remainder of this chapter deals with this argument in more depth, then looks at the interaction of diplomats and statesmen of Great Britain, France, the United States, and Germany at the negotiations, and the extent to which diplomats contributed to the outcomes of the Treaty of Versailles.

The procedural and organizational failures of the conference

On 2 and 3 December 1918, Clemenceau went to London to try to work out a program for the upcoming conference in Paris. Four points were discussed: that a Committee would immediately work on deciding the amount of German reparations, that the former Emperor would be tried in an International Tribunal, that the British dominions would be allowed representation in the relevant negotiations, and that a Committee would be set up to determine supply and relief for victims of the war devastation.[48] These initial agreements, however skeletal, were not followed at the conference. The French also made a strong effort to set up a preliminary plan and structure for the conference. Clemenceau requested that André Tardieu write a plan of procedure, and he submitted it to the conference in early January. This more detailed plan outlined the guiding principles and methods to address each of the territorial, financial, and economic problems as well as promoting the League of Nations. It also provided a breakdown of the conference into committees and subcommittees, and the precedence of issues according to urgency. The French plan was based on Wilson's Fourteen Points articulated in his speech on 27 September 1918 and his message of 8 January 1918.[49]

Ultimately, the negotiators followed neither the British nor French plan at the conference, and the Big Four adopted an ad hoc agenda. Rather than setting up commissions (topical committees) at the start of the conference to establish a firm pattern of division of labor and responsibility, they set up commissions as it occurred to them. This lack of organization and planning of any kind was unprecedented. At the Treaties of Westphalia, Vienna, and Berlin among others, procedures and precedence were decided upon in advance, and the diplomats adhered to them strictly. These professional negotiators appreciated the difficulties and obstacles to compromise and knew that contentious issues required organization and mediation for the negotiations to be effective. Thus, not only was the Treaty of Versailles much more complex than earlier treaties, it was written with no advance preparation or a preliminary treaty.

The disorganization of the conference existed in large part because as late as 19 March, the leaders had still not decided whether their discussions were to go toward a preliminary or final treaty. The ad hoc committees and disorganized meetings of the Big Four proceeded with no clear idea of what was to be discussed, nor in what order. They just continued to meet, and eventually decided that they had reached enough points of compromise for the treaty to be final. Of course, this had a strong bearing on the third major undecided component of conference procedure: whether the treaty would be imposed or negotiated with Germany. In a kind of unconscious domino effect, the German plenipotentiaries were not included in the negotiations because the preliminary treaty suddenly turned into the final treaty and, in turn, there was no real conference procedure. In November 1918, five seats had actually been set aside for the German delegation, but these seats were never filled. Clemenceau, Wilson, and Lloyd George were even absent for a time during a critical phase of completion of the treaty. This lack of procedure was mainly because they designated themselves, instead of professional diplomats, to conduct the peace negotiations, and subsequently followed the wartime practices of the Supreme War Council.

Historians cite many reasons for the failure of Versailles. Some argue that it was the overbearing and stubborn personalities of the leaders. Others argue that the Wilsonian ideal was simply not compatible with European needs at the time. Yet another popular argument is that the absence of German participation meant that the treaty lacked legitimacy violating the principle of "open covenants of peace, openly arrived at," and there was always the question of whether the enemy would follow its terms. I argue that the overwhelming reason was that the statesmen fell short of the abilities of professional diplomats, and that because they were not diplomats with negotiation expertise, knowledge, and shared norms of understanding, they could not find a workable solution. It is clear that they did not realize the importance of a solid agenda, rank ordering of precedence for the topics to be addressed, and who the participants would be. Also, because they were democratically elected, their attention was divided between the potential reactions of public opinion to the treaty and their duties of domestic leadership instead of focusing on finding the best solution to the problem of peace. It can be debated whether or not it was a good thing that those negotiating foreign policy were democratically elected, however it is the nature of any democratic system to delegate decision-making authority to nonelected officials who are then held accountable to their elected leaders and are typically more expert at the finer points of international negotiation.[50]

The strong influence of domestic public opinion went hand in hand with the role of statesmen in negotiating the Treaty of Versailles. Many historians draw comparisons between the 1815 Congress of Vienna and the Paris Peace Conference arguing that the former is a strong example of old diplomacy and the latter marked the beginning of new diplomacy. At Vienna, participants believed in secret diplomacy, the role of diplomats in determining outcomes based on whatever they saw fit, and the rationale of power-based outcomes. At Versailles, "open covenants of peace, openly arrived at" meant that the negotiations would be open to public scrutiny. Wilsonianism also emphasized national self-determination instead of power relationships. As the negotiations progressed, Wilson and other strong supporters of open diplomacy realized that public opinion could be very damaging to the prospects for cooperation. William R. Keylor argues,

> Wilson's mounting apprehension about the potentially deleterious effects of public opinion on the peace negotiations prompted him to join his European colleagues in sacrificing the cherished principle of open diplomacy before the negotiations began. The world press became the chief victims, and eventually the harshest critics, of this change of heart.[51]

Despite the fact that the statesmen abandoned the principle of open diplomacy from the start, each was still plagued by the strong pressures of public opinion. As politicians of democratic countries, they could not escape these pressures. It is important to look at the role and interaction of statesmen and diplomats in more detail, to provide a comparison with other conferences, and to show the extent to which diplomats did play a role despite the obstacles. The analysis proceeds with a country-by-country investigation.

Great Britain

The British state: Lloyd George

It is often argued that Lloyd George tried to seek a middle ground between the positions of Woodrow Wilson and Clemenceau.[52] He consistently tried to insure that the final treaty did not stray too far from the conditions expressed by Wilson, but he would often change his mind on many of the particular issues, sometimes even within the course of one speech. Lloyd George had a sociable personality that enabled him to get along with some, but his mercurial, spontaneous qualities disconcerted others. In particular, the French at the conference found him to be lacking in formality, and to be too merry, reckless, and unstable. He lacked knowledge of protocol and often acted unilaterally. Clearly, he was charismatic and unique, but had not acquired the dignity, knowledge, and reserve of a professional diplomat. He would often make quick decisions and then rely on his debating skills. As a result, the British position in Paris changed considerably and in unpredictable ways.

Antony Lentin writes, "Practiced diplomats like Lords Hardinge and Curzon, whom he kept in the dark, deplored what they saw as the 'complete absence of any system on the part of the Prime Minister, who declines to utilize the services of experts.'"[53] Indeed, he alienated some of his aides before the negotiations even began. Although not a professional diplomat, he did not want to take advice from his assistants, in particular Foreign Secretary Balfour. It is important to note that Lloyd George openly did not believe in the efficacy of professional diplomats and the Foreign Office. He himself enjoyed having personal contact with other states' representatives instead of sending plenipotentiaries, and he argued that negotiation by statesmen was preferable.

Woodrow Wilson described him as a "chameleon," but noted that he was also a very persuasive negotiator when the point of view he advocated happened to coincide with what he really needed to say. The British Prime Minister was at times a purposeful chameleon in light of his changing policy position during the negotiations, but he would also erroneously argue points that the British government did not support. For example, he would arrive late to the first session of the morning and start speaking without knowing the topic of discussion. Once his aides realized that he was presenting an argument against British interests, one of them would pass him a note and shortly after he would announce that he did not support the speech he had just given.[54] In general, Lloyd George's main priorities were Britain's naval power, a European balance of power, and protecting the boundaries of the Empire.[55]

Once the Council of Four more firmly isolated Lloyd George from his delegation, he was willing to accept the harsh terms of the treaty. Later, he became sharply aware of this mistake when British public opinion was strongly critical of the treaty. The Left newspapers in Britain and elsewhere were outraged at the terms of the treaty which literally violated the entire body of Wilson's Fourteen Points. The clauses on trade and reparation meant that Germany could not even feed its own people, and the League of Nations was an alliance of Victors, not an enlightened international organization of peace. At the same time, the Right complained that the terms were too lenient. In sum, their choice was, "either move toward appeasing both the Germans and the Left, even at the risk of further infuriating the Right extremists, or stand fast, even at the expense of paying off the ultra-Right, for fear that appeasement would dangerously embolden the Left."[56]

Lloyd George backed down from his united stance with Clemenceau, and argued for moderation, siding with the Left and Labor, during the crisis weeks between the draft and final treaties. In Britain, the Labor party had a loud voice against a harsh treaty, and as a politician, Lloyd George had to be careful as multiple strikes threatened to break loose. He chose to exaggerate the pressure of Labor to justify his support for German concessions or, at a minimum, gain popularity for his efforts at revision. He held Cabinet and Council meetings to try to push his case with the British government. As a result, Brockdorff-Rantzau, the German diplomat, sent a top-secret telegraph home, notifying Social Democrat Party Chairman Frederich Ebert that domestic pressure in the Allied countries was forcing the Big Four to concede to German requests. Eventually, his optimism would be checked as pressure from the Left and Labor only represented one facet of society.

British diplomats

The British delegation consisted of nearly 200 individuals, including typists and clerks.[57] They were housed in five hotels. William Tyrrell was the only member of the delegation that appealed to foreign diplomats because they could relate to him and they found he shared their worldview.[58] Tyrrell was the director of the Political Intelligence Department of the Foreign Office. It was a relatively new department established in 1917, and was the primary division of the Foreign Office dealing with the initial armistice notes and memoranda between the Allies and Germany. Despite this advance preparation and the wealth of knowledge gathered by the Political Intelligence Department, Lloyd George chose General Smuts to prepare the British proposals for the conference.

Smuts was wholly unqualified for this role and lacked an expert staff. Nevertheless, he put much effort into the task and did come up with several plans. He could not, however, produce a coherent plan of action and if it were not for the work of Philip Kerr, Lloyd George's private secretary, the British delegation would have left for Paris with little expert advice.[59] Later, however, Smuts, a strong Wilsonian, was one of the most radical supporters of revisions to the draft treaty, calling it a *war treaty* and inevitably leading to revolution.

Sir Headlam-Morley, who was the assistant director of the Political Intelligence Department, was also a key member of the British diplomatic delegation to Paris. He was on most of the territorial commissions and took part in an exchange of intelligence information with the United States starting in February 1919. He wrote many proposals for the treaty and most of these were contingent on his assumption that the League of Nations would be a permanent supervisory organization that would ensure the continued viability of the treaty. Headlam-Morley's memoirs are strikingly similar to other diplomatic accounts in Paris during the negotiations. He writes on 19 January 1919, "While all subordinate officials are producing their material and are ready to take up and to bring to a practical solution the matters with which they are charged, there remains as before a complete absence of leadership, statesmanship, decision and, apparently, of any sense of responsibility above."[60]

Thus, the diplomats yearned to contribute in the process, were prepared for the task, but were not permitted any autonomy to act.

France

The French state: Clemenceau

The French government played an important role in the negotiations, especially since France served as the host state for the conference. Whereas all the other countries had to prepare special representatives and teams of experts to travel to Paris, the French could call on their entire governmental apparatus. Although Geneva and Brussels were alternative locations for the Peace Conference, Paris won the bid as it was twice threatened by the enemy and because Versailles had been the wartime venue of the Supreme War Council of the Allies.

Clemenceau was the Chairman of the Peace Conference and along with the Secretary-General was in charge of devising the agenda for the delegates. Prior to the conference André Tardieu and officers of the Quai d'Orsay proposed several revisions to a general conference agenda. However, Clemenceau virtually wasted his right to determine the conference agenda through the Secretariat and to appoint the Secretary General. He selected an unenterprising bureaucrat, Henri Dutasta (rumored to be his illegitimate son), as the Chief Secretary. A more natural choice would have been Philippe Berthelot, the Secretary General at the Quai d'Orsay, who had expected to be appointed head of the delegation, and had served a vastly important diplomatic role since the beginning of the war. Because of Dutasta's lack of skill, the British diplomat Sir Maurice Hankey, chief secretary during the Supreme War Council meetings, promptly stepped in performing Dutasta's tasks, even though officially his title was only Deputy Secretary. Just as during the war, Hankey took the lead and always had the appropriate documents and information on hand, making him extremely useful to Clemenceau.

At the conference, Clemenceau gave the impression of not listening half the time. He would frame a proposition or resolution in rapid fire: "*y a-t-il d'objections? Non? . . . Adopté.*" (Are there any objections? No? . . . Adopted.) He was also extremely rude and condescending to the small powers. When he was tired, he would simply interrupt a speech and declare "*c'est tout*" (that's all), get up and leave the room regardless of pleas or protests.[61] In addition, when technical advisors were called in from the anteroom, he would often decide that they were unnecessary, promptly and unceremoniously asking them to leave. They were not even granted enough time to gather their maps and documents.

Clemenceau was known as "the tiger" of the conference. His realpolitik approach meant that he subordinated everything to France's national security interests. Seymour's impression was that Clemenceau was so permanently tied to old traditions that they constrained him. He often got his way at the conference. He had an insistent negotiating style that asked for much, but with soft words surrounding harsh demands. His main demands were French occupation of the Saar Valley, the left bank of the Rhine, and a high level of reparations from Germany. The German troops had left northern France with the most destruction; coal mines, factories, orchards, and farms all lay in ruin. Thus, Clemenceau and the pressure of public opinion, to a certain extent, naturally pushed for the harshest treaty possible. Like Wilson, he shared the principles of reparations, guarantees, and restitutions. It was ultimately Lloyd George who worked against severity in this regard, although at first he was more in agreement with Clemenceau's position.

French diplomats

The French diplomats' aim was to begin afresh with the peace negotiations to mark a separation between war and peace. They sought to establish a plan and procedure that would ensure the successful accommodation of everyone's desires to reach a workable compromise. However, the pull of the wartime procedures worked against them; with many of the same characters from the War Council present at the conference, the tendency was to continue to sideline the diplomats.

André Tardieu, who later became Premier of France three times, was the major French diplomat involved in the negotiations. He was the author of the French conference plan, and even after it was abandoned was chief among the proponents of following a program and adhering to precedence of issues. Lloyd George was concerned that a strong treaty would be unjust and would result in Bolshevism, an unsigned treaty, or both. Toward the end of the negotiations, Clemenceau threatened to resign if Lloyd George continued to support German concessions. Tardieu was instrumental in responding to Lloyd George's principle of extreme moderation; after the treaty was submitted to German representatives, he laid out his response in several Notes. Tardieu was a good person for the job as he got along well with the diplomats from other countries taking full advantage of the epistemic community.

Another major French diplomat participating in the negotiations was Jules Cambon, a diplomat since the end of the Franco-Prussian War in 1870–71. He was chairman of several commissions. Together, Tardieu and Cambon represented France in nearly all of the commissions.

Philippe Berthelot, who was really denied his rightful place as Secretary General, did, however, have some role at the conference. He was on the commission establishing the new states of Central Europe with the fall of the Austro-Hungarian Empire. Berthelot was involved in some way with most territorial clauses of the Treaty of Versailles. To the extent that Dutasta did live up to his appointment as Secretary General of the conferences, he relied on Berthelot's advice as they had a close relationship.

United States

Woodrow Wilson engaged in an ultimatum tactic, ordering the ocean liner, *George Washington*, to Brest on 7 April when the French would not back down from their position on German reparations. The French argued that the Germans should pay as high a figure as possible while the British and Americans believed that the German capacity to pay should be taken into consideration. The French position clashed with Woodrow Wilson's principles.

President Wilson was the creator of the Fourteen Points and the League of Nations. Among the principles he expressed on 11 February 1918 was that "there shall be no annexations, no contributions, no punitive damages."[62] He was also the first US president to travel abroad during his term. He attended the Paris Peace Conference against the advice of his Secretary of State, Robert Lansing, as well as many others in the United States, France, and Britain, and proceeded to push his own agenda at the conference. This was a dangerous step as the Republicans held the majority of seats in both the Senate and the House of Representatives. He would have to get approval for the treaty from the Foreign Relations Committee of the Senate, which was heavily Republican, and most Europeans knew that his views were not really those of the US government. His legitimacy was tenuous.

Because of Lansing's independent viewpoints, Wilson tried to push the Secretary of State to the sidelines at the negotiations, instead relying more heavily on his long-time friend, Colonel Edward M. House, a lawyer by training. Like Lansing, House eventually understood the extent to which the President was unwilling to compromise, and increasingly disagreed with Wilson's approach. By the end of the conference, House, like Lansing, had distanced himself from the President, and they never saw each other again. Wilson's personality combined idealism and uncompromising stubbornness, a mixture that was difficult to accommodate in Paris given the practical realities and complexities of the treaty.

Harold Nicolson, a British diplomat, argues that whatever stubbornness and arrogance the President naturally possessed became even more exaggerated once he arrived in Europe. Nicolson writes that compared with Lloyd George and Clemenceau, Wilson was much more informed and practical during the negotiations.[63] His abilities at the conference were not hampered by his style of negotiation and presentation, which André Tardieu describes as professorial, but rather by his "one-track mind" and unwillingness to consider other opinions. He was very predisposed against any Americans from the Republican Party because they were political opponents. He would request information from his expert advisors, but would rarely listen to their ideas or opinions either.

Throughout the conference, Wilson slowly shifted his emphasis from the Fourteen Points to the creation of the League of Nations. Naturally, this was disconcerting for many of the attendees whose sole reason for agreeing to the armistice was the hope they had for the fruition of the principles expressed in the Fourteen Points. Wilson shifted his focus because the League of Nations became a personal goal for him, and one he hoped would have a lasting impact. Seymour writes that at first the league was a "fantastic possibility," then a "desirability," and eventually an "absolute necessity."[64] One of the reasons he was less concerned about the viability of the actual stipulations of the treaty was because he trusted that the League of Nations would continuously review and alter the treaty as time passed. Thus, over time the treaty did not have to be as harsh as it at first appeared. The great tragedy was that nine months later, the US Senate rejected the treaty and US membership in the League; without the United States, the League was unworkable. Like Clemenceau and Orlando, Wilson was ruined by the political effects of their struggle to write the Treaty of Versailles.

US diplomats

Charles Seymour was one of the prominent diplomats who represented the US at the negotiations. In his diary, he writes that the diplomats often waited outside the room while the Big Four discussed the major issues. Occasionally one of them would come out and announce their most recent decision. It was not until 3 June 1919, that all of the American delegation met together in one grand room to discuss the treaty with the Germans. A major point of discussion was Lloyd George's new position, which advocated that the

Allies grant many concessions to prevent the treaty from being unjust, and to ensure that the Germans would be willing to sign. In this rare meeting, Wilson sought the expert advice of his diplomats, and each in turn gave their viewpoints to the American assembly on the issue of concessions to Germany. Wilson took a strong stance saying, "If the Germans won't sign the treaty as we have written it then we must renew the war; at all events we must not allow ourselves to flop and wobble trying to find something they will sign."[65]

Seymour backed up the President arguing that they must show resolve and respect for all the work that had already gone into the treaty. However, on 19 June 1919, with persisting gridlock about which concessions to make, Seymour vented his frustration about the powerlessness of the diplomats. "It all shows the futility of the organization which keeps the Four by themselves, separated from the foreign ministers and the other Commissioners. Actually things went more speedily in the old Council of Ten."[66] Balfour and Lansing were both angry that as foreign ministers they had virtually no authority in the decision-making. Thus, it appears that the decision to limit the talks to only the Big Four did not result in more efficiency, nor did it result in more success. Wilson's undiplomatic propensity to avoid social events and alienate his colleagues finally backfired. Overall, the American foreign service was particularly strong despite being largely ignored by Wilson.[67]

Germany

The German delegation stands out as an anomaly at the Paris Peace Conference as it was the only delegation consisting primarily of traditional, professional diplomats whose government granted them real decision-making power. In addition, these diplomats exercised agency, despite the mix of confusion, lack of information, and inability to negotiate. The original primary plenipotentiary for Germany was Ulrich Brockdorff-Rantzau, an aristocratic diplomat newly appointed as foreign minister. He was trained as an old-school diplomat, and was proud of this heritage. Thus, it is understandable that he firmly believed the treaty would be negotiated among equals, and that Germany would accept no treaty damaging to its honor. The delegation was largely traditional in its diplomatic approach. The Germans engaged in a great deal of advanced preparation for the negotiations they thought they would attend. Johann Bernstorff, the former German ambassador to the United States, provided much of the preparatory material.

In October of 1918, the Germans set up an armistice committee, chaired by Matthias Erzberger, with Kurt von Lersner as the representative of the Foreign Office. Although young, Lersner had a distinguished career and many personal contacts with the military and political leaders of the war. Lersner was a member of the delegation, but not a plenipotentiary; nevertheless, his strong diplomatic ties made him indispensable to the proceedings. During the armistice period, Lersner served as the intermediary between Erzberger and Brockdorff-Rantzau. This was a difficult task because Brockdorff-Rantzau refused to sign a dictated treaty, whereas Erzberger wanted to sign the treaty as quickly as possible. The conflict between the two grew and each tried to assert authority over the other. Ultimately, Brockdorff-Rantzau revamped the organization structure to make it necessary for Erzberger to report to him and severely constrained Erzberger's flexibility in negotiations.

Accompanying Brockdorff-Rantzau was a team of economic experts, diplomats, and a press group. The German delegation hoped to use public opinion in their favor, and they believed that as long as the Americans retained power over the decisions in Paris, they would be treated with leniency. When they arrived in France, a government-sponsored train took them to the North of the country where they could witness the great devastation caused by the departing German troops. The delegation remained there for four weeks wondering when the negotiations would begin. During that time, they only had five meetings, and the delegates slowly returned home until only Max Warburg, a banker, and Lersner were left when the Germans were, at long last, summoned to Paris and Versailles.

In Versailles, they stayed at the Hotel des Reservoirs and were virtual prisoners surrounded by French guards and caged gardens. On 29 April, the German delegates once more arrived in France, and they occupied the Hotel Vatel and Hotel Suisse as well. Telephones and telegraphs were set up in these two hotels, and the Germans, thinking that there were listening devices in the rooms, played music almost constantly to drown out their conversations.

The first task was the exchange of credentials, which took several days to verify. The German delegation was nervous during this waiting period because they were still in the dark about whether they would be negotiating the treaty. They were allowed full contact with their counterparts in Germany, but no means of communication with the Allied delegations in Paris. Lersner was critical in getting information because he had friends in the French foreign service. He used these connections to send a message to the Big Four that many of the Germans would have to return to Berlin if information was not forthcoming. Immediately, because of Lersner's initiative, they received a note from Clemenceau that the delegates were to meet to receive the treaty on 7 May. Only then did the Germans discover that it would be a dictated treaty.

On the afternoon of 7 May in the great hall of the Trianon Palace, Brockdorff-Rantzau famously did not stand to receive the treaty. There is much speculation as to why he dared to defy protocol in this way. Some of those present thought that he was nervous and a poor public speaker, others thought that he was enraged by the terms of the treaty, while some blamed his poor health. Whatever his true reason, he ultimately refused to sign because he saw this imposed treaty as an insult to Germany's honor that made slaves of the German people. The German delegation had prepared for Brockdorff-Rantzau several possible speeches depending on the circumstances of the treaty. Lersner and others urged him beforehand to accept the treaty as quickly as possible, instead he decided to read the strongest one in opposition to the terms. As Arno J. Mayer describes it,

> He chose to remain seated to deliver a speech which was pugnacious and defiant. He began by registering the victors' intense and passionate hatred for the vanquished, who, in line with their guilt, were to be punished. He then went on to contest Germany's war guilt, and stressed that only a peace consonant with Wilson's principles and the pre-Armistice agreement could be just and lasting.[68]

Clemenceau gave the German delegation two weeks to respond in writing, and the one-hour session was over. Lersner remained behind to get a copy of the treaty, had it translated into German, and disseminated to all the delegates. By this time, Lersner was a great necessity to Brockdorff-Rantzau for his diplomatic connections and good reputation among the European diplomatic corps.

The next evening, the German diplomats met together to discuss their response. While they must have been tempted to pack up and leave, as Orlando, Wilson, and Lloyd George had all done or had threatened to do at one point or other, the German diplomats stayed. They were unanimously opposed to the harsh terms, except for two exceptions, but decided to negotiate to the best of their abilities in true diplomatic fashion. On 8 May, each spoke in turn against the treaty until Albert Schwarz, the Saxon Socialist Minister for Labor who had previously remained quiet, stood up and said,

> Gentlemen! I cannot understand your despair. One would imagine, listening to your speeches, that Germany's last hour had struck. But the German People wants to live; it *shall* live. It may be that the consequences of this Treaty will keep us down for twenty – even twenty-five years – but sooner or later we shall rise.[69]

The speech urged the delegation to put an end to the evening and spawned a division in the delegation. Brockdorff-Rantzau opposed the treaty completely, while some members of the Cabinet and others argued that a harsh response would give the Entente powers an incentive to unite. Lovin writes, "Now the Germans were publicly divided; the entente powers were united; and Clemenceau was in the driver's seat."[70]

Throughout this period of crisis, from 9 May to 29 May, the Germans replied to the treaty through a series of 15 short Notes, and Lersner constantly used his diplomatic contact with French diplomat Saint Quentin to garner information for the isolated German delegation. The German Notes included, among other things, a protest about Germany's exclusion from the

League of Nations and the International Labor Organization, and the need to conduct oral negotiations to moderate the terms of the treaty. Brockdorff-Rantzau took the opportunity to travel to Spa to meet with cabinet members of the new German republic, and inform them of the recent developments. He emphasized many times that domestic public opinion in the Allied countries was opposed to a dictated peace, and therefore the Germans should refuse to sign. Interestingly, he did not take further instruction from them, but emphasized that he would not allow the German delegation to be burdened with political dissension in Berlin.[71] The diplomats would remain autonomous and keep the Paris decision-making in their own hands.

On 30 May, the German delegation's final counter-proposals were submitted in the form of a diplomatic brief, consisting of 443 pages of details. It included a covering letter, designed to appeal to public opinion at home, passionately requesting that the allies not consider Germany as the sole country to blame for the war, and to recognize the impossibility of the terms of the treaty.[72] They were willing to succumb to the economic and military stipulations of the treaty, but not the territorial ones. Lersner learned in advance that despite serious discussions to consider the German Notes, the allied powers were unwilling to make any major concessions. It turned out that domestic dissent and even strikes were not enough of a political threat for the Big Four. On the 16 June, the delegation received official word that they had one week to accept the final draft of the treaty, which did feature some minor concessions, or else the armistice would be called off. The German cabinet decided that it would be better to sign than to subject the struggling new republic to a takeover by the Independents and Communists, and subsequent anarchy.

Because of Lersner's inside knowledge and diplomatic relationships, he arranged for most of the delegation to return home before the official response from the Allies to minimize their loss of face and make their journey safer. Despite this, many inhabitants of Versailles gathered along the streets to throw stones at the German carriages, even inflicting permanent brain damage to one attendee. Lersner himself was left as the main German representative in Paris. Dr Müller and Dr Bell were designated to attend the signing ceremony at the Palace of Versailles on 28 June 1919, since Brockdorff-Rantzau would not sign the final treaty. Clemenceau began the ceremony stating, "We are here to sign a Treaty of Peace," and ended it shortly after with, "The meeting is over."

The epistemic community of diplomats: The commissions

Diplomats accomplished a great deal in writing the Treaty of Versailles, but they were uninformed and disorganized as a result of the lack of procedure and protocol. They had to proceed with their work based on certain critical assumptions. First, they thought that the suggestions of the commissions were only preliminary and would be further debated among the Big Four. As a consequence, they articulated the maximum level of punishment for Germany in their documents, and left certain clauses in skeletal form assuming that they would be filled in later. Second, the diplomats assumed that many of their suggestions would receive their due elaboration during the discussions of the Big Four. The diplomats and experts in the commissions were constrained because they lacked instruction, and thus had to be satisfied with a degree of imprecision. However, the Big Four often ran out of time, and after a quick glance at the commissions' documents would write them into the main treaty. When the final treaty went to the German representatives for approval the diplomats were indeed aghast at the harsh nature of the terms and the poor quality of the document. Third, the diplomats assumed that the German representatives would have the opportunity to negotiate the treaty so at the very least the terms could be moderated.

Setting these assumptions aside, what was the nature of the diplomats' interaction and ability to cooperate? The commissions were the key bodies in which the diplomats could shine at the Paris Peace conferences. There were fifty-two commissions, made up of the most renowned specialists from each country, that met 1646 times (according to Tardieu's count) before the treaty was signed. After the commissions submitted their decisions, three bodies considered them: the Council of Ten, the Council Four, and the Council of Ministers of Foreign Affairs.[73] From 24 March to 7 May, the focus was on the Council of Four, who produced the final treaty.

The diplomats hesitated when making decisions because they knew that they really did not have the power to do so. The heads of state could immediately change anything, without deference to their experts, if it suited them. However, it is important to recognize the extent to which the diplomats *did* have an impact on the outcomes of the treaty. The commissions set up by the Big Four were comprised of the best diplomats and experts on each particular issue. These commissions had the responsibility to deal with a specific question of fact and policy, and much of their work was taken word for word as part of the treaty.[74] Clive Day argues, "Some of these commissions were entrusted with questions so important that their contributions to the settlement appear positively greater than those of the Council of Ten itself."[75] Certainly, the selection of participants in these commissions was highly meritocratic and was less based on convention. The territorial commissions were the ones most populated by professional diplomats, while the finance ones consisted more often of bankers and businessmen. The Americans were prone to sending academics as representatives in the commissions. Diplomats were present, but conspicuously underrepresented of the various expert professions in Paris because of the rising influence of soldiers and other governmental departments during the war.[76] When the Big Four took over, around two months into the conference, they clearly proved themselves to trust more in the opinions of these commissions than even their own foreign ministers. As evidence of this, it was highly unusual for the Big Four to amend one of the draft articles of a commission, thus giving the diplomats an important, though uninformed role.

Diplomatic agency

What would have happened had diplomats served as true plenipotentiaries during the negotiations and drafting of the Treaty of Versailles? E.J. Dillon argues,

> Traditional diplomacy would have shown some respect for the law of causality. It would have sent to the Conference diplomatists more or less acquainted with the issues to be mooted and also with the mentality of the other negotiators, and it would have assigned to them a number of experts as advisers.[77]

The evidence in this chapter demonstrates the strong role of statesmen alongside their lack of diplomatic expertise.

As a case in point, Harold Nicolson, a professional diplomat of the British delegation, finished his preparatory work for the conference, and immediately set about making contacts with the American diplomats. He knew that these contacts would be extremely valuable in the future should they find themselves at the negotiating table. He formed relationships with several diplomats, including Mr Rhys Carpenter, a subordinate member of the American delegation, who introduced him to Dr Charles Seymour, Dr Clive Day, and Dr Lybyer. On one occasion he met with Mr Alan Dulles, and the two discussed their opinions on the issues at stake at the conference. He writes, "We compared notes. Our opinions on every one of the subjects within our particular orbit appeared to be identical. It seemed to us that the drafting of peace would be a brisk, amicable, and hugely righteous affair."[78] Even on issues where they had differences in opinion, they found that the details could easily be worked out with a little deliberation. This evident optimism of an outcome governed by diplomats was ultimately crushed as the conference progressed because "our relations were darkened by the wrangles of our respective chiefs."[79]

Nicolson was not the only British diplomat to undertake relationship building with other professional diplomats. His close colleague, Allen Leeper, had previously cultivated numerous relationships with the Americans and sought to foster them in Paris. The majority of diplomats spent days of boredom waiting for instructions that would never arrive from their respective statesmen. Nicolson writes in his diary entry of 24 May, "It is *such* a bore waiting on – without instructions. If I could be given a free hand I could easily settle all my stuff in a week."⁸⁰ He also argues that if the initial cooperative understandings reached between the American and British diplomats had been maintained, and not altered by the Chiefs of State, then the Treaty of Versailles would have been a much more workable document. Had professional diplomats been granted plenipotentiary power, instead of the statesmen and their pet advisors, a clear program would have been followed.

Bargaining theory as an alternative explanation

The Versailles case clearly points to the inadequacy of bargaining theory in predicting outcomes. Rationalist predictions of outcomes are different from what a historical process-tracing approach reveals. More importantly, it is clear that despite the existence of a strategic ranking of preferences, statesmen may simply lack the skills to realize and accomplish them. The preceding analysis proves that it matters *who* is negotiating. One cannot assume that the balancing out of competing preferences to find the Pareto optimum can actually occur in all cases. It is necessary to understand which actors are negotiating and what qualities they possess.

Lloyd George's preferences were to protect Britain's naval power, form a European balance of power, and protect the boundaries of the Empire.⁸¹ Clemenceau's was most strongly realist, thus he called for harsh terms in the treaty and his decisions were guided almost entirely by France's national-security interests. Lloyd George and Woodrow Wilson were more in line with each other, and both advocated toning down the terms of the treaty so that Germany would sign it and German domestic reaction would not trigger a Bolshevik revolution. The treaty was closer to Clemenceau's preferences, but the result was failure for everyone because the US government ultimately refused to accept it, dramatically diminishing the viability of the League of Nations.

Another problem with statesmen acting as diplomats was that they were neither knowledgeable enough to persuade their home governments, nor able enough to anticipate what they could or could not get away with. While diplomats cultivate relationships within their epistemic community, these statesmen did not have membership in an epistemic community. The strength of the epistemic community contributes to diplomats' anticipation of how much agency they can exercise. The Big Four did not have the tools to anticipate their room for maneuver, nor the collective strength to persuade governments of their decisions.

Conclusion

The Treaty of Versailles was supposed to insure that the Great War could not repeat itself. To accomplish the task, the Allied delegations redrew the borders of Germany, imposed war reparations in the form of payments and financial restrictions, and called for the establishment of the League of Nations. It is significant that all of the powers present signed this controversial treaty, except for the Chinese who were protesting the Shantung settlement.

Statesmen articulated the desire to transform the diplomatic process into a transparent, open one in which public opinion could have an impact as the negotiations went forward. In the example of the Treaty of Versailles, they could not accomplish this, and much of the decision-making occurred behind closed doors with vague procedures and ad hoc protocol. Moreover, the major discussions occurred in separate rooms creating a cleavage between the statesmen in attendance who were together in one room, and the professional diplomats in other rooms. In this case, the statesmen did not grant power to their diplomatic representatives to the detriment of outcomes of international cooperation. I argue in this chapter that failure may have been averted had diplomats truly acted as plenipotentiaries during the negotiations for the Treaty of Versailles.

There was also a division between the traditional diplomats and amateur diplomats. The traditional diplomats and foreign ministers were surprised that they were not involved in any meaningful way. Lovin argues, "All diplomats, regardless of rank, were disappointed because each of their political leaders expected to act directly in the activities of the peace conference as they had during the war. Their populist tendencies caused them to be suspicious of the elitist foreign-service bureaucracies."[82]

Public pressure eventually lashed out in full force with the dissemination of the treaty. The response was mixed, but the leaders decided to push for their original terms, with only a few minor concessions to the Germans. The meetings of the Big Four were secret, but lacking in organization and coherence. Too many times, one or another threatened to leave and issued an ultimatum. Diplomatic negotiations benefit from protection of scrutiny of the public eye. In the early twentieth century, public opinion became an important force in international relations and foreign policy. It was a reflection of growing democratization and democratically elected statesmen. While transparency and popular participation are positive developments, the diplomatic debate itself benefits from privacy. Diplomats are often more aware than statesmen of the invisible pressure of international opinion as they are members of international society.

The climate of new diplomacy during the postwar era provides an opportunity to examine the direction of diplomacy in the twentieth century: its move toward summitry and an increasingly bureaucratized profession. At the same time, this case study is a natural example of what happens to the agency of diplomats and the quality of the diplomatic epistemic community when status suffers, and what happens to the outcomes of international cooperation when diplomacy is performed by amateurs. One outcome of the conference, despite its poor treatment of diplomats, was to push diplomacy toward more professionalization as will be seen in the next chapter.

6
The Late Twentieth Century and the Treaty on European Union

> The question of whether or not ambassadors should be regarded as anachronistic relics, the eccentric survivors of the advent of electricity and steam, depends upon the activities ascribed to them.
> – Keith Hamilton and Richard Langhorne,
> *The Practice of Diplomacy*

Climate of the times

It is undeniably easier to identify and define the role of diplomats before the twentieth century, the growth of summitry, globalization, advances in technology, and the advent of international organizations. Before these contextual developments, diplomats formed a permanent elite international society and engaged in bilateral diplomacy in every major European capital. They held daily meetings to deliver démarches and maintained carefully cultivated relationships with kings or statesmen, members of court or parliament, and with other diplomats. When the occasion called for it, they represented states at major multilateral congresses. However, the diplomatic profession is marked by continuity as well as change. A diplomat of the seventeenth century could walk into an embassy today and recognize his profession, but bureaucratization, professionalization, and institutionalization have led to many structural transformations.

What is happening to the structural trajectory of diplomacy? The mid-seventeenth century witnessed the unprecedented event of a large-scale multilateral congress. By the end of the nineteenth century, multilateralism was still not the norm for diplomatic practice; the Congresses of Vienna and Berlin were exceptions to the century's more typical bilateral and secret diplomacy. After two world wars, the shortcomings of bilateralism became apparent and multilateral diplomacy took off. Since the beginning of the twentieth century, multilateral diplomacy, the rise in importance of international organizations, and the popularity of summitry have characterized international relations. The twentieth century marks the rise of international organizations as permanent multilateral institutions with regular meetings. This rise made it possible for international agreements to persist and for the idea of the Concert of Europe to reach actualization.

Modern professional diplomats are less involved in conference diplomacy, although they are still occasionally called upon to act as plenipotentiaries. Diplomats and embassies, however, remain an integral part of international society. In medieval times diplomats represented nonstate entities to other nonstate entities, from the mid-seventeenth century to the late nineteenth century diplomats represented states to other states, but for the past few decades diplomats are once again involved in the relations with nonstate entities. Whereas in medieval times the nonstate entities consisted of the church, merchants, members of the nobility, and land owners, today they consist of supranational institutions. The nature of the diplomatic profession is transformed such that embassy diplomacy is diminishing in importance in Europe, and diplomats are now called upon to represent their countries to institutions. In this respect, the diplomatic profession has taken a circular path to end up where it started, but the world is a very different place.

Because international organizations play such a central role in today's politics, theories abound on the nature of institutions: in particular, why they arise, whether they act independently, and how change occurs over time. The prime new factor, the advent of international organizations, is an institutionalized and legalized version of the community of diplomats. Now they do not just reside in embassies, but in the EU buildings in Brussels. Rather than cultivating bilateral relationships at Kings' courts, diplomats work along side each other on a daily basis in a modern, professional bureaucracy.

Preventive diplomacy is the *modus operandi* of international relations. Since no wars have occurred among the members of the EU since its inception in 1951, diplomacy to redraw territorial boundaries or deal with indemnities is not typical. As Peter Marshall writes, "The task is to look for signs of trouble and find ways of preventing the problem in question from arising. Preventive diplomacy is the most economical and efficient branch of the profession."[1] Diplomats and states consequently micromanage relationships with hundreds of meetings, memos, and messages. Information, efficiency, and transparency of institutions are assumed. Yet, a completely rational approach to diplomatic interactions does not ensue alongside increased bureaucratization. Diplomats exercise agency and maintain an influential epistemic community that exists to a significant extent outside of the rules, regulations, and structure of the Brussels bureaucracy.

Who are the diplomats of today's EU, and what is their role? The traditional embassy diplomats are less important to international relations as they tend to concentrate on consular, cultural, commercial, and informational work, and their numbers are declining. In Britain there were 221 embassy posts overseas in 1997, one-fifth less than in 1982.[2] In 1997, there were 253 overseas embassy posts for France, 229 for Germany, and 265 for Italy. The British embassy to the Council of the European Union, separate from the British embassy to Belgium, had around seventy individuals.[3] Today, many member states have their largest representations in Brussels. Diplomats who are assigned to represent their home states to international organizations such as the EU, NATO, and the UN are now increasing in numbers, and have taken over the political work of traditional embassy diplomats. It is worth noting that their role as multilateral interlocutors in international organizations is not strictly prescribed in treaties, but to a great extent determined by their own agency and their mutually constituted identity in an epistemic community. They themselves determine "the activities ascribed to them." The diplomats of today's EU are the Committee of Permanent Representatives (Coreper), and the Commission diplomats represent EU member states to outside countries. There is even talk of creating a European foreign service that would represent the EU to the outside world with one voice. Coreper was not a requirement in the Treaty of Rome, which stated that a committee of diplomats *may* be established and that this would be the prerogative of the Council of Ministers.[4] Now, the permanent representatives are arguably one of the most important contributors to the EU decision-making process. The foreign ministers increasingly rubber-stamp the prenegotiated agreements determined by Coreper in advance of ministerial meetings.

One tendency among EU scholars is to treat each EU institution as a black box, much the way realists treat states. Scholars rarely concentrate on what happens within institutions to produce outcomes.[5] Another tendency is to treat EU interactions as purely intergovernmental in the realist sense that only states, as black boxes, make decisions. Yet another approach is found at the individual level of analysis; sophisticated bargaining theories ascribe outcomes to state leader preferences alone, recognizing no significant impact from supranational or national representatives. I argue that it is necessary to look at diplomacy's *processes* to understand outcomes. Are diplomats agents of political cooperation in the EU or simply member states' transmission belts? In other words, to what extent do diplomats really deliberate, and why? Analysis of this question informs the larger debate among contemporary EU scholars about whether there is a "democratic deficit" in EU supranational governance and, if so, whether it will impact future efforts at integration.[6]

Europe's multileveled, mixed bag of foreign policy approaches means that each decision requires cooperation among member states to an unprecedented degree, and thus relies heavily on diplomatic skills and negotiations. Despite the fact that national differences remain, too many scholars speak of EU institutions as if they are unitary actors. To understand the process of diplomacy in the EU, it is necessary to disaggregate these "actors as institutions," and decipher how and why states agree to common policies. What processes bring about consensus and why? Can bargaining theories that emphasize state leaders' stable preferences predict outcomes or do diplomats exercise collective agency separate from their states?

The society of diplomats

Diplomatic corps today represent a culmination of centuries of professionalization and bureaucratization, followed by general democratization in the middle to late twentieth century, which has triggered an era of reforms. The evolution of the corps over time is neither unidirectional, nor characterized by constant improvement. Today, there is a particular lack of study devoted to European diplomatic corps. In English, there is only one book, two dissertations,[7] and a handful of articles that deal specifically with the role of the permanent representatives in today's EU. Brian Hocking and David Spence's important book, *Foreign Ministries of the European Union: Integrating Diplomats*, provides a comprehensive analysis of national foreign ministries, though the focus is not on the permanent representatives. Coreper is conspicuously understudied and underrecognized, evoking surprise whenever it is (accurately) characterized as *the* decision-making body of the EU. A journalist writes,

> Jacques Delores, president of the European Commission in 1985–94, thought it was the only European body that really counted. Heads of government? The council? No, he meant the Committee of Permanent Representatives, which every week brings together members' ambassadors to the EU, and which prepares for all council meetings and European summits. Coreper has huge clout.[8]

Only a handful of scholars recognize the importance of Coreper,[9] but the vast majority of scholars emphasize the foreign ministers and statesmen to the exclusion of this elite, powerful group of diplomats. A journalist's interview reveals, " 'Without us,' said one senior ambassador, 'the machinery of European government would collapse.' Yet who has heard of any of these players? Who has heard of Coreper – the name their unelected club adopts?"[10] Other scholars recognize their existence, but regard them as transmission belts for states, only acting within their delegated autonomy.[11]

Training, meeting frequency, social background, and status have consistently been important indicators of the strength of the epistemic community of diplomats since the seventeenth century, though they tend to vary significantly, and not in tandem. The professional norms that result from these factors create a widely recognized culture of compromise. Poul Christoffersen, Secretary-General of the Council of Ministers during Maastricht, wrote in a personal communication to me, "This culture of compromise has played an essential role in moving the Union forward, both in the daily work on the many practical issues that cross the table of Coreper, but also in the major negotiations."[12]

The remainder of this chapter will focus on the evidence for these variables in the make-up of today's European corps, and will then take the example of the 1992 Maastricht Treaty to further elucidate this process of decision-making among diplomats and to draw out the evidence for diplomatic agency. First, given increasing bureaucratization and the importance of institutions as umbrellas under which diplomats operate, it is necessary to specifically address the structure of Coreper, which provides both a hindrance and an incentive for diplomatic agency.

Structure of Coreper[13]

The Council of the European Union is the primary decision-making body of the EU, and within this intergovernmental institution is Coreper, founded in 1958.[14] It is divided into Coreper II, comprised of ambassadors, and Coreper I, comprised of deputy ambassadors. Coreper I typically deals with budget, transport, social, environmental, trade union, and institutional issues. Coreper II focuses more on general *dossiers* dealing with political issues.[15] Above Coreper is the Council of Ministers, and below Coreper are a variety of working groups, which are created and called to session based on Coreper's needs. The two most important groups are the Antici and Mertens groups. The working groups that are dedicated to more general or political issues often have diplomats as members, but scientists deal with more technical issues. In 1993, there were around 170 working groups in session. Today, there are around 250.

The purpose of this three tier structure – Ministers, Coreper, and working groups – is to divide up the necessary and daily task of negotiation within the Council (Figure 6.1). The ambassadors are not required to set aside their national interests in favor of the community interest, like Commissioners who have to swear an oath to this effect. However, over time, Coreper members have developed norms of collegiality and consensus as a result of their shared professional status, meeting frequency, social background, and training. Ironically, within Coreper the norms of collegiality and consensus are often stronger than within the Commission.[16]

The Council of Ministers is only called to Brussels if Coreper and the working groups cannot come to a resolution. By the time the policy issue reaches the level of the Ministers, it is most often rubber-stamped. In EU-speak, those policies resolved at the Coreper level are labeled *A* and those that are not are labeled *B*.

Weekly Coreper meetings typically deal with the preparation for up to six upcoming Council meetings, up to twenty policy decisions on a wide variety of topics, and very controversial issues such as the Common Foreign and Security Policy (CFSP) and voting rights that are too controversial for a

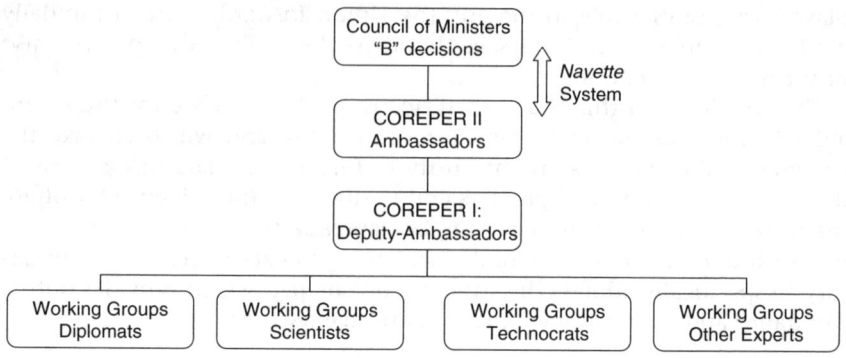

Figure 6.1 Council of the European Union organizational chart

ministerial-level meeting.[17] In all, ambassadors spend over 100 days of the year together; as Lewis argues, "they know each other extremely well, and this often leads to a mutual respect because of the workload, time pressures, and decisional demands that they must live with."[18]

All levels of the Council are granted a high degree of secrecy so that discussions can be direct, frank, and uninterrupted by external factors or domestic public opinion. Records of meetings are not required, and if they do exist are not openly distributed. Around 70 percent of negotiations are formally concluded at the working-group level, the remainder is divided by Coreper and the Ministers.[19] The creation of working groups is not stipulated in the EU treaty, but emerged as a result of Coreper initiative. Nevertheless, they accomplish a great portion of the work, and often achieve compromise so that further negotiation is unnecessary. Westlake argues, "In fact, working parties are the Council's lifeblood."[20] The working groups are primarily comprised of diplomats, some of which will become Coreper ambassadors when they gain more experience.

Coreper and its working groups together informally resolve around 90 percent of policy debates before the ministers even begin to address the issues.[21] Even when a decision is marked *B* and is passed on to the Council, a *navette* (shuttle service) occurs in which draft agreements are shuttled back and forth between the Ministers and Coreper. Coreper's official role is the preparation of all tasks assigned to the Council, and it has effectively taken over around 90 percent of these tasks from start to finish. Permanent representatives also sit in on Council meetings as they are the most familiar with the issues. Because of the *navette* and Coreper presence in Council meetings, diplomats are still heavily involved in the remaining 10 percent of decisions. Thus, combined with the negotiations conducted by the working groups, Brussels diplomats take on nearly all of the decision-making. However, the goal of ambassadors is to decide as much as possible so that issues are *not* passed to the Ministers. In effect, the rule of subsidiarity[22] metaphorically applies within the Council. An ambassador will negotiate with his or her capital to change the instructions so that a compromise can be reached before it gets to the ministerial level. A B decision is used as a last resort.

There remains a system of contact between the foreign ministries and Coreper. The permanent representatives are growing in significance as a community decision-making body, but Coreper officially remains an extension of nation-states, and thus foreign ministries. However, the foreign ministries are largely cut out of the process. Brian Hocking argues that foreign ministries serve as "gate-keepers" or "points of interface" between the domestic and the international realms.[23] Foreign ministries have a more hands-off relationship with the EU than they have with traditional embassies, tending to express viewpoints without really interfering in the technical aspects of EU processes.[24]

What does this mean for voting, a structural component of EU decision-making? Council voting is weighted so that countries with larger populations have more votes. As of September 2005, Germany, France, Italy, and the United Kingdom each had twenty-nine votes; Spain and Poland had twenty-seven; the Netherlands had thirteen; Belgium, the Czech Republic, Greece, Hungary, and Portugal had twelve; Austria and Sweden had ten; Denmark, Ireland, Lithuania, Slovakia, and Finland had seven; Cyprus, Estonia, Latvia, Luxembourg, and Slovenia had four; and Malta had three.[25] For most issues, the Council follows qualified majority voting, but on a few specific and more sensitive issues, decisions must be unanimous. Despite these finely chiseled rules on voting, it is only one mechanism for determining decisions, and is rarely used by the Council of Ministers.[26] Coreper, in fact, never votes. In light of this, the work of Coreper and the working groups, where most of the decisions are made through persuasion and unofficial agreement, is clearly of great significance to the decision-making process.[27] The Chairman knows which ministers will support a measure before they vote, and even the ministers themselves do not always vote.

Since the Maastricht Treaty came into effect, the responsibilities of Coreper have been substantially expanded. It is the only body which reviews all policies presented to the ministers, and is thus in charge of all the Council's activities, particularly in regard to Community political cooperation and the CFSP pillar. Since, as mentioned earlier, the ministers rarely meet, permanent representatives bear nearly the entire weight of political responsibility and consistency in the EU.[28]

Social background and training

As in the early twentieth century, foreign ministries still play an important role in the selection and training of diplomats. Foreign ministries emerged in the seventeenth and eighteenth centuries, and developed alongside the modern state as a kind of home base or coordinator for diplomats. In the nineteenth and most of the twentieth century, foreign ministries were not meritocratic and candidates often needed personal connections, a private income, or even a title to be considered for the diplomatic corps. In the early twentieth century, reforms were introduced in many European countries, but they were postponed with the devastation of World War I and again with World War II. During the late twentieth century, however, foreign ministries were finally able to take the steps necessary to accomplish a fully meritocratic system that at least seeks to be representative of society, professionalized, and standardized.

Diplomats today are selected through a regular exam system administered by the foreign ministries, where they receive their training and where they can alternate as diplomats or as foreign ministry officers. Many of the ambassadors of Coreper originate from this process and work their way up through the bureaucracy until they are experienced enough to receive an appointment as an ambassador. An ambassadorship in Brussels is one of the most prestigious posts to hold for the European corps. It was at a meeting of foreign ministers in Paris on 6 and 7 January 1958 that a decision was made that Coreper would be comprised of ambassadors, the highest rank of diplomats.[29] All permanent representatives receive the title "Ambassador Extraordinary and Plenipotentiary" except for the Italian and British permanent representatives who are simply called "Ambassador."[30]

Training on the job is particularly important as diplomats work their way up to the title of Ambassador. Whereas for statesmen, policy-makers, and European citizens many high-profile negotiations can reach crisis proportions, for the European corps, even the toughest scenarios are precisely where their training and expertise lies. In September 1992, when the post-summit Maastricht negotiations were on shaky ground, Coreper continued to work both on Maastricht drafts as well as budgetary issues. "While the world may be falling all around them, EC ambassadors continue to adopt a business-as-usual approach."[31]

Despite the numerous reforms that enable a more representative and meritocratic diplomatic corps in Brussels, opportunity still favors candidates of a similar social and educational background. They are largely white, male, and drawn from upper middle-class families. Until 1993, all permanent representatives were male. Even below the ranks of Ambassador and Deputy-Ambassador, the staff of Coreper was only 6 percent female in 1992 and 1993.[32] In this regard, the European corps retains some of the characteristics of the early twentieth century and the Paris Peace Conference, which historians describe as a collection of university reunions.[33] The corps is becoming more diverse with at least five women in the current Coreper. The first ever female Coreper, Irish Ambassador Anne Anderson, is still a relatively recent addition to the Brussels corps.

A greater variety of universities feed into the foreign service today and are more meritocratic in their own selection, but by the time graduates begin their professional diplomatic training, a large portion of the socialization has already taken place. This is particularly apparent at Oxford, Cambridge, and *Les Grandes Écoles* in Paris. French civil servants are required to receive a three-year postgraduate degree from the *École Nationale d'Administration* (ENA), a highly selective school of public administration, after attending one of *Les Grandes Écoles*. The new graduates then choose their assignment based on their ranking at ENA. Typically, the top quarter of graduates always pick the foreign service.

Most countries have an examination system to select diplomats. Denmark is one exception with no entrance exams except for the university entrance exam. In Denmark, usually a Master's degree is required, but some diplomats prove themselves to be very skilled and qualified for the job without one. Selection is based on grades and the profile behind each candidate, such as the languages they speak and any international experience. In some rare cases, they can even have no university degree at all, but prove themselves to be of a high enough quality.[34]

Diplomats are also socialized during prior bilateral diplomatic engagements in other countries, before they are sent to the EU. The elite of the British foreign service has a "clubbish" atmosphere formed through a sense of upper middle-class culture and the public school environment. Despite this clear similarity in social background, experts on Europe still debate the relevance of this variable. Edward Page argues that a similar educational background has no impact on social integration among EU officials while Fiona Hayes-Renshaw and her colleagues argue that it does.[35] While it may not be the only important variable, it certainly contributes to the cohesiveness and prior socialization of the corps.

The final stage of socialization occurs in Brussels. Ambassadors appointed for a post in Brussels have long prior diplomatic experience,[36] an expertise in European integration, an air of authority, and a high level of trust in their capitals.[37] They usually have copious multilateral and bilateral experience and by the time they are appointed ambassadors in Brussels they have experienced a little bit of everything.[38] Although diplomats tend to be generalists, the European ambassadors are different. Danish Ambassador Tranholm said, "There is an exception for European policies because in Brussels we prize specialization. It makes sense to know the institutions, how they work, and to know the people who work there."[39] Because of the prior experience at other posts, diplomats often know each other once they arrive in Brussels and these prior relationships help them in their work. French Ambassador Masset said, "I know three other ambassadors in Coreper with whom I worked with before – Luxembourg, Belgian, and Spanish. It is extremely useful to know people."[40] Irish Ambassador Anderson said, "Many are specialists and share memories of negotiations that happened a decade ago and have common points of reference."[41]

As a social group, members of Coreper engage in a similar lifestyle. Many live in the suburbs of Brussels, send their children to the European School, spend their weekend afternoons in Bruges and winters skiing.[42] They are also of a similar age. The average age of permanent representatives in 1993 was 46.7.[43]

The personal qualities of a diplomat remain, surprisingly, much the same as in the seventeenth century when François de Callières wrote *On the Manner of Negotiating with Princes*.[44] While there is no longer the requirement that a diplomat be handsome or engage in courtly manners, today's diplomat must possess an ease with foreign cultures and languages, an ability to negotiate without getting too passionate, a talent in probing the thoughts of others, and good judgment. Sharing these qualities gives the diplomat a step up in reaching consensus and establishing a common platform prior to negotiations.

Thomas Risse states that before the processes of arguing, deliberation, and persuasion can occur, there must be a basis of shared understanding.[45] He rightly differentiates between bargaining and "truth-seeking" in striving toward compromise. The latter emphasizes mutual understanding, while the former is indifferent to the actual personalities and qualities of the negotiators. Mutual understanding is a near constant within Coreper because of shared qualities, norms, and continual interaction. Thus, even though the process within the Council is officially intergovernmental, diplomats take the initiative to form a collective, and are facilitated in this endeavor by their similar qualities and identity. The convergence of worldviews and sense of Community is not unique to Coreper in the EU. Anne-Marie Burley (now Slaughter) and Walter Mattli made the same observation of judges in the European Court of Justice. Like judges, once diplomats arrive at their posts, they often "switch their loyalties"[46] from purely home-state interests to the community interest. Even if they are selected for their unswerving interest in their own state, the climate within Coreper and other international institutions makes this attitude difficult to maintain. Despite the fact that they do not swear an oath of loyalty to the EU, as the Commissioners do,[47] their professional background and subsequent socialization make this unnecessary.

Meeting frequency

Permanent representatives (Coreper) meet on a weekly basis, spending an average of 119 days per year in meetings together.[48] Coreper II has one formal meeting per week and Coreper I has two, every Wednesday and Friday. They are also responsible for preparing six Council meetings. They assist the minister and flank him on the right-hand side.[49] Their everyday interaction and informal "working lunches" or "working coffees" are also important in enhancing a collective identity and *esprit de corps*. Working lunches are particularly important when the issue to be discussed is sensitive and the diplomats want to be able to speak openly. Danish Ambassador Tranholm said, "From time to time we have a working lunch, when a Commissioner joins us to discuss an issue that is politically difficult. This way we can talk openly about a sensitive issue, without people taking notes, to better understand what is behind the issue."[50] In addition, every six months the Presidency organizes an informal trip to his member state, and diplomats go together to visit its institutions and companies. In this case, spouses are invited to the three to four-day trip and only with a very good excuse can they avoid the trip. Tranholm said, "This is clearly an occasion to get to know each other."[51] Other informal meetings are dinners and social events when someone leaves the EU. At the Coreper II level, ambassadors meet even more often, sometimes spending whole days together in meetings, and typically having dinner together at least once per week. "Even if we don't know each other prior to Brussels, we quickly develop intense relationships. We have a huge exposure to each other, and get to know each other's personalities and sense of humor quickly."[52]

Additionally, the level of cohesion brought about through the high number of meetings is unique to the Brussels diplomatic corps. At bilateral embassies, the focus is on the host country and not the other diplomats. In other multilateral settings such as the UN, diplomats rely more on informal meetings because the formal ones are so big. In Coreper, the formal meetings are where they get to know each other and where relationships are developed.[53]

Permanent representatives initiate and maintain a strong consensual ethos and camaraderie abounds. Although they come from many different countries, with centuries-long evolution in the diplomatic profession, they have similar systems of recruitment and training, and on the international level, they have shared status and membership in an elite international society.

Professional norms

There are two broad types of norms in the European corps. First are the enduring historical norms that are passed down through generations of diplomats and second are the new EU norms maintained through institutional memory and interaction in the multilateral, institutional setting. One major historical norm is the pomp and displays of status accompanying major diplomatic meetings. In Britain, diplomats are still sent out from Buckingham palace with their credentials stamped with the regal seal of the British monarchy. The flowery words that bestow plenipotentiary power on the diplomat bearing the letter of credence are so elaborate that they seem to empower him with the fate of the world.[54] Euro-diplomats regard themselves as the elite or *crème de la crème* of civil servants in every EU country.

At the same time, the new norms developing in the EU are far less formal than those of the past. Instead of following a strict protocol, the goal is to accomplish meetings efficiently and effectively. French Ambassador Masset explains,

Even though we may be on a first-name basis with the chairman outside of the meeting room, we all refer to him as Mr. Chairman inside the meeting room. We show him respect. We also speak only one at a time and it is important that we get our point across quickly. We have discipline instead of protocol.

Diplomats continue to develop and maintain norms of consensus and a shared desire to reach agreement more than a desire to gain the biggest concession for their own states. Westlake writes, "The ministers in the Council and their diplomatist assistants in Coreper are frequently prepared to forego unattainable excellence for an attainable good, and they are prepared to compromise and make concessions and package deals. This, understandably, is anathema to the pure scientist."[55] Thus, despite the official intergovernmental role of the Council, a norm of accomplishing results in the form of common agreement remains paramount. Diplomats today, as in the past, play a dual role. They represent their states to the Community, and the Community to their states. The latter case is even stronger because of the lasting nature of the Community.

Related to this, is a norm of collegiality. Diplomats strive to maintain working relationships. A news journalist writes, "Permanently in Brussels, ambassadors know each other well, and can feel out deals faster and more effectively than can most ministers."[56] An intergovernmental perspective would predict that Coreper simply reflects the Council as an intergovernmental body, but in actuality, the two are very different. The members of Coreper, by virtue of training, background, diplomatic qualities, and a high frequency of meetings, comprise an epistemic community, which makes consensus a much higher priority.

Many scholars have described the norm of collegiality among Eurodiplomats. Lewis, through extensive interviews and research, convincingly demonstrates that permanent representatives share a *vue d'ensemble*. Irish Ambassador Gunning said, "There is no question that there is an *esprit de corps*. It's absolutely tangible in a meeting of colleagues. It follows from that *esprit* that there is a willingness to find a solution."[57] Most are experienced diplomats, experts in EU affairs, who they want to successfully negotiate for a variety of reasons. According to Lewis, these include the shadow of the future (knowledge that negotiation will happen again), a desire to make the Council a strong EU institution, and the opportunity to report success back to their home states. This norm of collegiality is stronger than it was in the past because Coreper is a permanent body performing continuous work. Because of all the new issues on the table, new risks are involved and this is extremely important. French Ambassador Masset said,

> Each matter could be dealt with in separate streams, which increases the complication and creates a risk that there will no longer be synthesis

and coordination. Everything goes to Coreper so this is where you can find coordination and coherence. You need a body which makes the whole process consistent. Coreper does this for the day-to-day business. Coreper insures the coherence of the whole EU machinery.

More recent norms have emerged, though they often have elements of the past. For example, permanent representatives continuously lobby Commissioners on behalf of their states' interests, much the way that early modern ambassadors lobbied statesmen and kings at court. Other norms are true of many EU institutions, such as language. Although French was the predominate language of European diplomacy, English has continued to grow in importance; but they typically alternate among German, French, and English. The development of "EU-speak" is a norm of communication in the EU that includes a mixture of languages, use of particular sentence structure, and a whole new vocabulary invented in the EU. After many years in Brussels, even native English speakers have difficulty translating "EU-speak" into natural English.

It is customary for diplomats to remain in Brussels for five to seven years, more as they are appointed to Brussels several times. This is longer than the average diplomatic stay and indicates the importance of expertise and status over time, relationships held between diplomats, and the nature of the agreements in the EU.

Status

Ambassadors in Coreper II tend to have a slightly higher status than those in Coreper I. Whereas Coreper II is more involved in the typical work of ambassadors, Coreper I receives assignments that a diplomat does not expect to do. Irish Ambassador Gunning said, "Coreper I is not the most popular position. It does not involve traditional foreign policy. Coreper II is regarded by diplomats as an important and desirable post. Coreper II has all the responsibility for dealing with the entire EU. It deals with the European Council, ECOFIN, and the General Affairs Council."

Coreper I deals with much more technical legislative issues that are less political and have less of a grand-scale impact. However, Ambassador Gunning thoroughly enjoys his position. He said that diplomats tend to have preconceptions about the role of Coreper I, but it is actually a fascinating job. Posted in Brussels, he learns more about the Irish stance on a great multitude of issues that he would otherwise not be exposed to.

The status of Coreper in Brussels tends to be slightly lower than that of the Commissioners. As noted, many people have not heard of this elite, unelected group. Among the diplomatic community, they are the *crème de la crème*, but in the entire EU structure, they receive less attention than the Commissioners and Members of the European Parliament.

Technology

Since the advent of the telegraph in the mid-nineteenth century, scholars have speculated about the role that technology plays in diplomatic interactions. While it seems intuitive that greater technology would mean closer control by statesmen over diplomats, in practice this has not been the case. Technology such as the telegraph, telephone, fax, and email tend to change the means by which diplomats communicate with their home states, but not the substance of this communication.[58] If anything, the ease of communication associated with improved technology has made communication shorter, enabling diplomats to take more liberties with state instructions. In the seventeenth century, state instructions were elaborate and verbose, containing specific instructions for a variety of scenarios. In the late nineteenth century, with the advent of the telegraph, such instruction was shortened to 5–10 lines. Today, email and telephone are primary means of diplomatic communications, although in the early to middle 1990s, telegraph was still used. Telephone calls tend to be short, typically 5–10 minutes, and emails are used only to hint at future instructions because of the danger of Internet hackers.[59] Interestingly, emails face the same threats as ciphered documents of the seventeenth century that had to be carried by couriers across dangerous terrain.

Diplomatic autonomy and agency

Today's epistemic community of diplomats tends to have a low degree of autonomy, but it demonstrates a relatively high degree of agency. Thus, they take actions beyond the limits of their explicit autonomy; the ability and desire to do so rests on the strength of their epistemic community.

In terms of autonomy, Coreper officially has no decision-making authority and it is impermissible for any EU body to delegate powers to it, yet in practice it is the leading institutional decision-making body of the EU, indicating a high level of agency. Ambassador Christoffersen writes, "Of course the permanent representatives have not got unlimited possibilities to move national positions, but practice shows that a skilled permanent representative can obtain a considerable margin of maneuver."[60] The highly bureaucratized, institutionalized, and rule-bound nature of the EU means that there is far less structural autonomy than in past centuries.

Over time, since the creation of the EU, the level of diplomatic autonomy has become more operationalized in EU treaties and as the relationship between the institutions of the Court, Parliament, Commission, and Council becomes more defined, diplomatic autonomy is decreasing. However, there is also a growth in issue areas for which the diplomats (or the Council more generally) are responsible, giving some incentive for diplomats to act decisively to create new policies and keep the operations of the EU going.

Besides looking at factors that would encourage diplomats to act as an epistemic community, such as training, social background, status, and face-to-face interaction, to what extent do they actually take advantage of this and push the boundaries of their autonomy? Ambassadors receive instructions from their home governments, just as in the past. These instructions consist of an explanation of what stipulations state leaders are willing to accept in an upcoming negotiation. In some cases, the instructions will require strict adherence as well as formal approval from the capital. Based on these stricter instructions, an ambassador will express at meetings a *reservation* or a *scrutiny reservation*, meaning that he still needs to confer with his capital. If an ambassador supports a negotiated agreement, he can agree *ad referendum*, meaning that he believes the agreement is best for his state, but he does not formally approve it.[61] A final option is to express a *waiting reservation*, which leans much more strongly in favor of the potential agreement and indicates that approval from the home state is simply a formality. Christoffersen writes,

> In the actual negotiations he has to rely on his intuition as to how far he can move his own authorities. He will never accept anything that goes against an explicit instruction, but if he is confident that he has a chance of moving the national position, he will take a waiting reserve or announce in the meeting that he will recommend a certain solution.[62]

Because there is a high level of trust between the ambassador and the statesmen in his capital, in most instances, when the ambassador supports a proposed agreement, his home state will approve the decision. In the rare instance that the home state does not grant approval, the issue up for negotiation will formally pass out of the hands of Coreper to the level of the Council of Ministers.[63] As mentioned, even decisions marked *B* are typically sent back to Coreper for renegotiation, resulting in Coreper participation in 70–90 percent of decision-making.

Ambassadors exercise the agency to appeal their instructions before negotiations begin. By writing a *reasoned request*, they try to persuade statesmen to change their instructions or policy stance. In light of the increasing duties of the Council, the growth in the number of issues on the table, and the growing instances of qualified majority voting (as opposed to unanimity voting), Coreper's duties are multiplying rapidly. For cooperation to take place, statesmen realize the greater importance of granting autonomy to Coreper and accepting changes to their instructions. At the same time, the permanent representatives are better able to anticipate their ability to push the boundaries of their autonomy and persuade statesmen of their collective preferences within Coreper. Ejner Stendevad, former Head of Division in the Directorate General, writes, "The representative of a member state works of course with instructions, but I have seen many examples of very experienced diplomats taking the risk of going beyond the brief in order to contribute to a compromise."[64] The degree of diplomats' agency from their home states has increased over time because of their own initiative, ability to persuade those in their capitals, and success at producing compromised outcomes within their epistemic community. Ambassador Anderson said,

> It is common to make an effort to be creative in finding solutions. We are not prisoners of our instructions. We don't just sit on a position. There are situations in which everybody makes concessions.... If the capital's instructions will not be acceptable to the other member states, then we go back to our capitals and explain the negative dynamic created by those instructions.

Overall, diplomats do exercise a high level of agency and enjoy some degree of autonomy from their state leaders. However, in the highly bureaucratized institutional apparatus of the EU, Coreper's decisions can be restricted as draft agreements are passed back and forth among the European Parliament, Commission, and, to a lesser extent, the Council of Ministers. This degree of agency and goal of compromise contrasts sharply with the way the statesmen operate. French Ambassador Masset said,

> The capitals do not have the same consensus culture as us. When the politicians are confronted with a draft proposal from the Commission, they may immediately try to block it. If they don't like it, they will do everything they can to block it. They will aim to get their points accepted completely without compromise.

Ambassador Tranholm said that, if faced with an obstinate response, the diplomats will try to explain why this approach will not work, and what the consequences will be. They try to convince their home governments and offer a second-best alternative that will better incorporate the general will. They know what is or is not possible, and based on experience and knowledge of the other diplomats, they can convince the government of a workable alternative.

This overview of the European corps provides the basis for understanding not only the way diplomacy works today, but the extent to which it is professionalized, cohesive, and transnational. This inductive analysis provides the groundwork for looking at the Treaty of Maastricht and the role of the epistemic community of diplomats from a more deductive angle.

The lead-up to Maastricht: European Political Union

To provide some background, in the late 1980s, there were several worldwide factors pushing toward a reevaluation of the EU Treaty, and the push for the development of a more explicit political union. It was a period of economic downturn, the fall of the Berlin wall, and political crises in Iraq, Kuwait, the Soviet Union, and Yugoslavia. Statesmen from Germany and France, in particular, wanted to reemphasize Germany's commitment to the EU, in light of German reunification, by suggesting the formal creation of political union alongside monetary union.

The European Council in Dublin, 28 April 1990, issued special instructions to begin the process of political union and to plan an intergovernmental conference (IGC) to this effect.[65] The instructions from Dublin were as follows:

> A detailed examination will be put in hand forthwith on the need for possible Treaty changes with the aim of strengthening the democratic legitimacy of the union, enabling the Community and its institutions to respond efficiently and effectively to the demands of the new situation, and assuring unity and coherence in the Community's international action.[66]

The Ministers officially approved the IGC on Political and Economic Union in June 1990 and the diplomats began the specific preparatory negotiations shortly thereafter.

The Maastricht summit consisted of parallel talks concerning both monetary and political aspects of the union; however, the monetary issues were largely worked out before the summit under a long-term initiative by the Delors Committee and it was primarily the political issues that were still under debate. The summit agenda of the political union dealt with issues as broad and diverse as the "federal vocation" of the treaty, the role of defense, industrial policy, subsidiarity, immigration policy,[67] majority voting, CFSP, workplace regulations, future integration, reform of decision-making institutions, and whether to create a common social policy.[68] In particular, CFSP created the greatest controversy and at first it was difficult to reach consensus between the British and Danish representatives on the one side opposing CFSP, and the German and French on the other side. Spain and Greece[69] also threatened to block the possibility of compromise toward a political union and representatives of the Commission and Parliament demanded increased powers. It is important and interesting to note that the Maastricht Treaty significantly expanded the particular power of Coreper in decision-making regarding the political union. The Maastricht Treaty gave Coreper the responsibility for all the preparatory and follow-up work involving CFSP cooperation. Thus, the treaty elevated Coreper to the level of a major EU institution with regard to CFSP.

This case study will focus on negotiation processes, state positions, and Coreper involvement leading to the agreement on CFSP as the major and most controversial part of political union. The member states had been trying to reach some kind of agreement on common foreign policy since the early 1950s, but the worldwide concern over German rearmament, the idea of defense as an important part of national sovereignty, and the early beginnings of Coreper prevented it from reaching fruition at that time. The second major push toward CFSP was in 1961 when the French government proposed the "Fouchet Plan," but this also failed to gain support. Finally, in the 1990s, the effort to create CFSP was successful. The issue was again taken seriously because of the vacuum of power created with the collapse of Eastern European communist countries and the ongoing desire of German leaders to solidify Germany's ties with the European Community.

The strength and abilities of Coreper enabled a successful outcome. As early as January 1989, the Council of Ministers invited Coreper to draw up a European Defense Concept along with US input.[70] Negotiations and proposals continued and for approximately two years *before* the Maastricht summit, the ambassadors negotiated member states' positions. At the European Council of Rome on 14 and 15 December 1990, the official beginning of the negotiations for political union took place and the work of Coreper, the working groups, foreign ministers, and statesmen began in earnest.

The negotiations

While the press portrayed the Maastricht negotiations as a 21-hour event on 11 and 12 December 1991, the real negotiations began two years prior when foreign ministers invited EU ambassadors to draw up a European Defense Concept. Although Coreper is officially not responsible for IGCs, statesmen and ministers appointed Coreper ambassadors (or former Coreper ambassadors) as personal representatives to do the preparatory work in the lead-up to Maastricht. Most of the foreign ministers' personal representatives were members of Coreper[71] and were even chosen to accompany the statesmen in both the political and monetary union negotiations instead of foreign ministers. The cohesion, strength, and expertise that EU diplomats gained through their primary role as permanent representatives enabled a successful outcome in their secondary role as personal representatives. The treaty was not the product of the Maastricht summit, but of many meetings among the foreign ministers and ambassadors well before the IGC. The Ministers met once per month while the ambassadors met every week and even more often in the lead-up to the IGC. Once the statesmen arrived at Maastricht, they were handed a full draft of the treaty.[72]

The main controversy over CFSP in 1991 was that the governments of several member states were concerned that it would supercede the authority of NATO, thereby alienating the United States from European affairs. The three main CFSP points up for consideration were the so-called Asolo list of areas that would come under joint action, the procedure for implementing joint action, and whether the issue of defense would be portrayed in the treaty as federal or intergovernmental.[73]

European Political Cooperation was already in place, but it was significantly different from having a common foreign and security policy. While European Political Cooperation (EPC) had an intergovernmental method of cooperation, CFSP would have a common method (i.e., one based on supranational consensus). EPC had a larger role for the European Parliament, whereas CFSP would mainly just inform Parliament. EPC did not involve a transfer of powers to the EU while CFSP did, but specific actions would be decided on a case-by-case basis. EPC only entailed a moral obligation while CFSP was officially binding with a unified execution – a single, combined military effort. Table 6.1 summarizes the main differences between the existing EPC, the proposed changes to create CFSP, and how this differed from a completely federal system of common policy.

CFSP clearly represented a big step beyond the original EPC, but it also fell far short of a fully federalist agenda. This compromise solution created an unprecedented framework for security integration that would allow for a potentially much greater degree of common policy at the discretion of the Council. The following subsections analyze the specific role of the diplomats and their political counterparts in reaching this historic agreement from the perspectives of the individual delegations involved.

The diplomats

To what extent were the permanent representatives involved in the Maastricht negotiations and to what extent did they follow state instructions or exercise agency of their own? The processes leading to the Maastricht Treaty demonstrate the important role of the ambassadors as permanent representatives in Coreper alongside their role as "personal representatives." In addition, they were extremely active throughout the preparatory and follow-up negotiations.[74] Ambassador Tranholm said, "The personal representatives are the most effective negotiators because they have the network and understand the details."[75]

The role of the ambassadors extends beyond their day-to-day decision-making in Coreper and, in particular, included major contributions leading to the creation and acceptance of the Maastricht Treaty. In this regard, the ambassadors operated outside of the institutional boundaries of Coreper. Still, as in the past, the diplomatic epistemic community exists with or without the institutional boundaries of the EU. In other areas of policy, the ambassadors have no formal authority in relation to IGCs; however, as permanent and personal representatives they were constantly writing and distributing memoranda that related directly to the terms of the treaty.

Table 6.1 Summary of the proposed changes to create CFSP, provided by the Spanish delegation

Before Maastricht: European political cooperation	Proposed common foreign and security policy	Single foreign and security policy (hypothetical)
Intergovernmental cooperation	Integrated and common method	Federal method (single and exclusive)
Consistency between EEC and EPC	Consistency between political and economic areas within Union	Total unity
Sphere: depends on the will of the members	Initial sphere: community method (EEC external relations) and common method (foreign and security policy)	Initial and final sphere: no differentiation
Noncompulsory pooling	Compulsory pooling based on common policy, case-by-case transfers, national policies compatible with common policies	Total transfer: policies are single and exclusive, no national policies
No transfer of powers	Council decides on basis of unanimity and case-by-case, certain CFSP policies are exclusively within Union	Total transfer
Moral obligation only	CFSP policies are binding	Acts specific to Union are compulsory
Any improvements do not require amendments to SEA	CFSP necessitates amendment of Treaties	European Union Treaty
Diversified execution, decision-making, preparation, monitoring, implementation; no guarantees of coordination	Unified execution: CFSP is formulated through a single voice	Single execution
European Parliament "closely associated"	European Parliament is informed and consulted regularly, may or may not be asked to deliver assent	European Parliament fully integrated, federal model

Note: EU Documents 10356/90, 26 November 1990. ADD 1, Annex 3, p. 5. These stipulations clearly went further than the Commission's earlier proposal. On 23 October 1990, the Commission, represented by Jacques Delors, also contributed to the debate, writing to the President of the Council, Gianni De Michelis. Under Article 23, they proposed calling a Conference of member states to amend the treaty and incorporate political union. They explicitly agreed to the goal of establishing a common foreign policy, which would include security, with the aim of taking a "flexible and pragmatic approach."

Documentation of the memoranda distributed during 1990–92[76] demonstrates the ambassadors' role in creating initial proposals and preparing drafts of the Maastricht Treaty.[77] These memos and nonpapers also show compromise over time (see Table 6.2 for some states' initial positions and Table 6.3 for the ordering from least to most federalist) and the extent to which most issues were decided before the Maastricht summit of statesmen. After the first meeting in Dublin, Coreper along with the Political Committee

Table 6.2 Summary: Diplomat delegations' initial negotiation stances founded on state preferences

Countries	Major changes?	Negotiation emphasis
Belgium	Yes, with transition	Extend security definition – anything involving security in the international forum and anything involving disarmament. Should have a transitional phase. Federalist overall.
Britain	No	Consensus across all member states. Long-term perspective. No definition of community citizenship. Proceed with caution. WEU serves as bridge between the Union and NATO. NATO should be the cornerstone of defense.
Denmark	No	Economic benefits, close attention to relationships with third countries. No common military, no cooperation on defense policy. Proceed with caution.
Dutch Presidency	No	(1) Unity and coherence of the Community's international action (defense); (2) political union emphasizing transfer of competence, subsidiarity, and community citizenship; (3) democratic legitimacy; (4) effective and efficient institutions.[a]
France	Yes	Same as Germany. Also, supports single currency so Western Europe not dominated by German Mark.
Germany	Yes	CFSP shall embrace all fields of foreign relations; enhance security of all member states.
Greece		Wants admission to WEU.
Ireland	No	Initially, no explicit direction; maintain balance between political and economic integration, gradual development of political role.
Italy	Yes	The Union should control all aspects of security without limitations. Redefine decision-making process. Extensive and radical reform with institutional safeguards. Federalist overall.
Luxembourg Presidency	Yes	Three-pillar structure: CFSP and internal security policies separate from Community jurisdiction stipulated by the Treaty of Rome.

Table 6.2 (Continued)

Countries	Major changes?	Negotiation emphasis
Netherlands	No	Step-by-step approach: No increase in intergovernmental nature of the Union; decision-making must be in line with NATO. Put NATO and the United States before EPC.
Portugal	No	Preserve existing institutional balance, gradual progress toward political union, foreign policy necessarily implies a security component.
Spain	Yes	National policies must be compatible with the common policy. Greater degree of integration and unity. Amendment of the Treaties necessary. Consensus decision-making, explicit vote not necessary. Rich countries subsidize poorer ones.

[a] EU Documents 8724/1/90 European Communities: The Council, Brussels, 2 October 1990.

Table 6.3 Approximate order of negotiation stances from least federal to most federal

Least federal	UK
	Ireland
	Denmark
	Portugal
	Greece
	Luxembourg
	The Netherlands
	Spain
	Belgium
	Italy
	France
Most federal	Germany

were charged with work of determining the agenda for political union and summarizing the options available.[78] By the time the statesmen gathered in Maastricht in December 1991, the diplomats had prepared a tenable draft treaty for political and monetary union.

Overall, most countries supported a more federalist union, but only for the particular policy areas that they believed were best decided at the Community level. Because there are no records from Coreper meetings, printed summaries of opinions distributed among the delegations are the best means to follow the decision-making process. Unlike the historical cases, it is not possible to examine personal communications as the diplomats involved are in most cases still active and have not written memoirs.

Clear initial disagreement

From the beginning, there was a clear divide between those in favor of CFSP and those who opposed it. Primarily, the British and Danish were the most opposed while the French and Germans were fully in favor of it. In fact, the French and Germans actually wanted to work toward federalism and a *Single* Foreign and Security Policy, which was even more supranational than CFSP. The Danish were more interested in economic union and only wanted political union in so far as it was necessary to achieve economic union.

Danish ambassadors sent provisional points on political union to the Secretary-General of the Council, Niels Ersbøll, and the other delegations on 11 May 1990.[79] The Danish diplomats argued for improved democratic processes, transparency, and unity and cohesion in international actions. They also asked for closer cooperation with Central and Eastern European countries. Their emphasis, however, was more on the ways in which the European Economic Community can help political unity, instead of focusing on political union as an end in itself.

On 4 October 1990, Danish Ambassador Jakob Rytter distributed a memo expressing his country's skepticism about CFSP. The memo states, "The Government rejects the idea that European Political Cooperation should come to include cooperation in defense policies, *inter alia* the setting-up of common military forces." Rytter emphasized in particular his desire to be inclusive of countries outside of the European Community (third countries) since the need to expand EU membership was tied to the credibility of the Community. The Community would serve as the central structure for many countries to participate.[80] Overall, the main goals outlined aimed to keep integration at a broad level with gradual cooperation.

Like the Danish, the British diplomats expressed initial reservations to CFSP. They argued that above all it was necessary for consensus across all member states to be achieved. The British position, articulated in a letter from J.R. de Fonblanque to Council Secretariat Poul Christoffersen, was that caution was the essence of the day. Fonblanque writes on 25 September 1990, "We would favour a more tentative approach to new provisions on inter-governmental cooperation and do not accept an automatic link with any arrangements for foreign and security policy."[81] Fonblanque cautioned that nothing could be assumed until discussions between the member states had occurred, particularly when it came to Community citizenship.

However, the British and Danish skepticism was only one side of the spectrum of opinions being articulated at the time. An earlier letter sent to Ersbøll from the Belgians highlighted their optimistic vision for political union.[82] The Belgian ambassador writes that the European Community will only gain recognition in the international sphere by being unified in its policy stance. Moreover, this political purpose has been an integral part of the European Treaties. He writes, "We will be taken seriously only insofar as we assert ourselves."[83] Rather than cautioning the other delegations about moving forward with political integration, the Belgians urged that it was *necessary* for improvement of the democratic deficit and addressing the problems of Central and Eastern Europe. In particular, he advocated the convergence between political cooperation and Community policy, and recommended that Coreper and the Political Directors alongside the Ministers for Foreign Affairs should be vested with the power to devise a solution. Diplomatic delegations distributed many more memos expressing this basic division over the extent to which political cooperation should proceed. With such starkly opposing starting positions, why was CFSP ultimately accepted?

Naturally, the diplomats could draw upon their Coreper relationship even in their secondary role as personal representatives. In addition, the diplomats were concerned about the process of negotiation and convinced their statesmen of this. J.R. de Fonblanque, a British government official, wrote to the Council of "the need my Ambassador expressed yesterday to adopt a more open and interrogative approach, and to avoid either rejecting any options or exaggerating the extent of consensus at such an early stage in preparatory discussion."[84] Thus, the diplomats were not only involved in expressing and negotiating policy positions through gradual compromise, but were concerned with process and protocol.

Closer to CFSP

At this stage, the Presidency of the Council issued a paper representing the sum of the deliberations of the working parties and personal representatives thus far. One of the primary goals summarized by the Presidency was the proposal for CFSP and unity in the Community's international actions. The Presidency stipulated that CFSP should include the widening of the notion of security to include industrial and technological cooperation, involvement in UN mandated military initiatives, a common position for the EU in the UN Security Council, and initial moves toward a common defense policy.

One aspect of greater consensus suggested by the Presidency was increased cooperation between embassies in third countries and diplomatic protection of member states' citizens. In other words, the Presidency requested diplomatic recognition of "community citizenship" to aid in the workability of common policies.[85]

On 18 October 1990, the Presidency of the Council summarized the memos and areas of agreement put forward by the personal representatives. The memo stipulated that the key to making the European Community a significant actor in international relations is to establish a European identity and to create a structure that embodies common interests.[86] At this point, most delegations agreed that the creation of CFSP, going beyond the system in place, would be the necessary next step to accomplish the goal of a European identity. The Presidency stipulated that there was general agreement that CFSP, if it were to be adopted, should include the widening of the notion of security to include industrial and technological cooperation, involvement in UN mandated military initiatives, a common position for the EU in the UN Security Council, and initial moves toward a common defense policy. At the same time, some delegations still had reservations about CFSP and emphasized improving the Political Cooperation system in place rather than trying to go beyond it. One of the primary goals summarized by the Presidency was the proposal for CFSP and unity in the Community's international actions.

Illustrative of this continuing divide over CFSP were the proposals from Italy and the UK. The Italian delegation supported a real common foreign policy and recognized the necessity of redefining the decision-making process and rules of implementation. For CFSP to be of real value, they argued, "It would in fact be difficult to justify maintaining limitations with regard to security, which constitute the essential component of a foreign policy."[87] The British continued to disagree, but with a subtly different argument that change was possible; it should just be adapted gradually from the current path of EPC. The UK delegation argued that the kind of international recognition that the Italians want to strive for has already been achieved. They wrote, "Far from having to strive to make the Community voice heard, EC involvement is now expected and actively sought on most major international issues."[88] Consequently, according to the British delegation, the evolution in political cooperation that started twenty years earlier should continue on the same gradual path. At this stage, universal consensus on CFSP had not been reached, but some of the major positions and proposals were being clearly articulated by the ambassadors.

Points of agreement on CFSP

On 4 December 1990, the General Secretariat of the Council distributed a second round of opinions from the personal representatives, which consisted of nonpapers dealing with CFSP from the Spanish, Belgian, and Dutch delegations. These written contributions were the result of further negotiations among the personal representatives.[89]

The Spanish contribution stated that CFSP should include the Community's external relations, all areas of foreign policy that were previously performed by European Political Cooperation (EPC), and security issues. Along with emphasizing the community nature of CFSP, the Spanish diplomats argued that the national policies must be compatible with community policy. CFSP would have a higher degree of integration and consistency, a decision-making process involving consensus or unanimity, and a unified execution of decisions. They suggested that Coreper and the Political Committee integrate their processes to ensure the efficiency and continuity of CFSP, and that the General Affairs Council may become the central decision-making institution. These stipulations clearly went further than the Commission's earlier proposal.[90] The Spanish diplomats' proposal also specifically treated the issues surrounding the Common Security Policy (CSP). They argued that CSP should include commitment to mutual defense, nonproliferation arrangements, transfers of military technology to third countries, negotiations on disarmament, and participation and coordination of military initiatives.[91]

The Belgian delegation's nonpaper of 12 November 1990 examined CFSP with an emphasis on implementation.[92] They recognized that there would be a transition phase and that the key to successful implementation would involve gradualism. They also extended the domain of political union to incorporate all security matters in the international arena and all issues involving disarmament. They suggested a provision to expand the domain of CFSP even further by enabling the Council to add issue areas to the common policy upon receiving a proposal from a member state or the Commission and after consulting with Parliament. Moreover, the Belgian delegation proposed that the Council be permitted to act unilaterally on situations that are urgent based upon a qualified majority. In conclusion, the Belgian diplomats emphasized the conditions following the transitional phase of CFSP. After the transition, they argued, "All sectors of common interest will be the subject of a common policy."[93]

In the same packet of memos, the Dutch delegation contributed a nonpaper dated 23 November 1990.[94] Like the Belgian delegation, they advocated a step-by-step process of implementation for CFSP. Their approach, however, was decidedly less Community-oriented than the Spanish and Belgian proposals. They made a point emphasizing the need to respect the jurisdiction of NATO and to avoid deciding anything that would alienate NATO and the United States. At the same time, they wrote, "The inclusion of foreign policy and security in EPU should not lead to an increase in the intergovernmental character of European integration."[95] Thus, they did not want common policy to go backwards, but were cautious about the extent to which they wanted it to go forward.

The remainder of the memo provides many details on the qualities of CFSP. The Dutch diplomats stated that the issues belonging to CFSP should include: elements of defense industry policy, policies on arms exports, nonproliferation, participation in UN peacekeeping, and joint operations. In terms of defense policy, the memo emphasized that this is meant in a narrow sense. Ultimately, the nonpaper concluded that the boundaries of CFSP would depend greatly on the political will of the member states.

By November 1990, there was some degree of agreement among ambassadors about foreign and security policy, but several different visions for how it would be created. The points of agreement included: the Union should deal with all aspects of foreign and security policy; there would be a single decision-making body; the Commission would have a greater role; external representation would be with a single voice; and the European Parliament would be regularly informed and consulted.[96] The major area of difference was whether to strengthen the current form of political cooperation by increasing its scope and effectiveness or to entirely transform the current form to create CFSP. The second option would entail a unique decision-making procedure and transfer of powers from the member states to the Union.

The Luxembourg Presidency

The Foreign Ministers met for the first time in the middle of December 1990 to decide on the protocol and timetable for the upcoming IGC at Maastricht. They met twice and agreed that the personal representatives would continue the negotiations in the lead-up to Maastricht. The diplomats persisted with their step-by-step consensus until in January 1991 when all delegations had agreed that CFSP would be adopted. A whole new round of discussion ensued over what the precise stipulations would be. At the end of January, the Luxembourg Presidency once more issued a summary of the progress made toward an agreement on CFSP.[97]

The delegations agreed to implement common policy in the areas of "industrial and technological cooperation in the armaments field, the transfer of military technology to third countries, arms control, involvement in peacekeeping operations and humanitarian action."[98] Still to be debated was the relationship with the Atlantic alliance embodied in NATO and the UN.

The Italian delegation was the first to distribute a detailed plan regarding all aspects of CFSP. Italy's previous position on CFSP was favorable for reaching consensus as the diplomats advocated both gradualism and substantive change, and they addressed the issue of EU cooperation with NATO and the UN. In light of this, they changed the final clause of the four areas of common security policy to read, "Involvement in and coordination of military initiatives, notably peacekeeping operations, in particular in the framework of a United Nations mandate."[99]

As a sign of the continuously unified stance of the delegations, the German and French delegations issued a joint Note on 6 February 1991. They emphasized that CFSP represented the center principles involved in political cooperation and would encompass all fields of international relations. Moreover, the EU in their opinion was incomplete without aiming to establish a common defense. They argued that defense should not be restricted to only the political and economic aspects, as long as member states maintain their commitment to NATO and the United States. They added that the Council should have the power to decide which policy topics would become common policy as they arise. The Franco–German proposals became a cornerstone to the remaining negotiations. A few days later, it was clear that even the Dutch were convinced as they suggested going even further in the definition of foreign policy. The Dutch delegation tried to position themselves as being just as cooperative as the French and German delegations, if not more so.

With the Dutch convinced of a strong role for CFSP, all that remained were the Danish and British delegations. On 21 February 1991, Danish Ambassador Riberholdt sent proposals to Secretary-General Ersbøll for amendments to the EC Treaties. In a major turnaround from their previous stance, the Danish delegation proposed amendments to incorporate CFSP. They proposed six articles: (1) That CFSP shall protect and promote member states' common values, peace, security, democracy, and the rule of law; (2) it shall cover all aspects that member states agree upon, but still respect other defense commitments; (3) the Council shall unanimously establish CFSP, while the Presidency, member states, or the Commission can submit proposals; (4) the Parliament shall be involved; (5) the Presidency shall be responsible for CFSP's external conduct, with the Commission involved; and (6) for all ambiguous areas member states will systematically coordinate.[100] This proposal brought the Danish stance much closer in line with the general consensus.

On 12 April 1991, the Luxembourg Presidency presented the first full draft treaty proposal for Political Union to the delegations. It included the well-known "three-pillar" structure for the new EU. Although all member states generally supported CFSP, the UK and Denmark thought it went too far while Italy, France, Germany, and Belgium would have wanted to see more federalism in the document. To help assuage the desires of the more federalist members, on 18 June 1991, the Luxembourg Presidency created a second draft that introduced the "federal vocation" and a single framework to the Community's structure.

The Dutch Presidency: A temporary crisis

The Dutch leadership held the presidency during the lead-up to the Maastricht IGC (July–December 1991) and looked for a middle path between the French–German call for an independent EC military and concerns that this would harm transatlantic relations with United States. The Dutch draft treaty was an attempt to tie the economic union to the political union, but it faced immediate opposition from Britain and Spain. Only the Belgians and the Commission supported the plan.

On 25 September 1991, the Dutch Presidency warned that the final agreement on European political union would not be ready as scheduled for the 9–10 December 1991 Maastricht summit. The next day, the representatives met in Brussels to discuss the Dutch draft, which the Dutch Presidency did not officially publish and distribute until 11 November 1991. At this advance meeting, the British, Danish, and French diplomats were completely against it. It did not contain any of the concessions that the British had worked hard to secure and even contained the words "federal goal." The Germans and Belgians supported it, but the Italians and Irish criticized it for reopening already resolved questions. The proposal went against the popular precedence established by the Luxembourg presidency with its three-pillar approach. The Dutch proposed granting more power to the Commission and Parliament, creating a two-tier process with richer member states joining the economic and political union first and providing an "opting out" clause for all countries who did not want to be a part of the single currency.[101]

The new controversy over the Dutch draft led to gossip that French President François Mitterrand and German Chancellor Helmut Kohl would possibly convene a special meeting for only those countries that supported a security union.[102] On 30 September, also known as "Black Monday," all delegations except for the Belgians rejected the Dutch draft outright. The diplomats went back to the Luxembourg draft and started to negotiate amendments from this previous rendition, even before the official publication and circulation of the Dutch version.

Yes to CFSP, but how?

Although the second round of negotiations had resulted in universal support of CFSP, the details of the proposal still had to be worked out. There still existed a fundamental difference of opinion over CFSP between the French–German and the English–Italian perspectives. A Note circulated on 8 November 1991 outlined the differences in approach. Table 6.4 reproduces some of the major points in the Note. The italicized texts represent the text that was included in the joint provisions of the treaty, thus it is the compromise of the two positions. The table also indicates the areas of emerging compromise after a year of negotiations among the permanent representatives.

On 29 November 1991, a few weeks following the distribution of this Note, the Presidency had received new comments and proposals from the delegations and decided that the representatives would work out a compromise and agreed text of CFSP in time for the final Ministerial meeting on 2 and 3 December 1991, in Brussels.[103] Some examples of the new suggestions follow.

Table 6.4 Note (8 November 1991) outlining the differences between the French–German and the English–Italian texts

French–German text	English–Italian text
The purpose of the Union is to assert its identity on the international scene, particularly through the implementation of a common foreign and security policy *which in the longer term will include a common defense.*	Political union implies the *gradual elaboration and implementation of a common foreign and security policy and a stronger defense identity with the longer-term perspective of a common defense policy* compatible with the common defense policy in NATO. The development of a European identity in the field of security and defense shall be pursued through *an evolutionary process involving successive phases.*
This Article's provisions will be reviewed on the basis of a report presented by the Council at the latest in *1996,* in consultation with the competent WEU institutions and *in light of the progress achieved and experience acquired to date.* In accordance with the guidelines set by the European Council, the Council takes the necessary measures for the subsequent progress of the process.	The role of the WEU and its relationship with the Alliance and the Union will be reviewed by 1998 in the *context of Article 12 of the Brussels Treaty.*
Strengthening of the role of the WEU, which is *a full part* of the European unification process with Union as its goal. Need to form a genuine *European defense and security identity.* Construction in stages of the WEU as a defense *component* of the Union. Invitation to DK and GR to become members of the WEU and offer to IRL of observer status. Consultation of the Commission in areas within its competence.	Nothing
Development of a *clear organic relationship* between WEU and the Union: harmonization of the sequence and duration of the Presidencies; synchronization of sessions; cooperation between the secretariats and between the assemblies. *Transfer of the WEU Secretariat to Brussels.*	Better coordination via synchronization of meetings and appropriate links between Secretariats, Presidencies, and Parliamentary Assemblies. *Transfer of the WEU Secretariat to Brussels.*
Creation of a WEU planning and military coordination group. Closer military cooperation complementing the Alliance. European arms agency, regular meetings of Chiefs of Staff, etc.	*Autonomous European Reaction Force* outside the NATO area, developed by Member States of WEU.

Strengthening of the Atlantic Alliance as a whole by strengthening the role and responsibility of the Europeans and by forming a *European pillar* within it. Establishment of practical provisions ensuring *transparency and complementarity between WEU and the Alliance.*	The review of the Alliance's tasks and strategy and the development of a common foreign and security policy in the context of political union are *complementary* and must proceed in *parallel.* The development of a European defense identity should be construed in such a way as to *reinforce the Alliance.*

Note: Italicized text denotes actual treaty language adopted.

"Consideration should be given for allowing Member States in case of imperative need to take action.... They shall inform the Council immediately of any such decision."

"A member State shall not be obliged to take or refrain from action if to do so would damage a supreme national interest."

"Member States who are also Members of the United Nations Security Council will consult and keep the other Member States fully informed. France and the United Kingdom will, as permanent members of the Security Council, in the execution of their functions ensure the defense of the positions and interests of the Union, without prejudice to their responsibilities under the provisions of the UN Charter."

"A Political Committee consisting of Political Directors shall monitor the international situation in the area covered by CFSP and deliver opinions to the Council at the request of the Council or at its own initiative."

"If there is a change in circumstances having substantial effect on a question subject to joint action, the Council shall review the principles and objectives of that action and take the necessary decisions."

"The Council shall by unanimity define those matters on which decisions are to be taken by qualified majority."

In addition to these proposals, several proposals had already been agreed upon by the delegations:[104]

Long-term goal: objective "Formulation of a common defense policy."
Short-term goals: The CFSP shall include all questions related to the Security of the Union; the Union may request the WEU, which is an integral part of the process leading to EU, to elaborate and implement decisions and actions of the Union which have defense implications.

Activities under CFSP shall respect NATO policies and not affect the specific character of the defense policy of certain member states.

The Dutch were among the most concerned over the French–German approach. While previously they had been the most pro-integrationist, they feared at this point that the French motivation was to diminish US dominance within NATO, a move that would ultimately harm the longevity of the Atlantic Alliance.[105] Meanwhile, the British delegation still tried to push for intergovernmentalism within the stipulations of CFSP. On 18 July 1991, they had proposed a case-by-case formula for decision-making. The response from other delegations was that such a procedural debate would result in delays every time there was another issue to consider.[106]

Only four months later and a few weeks before Maastricht, consensus was once more on track.[107] The UK delegation agreed to grant more power to the European Parliament. However, they downgraded their rejection of CFSP to an expression of serious reservations about CFSP and a European defense identity. The Danish, Irish, and Portuguese delegations followed the UK in this opinion. One week before Maastricht, explicit reference to common defense was included in the draft treaty and no longer posed a problem for any of the delegations. It was agreed that "federal" would be left out (although the Dutch claimed it was still there). Meanwhile, the United States had also approved of European efforts at creating an independent common foreign and security policy, making discussions even more relaxed.[108]

The foreign ministers met one last time only a few days before the summit, but decided that the final decisions about defense should be left to the statesmen. Nevertheless, as the draft treaty stood, agreement on CFSP was all but accomplished. The British had agreed to support it and only expressed reservations about using qualified majority voting as the decision-making procedure for common foreign or defense action. They pushed for unanimity of votes and also continued to emphasize the primary importance of NATO. The draft treaty contained a list of areas for joint action including arms control, restriction of arms sales, and nuclear proliferation. It did not include reference to EC relations to the United States and the former Soviet Union.

While the EU documents cannot express motivations of diplomats, the culture of consensus among the European diplomats, the documented process of gradual compromise, and the ability of diplomats to persuade recalcitrant statesmen (discussed in the next section) provide evidence that agreement on CFSP rested on the strength of the epistemic community of diplomats and their willingness to negotiate with their capitals. An ambassador described how on occasion a minister would be sent to Brussels to negotiate particularly important components of treaties; however, he would never show up at the relevant meetings. The ambassador said,

I have seen how they have flown in ministers or deputy ministers and they did not show up for meetings because their permanent representative went for them.... They are very intelligent, high-profile, and able men but it is difficult for them to do it if they are not used to negotiating or do not know the treaty. Even those who have chosen others rely on their Personal Representative.[109]

The next section describes the role of the statesmen at Maastricht to emphasize the difference in their role and preferences compared to those of the diplomats.

The statesmen at Maastricht

To what extent were the statesmen involved in the negotiations leading to the new Treaty on European Union? The Maastricht agenda for political union was replete with an expansive array of issues on the table. There was not enough time in the 21 hours of the summit to even *mention* all of the policies up for consideration let alone engage in substantive negotiation. Even with the issue of subsidiarity, for example, state leaders could not agree upon a definition. Some statesmen, such as Britain's John Major, insisted that subsidiarity stopped at the government level, whereas others argued that it extended down to the individual level.[110]

Most issues were worked out ahead of time by the permanent representatives and those which were still outstanding after Maastricht were passed back to the diplomats for renegotiation. At the summit itself, only the heads of state and foreign secretaries were allowed in the room, but a buzzer was provided for each delegate to summon his ambassador or aide. The negotiations were highly complex as there were not just compromises on single policy areas, but negotiations among multiple issues as well as ultimatums that statesmen had issued in the lead-up to the Maastricht summit.[111] The statesmen's stubborn personalities and personal agendas did not help in resolving these outstanding issues at the summit itself. As at Westphalia, Berlin, and Versailles, the statesmen at Maastricht proved once more how diplomacy by amateurs falls short of professional diplomacy and the extent to which diplomats were able to accomplish a great deal in comparison.

Germany and France

German Chancellor Helmut Kohl set the most drastic agenda in the run-up to Maastricht. His firm belief was that economic union could not progress further without a strong commitment to political union.[112] This would enable him to overcome domestic trepidation over rebuilding Germany's military role and enable the German government to exert influence in European relations through legitimate, institutional means. Kohl's motive was to strive toward German unification, while supporting the Atlantic Alliance and the EU. Compared to the statesmen from Paris, London, and Rome, Kohl had the most radical agenda.[113] He was so determined to gain real progress on political union that he threatened to withdraw support for the economic union treaty.

An important feature of the two-day meeting was the partnership of Helmut Kohl and French President François Mitterrand, and their efforts to avoid marginalizing British Prime Minister John Major. Mitterrand mostly spoke with rhetoric, was uninterested in the details, and was described as really showing his old age.[114] Kohl was adamant about EMU as necessary and irreversible. He was known as "a doer and not a thinker" who, like Mitterrand, also avoided the details.[115] His chief motivation was his belief that the European institutions would act as a safeguard for Germany's recent unification.

The French and German leaders have traditionally been profederalist, while the British have tried to maintain the intergovernmental nature of the EU. The issue of defense was a sensitive issue for the British delegates because of their preference to maintain the security apparatus embedded in NATO. In the words of one journalist,

> The wording on defense in the Maastricht treaty is an uneasy compromise between France, which wants the WEU – a group of nine EC countries that are also members of NATO – to become the Community's military wing, and Britain, which would limit EC ambitions in this field, lest they undermine NATO.[116]

Kohl was prepared to make the most sacrifices to strengthen the European parliament and assure Germany's position as an integrated European power. Yet, Mitterrand's stance differed from Kohl's in terms of political union because he did not want to strengthen the powers of the European parliament in any meaningful way. Mitterrand was able to rely on the support of the Italians. The French government's objective was to reduce the influence of the United States and NATO in Europe, thereby gaining more autonomy. To accomplish this, it was necessary to advocate increased integration. If not for diplomatic flexibility in the lead-up to the summit, it would have been impossible for the leaders to agree, each with their own hard-line approaches.

Britain, Denmark, and Spain

At Maastricht, the UK and Denmark had to make concessions regarding CFSP. Because of this, all statesmen agreed that the European Council would have the role of deciding the specific areas of joint action and that a degree of joint implementation would be decided by majority voting. By the time statesmen arrived at Maastricht, the Asolo list, stipulating the areas of joint action, had already been negotiated and added as an annex to the treaty to be approved. These joint action areas included the process of the Conference on Security and Cooperation in Europe, the issues of nuclear nonproliferation, the economic aspects of security, and the policy of disarmament and arms control.[117]

Belgian Prime Minister, Wilfried Martens, and Minister of Foreign Affairs, Mark Eyskens, had a federalist goal in mind, but their proposal for CFSP was cautious. Like British Prime Minister John Major, the Belgian statesmen wanted intergovernmentalism within the parameters of CFSP. When Martens left the Maastricht summit, he was unhappy with the final results.[118]

Major was described as the most "pugnacious" statesman at the summit. Despite the fact that most of the delegations did not share his position, he was the most determined to stick to his negotiation stance. A journalist writes, "'Disaster for Europe, success for Britain,' was how one diplomat put it, after an often-chaotic summit which showed, he claimed, just how unsuited heads of state and government are to negotiating detailed treaty texts."[119] Another diplomat said, "Most of them did not know what they were doing."[120]

The British government's approach was more to define issues according to what they did not want, instead of what they would accept. Ultimately, such an inflexible stance meant that they were willing to threaten the possibility of a veto to the whole treaty in the worst-case scenario. Sir John Kerr, the British permanent representative, was probably the most visibly outspoken and involved in the Maastricht summit. A British journalist in 1991 writes, "If there is a deal at the end of the day in Maastricht, the glory should be claimed more by Sir John [the British Ambassador] and his fellow permanent representatives than any other single group of negotiators."[121] Kerr was widely recognized as the British man who most contributed to the Maastricht Treaty, making it a success despite the British government's stubbornness.

Following British opinion, the Danish also gave an initial "no" to the Maastricht Treaty in June stipulating that the NATO defense structure should have clear priority and that the United States should be encouraged to have troops in Europe as well. Denmark's foreign minister, Uffe Ellemann-Jensen, said, the WEU "should not have its own standing forces or duplicate the command structure of NATO, which should have primacy."[122] Ultimately the treaty was passed with a final "no" from the Danes and an "opt-out" clause for the British in regard to the currency union and social legislation. Nevertheless, as late as September 1992, the eleven member states' representatives were still trying to seek a compromise solution that would include the Danes; otherwise the whole treaty would be untenable.

The Spanish leadership also fell more on the side of the British, hesitating to so closely adhere political and economic union. Prime Minister Felipe Gonzalez demanded that richer EC countries give more money for development of poorer countries such as Spain, Portugal, Greece, and Ireland.

The Maastricht ratification process

In 1992, it was then given to the personal representatives once more to work out the application of the Maastricht Treaty. Once ratified by national parliaments it would begin to take effect on 1 January 1993. European statesmen and foreign ministers played a big role in getting the treaty accepted in their states from around September 1992 to August 1993, when Germany ratified the treaty. Coreper worked alongside the statesmen, who had to appeal to domestic concerns to find a workable solution at the international level. Referenda were held in many countries to enable citizens to play a role in the process. The treaty was ultimately passed with ratification from each member state almost two years after the summit. Britain was the eleventh to ratify it on 2 August 1993 and Germany was the last. The most difficult part, however, was to create a treaty document that was likely to be passed in the ratification process and this was Coreper's job.

The Maastricht summit resulted in an 18-month political struggle in British parliament. Tory Euro-skeptics did not want to approve the Maastricht Treaty at all. For them it represented the "end of the road" for their cause because of the strong moves toward increased supranationalism, particularly in regard to majority voting on issues that would impact British politics. The Maastricht Treaty was described as an "immensely damaging episode for the Conservative party."[123]

Diplomatic agency

It is important to note that the Maastricht Treaty significantly expanded the particular power of Coreper in decision making regarding the political union. Coreper was made responsible for all the preparatory and follow-up work for cooperation relating to CFSP. Thus, the Maastricht Treaty elevated Coreper to the level of the EU institutions (Court of Justice, Parliament, Commission, and Council) in this regard. The agreement on CFSP represents an unprecedented level of community method plus "common" method instead of intergovernmental cooperation. It is also officially binding through treaty amendments and highlights the important role of Coreper, despite being an intergovernmental body in carrying through this policy.

In the case of Maastricht, the ambassadors were, both before and after the summit, absolutely necessary and determined the outcome of the political union by producing a treaty that was tenable for the member states. The Head of Division in the Directorate General Agriculture of the European Commission Ejner Stendevad commented on the nature of the diplomatic epistemic community.[124] He wrote:

> The representative of a member state works of course with instructions, but I have seen many examples of very experienced diplomats taking the

risk of going beyond the brief in order to contribute to a compromise. The decision process of the EU of today is based on a negotiation culture: A constant process of finding a realistic and balanced compromise. In this process, the skilled and experienced diplomat has a platform of his own. It is very often so, that there is an understanding between the negotiators, that nothing is agreed before everything is agreed, a kind of single undertaking.... The risk of being overruled exists always, but when I look back on the many cases I have been involved in, it is very rare it has happened.

While it is clear that diplomats played an important role in negotiating the Maastricht Treaty, it is valuable to highlight here their impact in determining the outcomes even beyond their delegated autonomy.

Alternative explanations

In today's environment, it is difficult to conceive of a purely realist world. With the exception of the leader of the world's superpower, it would be hard for states to act purely according to relative power, with no consideration of the larger international society. The very existence of the EU is a case in point. The huge bureaucratic apparatus that supports the EU institutions is obviously populated with thousands of officials who make important contributions to the effective operation and decision-making of this supranational entity. The interesting question is to what extent diplomats exercise agency to impact outcomes of cooperation beyond what rational choice theories would expect.

While it is clear that diplomats played an important role in negotiating the Maastricht Treaty, it is valuable to highlight here their impact in determining the outcomes even beyond their delegated autonomy. What would rationalist bargaining theory predict? To reiterate, the premise of bargaining theory is that state preferences are determined early in negotiations and remain stable despite any influence from supranational or transnational actors. In the lead-up to Maastricht, state preferences were clearly articulated as summarized in Table 6.2 earlier in this chapter. There were major divisions in state preferences with Britain, Denmark, the Netherlands, Ireland, and Portugal generally against major changes to the common foreign policy in place, and Germany, France, Italy, Spain, and Belgium generally in favor of major changes. The most vociferous and influential statesmen were Mitterrand, Kohl, and Major.

I argue that these leaders would not have expected at the beginning to agree to the terms that they ultimately accepted at the end. Mitterrand and Kohl were adamant about a federalist vision of the future EU and wanted this to be reflected in the new treaty with the use of the word "federal." It was not until late in the negotiations that "federal" was removed from the draft treaty, thereby making it more acceptable to other countries. Major was perhaps the strongest case of a statesman who had to agree to terms that were far different from his initial expectations. This was in large part due to Sir Johnkerr's role and his willingness to compromise. When Major arrived at the Maastricht summit, he did not have the same skills of treaty negotiation and creation and he did not have the same membership in the diplomatic epistemic community. It would be difficult for bargaining theory to predict the outcome of the negotiations without considering the collective agency of the diplomats.

The preceding analysis demonstrates the process whereby diplomats sent a multitude of memos, working papers, and draft treaties to each other, and the secretariat summarized the points of common agreement as the debate proceeded. The drafts and points of agreement were a clear product of compromise and shared understandings. As usual, diplomats defined success as a compromise agreement, and this trumped pure appeasement of state preferences. Since the statesmen ultimately signed off on the agreement during the two-day summit at Maastricht, it is evident that diplomats were skilled at persuading statesmen to change their preferences throughout the negotiations and were able to anticipate the degree of change that would be acceptable (see Table 6.5 for a summary of those involved in the negotiations). Their confidence about their ability to persuade was borne out of the strength of their epistemic community.

Conclusion

Within the case of the EU, there is still much debate about the extent to which it is intergovernmental or transnational, and whether deliberation actually occurs in the international meetings or whether there is a democratic deficit that precludes any real negotiation and compromise from taking place. There is much criticism of EU decision-making processes particularly concerning the role of Coreper. This body of ambassadors is permitted complete secrecy, they are appointed officials, and many of their decisions are rubber-stamped. Such a process leads many Euro-citizens and scholars to point to a large democratic deficit at the supranational level. Whether one can expect a supranational, nonstate entity to adhere to the same criteria as a democracy is a hotly debated issue. Moravcsik argues that the EU is not a state therefore it is not necessary to hold it up to the same standards as states. Thomas D. Zweifel argues that even if you compare the EU to "model democracies" like the United States and Switzerland it still scores well in comparison.[125]

Hayes-Renshaw also emphasizes the importance that Coreper's preparation of issues for the Council of Ministers. In her case study of the negotiation of the public supplies directive in the 1980s, statesmen met in London for four days to agree to instruct their permanent representatives to reach an agreement.[126] However, for Hayes-Renshaw, Coreper is equated with member state involvement and their role as a community-based entity is

Table 6.5 Statesmen and diplomats involved in the Maastricht negotiations

EU member states	State leaders	Foreign ministers	Coreper
United Kingdom	John Major	Douglas Hurd	Sir John Kerr David Durie
The Netherlands	Ruud Lubbers (Chair) Queen Beatrix	Hans van Den Broek	Pieter Nieman Ate Oostra
Germany	Helmut Kohl (Chancellor)	Hans-Dietrich Genscher	Jurgen Trumpf Jochen Gruenhage
France	François Mitterrand	Roland Dumas	François Scheer Pierre Sellal
Spain	Felipe Gonzalez (PM)	Carlos Westendorp (State secretary for EU affairs)	Camilo Garcia-Villamil Carlos Sagües
Italy	Giulio Andreotti (PM)	Gianni De Michelis	Frederico di Roberto Rocco Antonio Cangelosi
Luxembourg	Jacques Santer (PM)	Jacques Poos	Jean-Jacques Kasel Jim Cloos
Belgium	Wilfried Martens	Mark Eyskens	Philippe de Schoutheete Jan de Bock
Portugal	Anibal Cavaco Silva	João de Deus Pinheiro	José Paulouro Vasco Valente
Ireland	Gerard Collins Charles Haughey (PM)	Gerard Collins	Padraic MacKernan Eamonn Ryan
Denmark	Poul Schlüter	Uffe Ellemann-Jensen	Gunnar Riberholdt Niels Henrik Sliben
Greece	Constantine Mitsotakis (PM)	Antonio Samaras	Leonidas Evangelidis Jean Corantis
European Commission	Jacques Delors (President) Frans Andriessen (VP)		
Council	Niels Ersbøll (General Secretary) Gianni de Michelis (President)		

overlooked as she does not look *within* Coreper to the deliberations of the ambassadors themselves.

Like in the seventeenth century, diplomats in today's EU continue to be torn between duty to the state and duty to the international community. The dual role of diplomats represents a common signal that international society exists and has an impact on international relations beyond issues of relative power. Ambassador Christoffersen writes,

> To prevent conflict between the two roles, the Permanent Representative is in constant dialogue with his national authorities (not just the Foreign minister or the foreign ministry, but all parts of the national administration) to make sure that the authorities have a full picture of how the negotiations are moving, and to suggest adaptation where it is difficult to find an overall compromise on the basis of the original position.[127]

The epistemic community of European diplomats constitutes a highly professionalized community with shared norms and a culture of compromise by virtue of their social background, training, meeting frequency, and status Despite the constraints of bureaucracy brought about by the institutional structure of the EU, diplomats continue to play a strong role in outcomes of international cooperation. Whether this will remain the case in the new, enlarged EU is the topic of the next chapter.

7
The Twenty-first Century European Corps

Climate of the times: Euro-skepticism

The member states of the EU deal with conflicting preferences. On the one hand, they must integrate further to combine power and gain influence in the international arena. On the other hand, they are still nation-states driven by the classic realist interests of sovereignty and security. Much political science scholarship about the EU, as well as public commentary in Brussels, focuses on the ways the EU falls short of supranational cooperation, particularly political and military integration.[1] These Euro-skeptics argue that the member states are fundamentally sovereign, and only cede authority to the supranational level if it is secondary to their fundamental interests. Therefore, according to this logic, the member states continuously grant increased authority to the Brussels institutions to control economic, monetary, and commercial policy, but hesitate when it comes to more important spheres like political, military, and diplomatic sovereignty.[2]

Another source of skepticism on the part of political scientists and European experts arises from a belief that political and military policies agreed to on paper and codified as law in treaties are of little importance. The unprecedented Common Foreign and Security Policy (CFSP) of the Maastricht Treaty, which states that "the common foreign and security policy shall include all questions related to the security of the Union, including the eventual framing of a common defense policy, which might in time lead to a common defense," is nonetheless regarded as inconsequential, despite the fact that CFSP has since evolved into the EU Security and Defense Policy (ESDP) in 1999, and includes an EU military force of 60,000 troops and a staff of 200 in 2004. Fifty-five years ago the idea of the EU emerged and its political aim to eradicate war in Europe was laid out in the 1957 Treaty of Rome. Javier Solana writes in 2004,

It is today on the basis of that fundamental historical *acquis* that the Union wishes to project to the outside world the stability that it has patiently constructed within by adding a common security policy to its traditional competencies; this is why it now wishes to promote, in the international system, a European Security Strategy, based on values, norms and capabilities shared by the 25.[3]

Thus, alongside Euro-skepticism, there still remains the overarching belief, shared by all EU members, that a strong Europe with international influence can only be accomplished through a common European identity and a single European voice, and this is based on values developed through the lessons of war.

Rather than examining the ways in which the EU falls short of supranationalism, this book provides one theory to understand the extent to which it actually achieves supranationalism. It focuses on a particular network of influential actors, the diplomats, to demonstrate how processes of international cooperation reveal much more than simply looking at the end results. The processes among diplomats show that even the Council, the major intergovernmental institution of the EU, includes supranational processes by virtue of the cohesiveness and community among Committee of Permanent Representatives (Coreper). Gnesotto writes, "In 1999 no one would have reasonably bet that the Union would, in 2005, have a Minister for Foreign Affairs, a mutual solidarity clause and a common security strategy."[4] Although the bid for an EU Constitution has failed, these aims will eventually be achieved. I argue that a consideration of diplomatic agency and epistemic communities can predict the degree to which consensus and cooperation will occur and, in light of this, the potential for agreement on contentious issues is strong going forward. Statesmen must continue to appoint professional, high-level diplomats to positions of decision-making authority as they have been so far. Before discussing the implications of this study, it is important to first summarize the findings.

The diplomatic epistemic community: A cross-time comparison

The evidence tends to suggest that diplomats are agents of international cooperation in Western Europe. They exercise agency independent of state instructions depending on the strength of the norm of consensus within their epistemic community. If their epistemic community is strong, they impact outcomes of cooperation in ways that neorealist and bargaining theories would not predict because the diplomats' preferences change during the course of negotiation. The cases illustrate that across time the strength of the diplomatic epistemic community has waxed and waned, and this has triggered a similar pattern with the level of diplomatic agency. Table 7.1

Table 7.1 Summary of results

Time period	Professional training	Similar social background	Professional status	Meeting frequency	Strength of shared norms	Demonstrated agency of diplomats
Mid-seventeenth-century Westphalia	Low, only on the job	High	Medium	Low	Medium	Medium
Late nineteenth-century Berlin	Medium	High	High	Medium	High	High
Early twentieth-century Versailles	Medium	High	Low	Low	Medium	Low
Late twentieth-century Maastricht	High	High	High	High	High	High

shows the compiled results of the four cases examined in the preceding chapters.

It is important to note the value of a cross-time analysis in contributing to these conclusions. Just looking at diplomacy today does not show the weight of each variable, but merely its presence or absence. By looking to the past, it is possible to decipher which variables have had a lasting impact on the formation of the epistemic community of diplomats, and hence which are likely to endure.

During the mid-seventeenth century, diplomats had a relatively medium-strength epistemic community. This was the stage at which diplomats were a distinctive professional group residing in major capitals throughout Europe. They were not yet fully bureaucratized, with training on the job and selection by appointment. However, they had acquired a degree of status for themselves as well as a practice of meeting informally at courts across Western Europe. They also corresponded regularly with each other, which created a nascent international society and a European transnational network. Diplomats cultivated relationships with each other and relied on these relationships when it was time to make major decisions impacting the cooperative outcomes in the fledgling state system. While bilateral meetings were commonplace, multilateral meetings were extremely rare and disorganized leadership meant that there was rivalry and competition among diplomats from the same state. During the Treaty of Westphalia, arguably the first major multilateral conference among states, diplomats made their mark by exercising some degree of agency in the decision-making process.

The late nineteenth century is characterized as the golden age of diplomacy. With the bureaucratization of the state and early beginnings of democratization, it was a new era of diplomacy. Diplomats were fully professionalized with a high degree of status and shared strong norms. They met quite frequently, but not as often as the diplomats in the EU's multilateral setting. Their similar social background also contributed to a cohesive diplomatic corps, but selection was not yet meritocratic. Although the invention of the telegraph revolutionized communication, it did not impact the ability of diplomats' to exercise agency as much as would be expected. Rather, diplomats found themselves supplementing their own instructions just as much as in the past because of the shortness of these high-speed communications. Instructions were skeletal, and allowed diplomats to take license with them. The role of diplomats at the 1878 Congress of Berlin demonstrated their level of professionalism and abilities. Advances in technology such as the steam engine and railroad enabled statesmen to attend the conference with relative ease; however, it was the diplomats who carried them through the negotiations.

Following the Great War, the nature of professional diplomacy was once more transformed. This time, it took a turn for the negative because diplomats had lost their status as a result of the breakdown in the alliance system that occurred in the lead-up to the war. Prior to the war, diplomats had begun a round of reforms to the diplomatic profession with the aim of making it more meritocratic, professional, and career-oriented. At last, the aim was to allow people who were not independently wealthy to pursue a career in the foreign service. However, these reform efforts were put on hold during the war, and instead of multilateral meetings of diplomats, we find summitry among statesmen forming the Supreme War Council. Diplomats maintained the shared norms that had characterized the profession for centuries, but they did not have any influence. The negotiations leading to the 1919 Treaty of Versailles demonstrated the culmination of this decline in status. Diplomats attended the Paris Peace Conference alongside statesmen, but they met in separate rooms and had a debilitating lack of information during the negotiations. The so-called "Big Four," George, Wilson, Orlando, and Clemenceau, attempted to design a workable peace on their own, but it was doomed to fail. The statesmen's radical personalities, stubbornness, and lack of diplomatic experience made it difficult for them to engage in treaty creation, something for which only the professional diplomats were wholly qualified.

Finally, in the most recent case, the 1992 Treaty on European Union at Maastricht, diplomats exhibited a strong epistemic community, as they do today. The advent of international organizations in the twentieth century with permanent negotiations marks another distinctive phase of diplomacy. Professional diplomats posted to multilateral organizations now have a greater political role than did their bilateral embassy counterparts. Selection of diplomats is highly meritocratic, yet diplomats continue to be drawn largely from a similar social background. Representatives to the EU have a very high status, and meet several times per week. For the most part, they receive specialized training prior to beginning a career in the foreign service followed by years of on-the-job training. During the negotiation leading to the Maastricht summit, members of the Coreper, serving as personal representatives, played a significant role. They exercised agency by constantly negotiating with their statesmen to change their instructions based on the climate in Brussels and their knowledge of how far the other diplomats could go to reach a compromise. Without a strong epistemic community of diplomats and without their ability to convince statesmen, an agreement would have been impossible.

The four cases show under what conditions diplomats really deliberate and the variables that lead to a stronger epistemic community. The counterpart to diplomatic agency is structure, defined as the rules, norms, and institutions that restrict diplomatic agency. Structure provides the context or environment for the diplomatic epistemic community in a given time period. Rather than looking simply at the absolute level of agency exercised by diplomats, it is necessary to consider agency relative to autonomy.

To what extent do diplomats, as an epistemic community, go beyond their granted autonomy? Autonomy is provided by state leaders, norms, and, more recently, institutions. Leaders delegate to diplomats space for decision-making authority through their instructions. Norms or rules govern diplomatic behavior, protocol, and precedence during negotiations. For example, if a diplomat independently violates protocol or issues an ultimatum as a negotiation tactic, he has violated the rules of the game and is unlikely to be included in consensus shaping. Diplomats define their own norms, so although norms restrain autonomy in certain aspects, they simultaneously strengthen the epistemic community by reinforcing a collective identity through shared knowledge of these norms. Institutions also set the bounds of autonomy as any bureaucracy typically does.

If diplomats as a collective push the boundaries of their autonomy, they have exercised agency. In most instances, they do this by going beyond or even violating their instructions. As presented in Table 7.2, in the seventeenth century, diplomats had little autonomy and exercised some agency. In the late nineteenth century, the golden age of diplomacy, they had some autonomy and exercised a high level of agency. In the early twentieth century, they had no autonomy because of fallen status, but still exercised a little agency. Finally, in the late twentieth century, bureaucracy restricts autonomy, but diplomats exercise a high degree of agency.

Table 7.3 shows examples in which diplomats exercised the strongest type of agency, acting against state instructions, in the case studies considered here.

These few examples highlight some of the instances in which diplomats have openly and blatantly exercised agency against the state. However, there are many more subtle examples, which can be understood by process tracing the diplomatic negotiations.

Table 7.2 Autonomy vs. agency

Time period	Level of delegated autonomy	Strength of epistemic community	Demonstrated agency of diplomats
Mid-seventeenth-century Westphalia	High	Medium	Medium
Late nineteenth-century Berlin	Medium	High	High
Early twentieth-century Versailles	Low	Medium	Low
Late twentieth-century Maastricht	Medium	High	High

Table 7.3 Examples of diplomatic agency against state instructions

Negotiation	State instructions	Diplomatic agency	Outcome
Westphalia	May 1646, Mazarin demanded that the diplomats compromise over Philippsburg as soon as possible.	French diplomats continued to demand Philippsburg.	Diplomats were successful.
Westphalia	Mazarin wanted an immediate truce with Italy.	French diplomats sought a different compromise.	Diplomats acted against Mazarin's instruction.
Westphalia	Mazarin thought that Bavaria was predisposed toward France.	Diplomats knew that Bavaria did not favor French interests.	Diplomats convinced Mazarin of their opinion.
Westphalia	Mazarin insisted on the exchange of Catalonia for the Spanish Low Countries.	Diplomats advised against this.	Mazarin did not listen to the diplomats, and this ended in disaster.
Westphalia	Chancellor Oxenstierna believed that the only way to protect the long Swedish coastline was to control the opposite shore at the same time.	Swedish diplomat Salvius argued that negotiations should be based on international consensus, not Sweden's fear of its neighbors.	Instructions of 11 July 1643 were changed to reflect Salvius' goal of international consensus.
Westphalia	Queen Kristina and Axel Oxenstierna maintained Sweden's controversial occupation of Pomerania, an important principality along the German Baltic coast that belonged to the Brandenburg elector, Frederick William, by treaty.	Swedish diplomats argued that Sweden had no right to control Pomerania and, despite personal differences, wrote letters to Stockholm strongly opposing the occupation of Pomerania.	The state eventually gave ground to their diplomats allowing that Salvius' partition idea could serve as a last resort during the negotiations.

Table 7.3 (Continued)

Negotiation	State instructions	Diplomatic agency	Outcome
Berlin	Emperor Francis Joseph and other realists in the government believed that nationalism did not matter, and their main aim was to acquire more land.	Andrássy, a diplomat and statesman, like Metternich in the past, believed that Austria's stable position rested on the integrity of Turkey.	Andrássy remained faithful to his alliance with the German and Russian leaders and did not threaten war to protect Austrian interests during Russia's advance toward Constantinople. At the congress, he could have demanded territory for Austria, but he sought economic and political ties, as well as to uphold the idea of sovereignty.
Maastricht	Several statesmen of the EU did not want any move toward CFSP because they saw it as a heavy encroachment on state sovereignty.	The Brussels ambassadors carefully worked out a compromise that all states could accept, vesting power in the Council on decisions about CFSP and significantly augmenting their own power in the process.	After referenda in nearly all of the member states, CFSP was approved as part of the Maastricht Treaty on Political Union in 1992.

Trends across time

To the extent that there is a grander historical trajectory in the development of European diplomacy and epistemic community, it can be found in increased bureaucratization, longer-lasting international cooperation, and democratization. These three factors affect the rules that constrain diplomats, the types of issues they negotiate, and the worldviews they bring to the table. From the seventeenth century to the late nineteenth century, bureaucracy was nonexistent or extremely limited. From the late nineteenth century to the mid-twentieth century, democracy and international cooperation were very limited. From the mid-twentieth century to today, all three factors are strong. Western Europe is comprised of democratic states that are fully bureaucratized and engage in large-scale international cooperation. Democracy and bureaucracy go hand in hand,[5] but now it is international cooperation that enforces this further, particularly as enlargement of the EU progresses and newly transitioned democracies seek membership.

Although bureaucracy, democracy, and international cooperation are exogenous to the variables affecting the strength or weakness of the epistemic community of diplomats, the growing presence of these three factors would lead us to expect that the role of diplomats has declined. While bureaucratization constrains diplomats to strict rules of the game, hierarchy, and limited autonomy, democracy holds states democratically accountable. Even though diplomats are not democratically elected, they represent democratic nations abroad and if they overstep their bounds, citizens have a right to complain to their democratically elected leaders and call for restraint. Permanent international cooperation also emphasizes intergovernmentalism among states as actors, not diplomats. The institutions created to serve permanent international cooperation are regarded as extensions of domestic bureaucracies and of domestic policies, further constraining the role of professional diplomats.

The preceding chapters show that diplomats do exercise collective agency depending on the strength of their epistemic community, and they do so despite these exogenous factors. Whatever the issues up for negotiation – whether to end war, prevent war, or sustain a lasting peace – European diplomats have behaved professionally and relied on their shared professional norms to get the job done. In several cases, they have gone beyond getting the job done to accomplish outcomes that are even more cooperative than would have otherwise been expected.

At the same time, the results show that the diplomatic epistemic community has by no means augmented in cohesiveness across time. There is no historical trajectory for the strength of the epistemic community. Rather, at times the European corps is strong, and at other times weak. This fact highlights the need to recognize the role that diplomats play. Despite the lack of any continuous effort on the part of state leaders to improve the quality of their foreign services, the diplomats themselves have pushed for their own professionalization.

Thus, one endogenous factor that creates a notable historical trend is the professionalization of the foreign service. A profession has distinct membership, skills, selection, and knowledge. Professionalism from today's perspective also includes meritocratic selection and promotion. It was only late in this past century that diplomats were paid enough that people from any social class could earn an independent living as a diplomat. It was only in the past ten years that women were assigned as ambassadors to the EU.

The process of professionalization in Western Europe lasted for centuries, and this may explain to some extent why other regions of the world have not yet progressed as far.

There is another endogenous factor in this analysis and that is time. While causality can be shown between the strength of the epistemic community and outcomes of a particular negotiation, if one were to take a longer-term perspective even outcomes of the negotiation are mutually constitutive with the epistemic community itself. As can be observed with the Treaty of Vienna and the 1992 Maastricht Treaty, often outcomes of particular negotiations provide stipulations for the future role of diplomats. Thus, the treaties that diplomats negotiate in turn affect their epistemic community.

Overall, the diplomatic epistemic community is stronger now than it has been in the past, but it may not continue to become more cohesive. With enlargement of membership, more diplomats are coming to Brussels to become part of the diplomatic corps serving the EU, yet they may have less in common with their counterparts who have been in Brussels for decades and have cultivated certain professional norms for much longer. It is likely that new members will adapt quickly, but there may be a significant period of transition before the diplomatic epistemic community increases in strength. At the same time, the intensification and increasing permanence of bureaucratic rules may work against this trend.

Democracy or deception?

To what extent do the processes of diplomacy in the EU help or harm supranational democracy? In other words, do European diplomats contribute to supranational democracy or instead to the democratic deficit? The issue of democracy is perhaps the most important implication of this study. If diplomats exercise agency different from state preferences, should we not be concerned? In general, there is much criticism about the growing delegation of authority to EU institutions because the additional layer of governance removes member-state citizens from the decision-making process. Since the member states are all now democratic countries, these critics point to a growing democratic deficit as a result of increased supranational integration without democratization. Some argue that representative democracy has been replaced with big and unwieldy supranational bureaucracies.

Should we be alarmed knowing that a group of unelected technocrats can have such a big role in international-policy formation? One argument is that democracy only applies to nation-states and the EU is not a nation-state; therefore, it is impossible for a democratic deficit to exist. During the Maastricht Treaty referendum, the Danish and French citizenry hotly debated the potential for a democratic deficit embodied in the Maastricht Treaty. At the time, the German constitutional court issued an objection to the Maastricht Treaty for this reason, but later ruled that the treaty was still governed by a union of sovereign states.[6] How can it be appropriate to speak of democracy if not in the context of a state? Thus far, the EU is not a superstate, nor is it even a federalist collection of states.

Beyond the fundamental point that the EU is not a state, it is nevertheless an institution with the mandate to continue domestic policy at the supranational level. Thus, it is a reasonable endeavor to investigate whether or not it does this democratically. One of the key definitions of democracy is accountability. Ironically, diplomats may be a part of the democratic deficit because of their behind-closed-doors decision-making, but they may also be instrumental in pushing democratization forward because of their shared norms and worldviews. They all typically seek fairness among member states, cooperative outcomes that protect the economy and society simultaneously, as well as a means to hold these decision-makers accountable. It would require another study to fully account for the types of norms that diplomats have tended to uphold during the course of decision-making over the past fifty-five years.

From a quick survey of the evolution of the EU more recently, the evidence suggests that diplomats, for the most part, are not harming national and supranational democracy in *today's* EU. In the past, when democracy was not a regime-type at the state-level, diplomatic accountability was not an issue. Citizens did not participate in international decisions anyway. As democracy became widespread throughout the course of the last century, popular participation became an important issue. With the advent of the EU, European leaders created an additional layer of governance. As more decision-making authority is ceded to the supranational level, it is important to pay attention to how these decisions are made, and whether democratic processes are followed.

I conclude that in today's environment, EU diplomats do not contribute to the democratic deficit, and it is unlikely that they will. First, no elected leader is expected to make all of the decisions himself, and even at the domestic level a statesman will delegate decision-making authority to unelected officials. Second, a diplomat is ultimately held accountable to his or her statesman who in turn is accountable to the people who elected him. Even if and when diplomats do make decisions behind closed doors, they still need to persuade statesmen or elected officials of their decisions. Persuasion is a major part of the processes of diplomacy, and is a form of agency in itself. Diplomats bank on their ability to persuade their statesmen of their decisions when they are still at the negotiation table. Third, international norms of democracy and the strength of international public opinion also serve as a final check on diplomatic decision-making. Overall, although it may seem to some observers that diplomats are contributing to the democratic deficit, it is in the nature of representative democracy to allow some individuals to make decisions as long as they are ultimately accountable for them.

Toward a single voice: European diplomacy with the world

A stated goal for the near future is to create the post of European Foreign Minister, and alongside this, a European foreign service. While such developments have been delayed because of recent setbacks to the EU Constitutional Treaty, they will certainly change the nature of the EU's diplomacy with the rest of the world. However, if and when a revised Constitution is passed, it is unlikely to fundamentally change Coreper's role, which will remain to resolve issues within the EU. After all, the EU is still fundamentally international relations among states. As political integration continues, issues within the EU will come to include the EU's common position with the rest of the world. It is likely that as a true European foreign service evolves, it will have to keep close contacts with Coreper as the permanent representatives will still be critical to determining the content of Europe's single voice.

If there is a more general policy recommendation to be advanced from this study, it is that epistemic communities of diplomats are better able to reach agreement on issues than their statesmen counterparts. Critically, they must be given the autonomy to use this epistemic community to the best of their abilities. Diplomats are in a unique position to resolving conditions of uncertainty because they are able to draw upon cultivated relationships, professional experiences, and shared norms.

Since the recent Iraq war and America's decision to act unilaterally, the need for a single European foreign policy has become more critical. Since its inception, EU officials and member state leaders have been careful about confirming US support in their initiatives, whether in creating a free-trade zone or a common defense policy. Until US President George W. Bush demonstrated his will to act with complete freedom, regardless of international consensus, the fate of the EU was fundamentally tied to the United States through NATO. Europeans would not pursue purely European military integration out of respect for the preexisting role of NATO and the promise it held for US support. The EU is now emerging from the shadows of the United States, and it is clear that at least in the near term, a European identity will be critical.

Notes

1 An epistemic community of diplomats

1. The diplomats considered in this project deal with political issues and tend to be ambassadors or deputy ambassadors since, historically, they are the actors actually granted plenipotentiary power. Thus, lower-ranked diplomats and those dealing solely with consular, commercial, economic, or cultural work are outside the scope conditions of this analysis. I define transnational as nonstate networks of people, institutions, ideas, and so on. My emphasis in this book is that diplomats are not entirely tied to the state. Rather, statesmen such as Kings, Princes, Prime Ministers, and Presidents are the embodiment of the state. Diplomats are representatives of the state, but also have elements of being nonstate actors by virtue of their ties to each other. They may also have different goals from statesmen as will be described.
2. Peter M. Haas, "Introduction: Epistemic Communities and International Policy Coordination." *International Organization* 46, no. 1 (1992): 3. In addition, he argues that an epistemic community is "a knowledge-based network of specialists who shared beliefs in cause-and-effect relations, validity tests, and underlying principled values and pursued common policy goals."
3. Ibid.
4. Emanuel Adler and Peter M. Haas, "Conclusion: Epistemic Communities, World Order, and the Creation of a Reflective Research Program." *International Organization* 46, no. 1 (1992): 367–90.
5. Some examples of this are Anthony R. Zito, "Epistemic Communities, Collective Entrepreneurship and European Integration." *Journal of European Public Policy* 8, no. 4 (2001): 585–603; Claudio M. Radaelli, "The Public Policy of the European Union: Whither Politics of Expertise?" *Journal of European Public Policy* 6, no. 5 (1999): 757–74; and Andreas Antoniades, "Epistemic Communities, Epistemes and the Construction of (World) Politics." *Global Society* 17, no. 1 (2003): 21–38.
6. Examples of epistemic communities are environmentalists, lawyers, human-rights advocates, health networks like the Red Cross, and other scientists. Many of these groups rely on diplomats to help achieve their goals at the policy level. An interesting future study would be to look more closely at the interaction between diplomats and other epistemic communities and to consider the role of other epistemic communities in devolving international norms.
7. Ethan Barnaby Kapstein, "Between Power and Purpose: Central Bankers and the Politics of Regulatory Convergence." *International Organization* 46, no. 1 (1992): 267.
8. See, for example, Mark A. Pollack, *The Engines of European Integration: Delegation, Agency, and Agenda Setting in the EU*, Oxford: Oxford University Press, 2003.
9. Harold Nicolson, *Diplomacy*, London: Oxford University Press, 3rd ed., 1969, p. 4; and Adam Watson, *Diplomacy: The Dialogue between States*, London: Eyre Methuen, 1982.
10. The distinction is made a bit differently here, but the idea of differentiating between superficial and procedural diplomacy is the same. Watson does not explicitly require a preference for words before force and/or liberalism in his definition of diplomacy as foreign policy.

11. José Calvet De Magalhaes, *The Pure Concept of Diplomacy*, translated by Bernardo Futscher Pereira, *Global Perspectives in History and Politics*, Westport, CT: Greenwood Press, 1988, p. 13.
12. Nicolson, *Diplomacy*, p. 4.
13. Watson, *Diplomacy: The Dialogue between States*, p. 11. See also Bull, Hedley, *The Anarchical Society*. 2nd ed. New York: Columbia University Press, 1995.
14. Watson, *Diplomacy: The Dialogue between States*, Chapter 5 "Power and Persuasion."
15. Robert Jervis, *Perception and Misperception in International Politics*, Princeton, NJ: Princeton University Press, 1976.
16. The most significant works on this topic are Robert D. Putnam, "Diplomacy and Domestic Politics: The Logic of Two-Level Games." *International Organization* 42, no. 3 (1988): 427–60; Jeffrey T. Checkel, "Taking Deliberation Seriously." European Union Center, Harvard University, Cambridge, MA, 11–12 May 2001; Andrew Moravcsik and Kalypso Nicolaïdis, "Explaining the Treaty of Amsterdam: Interests, Influence, Institutions." *Journal of Common Market Studies* 37, no. 1 (1999): 59–85; and Thomas Risse, " 'Let's Argue!': Communicative Action in World Politics." *International Organization* 54, no. 1 (2000): 1–39.
17. States are defined as the central decision-making authority of foreign policy, whether it involves a monarchical ruler or a democratically elected president constrained by public opinion.
18. See discussion on the distinction between autonomy and agency in Chapter 2.
19. Technology is also considered in each case study, but is shown to not be a critical variable in determining the strength of the diplomatic epistemic community.
20. James K. Sebenius, "Challenging Conventional Explanations of International Cooperation: Negotiation Analysis and the Case of Epistemic Communities." *International Organization* 46, no. 1 (1992): 325.
21. In a future project, I will look at outcomes substantively to determine whether shared worldviews among diplomats help or harm supranational democracy in the European Union. The current project, however, is confined to proving whether and under what circumstances the epistemic community of diplomats impacts outcomes more broadly. This is a necessary first step to determining how values or worldviews impact the actual substance of outcomes.
22. I take a broad definition of epistemic communities. That is, any individual or group which shares a particular kind of expertise and knowledge may belong to the epistemic community. Naturally, some participate more in the epistemic community than others, and may constitute an important transnational core. For the purposes, of understanding outcomes, I focus on a particular core of diplomats involved in particular negotiations while still recognizing that there *is* a wider epistemic community.
23. Jan Beyers and Guido Dierickx, "The Working Groups of the Council of the European Union: Supranational or Intergovernmental Negotiations?" *Journal of Common Market Studies* 36, no. 3 (1998): 259–317.
24. Kenneth Glarbo. "Wide-Awake Diplomacy: Reconstructing the Common Foreign and Security Policy of the European Union." *Journal of European Public Policy* 6, no. 4 (1999): 634–51.
25. Martin Westlake, *The Council of the European Union*, London: Cartermill International Ltd, 1995, pp. 319–20.
26. Pollack, *The Engines of European Integration*.
27. See, for example, Colette Mazzucelli, *France and Germany at Maastricht: Politics and Negotiations to Create the European Union*, New York: Garland Publishing,

Inc., 1997; Barnett, Michael N. and Martha Finnemore, "The Politics, Power, and Pathologies of International Organizations." *International Organization* 53, no. 4 (1999): 699–732; Risse, "'Let's Argue!'"; John Gerard Ruggie, "What Makes the World Hang Together? Neo-Utilitarianism and the Social Constructivist Challenge." *International Organization* 52, no. 4 (1998): 855–85; Watson, *Diplomacy: The Dialogue between States*; Oran R. Young, "Political Leadership and Regime Formation: On the Development of Institutions in International Society." *International Organization* 45, no. 3 (1991): 281–308; and Paul Pierson, *Politics in Time: History, Institutions, and Social Analysis*, Princeton, NJ: Princeton University Press, 2004.

28. Diplomats may agree to something that does not benefit the common good, as they did at the Munich Conference in 1938.
29. For example, see Michael Barnett and Martha Finnemore, *Rules for the World*, Ithaca, NY: Cornell University Press, 2004; Frank Dobbin, *The New Economic Sociology*, Princeton, NJ: Princeton University Press, 2004; and Neil Fligstein and Iona Mara-Drita, "How to Make a Market: Reflections on the Attempt to Create a Single Market in the European Union." *The American Journal of Sociology* 102, no. 1 (1996): 1–33.
30. Martha Finnemore and Kathryn Sikkink use the term "norm entrepreneurs" in describing their model of a norm life cycle in Martha Finnemore and Kathryn Sikkink, "International Norm Dynamics and Political Change." *International Organization* 52, no. 4 (1998): 887–917.
31. There is much criticism directed at the use of diplomatic interviews as data as diplomats are obviously skilled orators who may phrase their opinions according to what they want to consciously convey rather than what is the most accurate. Diplomatic interviews are thus used here to back up other forms of research rather than as the primary evidence.
32. Secondary historical accounts are from the Princeton University Library, Columbia University Library, Bibliothèque Nationale – Richelieu and Mitterrand (Paris), Institutes des Sciences Politiques (Paris), British Library, European University Institute (Florence), Documentation Centre (Brussels).
33. Archival documentation is from the Bibliothèque Richelieu Salle des Manuscrits (Paris) for the Westphalia case study, the British Library Manuscript Room for the Congresses of Berlin and Versailles case studies, and Princeton's Firestone Library microfiche room.
34. Governmental documentation was obtained from the Ministry of Foreign Affairs in Paris (Congress of Berlin and Versailles), the European University Institute in Florence (translated German documents for the Congress of Berlin case study), the Council of the European Union (Maastricht case study), and the British Library (Congresses of Berlin, Versailles, and Maastricht).
35. Carl von Clausewitz, *On War*, translated by Michael Howard and Peter Paret, Princeton, NJ: Princeton University Press, 1976, p. 170.
36. Martha S. Feldman, *Strategies for Interpreting Qualitative Data*, Newbury Park, CA: Sage, 1995.
37. Beth L. Leech, "Asking Questions: Techniques for Semistructured Interviews." *Political Science and Politics* 35, no. 4 (2002): 665–8.
38. Gary Goertz, *Social Science Concepts: A User's Guide*, Princeton, NJ: Princeton University Press, 2005.
39. Alexander L. George and Andrew Bennett, "Process Tracing and Historical Explanation." *Case Studies and Theory Development in the Social Sciences*, Chapter 10, Cambridge: MIT Press, 2004.
40. Charles Ragin, *Fuzzy Set Social Science*, Chicago: University of Chicago, 2000.

41. Some historians refer to early to middle twentieth-century international treaties or congresses as international organizations, but for the purposes of clearly delineating and recognizing the relatively permanent, concrete, transnational, and formal institutional quality of modern international organizations, this book will refer to middle to late twentieth-century international organizations.
42. Pierson, *Politics in Time*.
43. Moravcsik and Nicolaïdis, "Explaining the Treaty of Amsterdam."

2 The diplomatic dialogue: Between power and cooperation

1. Kenneth Waltz, *Theory of International Politics*, Reading, MA: Addison-Wesley Pub. Co., 1979.
2. J.W. Burton, *Systems, States, Diplomacy, and Rules*, Cambridge: Cambridge University Press, 1968.
3. Ibid., p. 199.
4. Each state acts in its own best interests unless another state directly changes the composition of those interests by the way in which that state pursues its own interests.
5. Kenneth Glarbo, "Wide-Awake Diplomacy: Reconstructing the Common Foreign and Security Policy of the European Union." *Journal of European Public Policy* 6, no. 4 (1999): 634–51.
6. Andrew Moravcsik, "Negotiating the Single European Act: National Interests and Conventional Statecraft in the European Community." *International Organization* 45, no. 1 (1991): 19–56.
7. Ibid., p. 25.
8. Functionalism is the theory that actors will change their behavior based on pragmatic need. For example, a functionalist would argue that religions exist because they serve a function to the survival of a society: providing a spiritual system of guidance. Functionalism is one explanation for the growth of the European Coal and Steel Community into the European Union.
9. Barry Buzan, "From International System to International Society: Structural Realism and Regime Theory Meet the English School." *International Organization* 47, no. 3 (1993): 327–52.
10. Hedley Bull and Adam Watson, "Introduction." In *Expansion of International Society*, edited by Hedley Bull and Adam Watson. Oxford: Clarendon Press, 1984, p. 1.
11. During the middle to late seventeenth century, diplomats may have been the only nonreligious members of international society. Merchants also interacted at the transnational level, but they were driven by personal self-interest and thus did not have a meaningful collective identity.
12. Buzan, "From International System to International Society." p. 334.
13. A spillover effect is defined as the inadvertent political consequences of units engaging in interest maximization.
14. Soft power is defined as factors that indirectly impact a state's influence in the international realm, such as ability to persuade, to inspire trust, or to be considered an important element in other states' calculations. See Joseph S. Nye, Jr., *Soft Power: The Means to Success in World Politics*, New York: Public Affairs, 2004.
15. Throughout this book, common good often refers to peaceful outcomes or avoidance of war even though militarily powerful states could actually maximize interests through engaging in war.

16. For example, Pope Julius II wrote a table of precedence in 1504, and William Penn (intellectual and founder of Pennsylvania) created one in 1691.
17. Evan Luard, *The Balance of Power: The System of International Relations, 1648–1815*, London: Macmillan, 1992, p. 133.
18. Bibliothèque Nationale Richelieu, Manuscrits Françaises, 4144, "Instructions to Longueville," January 1644.
19. Andrew Moravcsik argues that the EU is the world's super power because of its civilian power. European Conference, Princeton University, Princeton, NJ, 3–5 October 2003.
20. Jeffrey T. Checkel, "Ideas, Institutions, and the Gorbachev Foreign Policy Revolution." *World Politics* 45, no. 2 (1993): 271–300.
21. Robert D. Putnam, "Diplomacy and Domestic Politics: The Logic of Two-Level Games." *International Organization* 42, no. 3 (1988): 427–60.
22. James N. Rosenau, "The Relocation of Authority in a Shrinking World." *Comparative Politics*, 24, no. 3 (April 1992): 253–72.
23. Robert O. Keohane and Joseph S. Nye, Jr., *Power and Interdependence: World Politics in Transition*. 2nd ed. Boston: Little-Brown, 1989.
24. Peter J. Katzenstein, *Between Power and Plenty*, Madison: University of Wisconsin Press, 1978.
25. Richard Katz and Bernhard Wessels. *The European Parliament, the National Parliaments, and European Integration*, London: Oxford University Press, 1999.
26. Hussein Kassim and Anand Menon, "The Principal–Agent Approach and the Study of the European Union: Promise Unfulfilled?" *Journal of European Public Policy* 10, no. 1 (2003): 123.
27. Ibid., p. 124.
28. Andrew Moravcsik and Kalypso Nicolaïdis, "Explaining the Treaty of Amsterdam: Interests, Influence, Institutions." *Journal of Common Market Studies* 37, no. 1 (1999): 59–85.
29. Other studies that assume actors' preferences remained fixed are G. Tsebelis, *Nested Games*, Berkeley and Los Angeles: University of California Press, 1990; K. Shepsle, *Perspectives on Positive Political Economy*, Cambridge: Cambridge University Press, 1990; and Robert O. Keohane, *After Hegemony*, Princeton, NJ: Princeton University Press, 1984.
30. In an earlier article (Moravcsik, "Negotiating the Single European Act"), Moravcsik argues that changes in national preferences are a key component of institutional intergovernmentalism. In a more recent article (Moravcsik and Nicolaïdis, "Explaining the Treaty of Amsterdam"), he argues that initial state preferences remain stable throughout the negotiations.
31. For an analysis of these two approaches, see Thomas Risse-Kappen "Did 'Peace through Strength' End the Cold War? Lessons from INF." *International Security* 16, no. 1 (1991): 162–88.
32. Robert Axelrod, *Evolution of Cooperation*, New York: Basic Books, 1984.
33. Glenn Snyder and Paul Diesing, *Conflict among Nations*, Princeton, NJ: Princeton University Press, 1977.
34. Kassim and Menon, "The Principal–Agent Approach."
35. See Chapter 1, pp. 3–4, or p. 40 of this chapter, for my discussion of the critical difference between autonomy and agency.
36. Mark A. Pollack, "Delegation, Agency, and Agenda Setting in the European Community." *International Organization* 51, no. 1 (1997): 101.
37. Ulf Sverdrup, "An Institutional Perspective on Treaty Reform: Contextualizing the Amsterdam and Nice Treaties." *Journal of European Public Policy* 9, no. 1 (2002): 120–40.

38. Ibid., p. 20.
39. Anthony R. Zito, "Epistemic Communities, Collective Entrepreneurship and European Integration." *Journal of European Public Policy* 8, no. 4 (2001): 585–603.
40. Except in the rare case that instructions from all the states involved in the negotiation happen to coincide.
41. Frank Dobbin, *The New Economic Sociology*, Princeton, NJ: Princeton University Press, 2004. Introduction.
42. Ibid.
43. For a good overview, see Elisabeth S. Clemens and James M. Cook, "Politics and Institutionalism: Explaining Durability and Change." *Annual Review of Sociology* 25 (1999): 445. Also, Neil Fligstein and Iona Mara-Drita, "How to Make a Market: Reflections on the Attempt to Create a Single Market in the European Union." *The American Journal of Sociology* 102, no. 1 (1996): 1–33.
44. Clemens and Cook, "Politics and Institutionalism." p. 446.
45. Krasner's "Punctuated equilibrium" is the argument that institutions are stable unless forced to change by an "exogenous shock" or sudden influence from outside the institution.
46. Fligstein and Mara-Drita, "How to Make a Market." p. 2.
47. Dobbin, *The New Economic Sociology*.
48. DiMaggio and Powell define organizational fields as "organizations that, in the aggregate, constitute a recognized area of institutional life." Paul J. DiMaggio and Walter W. Powell, "The Iron Cage Revisited: Institutional Isomorphism and Collective Rationality in Organizational Fields." *American Sociological Review* 48, no. 2 (1983): 149.
49. Ibid., p. 148.
50. For an overview of this, see Neil Fligstein and Peter Brantley, "Bank Control, Owner Control, or Organizational Dynamics: Who Controls the Large Modern Corporation?" *The American Journal of Sociology* 98, no. 2 (1992): 280–307.
51. Ibid., p. 286.
52. Fligstein and Mara-Drita, "How to Make a Market." p. 2.
53. Ibid., p. 5.
54. Andreas Antoniades, "Epistemic Communities, Epistemes and the Construction of (World) Politics." *Global Society* 17, no. 1 (2003): 21–38.
55. Ernst B. Haas, *The Uniting of Europe. Political, Social and Economic Forces 1950–57*, Stanford, CA: Stanford University Press, 1958.
56. Ernst B. Haas, "Is There a Hole in the Whole? Knowledge, Technology, Interdependence, and the Construction of International Regimes." *International Organization* 29, no. 3 (1975): 827–76.
57. For a good summary of Ernst Haas's approach, labeled neofunctionalism, see Fiona Hayes-Renshaw and Helen Wallace, *The Council of Ministers*, London: Macmillan Press Ltd, 1997, pp. 254–5. The first part of Haas's theory is a variant of functionalism, although it considers individual actors' (diplomats') preferences rather than simply state interest. However, it quickly becomes a constructivist theory of worldviews, socialization, and loyalty when cooperation over time becomes a factor, particularly in the case of the EU.
58. Instituted with the 1992 Maastricht Treaty.
59. Glarbo, "Wide-Awake Diplomacy." p. 635.
60. Emanuel Adler and Peter M. Haas, "Conclusion: Epistemic Communities, World Order, and the Creation of a Reflective Research Program." *International Organization* 46, no. 1 (1992): 367–90.
61. Ibid.

62. James K. Sebenius, "Challenging Conventional Explanations of International Cooperation: Negotiation Analysis and the Case of Epistemic Communities." *International Organization* 46, no. 1 (1992): 323–65.
63. Checkel, "Ideas, Institutions, and the Gorbachev Foreign Policy Revolution."
64. Thomas Risse-Kappen, "Ideas Do Not Float Freely: Transnational Coalitions, Domestic Structures, and the End of the Cold War." *International Organization* 48, no. 2 (1994): 185–214.
65. Ibid., p. 187.
66. Jeffrey T. Checkel, "Norms, Institutions, and National Identity in Contemporary Europe." *International Studies Quarterly* 43, no. 1 (1999): 83–114.
67. Margaret Keck and Kathryn Sikkink, *Activists Beyond Borders*, Ithaca, NY: Cornell University Press, 1998.
68. Clemens and Cook argue, "The patterning of social life is not produced solely by the aggregation of individual and organizational behavior but also by institutions that structure action." Clemens and Cook, "Politics and Institutionalism."
69. Dobbin, *The New Economic Sociology*, Introduction.
70. For an excellent analysis of the rules of the game provided by states and institutions, see Brian Hocking and David Spence (eds), *Foreign Ministries of the European Union: Integrating Diplomats*, Houndmills, UK: Palgrave, 2002. This book tells the story of the interaction between member states and the EU from the perspective of the foreign ministries.
71. Kathleen R. McNamara, *The Currency of Ideas*, Ithaca, NY: Cornell University Press, 1998, p. 4.
72. Jon Elster, *The Cement of Society: A Study of Social Order*, Cambridge: Cambridge University Press, 1989.
73. Martha Finnemore and Kathryn Sikkink, "International Norm Dynamics and Political Change." *International Organization* 52, no. 4 (1998): 887–917.
74. I will refer to its contribution to international rules of diplomatic protocol in Chapter 4. In general, the spirit of the Congress of Vienna was to glorify past diplomacy.
75. In several instances, diplomatic decisions have resulted in highly detrimental policies going against the common good; consider the 1938 Munich Pact that secured France and Britain's support of Adolf Hitler. It is important to remember, however, that statesmen (British Prime Minister Neville Chamberlain, French Premier Édouard Daladier, Germany's Adolf Hitler, and Italy's Benito Mussolini), not diplomats, negotiated the terms of the agreement.
76. Adam Watson, *Diplomacy: The Dialogue between States*, London: Eyre Methuen, 1982.
77. For example, in 1864, Great Britain, Denmark, France, Austria, the German Confederation, Germany, Sweden–Norway, and Russia held a meeting to prevent war between Austria–Germany and Denmark. Another example is the London conference of 1867, where all the states of Europe and the new Kingdom of Italy met to decide on the permanent neutrality of Luxembourg. This served to prevent conflict between France and Germany over the future of Luxembourg. Examples from Gerard J. Mangone, *A Short History of International Organization*, New York: McGraw-Hill Book Company, Inc., 1954, p. 54.
78. Keith Hamilton and Richard Langhorne, *The Practice of Diplomacy: Its Evolution, Theory and Administration*, London: Routledge, 1995, Chapter 4.
79. Mangone, *A Short History of International Organization*, p. 54.
80. Claudio Radaelli, another author who addresses the epistemic community approach, argues that epistemic communities play a role in international cooperation only under the constrained conditions of high uncertainty and high salience

of the issue at hand. (Claudio M. Radaelli, "The Public Policy of the European Union: Whither Politics of Expertise?" *Journal of European Public Policy* 6, no. 5 (1999): 757–74.) However, an examination of the epistemic community of diplomats demonstrates that diplomats often exercise agency for issues that are neither of high salience nor uncertain.

3 The seventeenth century and the Treaty of Westphalia

1. Evan Luard, *The Balance of Power: The System of International Relations, 1648–1815*, London: Macmillan, 1992, p. 48.
2. During the Middle Ages, the conduct of diplomacy was vaguely defined. Merchants, bishops, and other nonsovereigns could send diplomatic representatives just as kings and princes could. See M.S. Anderson, *The Rise of Modern Diplomacy 1450–1919*, London and New York: Longman, 1993, p. 42.
3. "Professionalization" is defined as the process by which norms, rules, behavior, and duty become standardized among a group of individuals who share a profession. For diplomats, professionalization is inherently transnational.
4. Thomas Risse, "'Let's Argue!': Communicative Action in World Politics." *International Organization* 54, no. 1 (2000): 1–39.
5. Garrett Mattingly, *Renaissance Diplomacy*, London: Butler & Tanner Ltd, 1955, Chapter 27.
6. Training can strengthen the epistemic community of diplomats, but is not a necessary component of many professional groups. For example, many merchants during the seventeenth century were not trained in business, and for that matter, many businessmen today do not receive training. However, they were and are still professional merchants.
7. As stated in Chapter 1, epistemic community is defined by Peter Haas as "a network of professionals with recognized expertise and competence in a particular domain and an authoritative claim to policy-relevant knowledge within that domain or issue area." Peter M. Haas, "Introduction: Epistemic Communities and International Policy Coordination." *International Organization* 46, no. 1 (1992): 3.
8. Adam Watson, *Diplomacy: The Dialogue between States*, London: Eyre Methuen, 1982.
9. François de Callières, *On the Manner of Negotiating with Princes*, Boston: Houghton Mifflin Co., 1919.
10. Richelieu, Armand du Plessis, *Testament Politique*, Amsterdam, The Netherlands: chez Henry Desbordes, 1688.
11. Callières, *On the Manner of Negotiating with Princes*.
12. Many books were written during the seventeenth century providing guidelines for the ideal qualities of diplomats. De Callières' is the most well known. Another good example is Juan Antonio de Vera, El Embajador translated into French (Le Parfait Ambassadeur).
13. Anderson, *The Rise of Modern Diplomacy 1450–1919*, p. 45.
14. Luard, *The Balance of Power*, p. 50.
15. Anderson, *The Rise of Modern Diplomacy 1450–1919*, p. 91.
16. The French term "démarche" is still used today in reference to meetings among diplomats for the express purpose of conveying information contained in instructions from the state.

17. Plenipotentiary is defined in the Webster's New World Dictionary as "a person, especially a diplomatic agent, given full authority to act as diplomatic representative of a government."
18. Anderson, *The Rise of Modern Diplomacy 1450–1919*, p. 42.
19. Watson, *Diplomacy: The Dialogue between States*, p. 103.
20. Extraordinary ambassadors were sent for a specific event or issue, such as the celebration of a royal wedding or to take a king's oath to support a newly signed treaty. Ordinary ambassadors were those who resided in the foreign capital on a permanent basis.
21. Anderson, *The Rise of Modern Diplomacy 1450–1919*, p. 56.
22. Bibliothèque Nationale Richelieu, Manuscrits Françaises, 4144, "Instructions to Longueville" January 1644.
23. Andreas Osiander, *The States System of Europe, 1640–1990: Peacemaking and the Conditions of International Stability*, Oxford: Clarendon Press, 1994, pp. 82–3.
24. Luard, *The Balance of Power*, p. 134.
25. M.S. Anderson's translation (p. 63) of F. Dickmann, *Der Westfälische Friede*, Münster, 1959, p. 210. For example, King Gustavus Adolphus in dealing with a struggle between the English and the French ambassadors argued that all kings should be considered equal because they get their authority from God.
26. Anderson, *The Rise of Modern Diplomacy 1450–1919*, p. 64.
27. Ibid., p. 61.
28. Ibid., p. 63.
29. "After the negotiations of Westphalia a new diplomatic style was established directed by members of a high status and prestige." (translation) from Porfirio Sanz Camañes, *Diplomacia Hispano-Inglesa en el Siglo XVII*. Cuenca: Ediciones de la Universidad de Castilla-La Mancha, p. 25.
30. Anderson, *The Rise of Modern Diplomacy 1450–1919*, p. 65. By the mid-eighteenth century, status, protocol, and ceremony were very clearly on the decline.
31. Strasbourg lies on the border between France and Germany, and Brussels and Luxembourg have been historically neutral locations, relatively equidistant from the various large states.
32. Garrett Mattingly, *Renaissance Diplomacy*, pp. 223–32.
33. Geoffrey G. Butler and Simon Maccoby, *The Development of International Law*, London and New York: Longmans, Green and Co., Ltd, 1928.
34. Hugo Grotius, *The Laws of War and Peace*, translated by Johan Blaeu and Francis W. Kelsey, Birmingham, AL: Gryphon, 1984.
35. Mattingly, *Renaissance Diplomacy*, Chapter 27.
36. Merchants and Catholic religious figures were the only other major transnational actors. However, merchants were driven by personal self-interest and thus did not have a meaningful collective identity. It could be argued that Catholic religious figures may have had an epistemic community, but that is a topic for another essay.
37. Much of this background is from Derek Croxton and Anuschka Tischer, *The Peace of Westphalia: A Historical Dictionary*, Westport: Greenwood Press, 2002, which provides a concise and thorough summary of the Thirty Years' War.
38. The Holy Roman Empire was, essentially, a loose confederation of literally hundreds of various sovereign states, some as small as a mere town. Its borders encompassed virtually all of the German- and Czech-speaking lands, and also included parts of what is now eastern France, the low countries, and the fringes of northern Italy.

39. The estates of the Holy Roman Empire consisted of the electors, who were the seven princes in charge of choosing each Emperor; the Imperial Princes; and the Imperial Free Cities. They each formed their own college in parliament, and each territory had one vote. Thus, many individuals who controlled more than one territory could vote more than once. See Croxton and Tischer, *The Peace of Westphalia*, pp. 128–9.
40. The Treaty of Hamburg was a three-year agreement between France and Sweden that they would not conclude a separate peace with the Empire. In addition, France gave Sweden one million livres per year, and in return the Swedes carried the war into the Eastern Habsburg dominions, and the French continued fighting in the Rhineland.
41. The French treated the Dutch representatives as "Excellencies" and were "ordered" by the six-year-old Louis XIV not to harm the Franco–Dutch alliance. Osiander, *The States System of Europe*, p. 183.
42. Because of a losing military campaign on 29 August 1645, the Emperor was forced out of desperation to summon the Imperial estates to participate in the peace conference. Significantly, he had to acknowledge that he was not the sole voice of the Empire. See Konrad Repgen, "Negotiating the Peace of Westphalia." In *1648: War and Peace in Europe*, edited by Klaus Bussmann and Heinz Schilling, Münster, Germany: S.N., 1999, p. 357.
43. Bibliothèque Nationale Richelieu, Manuscript Room, MSS Français, Number 4148, Memoirs of the negotiations of the general peace in 1648.
44. Derek Croxton, *Peacemaking in Early Modern Europe: Cardinal Mazarin and the Congress of Westphalia, 1643–1648*, London: Associated University Press, 1999, p. 103.
45. As Osiander writes, the participants in the congress accepted the concept of legality in customary and written law. They had hoped that the treaty would be a final and binding agreement. Osiander, *The States System of Europe*, pp. 43–72.
46. A total of sixteen European states were present.
47. Repgen, "Negotiating the Peace of Westphalia," p. 355.
48. Ibid.
49. Osiander, *The States System of Europe*, p. 21.
50. Bibliothèque Nationale Richelieu, Manuscrits Françaises, 4144, "Instructions to Longueville," January 1644. Section Première.
51. Figures from Klaus Bussmann and Heinz Schilling, *1648: War and Peace in Europe*, Münster, Germany: S.N., 1999, p. 356.
52. "That those in the Confession of Augsburg, and particularly the Inhabitants of Oppenheim, shall be put in possession again of their Churches, and Ecclesiastical Estates, as they were in the Year 1624. As it shall have the free Exercise of their Religion, as well in publick Churches at the appointed Hours, as in private in their own Houses, or in others chosen for this purpose by their Ministers, or by those of their Neighbours, preaching the Word of God." Article XXVIII, Treaty of Westphalia. Münster, 24 October 1648.
53. Croxton, *Peacemaking in Early Modern Europe*, p. 40.
54. Ibid., p. 41.
55. Ibid., pp. 23–4.
56. Ibid.
57. Ibid., p. 29
58. Ibid., p. 33.
59. France became the most powerful country in Western Europe by 1648, with the largest population and greatest resources. During the Congress of Westphalia, the

French state and diplomats still felt insecure in this new position of power, and thus wanted to assert their rank whenever possible.
60. Croxton, *Peacemaking in Early Modern Europe*, p. 38.
61. Osiander, *The States System of Europe*, p. 85.
62. Translated by Osiander, p. 86 from APW II B. ii. 73.
63. Croxton, *Peacemaking in Early Modern Europe*, p. 40.
64. Lionne wrote on behalf of Mazarin: "We have received your memorandum from the 14th of this month. You will recognize this easily by several items included in the royal memo."
65. Bibliothèque Nationale Richelieu, Manuscrits Françaises, 4144, "Instructions to Longueville" January 1644.
66. Osiander, *The States System of Europe*, p. 23 from APW II C. iii. 383 f.
67. Translated by Osiander, p. 83 from APW I. I. 244f/.
68. Ibid., p. 25.
69. APW II C. i. 4.
70. This was true particularly on the issue of encouraging the various estates of the Empire to send delegates to the negotiations, warning them that they risked losing their liberty and constitutional rights.
71. Osiander, *The States System of Europe*, p. 30.
72. Anderson, *The Rise of Modern Diplomacy 1450–1919*, p. 47.
73. Osiander, *The States System of Europe*, p. 31.
74. Most notably during the Italian wars of the fifteenth and sixteenth centuries.
75. Osiander, *The States System of Europe*, p. 31.
76. Translated by Osiander, p. 37. A letter from the Imperial ambassadors to Ferdinand III. 16 February 1645, APW II A. ii. 189f.
77. It was also not the lowest, as will be seen in Chapter 5.
78. The following description of procedure is from Repgen, "Negotiating the Peace of Westphalia," pp. 357–9.
79. Watson. *Diplomacy: The Dialogue between States*, p. 103.
80. Article XLI. Treaty of Westphalia.
81. Osiander, *The States System of Europe*, p. 43. The term "balance of power" was not explicitly stated (instead, "aid the weaker against the stronger") as the concept had not yet come into use, nor was there enough empirical proof available to generalize about its impact on international security. Interestingly, the diplomat Salvius thought about balance of power in more theoretical terms and wrote about it to Queen Kristina.
82. Luard, *The Balance of Power*.
83. Ibid., p. 41.
84. See Waltz, *Theory of International Politics*, Reading, MA: Addison-Wesley Pub. Co., 1979; and John Mearsheimer, "Back to the Future: Instability after the Cold War." *International Security* 15, no. 4 (1990): 5–56.
85. See Hans Morgenthau, *Politics among Nations: The Struggle for Power and Peace*, New York: Knopf, 1978.
86. See Robert Jervis, *Perception and Misperception in International Politics*, Princeton, NJ: Princeton University Press, 1976; and Gideon Rose, "Neoclassical Realism and Theories of Foreign Policy." *World Politics* 51, no. 1 (1998): 144–72.
87. Wendt refers to this as "rump materialism." Alexander Wendt, *Social Theories of International Politics*, Cambridge: Cambridge University Press, 1999.
88. Luard, *The Balance of Power*, p. 40.
89. David J. Hill, *A History of European Diplomacy*, Vol. 2, London: Longmans, 1906, pp. 569–607.

90. Quote of Callières from Ibid., p. 256.
91. Ibid., p. 269.
92. Translated by Osiander, *The States System of Europe*, p. 83 from APW I. I. 244f.
93. The Treaty of Westphalia, Article 17.5–6.
94. Knutsen, Torbjørn L., *A History of International Relations Theory*, Manchester: Manchester University Press, 1997.
95. Many scholars of international relations subscribe to the notion that the Treaty of Westphalia was a watershed event for the concept of sovereignty. The congress, however, was not about sovereignty in a formal and legal sense but, as Osiander argues, about autonomy. See p. 78 of Osiander, *The States System of Europe*. The Spanish–Dutch treaty, negotiated alongside the Treaty of Westphalia, did stipulate legal sovereignty in terms of Dutch independence from Spain, but this was not an issue involving the Emperor.
96. Luard, *The Balance of Power*.
97. Anderson, *The Rise of Modern Diplomacy 1450–1919*, p. 42. Before around the mid-seventeenth century, nonsovereign or quasi-sovereign authorities could send representatives to negotiations in Europe.
98. Luard, *The Balance of Power*, p. 31.
99. Ibid., Chapter 5 Status.

4 The late nineteenth century and the Congress of Berlin

1. France, Britain, Italy, Austria-Hungary, Russia, and Germany.
2. Bismarck brought together the German states in 1862. In 1866, Germany defeated Austria, putting a long-time rivalry to an end and asserting German control. The Austrian Habsburgs fled to Hungary, creating the Austria-Hungary state. When Bismarck gave support to a Hohenzollern prince to take the throne in Spain, France declared war on Germany. This resulted in even further German consolidation.
3. Shifts in long-held alliances would have disastrous consequences. Bismarck tried to prevent this by insisting on compromise between the Russian and Austrian leaders who were on increasingly shaky ground. Eventually the alliances were severed in the aftermath of the Congress of Berlin and this lead to World War I.
4. G.P. Speeckaert, "Un siècle d'Expositions Universelles, leur influences sur les congres internationaux," *Bulletin NGO-ONG* 3, no. 10 (1951): 270.
5. M.S. Anderson, *The Rise of Modern Diplomacy 1450–1919*, London and New York: Longman, 1993, p. 105.
6. In the late nineteenth century, Britain was a constitutional monarchy with a functioning parliament and Cabinet, but power was still heavily weighted toward the upper class. France had embarked upon its third experiment in democracy, the Third Republic. Like Britain, Germany had a parliament and Cabinet, and the Social Democratic party in Germany was gaining some momentum.
7. A.H. Layard, *Layard Papers*, British Library, 1877–78.
8. Chester Wells Clark, Franz Joseph and Bismarck: The Diplomacy of Austria before the War of 1866, *Harvard Historical Studies*, Cambridge: Harvard University Press, 1934, p. 491.
9. Lord Granville to Mr. Gladstone 18 March 1877. *The Political Correspondence of Mr. Gladstone and Lord Granville 1876–1886*, Vol. 1, Gladstone and Granville. Oxford University Press, 1962, p. 34.

10. Layard, "Confidential Print. Turkey. 31 July–August 1877. MSS 39145." The Earl of Derby to Mr. Layard.
11. Peter Marshall, *Positive Diplomacy*, London: Macmillan Press, 1997, p. 145.
12. Anderson, *The Rise of Modern Diplomacy 1450–1919*, p. 111.
13. Ibid., p. 123.
14. Edward A. Whitcomb, *Napoleon's Diplomatic Service*, Durham: Duke University Press, 1979, p. 149.
15. Ibid., p. 152.
16. Ibid., p. 150.
17. Keith Hamilton and Richard Langhorne, *The Practice of Diplomacy: Its Evolution, Theory and Administration*, London: Routledge, 1995, p. 108.
18. Dame Lillian Penson, *Foreign Affairs under the Third Marquis of Salisbury, The Creighton Lecture in History 1960*, London: The Athlone Press, 1962.
19. There was a noticeable decline in interception and deciphering of British diplomatic correspondence in the second half of the nineteenth century as they made greater use of the diplomatic bag. In France, Russia, and the Habsburg Empire, deciphering was even more widespread and each had its cabinet noir. See Anderson, *The Rise of Modern Diplomacy 1450–1919*, pp. 116–17.
20. Penson, *Foreign Affairs under the Third Marquis of Salisbury*.
21. Hamilton and Langhorne, *The Practice of Diplomacy*, p. 98.
22. Ibid., pp. 90–1.
23. Paul Gordon Lauren, *Diplomats and Bureaucrats: The First Institutional Responses to Twentieth-Century Diplomacy in France and Germany*, Stanford, CA: Hoover Institution Press, 1976, p. 3.
24. Anderson, *The Rise of Modern Diplomacy 1450–1919*, p. 114.
25. Ibid., pp. 114–15.
26. These lowest ranking diplomats were finally paid in Britain in 1904. Hamilton and Langhorne, *The Practice of Diplomacy*, p. 108.
27. Lauren, *Diplomats and Bureaucrats*, p. 28.
28. Anderson, *The Rise of Modern Diplomacy 1450–1919*, p. 121.
29. Lauren, *Diplomats and Bureaucrats*.
30. Hamilton and Langhorne, *The Practice of Diplomacy*, p. 96.
31. Disraeli wrote to his Queen that he witnessed Gorchakov leaning on Bismarck as they were walking with Bismarck's dog. Bismarck was overcome with a coughing fit and fell, causing the weak Gorchakov to fall on top of him. Bismarck's dog started attacking Gorchakov out of concern for his master underneath and Bismarck had to immediately save his friend from the dog; but only after Bismarck himself had recovered from his attack of rheumatism. Hesketh Pearson, *Dizzy: A Life of Benjamin Disraeli*, London: Penguin Books, 2001, p. 248.
32. Hamilton and Langhorne, *The Practice of Diplomacy*, p. 105.
33. Ibid.
34. Letter from Bismarck to Bülow, 14 August 1876. E.T.S. Dugdale, "The Bismarck Period." *German Diplomatic Documents 1871–1914*, New York: European University Institute, 1928, p. 24.
35. Anderson, *The Rise of Modern Diplomacy 1450–1919*, p. 126.
36. Mr Gladstone to Lord Granville, 20 August 1876, *The Political Correspondence of Mr. Gladstone and Lord Granville 1876–1886*, p. 1.
37. Hastings Eells, "Recent Progress in Science." *Europe Since 1500*, New York: Henry Holt and Company, 1933.
38. G.D. Clayton, *Britain and the Eastern Question: Missolonghi to Gallipoli*, London: Lion Library, 1971. Part V.

39. David Harris, *Britain and the Bulgarian Horrors of 1876*, Chicago: University of Chicago Press, 1939, p. 25.
40. George Earle Buckle, ed., *The Letters of Queen Victoria (Second Series) A Selection from Her Majesty's Correspondence and Journal between the Years 1862–1878*, Vol. 2, London: His Majesty the King, London: Murray, 1926, p. 622.
41. Hamilton and Langhorne, *The Practice of Diplomacy*, p. 90.
42. "Peace at any price" was what Gladstone, leader of the Liberal party in Britain, and Lord Derby, Secretary of State, fought for.
43. Charles Dunlop, *Beaconsfield Brilliants: Being Choice Selections from the Speeches and Works of the Late Benjamin Disraeli, Earl of Beaconsfield*. London: Bates, Hendy and Co., 1881(?), p. 8.
44. *Hansard's Parliamentary Debates*, Vol. 240, 16 May–20 June 1878, London: Cornelius Buck, 1878, pp. 721–2.
45. For a good, quick survey of the events leading to the Congress of Berlin, see A.J.P. Taylor, *The Struggle for Mastery in Europe 1848–1918*, Oxford: Clarendon Press, 1954, pp. 228–54; or Clayton, *Britain and the Eastern Question*.
46. R.T. Shannon, *Gladstone and the Bulgarian Agitation 1876*. 2nd ed. Sussex, UK: The Harvester Press, 1975, p. 22.
47. Taylor, *The Struggle for Mastery in Europe 1848–1918*, p. 235.
48. For a concise analysis of this alliance, see Wrigley, Chris, ed. *Struggles for Supremacy: Diplomatic Essays by A.J.P. Taylor*, Aldershot, UK: Ashgate, 2000, Chapter 5.
49. Historical Section of the Foreign Office. *Foreign Policy of Austria-Hungary*, Vol. 1, *Foreign Office Historical Handbooks*, London: H.M. Stationery Office, 1920, p. 73.
50. In hindsight, the Russian leaders regretted this move fueled by popular opinion and wished they had acted according to geostrategic interests alone. This is an example of how states may want to behave according to realist principles, but are often persuaded by other concerns.
51. *Hansard's Parliamentary Debates*, p. 1057.
52. R.W. Seton-Watson, *Disraeli, Gladstone and the Eastern Question: A Study in Diplomacy and Party Politics*, London: Macmillan and Co., Limited, 1935, p. 433.
53. At first, the Queen did not even want him to attend the congress for fear of his old age and poor health, but her son convinced her to let him go describing him as "not only the right man to represent us at the Congress, but the only man who can go, as he will show Russia and the other Powers that we were really in earnest." See J. Pudney and Lord Sudley, Trans. "Further Letters of Queen Victoria from the Archives of the House of Brandenburg-Prussia." London, 1938, p. 230.
54. He resigned shortly after his return to Austria, though he later regained his health and popularity during the 1880s.
55. Seton-Watson, *Disraeli, Gladstone and the Eastern Question*, p. 438.
56. Letter from Prince Bismarck to Bülow, Foreign Minister, 14 August 1876. Dugdale, "The Bismarck Period." p. 23.
57. Seton-Watson, *Disraeli, Gladstone and the Eastern Question*, pp. 433–6.
58. René Albrecht-Carrié, *A Diplomatic History of Europe since the Congress of Vienna*. Revised ed., New York: Harper & Row, Publishers, 1973, p. 176.
59. B.H. Sumner, *Russia and the Balkans 1870–80*, London: Archon Books, 1962, p. 511. Translated by Mai'a K. Davis Cross, from French.
60. The importance of Bismarck's relationship to Andrássy will be discussed further.
61. Joseph Vincent Fuller, *Bismarck's Diplomacy at Its Zenith*, Cambridge: Harvard University Press, 1922, p. 7 (text and footnote).
62. Penson, *Foreign Affairs under the Third Marquis of Salisbury*, p. 2.
63. Buckle, *The Letters of Queen Victoria (Second Series)*.

64. Queen Victoria to the Earl of Derby 10 February 1878. Ibid.
65. To characterize the relationship between Queen Victoria and Disraeli: The Queen wrote to Lord Rowton when Disraeli died, "Never had I so kind and devoted a Minister and very few such devoted friends. His affectionate sympathy, his wise counsel – all were invaluable to me even out of office... the bitterness and suffering are not the less severe." Blake, Robert, *Gladstone, Disraeli, and Queen Victoria*, The Centenary Romanes Lecture, Delivered before the University of Oxford on 10 November 1992. Oxford: Clarendon Press, 1992, pp. 3–4. Disraeli wrote to her during the lead-up to the congress, "He feels there is no devotion that your Majesty does not deserve, and he only wishes he had youth and energy to be the fitting champion of such an inspiring Mistress as your Majesty.... He lives only for Her, and works only for Her, and without Her all is lost." Pearson, *Dizzy: A Life of Benjamin Disraeli*, p. 246.
66. Despite their strongly and heatedly opposed stances, Gladstone recognized Disraeli's contribution at Berlin. On 9 May 1881, less than a month after Disraeli's death, Gladstone is reported as saying to parliament, "The career of Lord Beaconsfield was in many respects the most remarkable and the most surprising in our Parliamentary history, and especially he dwelt on his connection with the last measure of Parliamentary reform, and the magnitude of the part he played in the great transactions of Berlin." See Dunlop, *Beaconsfield Brilliants*, p. 2.
67. Seton-Watson, *Disraeli, Gladstone and the Eastern Question*, p. 379.
68. For a transcript of the April 1 Circular, see Harold Temperley and Dame Lillian Penson, *Foundations of British Foreign Policy from Pitt (1792) to Salisbury (1902)*, Cambridge: Cambridge University Press, 1938, pp. 372–80.
69. David Steele, *Lord Salisbury: A Political Biography*, London: UCL Press, 1999, p. 106.
70. Ibid., p. 108.
71. Seton-Watson, *Disraeli, Gladstone and the Eastern Question*, p. 435.
72. Ibid., p. 379.
73. Pearson, *Dizzy: A Life of Benjamin Disraeli*, p. 249.
74. Taylor, *The Struggle for Mastery in Europe 1848–1918*, p. 231.
75. Julius Andrássy, *Bismarck, Andrássy, and Their Successors*, London: T. Fisher Unwin Ltd, 1927, p. 15.
76. Julius Andrássy, *Diplomacy and the War*, translated by J. Holroyd Reece, London: John Bale, Sons & Danielsson, Ltd, 1921, p. 12.
77. Andrássy, *Bismarck, Andrássy, and Their Successors*, p. 19. This sovereign had ended the independence of the Magyars.
78. Mason, John W., *The Dissolution of the Austro-Hungarian Empire 1867–1918*. 2nd ed. *Seminar Studies in History*, London: Longman, 1997, p. 54.
79. Andrássy, *Diplomacy and the War*.
80. Mason, *The Dissolution of the Austro-Hungarian Empire 1867–1918*, p. xiii.
81. Andrássy, *Diplomacy and the War*, pp. 12–13.
82. George Hoover Rupp, *A Wavering Friendship: Russia and Austria 1876–1878*, Philadelphia: Porcupine Press, 1976, Appendix I.
83. David Harris, *A Diplomatic History of the Balkan Crisis of 1875–1878: The First Year*, Hoover War Library Publications – No. 11. Stanford, CA: Stanford University Press, 1936, p. 291.
84. Andrássy, *Bismarck, Andrássy, and Their Successors*, p. 20.
85. Ibid. For a good comparison of the personalities of Bismarck and Andrássy. pp. 40–53.
86. W.N. Mendlicott, *The Congress of Berlin and After: A Diplomatic History of the near Eastern Settlement 1878–1880*, London: Frank Cass & Co. Ltd, 1963, p. 143.

87. Historical Section of the Foreign Office, *The Congress of Berlin*, Vol. 167, *Foreign Office Historical Handbooks*, London, February 1919, p. 24.
88. Andrássy, *Bismarck, Andrássy, and Their Successors*, p. 17.
89. Seton-Watson, *Disraeli, Gladstone and the Eastern Question*, pp. 440–1.
90. Andrássy, *Bismarck, Andrássy, and Their Successors*, p. 18.
91. Count Waddington's Telegram of 18 June 1878. Archives des Affaires Étrangères, "Mémoires et documents, Bulgarie." In Ministry of Foreign Affairs, Paris, 1878–91.
92. The third plenipotentiary, M. d'Oubril, served to bridge the gap between his two rival colleagues.
93. Historical Section of the Foreign Office, *The Congress of Berlin*, p. 28.
94. Sumner, *Russia and the Balkans 1870–80*, p. 501.
95. Lord Granville to Mr. Gladstone, 20 December 1877, *The Political Correspondence of Mr. Gladstone and Lord Granville 1876–1886*, pp. 62–3.
96. Archives des Affaires Étrangères, "Mémoires Et Documents, Bulgarie." Translation of "Monsieur le Ministre et Cher Président, Je suis arrivé à Berlin le 10 de ce mois et dès le lendemain, grâce aux dispositions prises par Mr Le Cte de St. Vallier, j'ai pu immédiatement entrer en rapports avec le haut personnel du Gouvernement Allemand." 14 June 1878.
97. Ibid., *Letter*, 18 June 1878.
98. Ibid., 11 July.
99. Correspondence Relating to the Congress of Berlin, with the Protocols of the Congress. Vol. 83ii, Accounts and Papers 1878, Turkey. No. 39. London: Harrison and Sons, 1878. Protocols.
100. Robert Taylor, *Lord Salisbury*, London: British Political Biography, 1975, p. 63.
101. Sumner, *Russia and the Balkans 1870–80*, p. 512.
102. Ibid., pp. 512–13.
103. German Crown Princess to Queen Victoria, 13 July 1878. *The Letters of Queen Victoria (Second Series)*, p. 628.
104. Historical Section of the Foreign Office, *The Congress of Berlin*, p. 25.
105. A.H. Layard, "Confidential Print. Turkey. 20 April–15 Aug 1878. MSS 39149." Telegraphic, 1 July 1878, Layard to Salisbury.
106. Ibid., Telegraphic, 11 July 1878, Layard to Salisbury.
107. Ibid., Telegraphic Therapia, 17 July 1878. Layard to Salisbury.
108. A.H. Layard, "Confidential Print. Turkey 17 March–5 June 1878. MSS 39148." Marquis of Salisbury first telegraph to Layard, 2 April 1878.
109. A.H. Layard, "Confidential Print. Turkey. Apr.–June 1877. MSS 39144." Telegraphic, Mr. Layard to the Earl of Derby, 24 April 1877.
110. Ibid., Layard to Derby, 25 April 1877.
111. Wrigley, ed., *Struggles for Supremacy*, Chapter 5.
112. Harris, *A Diplomatic History of the Balkan Crisis*, Chapter 6, "The Berlin Memorandum."
113. Gerard J. Mangone, *A Short History of International Organization*, New York: McGraw-Hill Book Company, Inc., 1954, p. 57.
114. Ibid., p. 57.

5 The early twentieth century and the Treaty of Versailles

1. Keith Hamilton and Richard Langhorne, *The Practice of Diplomacy: Its Evolution, Theory and Administration*, London: Routledge, 1995, p. 136.

2. Ibid., p. 168.
3. José Calvet De, Magalhaes, *The Pure Concept of Diplomacy*, translated by Bernardo Futscher Pereira, *Global Perspectives in History and Politics*, Westport, CT: Greenwood Press, 1988, p. 48. He argues against the efficacy of direct negotiations across history.
4. Stefan Zweig, *The World of Yesterday, an Autobiography*, New York: The Viking Press, 1943, p. 223.
5. Gordon A. Craig, and Felix Gilbert, *The Diplomats: 1919–1939*, Princeton, NJ: Princeton University Press, 1953, p. 17.
6. Magalhaes, *The Pure Concept of Diplomacy*, pp. 33–4.
7. M.S. Anderson, *The Rise of Modern Diplomacy 1450–1919*, London and New York: Longman, 1993, p. 103.
8. Lamar Cecil, *The German Diplomatic Service, 1871–1914*, Princeton, NJ: Princeton University Press, 1976, p. 322.
9. Ibid., p. 320.
10. Anderson, *The Rise of Modern Diplomacy 1450–1919*, p. 110.
11. Zara S. Steiner, *The Foreign Office and Foreign Policy, 1898–1914*, London: The Ashfield Press, 1969, p. 174.
12. Ibid., p. 175.
13. Ephraim Maisel, *The Foreign Office and Foreign Policy, 1919–1926*, Brighton, UK: Sussex Academic Press, 1994, p. 12.
14. Ibid., p. 14.
15. Raymond A. Jones, *The British Diplomatic Service 1815–1914*, Waterloo, Ontario: Wilfrid Laurier University Press, 1983, p. 171.
16. Craig and Gilbert, *The Diplomats: 1919–1939*, p. 50.
17. Ibid., p. 51.
18. Jones, *The British Diplomatic Service 1815–1914*, p. 139.
19. Anderson, *The Rise of Modern Diplomacy 1450–1919*, p. 121.
20. Cecil, *The German Diplomatic Service, 1871–1914*.
21. Ibid., p. 49.
22. Walter Sharp, *French Civil Service: Bureaucracy in Transition*, New York: Macmillan, 1931, p. 12.
23. Jones, *The British Diplomatic Service, 1815–1914*, p. 143.
24. Ibid., p. 159.
25. Cecil, *The German Diplomatic Service, 1871–1914*, p. 21.
26. Ibid.
27. Jones, *The British Diplomatic Service 1815–1914*, p. 168.
28. Steiner, *The Foreign Office and Foreign Policy, 1898–1914*.
29. Cecil, *The German Diplomatic Service, 1871–1914*, p. 27.
30. King Edward was easily swayed by personalities and networking relationships. After 1901 many of the diplomatic appointments were based on personal friendships with the King. For example, Charles Hardinge and Francis Bertie were known to exploit their relationship with the King to secure appointments that they wanted. Lord Hardinge used his influence with the King to get an appointment in London in 1903 and gain a more influential position at Court. He was later appointed to St Petersburg in February 1904, and Bertie got a Paris appointment in August of the same year.
31. In Britain, the autonomy granted to individual diplomats declined from its high point in the late nineteenth century, but diplomats sent to smaller countries had more autonomy than others. For example, the British ambassadors in Peking, Morocco, Persia, and Tokyo had more autonomy than those in Paris, Berlin, and Vienna. While interesting theories may be drawn about the relationship between

autonomy and distance from the capital, regional European diplomacy was not affected by this phenomenon.
32. Jones, *The British Diplomatic Service 1815–1914*, p. 196.
33. Craig and Gilbert, *The Diplomats: 1919–1939*, p. 58.
34. Hamilton and Langhorne, *The Practice of Diplomacy*, p. 167.
35. Craig and Gilbert, *The Diplomats: 1919–1939*, p. 60.
36. Cecil, *The German Diplomatic Service, 1871–1914*, p. 9.
37. Ibid., p. 11.
38. Anderson, *The Rise of Modern Diplomacy 1450–1919*, p. 121.
39. Hamilton and Langhorne, *The Practice of Diplomacy*, pp. 246–7.
40. See Lord Strang, *The Foreign Office*, London: George Allen & Unwin Ltd, 1957, p. 35.
41. Hajo Holborn, "World War, World Settlement and the Aftermath." In *The Versailles Settlement: Was It Foredoomed to Failure?* edited by Lederer, Ivo J.; *Problems in European Civilization*, edited by Ralph W. Greenlaw, Boston: D.C. Heath and Company, 1960.
42. H.M.V. Temperley, *A History of the Peace Conference of Paris*, Vol. 1, London: Oxford University Press, 1920. Footnote, p. 245. This figure is from the French official Composition et Fonctionnement of 1 April 1919, counting the number of delegates, not including plenipotentiaries. It was not a complete count.
43. F.S. Marston, *The Peace Conference of 1919: Organization and Procedure*, London: Oxford University Press, 1944, p. 10.
44. Temperley, *A History of the Peace Conference of Paris*, pp. 250–1.
45. The translator present at Council of Four meetings did manage to provide a thorough text of the meetings post-facto. Paul Mantoux, *The Deliberations of the Council of Four (24 March–28 June 1919)*, translated by Arthur S. Link, Vol. 1, Princeton, NJ: Princeton University Press, 1992.
46. Clifford R. Lovin, *A School for Diplomats: The Paris Peace Conference of 1919*, Lanham, MD: University Press of America, 1997, p. 5.
47. These criticisms are mentioned by many scholars, but particularly conform to the emphasis of Harold Nicolson. See Harold Nicolson, *Peacemaking*, London: Oxford University Press, 1933.
48. Ibid., p. 82.
49. André Tardieu, *The Truth about the Treaty*, London: Hodder and Stoughton, 1921, pp. 88–93.
50. Whether democratically elected leaders should negotiate treaties and participate in all international decision-making is a debate that continues today in reference to the EU. One source of the "democratic deficit" is the fact that nonelected officials engage in a great deal of decision-making.
51. William R. Keylor, "Versailles and International Diplomacy." In *The Treaty of Versailles: A Reassessment after 75 Years*, edited by Manfred F. boemeke, Gerald D. Feldman, and Elisabeth Glaser. German Historical Institute, Washington DC: Cambridge University Press, 1998, p. 481.
52. The same is said of Woodrow Wilson. See Edward Mandell House and Charles Seymour, eds, *What Really Happened at Paris: The Story of the Peace Conference, 1918–1919*, New York: Charles Scribner's Sons, 1921. However, Clemenceau does not have a similar reputation.
53. Anthony Lentin, *Lloyd George and the Lost Peace: From Versailles to Hitler, 1919–1940*, New York: Palgrave, 2001, p. 4.
54. Charles L. Mee Jr, *The End of Order: Versailles 1919*, New York: Elsevier-Dutton Publishing Co., Inc., 1980.

55. Maisel, *The Foreign Office and Foreign Policy, 1919–1926*, p. 91.
56. Arno J. Mayer, *Politics and Diplomacy of Peacemaking: Containment and Counterrevolution at Versailles, 1918–1919*, New York: Alfred A. Knopf, 1967, p. 775.
57. Temperley, *A History of the Peace Conference of Paris*, p. 243.
58. Maisel, *The Foreign Office and Foreign Policy, 1919–1926*, p. 54.
59. James Headlam-Morley, *A Memoir of the Paris Peace Conference 1919*, London: Methuen, 1972, p. xxiv.
60. Ibid., p. 4.
61. Mee Jr, *The End of Order*.
62. See Michael L. Dockrill and Douglas J. Goold, *Peace without Promise: Britain and the Peace Conferences, 1919–23*, Hamden, CT: Archon Books, 1981, p. 32.
63. Nicolson, *Peacemaking*, pp. 196–7.
64. Charles Seymour, *Letters from the Paris Peace Conference*, New Haven, CT: Yale University Press, 1965, p. 44.
65. Ibid., p. 256.
66. Ibid., p. 273.
67. The whole event also served as a reunion for the Harvard class of 1915 as most of the diplomats graduated in the same class.
68. Mayer, *Politics and Diplomacy of Peacemaking*, p. 767.
69. Lovin, *A School for Diplomats*, p. 63.
70. Ibid., p. 67.
71. Mayer, *Politics and Diplomacy of Peacemaking*, p. 770.
72. Temperley, *A History of the Peace Conference of Paris*, p. 270.
73. Tardieu, *The Truth about the Treaty*, p. 97.
74. Clive Day, "The Atmosphere and Organization of the Peace Conference." In *What Really Happened at Paris: The Story of the Peace Conference, 1918–1919*, edited by Edward Mandell House and Charles Seymour. New York: Charles Scribner's Sons, 1921, pp. 33–4.
75. Ibid., p. 26.
76. Temperley, *A History of the Peace Conference of Paris*, p. 244.
77. E.J. Dillon, *The Inside Story of the Peace Conference*, New York: Harper & Brothers Publishers, 1920, pp. 102–3.
78. Nicolson, *Peacemaking*, p. 106.
79. Ibid., p. 107.
80. Ibid., p. 348.
81. Maisel, *The Foreign Office and Foreign Policy, 1919–1926*, p. 91.
82. Lovin, *A School for Diplomats*, pp. 4–5.

6 The late twentieth century and the Treaty on European Union

1. Peter Marshall, *Positive Diplomacy*, London: Macmillan Press, 1997, p. 167.
2. Ibid., Chapter 8.
3. Chris Moncrieff and Geoff Meade, *The Press Association*, 1 July 1992, Home News.
4. Philippa Sherrington, *The Council of Ministers: Political Authority in the European Union*, London: Pinter, 2000, p. 45.
5. Some exceptions include Fiona Hayes-Renshaw and Helen Wallace, *The Council of Ministers*, London: Macmillan Press Ltd, 1997; Neill Nugent (ed.), *At the Heart of the Union: Studies of the European Commission*, 2nd ed. London: Macmillan Press Ltd, 1997; and Jan Beyers and Guido Dierickx, "The Working Groups of the Council of

the European Union: Supranational or Intergovernmental Negotiations?" *Journal of Common Market Studies* 36, no. 3 (1998): 259–317.
6. "Democratic deficit" is defined as a lack of open and transparent processes in EU institutions when compared to the standards of democratic processes in domestic institutions.
7. Jaap W. de Zwaan, *The Permanent Representatives Committee: Its Role in European Union Decision-Making*, Amsterdam: Elsevier, 1995. Dissertations by Jeffrey Lewis and Fiona Hayes-Renshaw.
8. "The Power-House." *The Economist*, 8 March 1997, 62.
9. For example, Jeffrey Lewis, "Is the 'Hard Bargaining' Image of the Council Misleading? The Committee of Permanent Representatives and the Local Elections Directive." *Journal of Common Market Studies* 36, no. 4 (1998): 479–504; Beyers and Dierickx, "The Working Groups of the Council of the European Union"; and Hayes-Renshaw and Wallace, *The Council of Ministers*.
10. Sarah Helm, "The 15 Men Who Run Europe on Our Behalf; EU/the Real Decision-Makers." *The Independent*, 18 June 1995, 17.
11. Andrew Moravcsik and Kalypso Nicolaïdis, "Explaining the Treaty of Amsterdam: Interests, Influence, Institutions." *Journal of Common Market Studies* 37, no. 1 (1999): 59–85.
12. Personal Communication, September 2004. Poul S. Christoffersen is currently the Danish ambassador to Italy in Rome. He was Secretary General of the Council of Ministers 1980–95, and the Danish Permanent Representative to the EU 1995–2003.
13. For a good overview of the structure of Coreper, see Christopher Bright, *The EU: Understanding the Brussels Process*, Colorado Springs: Wiley Law Publications, 1995, p. 18.
14. The Council of the European Union (the Council) should not be confused with the Council of Europe, a non-EU institution in Strasbourg, and the European Council, which is a summit forum for policy formulation that meets twice per year.
15. Sherrington, *The Council of Ministers*, p. 47.
16. With the 2004 enlargement from 15 to 25 member states, the Commission and Parliament lag behind Coreper in terms of assimilation of the new members. Among other things, there is a lack of translators to handle the new official languages of the EU and many new Commission delegations cannot understand the proceedings. By contrast, in Coreper, assimilation was rapid and the language barrier did not pose a problem since professional diplomats all speak English. Ambassador Tranholm said, "In Coreper, the enlargement has taken place and has been carried through, but in most parts of union it is not a reality. In Coreper, the new members have become fully integrated. There are no language barriers, these are professional diplomats" (Interview).
17. Jeffrey Lewis, "The Methods of Community in EU Decision-Making and Administrative Rivalry in the Council's Infrastructure." *Journal of European Public Policy* 7, no. 2 (2000): 261–89.
18. Ibid., p. 265.
19. This statistic is from Hayes-Renshaw and Wallace, *The Council of Ministers*. Other scholars argue that as much as 90 percent of the Council's work is accomplished at the working group level. For a summary of data pertaining to working groups, see Beyers and Dierickx, "The Working Groups of the Council of the European Union."
20. Martin Westlake, *The Council of the European Union*, London: Cartermill International Ltd, 1995, p. 312.

21. David Spence, "Foreign Ministries in National and European Context." In *Foreign Ministries: Change and Adaptation*, edited by Brian Hocking. New York: St. Martin's Press, 1999, pp. 247–68.
22. Subsidiarity means that if the policy is best tackled by regional or national government, it should not be brought to the EC level. Decisions should be taken at the lowest level of government possible.
23. Ibid., Introduction.
24. Paulette Enjalran and Philippe Husson, "France the Ministry of Foreign Affairs: 'Something New, But Which Is the Legitimate Continuation of Our Past. . . .'" in *Foreign Ministries: Change and Adaptation*, edited by Brian Hocking. New York: St. Martin's Press, 1999, pp. 59–74.
25. See http://europa.eu.int/institutions/council/index_en.htm for the most current vote weighting information.
26. Fiona Hayes-Renshaw and Helen Wallace, "Executive Power in the European Union: The Functions and Limits of the Council of Ministers." *Journal of European Public Policy* 2, no. 4 (1995): 565.
27. It is important to note that consensus decision systems have become commonplace in most international organizations. However, Ambassador Christoffersen writes that with enlargement, the consensus mechanism becomes more difficult and majority voting may take over a greater percentage of the decision-making process going forward (Personal Communication, September 2004).
28. Ton Heukels and Jaap de Zwaan, "The Configuration of the European Union." In *Institutional Dynamics of European Integration: Essays in Honour of Henry G. Schermers*, Vol. 2, edited by Dierdre Curtin and Ton Heukels. Boston: Martinus Nijhoff, 1994, pp. 195–228.
29. Zwaan, *The Permanent Representatives Committee*, p. 15.
30. Ibid.
31. Sean Flynn, "Windfall in Structural Funds Now under Threat." *The Irish Times*, 23 September 1992, City Edition, 8.
32. Edward C. Page, *People Who Run Europe*, Oxford: Clarendon Press, 1997, p. 71. Data drawn from The European Companion (1992, 1993).
33. The Versailles Treaty was negotiated by diplomats from Harvard class of 1915 and École Libre des Sciences Politiques.
34. Danish Ambassador Tranholm, personal interview, 11 October 2004.
35. Fiona Hayes-Renshaw, C. Lequesne, and P.M. Lopez, "The Permanent Representations of the Member States to the European Communities." *Journal of Common Market Studies* 38, no. 2 (1989): 119–37; Page, *People Who Run Europe*.
36. This differs from the American ambassadors, who are usually appointed from outside of the diplomatic corps. Interestingly, unlike in the past, the European ambassadors do not need to bring a letter of credence to their posts in Brussels. They are afforded the same privileges, immunities, and diplomatic status as in the past.
37. Zwaan, *The Permanent Representatives Committee*, p. 15.
38. Danish Ambassador Tranholm, personal interview, 11 October 2004.
39. Tranholm interview, 11 October 2004.
40. French Ambassador Masset, personal interview, 11 October 2004.
41. Anderson, personal interview.
42. Page, *People Who Run Europe*, p. 69.
43. Ibid., p. 73. Data drawn from The European Companion (1992, 1993).
44. François de Callières, *On the Manner of Negotiating with Princes*, Boston: Houghton Mifflin Co., 1919.

45. Thomas Risse, " 'Let's Argue!': Communicative Action in World Politics." *International Organization* 54, no. 1 (2000): 1–39.
46. Anne-Marie Burley and Walter Mattli, "Europe before the Court: A Political Theory of Legal Integration." *International Organization* 47, no. 1 (1993): 41–76. They cite Ernst Haas in regards to shifting loyalties.
47. See Nugent, ed., *At the Heart of the Union.*
48. Sherrington, *The Council of Ministers*, p. 46.
49. Irish Ambassador Gunning, personal interview, 12 October 2004.
50. Personal Interview, Brussels, 11 October 2004.
51. Personal Interview, Brussels.
52. Personal Interview, Ambassador Anderson, 13 October 2004.
53. Ibid.
54. For the exact wording of the credentials, see John Dickie, *Inside the Foreign Office*, London: Chapmans, 1992, pp. 12–13.
55. Westlake, *The Council of the European Union*, p. 320.
56. "The Power-House."
57. Irish Ambassador Gunning, personal interview, 12 October 2004.
58. See M.S. Anderson, *The Rise of Modern Diplomacy 1450–1919*, London and New York: Longman, 1993.
59. Personal Interview, March 2004.
60. Personal Communication, September 2004.
61. Zwaan, *The Permanent Representatives Committee*, p. 192.
62. Personal Communication, September 2004.
63. Zwaan, *The Permanent Representatives Committee*, p. 193.
64. Personal Communication, Ejner Stendevad, 24 April 2004.
65. Article 48 of the EU Treaty stipulates that a member state or the Commission can initiate an IGC by submitting a proposal to the Council. The Council, in consultation with the Parliament and the Commission, then decides whether or not to hold the IGC. The President of the Council convenes the conference, Coreper performs the preparatory work, and the foreign ministers conduct the preliminary decision-making. The heads of state have final ratification and negotiation power.
66. European Documents 9431/90.
67. Immigration came under the umbrella of "questions of common interest," which dealt also with political asylum, employment and residency rights, narcotics, terrorism, and Europol.
68. Finn Laursen and Sophie Vanhoonacker, eds, *The Intergovernmental Conference on Political Union: Institutional Reforms, New Policies and International Identity of the European Community*, European Institute of Public Administration. Leiden, The Netherlands: Martinus Nijhoff Publishers, 1992.
69. The Greek Prime Minister threatened to veto if Greece did not gain membership in the Western European Union (WEU). Denmark and Ireland were also excluded from membership. The concern with Greece was that it may bring the WEU into conflict with Turkey.
70. Edward Mortimer. "European Union Advocated." *Financial Times*, 16 January 1989, 3.
71. Personal Communication, Poul S. Christoffersen, September 2004.
72. The foreign ministers approved the Treaty on 7 February 1992. After the Maastricht summit, the treaty was approved by all member states in August 1993.
73. Laursen and Vanhoonacker, eds, *The Intergovernmental Conference*, p. 18.
74. Westlake, *The Council of the European Union*, p. 298.
75. Interview, October 2004.

76. Documents provided by the General Secretariat of the Council of the European Union. Through special consideration, they granted access to these documents despite the thirty-year rule that typically determines declassification of documents (i.e., Once the documents are more than thirty years old, they are declassified).
77. Gerda Falkner, "How Intergovernmental are Intergovernmental Conferences? An Example from the Maastricht Treaty Reform." *Journal of European Public Policy* 9, no. 1 (2002): 98–119.
78. Colette Mazzucelli, *France and Germany at Maastricht: Politics and Negotiations to Create the European Union*, New York: Garland Publishing, Inc., 1997, p. 70.
79. EU Documents 6356/90.
80. EU Documents 9046/90 Annex.
81. Fonblanque Letter, 25 September 1990, EU Documents 521497.
82. EU Documents 5519/90, 21 March 1990.
83. Ibid.
84. Fonblanque Letter 521497.
85. EU Documents 8724/1/90 Revtrat 12, p. 10.
86. EU Documents 9233/90 Revtrat 16: 2.
87. European Documents 9233/90 Add 1, Revtrat 16, Annex 1.
88. Ibid., Annex 2.
89. EU Documents 10356/90, Add 1.
90. On 23 October 1990, the Commission represented by Jacques Delors also contributed to the debate, writing to the President of the Council, Gianni De Michelis. Under Article 23, they proposed calling a conference of member states to amend the treaty and incorporate political union. They explicitly agreed to the goal of establishing a common foreign policy which would include security, with the aim of taking a "flexible and pragmatic approach."
91. Ibid., Annex 3.
92. Ibid., Annex 4.
93. Ibid.
94. Ibid., Annex 5.
95. Ibid.
96. EU Documents 10356/90, p. 14.
97. EU Documents SN 1030/91 (UP).
98. Ibid., Annex I, "Implementation of a Common Security."
99. EU Documents CONF-UP 1720/91 Annex.
100. EU Documents CONF-UP 1777/91 Annex, p. 34.
101. Jacques Lhuillery, "'Federal' Row Revives Doubts over Dutch Tenure of EC Presidency." *Agence France Presse*, 4 December 1991.
102. John Palmer, "Federalists Set to Leave Britain in Cold." *The Guardian*, 19 November 1991.
103. EU Documents CONF_UP 1858/91. NOTE from the Presidency.
104. Ibid.
105. "European Defence: Initial Rapprochement among the Twelve." *European Information Service*, 28 March 1991, 5.
106. "Political Union: UK Proposes Taking Foreign Policy Decisions on a Case-by-Case Basis." *Europe Information Service*, 20 July 1991, 2.
107. "Political Union: Ministers Move Ahead Inch by Inch." *Europe Information Service*, 26 November 1991.
108. "Political Union: A Week before Maastricht, Compromise Begins to Emerge." *European Information Service*, 30 November 1991, 4.

109. Anonymous, personal interview.
110. See "EC Finance Ministers Meet on EMU Transition Compromise." *Agence France Presse*, 19 September 1991.
111. For example, the Netherlands dropped a directive on working hours because the UK threatened to veto a range of compromises at Maastricht.
112. John Eisenhammer, "Germany's True Believer Who Will Not Be Fobbed Off." *The Independent*, 28 June 1991, 10.
113. Ibid.
114. Andrew Duff, John Pinder, and Roy Pryce, eds, *Maastricht and Beyond*, London: Routledge, 1994.
115. Elizabeth Pond, "German Unification and Maastricht, 1989–93." *The Rebirth of Europe*, Washington, DC: Brookings Institution Press, 1999, p. 39.
116. "European Community; Thunder Off." *The Economist*, 12 September 1992, 48.
117. Laursen and Vanhoonacker, eds, *The Intergovernmental Conference*, p. 22.
118. Ibid., p. 46.
119. David Buchan, "Pugnacious Major Outshines His Counterparts – The UK Prime Minister Impressed, the Italian One Slept, the French President 'Was Just Plain out of It.'" *Financial Times*, 12 December 1991, 2.
120. Ibid.
121. John Palmer, "The Road to Maastricht: The Dapper Scot with a Firm Hand on the Minister's Elbow – Key Player: Sir John Kerr." *The Guardian*, 2 December 1991.
122. "European Community; Thunder Off." p. 48.
123. Robert Rice and David Owen, "Maastricht Ratified as Rees-Mogg Bows Out." *Financial Times*, 3 August 1993, 6.
124. Personal Correspondence, 2004.
125. Thomas D. Zweifel, "Who Is Without Sin Cast the First Stone: The EU's Democratic Deficit in Comparison." *Journal of European Public Policy* 9, no. 6 (2002): 812–40.
126. Fiona Hayes-Renshaw, "The Role of the Committee of Permanent Representatives in the Decision-Making Process of the European Community." PhD dissertation, University of London, 1990, Chapter 7.
127. Personal Communication, September 2004.

7 The twenty-first century European corps

1. Andrew Moravcsik and Kalypso Nicolaïdis, "Explaining the Treaty of Amsterdam: Interests, Influence, Institutions." *Journal of Common Market Studies* 37, no. 1 (1999): 59–85; and Nicole Gnesotto, "Introduction ESDP: Results and Prospects." In *EU Security and Defence Policy: The First Five Years (1999–2004)*, edited by Nicole Gnesotto. Paris: EU Institute for Security Studies, 2004.
2. Gnesotto, "Introduction ESDP: Results and Prospects." p. 19.
3. Javier Solana, "Preface." In *EU Security and Defence Policy: The First Five Years*, edited by Nicole Gnesotto. Paris: EU Institute for Security Studies, 2004.
4. Gnesotto, "Introduction ESDP: Results and Prospects." p. 20.
5. Suleiman, Ezra, *Dismantling Democratic States*, Princeton, NJ: Princeton University Press, 2003.
6. Thomas D. Zweifel, "Who Is Without Sin Cast the First Stone: The EU's Democratic Deficit in Comparison." *Journal of European Public Policy* 9, no. 6 (2002): 812–40.

Bibliography

Abbott, Kenneth W., Robert O. Keohane, Andrew Moravcsik, and Duncan Snidal. "The Concept of Legalization." *International Organization* 54, no. 3 (2000): 401–19.
Adler, Emanuel, and Peter M. Haas. "Conclusion: Epistemic Communities, World Order, and the Creation of a Reflective Research Program." *International Organization* 46, no. 1 (1992): 367–90.
Albrecht-Carrié, René. *A Diplomatic History of Europe since the Congress of Vienna.* Revised ed. New York: Harper & Row Publishers, 1973.
Alcide, Ebray. *A Frenchman Looks at the Peace.* Translated by E.W. Dickes. New York: Alfred A. Knopf, 1927.
Anderson, M.S. *The Eastern Question 1774–1923: A Study in International Relations.* London: Macmillan Press, 1966.
———. *The Rise of Modern Diplomacy 1450–1919.* London and New York: Longman, 1993.
Andrássy, Julius. *Bismarck, Andrássy, and Their Successors.* London: T. Fisher Unwin Ltd, 1927.
———. *Diplomacy and the War.* Translated by J. Holroyd Reece. London: John Bale, Sons & Danielsson, Ltd, 1921.
Antoniades, Andreas. "Epistemic Communities, Epistemes and the Construction of (World) Politics." *Global Society* 17, no. 1 (2003): 21–38.
Archives des Affaires Étrangères. "Mémoires et Documents, Bulgarie." In *Ministry of Foreign Affairs, Paris*, 1878–91.
Axelrod, Robert. *Evolution of Cooperation.* New York: Basic Books, 1984.
Axelrod, Robert, and Robert O. Keohane. "Achieving Cooperation under Anarchy: Strategies and Institutions." *World Politics* 38, no. 1 (1985): 226–54.
Barnett, Michael N., and Martha Finnemore. "The Politics, Power, and Pathologies of International Organizations." *International Organization* 53, no. 4 (1999): 699–732.
———. *Rules for the World.* Ithaca, NY: Cornell University Press, 2004.
Baun, Michael J. *An Imperfect Union: The Maastricht Treaty and the New Politics of European Integration.* Boulder, CO: Westview Press, 1996.
Bennett, G., and K.A. Hamilton, eds. *The Conference on Security and Cooperation in Europe, 1972–75.* Vol. 2, Series 3, *Foreign and Commonwealth Office: Document on British Policy Overseas.* London: The Stationery Office, 1997.
Berkholz, G. *Tracts on the Eastern Question 1863–79.* Brussels: A L'office de publicité, 1863.
Berman, Sheri. "Review Article: Ideas, Norms, and Culture in Political Analysis." *Comparative Politics* 33, no. 2 (2001): 231–50.
Berridge, G.R. *Diplomacy: Theory and Practice.* New York: Palgrave, 1995.
Beyers, Jan, and Guido Dierickx. "The Working Groups of the Council of the European Union: Supranational or Intergovernmental Negotiations?" *Journal of Common Market Studies* 36, no. 3 (1998): 259–317.
Blake, Robert. *Gladstone, Disraeli, and Queen Victoria,* The Centenary Romanes Lecture, Delivered before the University of Oxford on November 10, 1992. Oxford: Clarendon Press, 1992.
Boemeke, Manfred F., Gerald D. Feldman, and Elisabeth Glaser. *The Treaty of Versailles: A Reassessment after 75 Years.* German Historical Institute, Washington DC: Cambridge University Press, 1998.

Bond, Martyn, and Kim Feus. *The Treaty of Nice Explained.* Vol. 3, *Constitution for Europe Series.* London: The Federal Trust for Education and Research, 2001.
Bonnell, Victoria E., and Lynn Hunt. *Beyond the Cultural Turn: New Directions in the Study of Society and Culture.* Berkeley: University of California Press, 1999.
Borzel, Tanja A. *States and Regions in the European Union.* Cambridge: Cambridge University Press, 2002.
Borzel, Tanja A., and Rachel A. Cichowski. *The State of the European Union.* Oxford: Oxford University Press, 2003.
Boyce, Robert, ed. *French Foreign and Defence Policy 1918–1940.* New York: Routledge, 1998.
Braubach, M., and K. Repgen, eds. *Acta Pacis Westphalicae.* 60 vols. Vol. 1:1, *Instruktionen.* Munster Westfalen: Aschendorffsche Verlagsbuchhandlung, 1962.
Bright, Christopher. *The EU: Understanding the Brussels Process.* Colorado Springs: Wiley Law Publications, 1995.
British Management Data Foundation. "The Treaty of Nice in Perspective." Gloucestershire, 2001.
Bruter, Michael. "Diplomacy without a State: The External Delegations of the European Commission." *Journal of European Public Policy* 6, no. 2 (1999): 183–205.
Buchan, David. "Countdown to Maastricht: Special Teams Pass on the European Treaty Baton." *Financial Times*, 12 November 1991, 3.
——. "Pugnacious Major Outshines His Counterparts – the UK Prime Minister Impressed, the Italian One Slept, the French President 'Was Just Plain out of It.'" *Financial Times*, 12 December 1991, 2.
Buckle, George Earle, ed. *The Letters of Queen Victoria (Second Series) A Selection from Her Majesty's Correspondence and Journal between the Years 1862–1878.* Vol. 2. London: His Majesty the King. London: Murray, 1926.
Bull, Hedley. *The Anarchical Society.* Second ed. New York: Columbia University Press, 1995.
Bull, Hedley, and Adam Watson. "Introduction." In *Expansion of International Society*, edited by Hedley Bull and Adam Watson. Oxford: Clarendon Press, 1984, p. 1.
Bulmer, Simon, Charlie Jeffery, and William E. Paterson. *Germany's European Diplomacy: Shaping the Regional Milieu.* Manchester: Manchester University Press, 2000.
Burley, Anne-Marie, and Walter Mattli. "Europe before the Court: A Political Theory of Legal Integration." *International Organization* 47, no. 1 (1993): 41–76.
Burton, J.W. *Systems, States, Diplomacy, and Rules.* Cambridge: Cambridge University Press, 1968.
Bussmann, Klaus, and Heinz Schilling. *1648: War and Peace in Europe.* Münster, Germany: S.N., 1999.
Butler, Geoffrey G., and Simon Maccoby. *The Development of International Law.* London and New York: Longmans, Green and Co., Ltd, 1928.
Buzan, Barry. "From International System to International Society: Structural Realism and Regime Theory Meet the English School." *International Organization* 47, no. 3 (1993): 327–52.
Calleo, David P. *Rethinking Europe's Future.* Princeton, NJ: Princeton University Press, 2001.
Callières, François de. *On the Manner of Negotiating with Princes.* Boston: Houghton Mifflin Co., 1919.
Campbell, Lord. "Policy of Great Britain in the War between Russia and the Porte." In *Tracts on the Eastern Question 1877–78.* London, 1877.

Campbell, Sir George. *A Handy Book on the Eastern Question: Being a Very Recent View of Turkey*. London: John Murray, Albemarle Street, 1876.
Carter, Charles H. "The Ambassadors of Early Modern Europe: Patterns of Diplomatic Representation in the Early Seventeenth Century." In *From the Renaissance to the Counter-Reformation: Essays in Honor of Garrett Mattingly*, edited by Charles H. Carter. New York: Random House, 1965, pp. 269–95.
Cecil, Lamar. *The German Diplomatic Service, 1871–1914*. Princeton, NJ: Princeton University Press, 1976.
Checkel, Jeffrey T. "Ideas, Institutions, and the Gorbachev Foreign Policy Revolution." *World Politics* 45, no. 2 (1993): 271–300.
———. "Norms, Institutions, and National Identity in Contemporary Europe." *International Studies Quarterly* 43, no. 1 (1999): 83–114.
———. "Taking Deliberation Seriously." Paper presented at a workshop on "Ideas, Discourse and European Integration," European Union Center, Harvard University, Cambridge, MA, 11–12 May 2001.
Childs, John Charles Rogers. *Armies and Warfare in Europe, 1648–1789*. New York: Holmes & Meier Publishers Inc., 1983.
Christiansen, Thomas. "The European Commission: Administration in Turbulent Times." In *European Union: Power and Policy-making*, Second ed., edited by J. Richardson. London: Routledge, 2001, pp. 95–114.
Chryssochoou, Dimitris N., Michael J. Tsinisizelis, Stelios Stavridis, and Kostas Infantis. *Theory and Reform in the European Union*. Manchester: Manchester University Press, 2003.
Cini, Michelle. *The European Commission: Leadership, Organisation and Culture in the EU Administration*. Manchester: Manchester University Press, 1996.
Clark, Chester Wells. *Franz Joseph and Bismarck: The Diplomacy of Austria before the War of 1866, Harvard Historical Studies*. Cambridge: Harvard University Press, 1934.
Clausewitz, Carl von. *On War*. Translated by Michael Howard and Peter Paret. Princeton, NJ: Princeton University Press, 1976.
Clayton, G.D. *Britain and the Eastern Question: Missolonghi to Gallipoli*. London: Lion Library, 1971.
Clemens, Elisabeth S., and James M. Cook. "Politics and Institutionalism: Explaining Durability and Change." *Annual Review of Sociology* 25 (1999): 441–66.
Coombes, David. *Politics and Bureaucracy in the European Community: A Portrait of the Commission of the E.E.C.* London: George Allen & Unwin Ltd, 1970.
Correspondence Relating to the Congress of Berlin, with the Protocols of the Congress. Vol. 83ii, *Accounts and Papers 1878, Turkey. No. 39*. London: Harrison and Sons, 1878.
"Correspondence Respecting the Convention between Great Britain and Turkey of June 4, 1878." In *Accounts & Papers Session 17 January–16 August 1878, Parliamentary Papers Volume LXXXII*. London, 1878, pp. 1–19.
Craig, Gordon A., and Felix Gilbert. *The Diplomats: 1919–1939*. Princeton, NJ: Princeton University Press, 1953.
Cram, Laura. "The Commission." In *Developments in the European Union*, edited by Laura Cram, Desmond Dinan, and Neill Nugent. London: St. Martin's Press, 1999.
Cram, Laura, Desmond Dinan, and Neill Nugent, eds. *Developments in the European Union*. New York: St. Martin's Press, 1999.
Cromwell, Valerie, and Zara Steiner. "Reform and Retrenchment: The Foreign Office between the Wars." In *The Foreign Office 1782–1982*, edited by Roger Bullen. Frederick, MD: University Publications of America, Inc., 1984.
Croxton, Derek. *Peacemaking in Early Modern Europe: Cardinal Mazarin and the Congress of Westphalia, 1643–1648*. London: Associated University Press, 1999.

Croxton, Derek, and Anuschka Tischer. *The Peace of Westphalia: A Historical Dictionary*. Westport, CT: Greenwood Press, 2002.

Cruz, Consuelo. "Identity and Persuasion: How Nations Remember Their Pasts and Make Their Futures." *World Politics* 52 (2000): 275–312.

Cullen, Holly, and Andrew Charlesworth. "Diplomacy by Other Means: The Use of Legal Basis Litigation as a Political Strategy by the European Parliament and Member States." *Common Market Law Review* 36 (1999): 1243–70.

Czalet, Edward. "The Berlin Congress and the Anglo-Turkish Convention: Address Delivered to the Working Men's Club at Plaxtol." In *Tracts on the Eastern Question 1877–78*. London, 1878.

Daly, John C.K. *Russian Sea Power and 'the Eastern Question' 1827–41*. London: Macmillan, 1991.

Day, Clive. "The Atmosphere and Organization of the Peace Conference." In *What Really Happened at Paris: The Story of the Peace Conference, 1918–1919*, edited by Edward Mandell House, and Charles Seymour. New York: Charles Scribner's Sons, 1921, pp. 33–4.

Delouche, Frédéric ed. *Illustrated History of Europe: A Unique Portrait of Europe's Common History*. New York: Barnes & Noble Books, 2001.

Denza, Eileen. *Diplomatic Law: Commentary on the Vienna Conventions on Diplomatic Relations*. Second ed. Oxford: Clarendon Press, 1998.

Despatch from the Marquis of Salisbury. Vol. 83ii, Accounts and Papers 1878, Turkey. No. 38. London: Harrison and Sons, 1878.

Dickie, John. *Inside the Foreign Office*. London: Chapmans, 1992.

Dillon, E.J. *The Inside Story of the Peace Conference*. New York: Harper & Brothers Publishers, 1920.

DiMaggio, Paul J., and Walter W. Powell. "The Iron Cage Revisited: Institutional Isomorphism and Collective Rationality in Organizational Fields." *American Sociological Review* 48, no. 2 (1983): 147–60.

———. *The New Institutionalism in Organizational Analysis*. Chicago: University of Chicago Press, 1991.

Dobbin, Frank. *The New Economic Sociology*. Princeton, NJ: Princeton University Press, 2004.

Dockrill, Michael L., and Douglas J. Goold. *Peace without Promise: Britain and the Peace Conferences, 1919–23*. Hamden, CT: Archon Books, 1981.

Duff, Andrew, John Pinder, and Roy Pryce, eds. *Maastricht and Beyond*. London: Routledge, 1994.

Dugdale, E.T.S. "The Bismarck Period." In *German Diplomatic Documents 1871–1914*. New York, 1928.

Dunlop, Charles. *Beaconsfield Brilliants: Being Choice Selections from the Speeches and Works of the Late Benjamin Disraeli, Earl of Beaconsfield*. London: Bates, Hendy and Co., 1881.

Dunn, David H. *Diplomacy at the Highest Level: The Evolution of International Summitry*. New York: Macmillan Press, 1996.

Duroselle, Jean-Baptiste. *France and the Nazi Threat: The Collapse of French Diplomacy 1932–1939*. New York: Enigma Books, 2004.

"Eastern Question. Confidential Papers Respecting Separate Negotiations with Austria, Russia, and Turkey." In *Salisbury Papers*, 1878.

"EC Finance Ministers Meet on EMU Transition Compromise." *Agence France Presse*, 19 September 1991.

"EC Ministers Say Agreement on Currency Union Will Come by December." *Agence France Presse*, 21 September 1991.

Edwards, Geoffrey, and David Spence. *The European Commission*. Second ed. London: Cartermill International Ltd, 1995.
Eells, Hastings. "Recent Progress in Science." In *Europe Since 1500*. New York: Henry Holt and Company, 1933.
Eisenhammer, John. "Germany's True Believer Who Will Not Be Fobbed Off." *The Independent*, 28 June 1991, 10.
Elcock, Howard. *Portrait of a Decision: The Council of Four and the Treaty of Versailles*. Birkenhead, UK: Eyre Methuen Ltd, 1972.
Elgstrom, Ole, and Christopher Jonsson. "Negotiation in the European Union: Bargaining or Problem Solving?" *Journal of European Public Policy* 7, no. 5 (2000): 684–704.
Elgstrom, Ole, and Michael Smith. "Introduction: Negotiation and Policy-Making in the European Union – Processes, System and Order." *Journal of European Public Policy* 7, no. 5 (2000): 673–83.
Elster, Jon. *The Cement of Society: A Study of Social Order*. Cambridge: Cambridge University Press, 1989.
Endo, Ken. *The Presidency of the European Commission under Jacques Delores*. London: Macmillan Press Ltd, 1999.
Enjalran, Paulette, and Philippe Husson. "France the Ministry of Foreign Affairs: 'Something New, but Which is the Legitimate Continuation of Our Past....' " In *Foreign Ministries: Change and Adaptation*, edited by Brian Hocking. New York: St. Martin's Press, 1999, pp. 59–74.
Ernst, Manfred. "Attitudes of Diplomats at the United Nations: The Effects of Organizational Participation on the Evaluation of the Organization." *International Organization* 32, no. 4 (1978): 1037–44.
Esteban, Maria Luisa Fernandez. *The Rule of Law in the European Constitution*. London: Klumer Law International Ltd, 1999.
"European Community; Thunder Off." *The Economist*, 12 September 1992, 48.
"European Defence: Initial Rapprochement among the Twelve." *European Information Service*, 28 March 1991, 5.
Evans, Peter B., Harold K. Jacobson, and Robert D. Putnam. *Double-Edged Diplomacy: International Bargaining and Domestic Politics*. Berkeley: University of California Press, 1993.
Falk, Richard A., and Wolfram F. Hanrieder. *International Law and Organization: An Introductory Reader*. Philadelphia: J.B. Lippincott Company, 1968.
Falkner, Gerda. "The Council or the Social Partners? EC Social Policy between Diplomacy and Collective Bargaining." *Journal of European Public Policy* 7, no. 5 (2000): 705–24.
———. "How Intergovernmental Are Intergovernmental Conferences? An Example from the Maastricht Treaty Reform." *Journal of European Public Policy* 9, no. 1 (2002): 98–119.
Feldman, Martha S. *Strategies for Interpreting Qualitative Data*. Newbury Park, CA: Sage, 1995.
Feltham, R.G. *Diplomatic Handbook*. Fifth ed. London: Longman, 1988.
Feus, Kim. *A Simplified Treaty for the European Union?*, *The Federal Trust Constitution for Europe Series 2*. London: The Federal Trust for Education and Research, 2001.
Finnemore, Martha, and Kathryn Sikkink. "International Norm Dynamics and Political Change." *International Organization* 52, no. 4 (1998): 887–917.
Fligstein, Neil, and Iona Mara-Drita. "How to Make a Market: Reflections on the Attempt to Create a Single Market in the European Union." *The American Journal of Sociology* 102, no. 1 (1996): 1–33.

Fligstein, Neil, and Peter Brantley. "Bank Control, Owner Control, or Organizational Dynamics: Who Controls the Large Modern Corporation?" *The American Journal of Sociology* 98, no. 2 (1992): 280–307.
Flynn, Sean. "Windfall in Structural Funds now under Threat." *The Irish Times*, 23 September 1992, City Edition. 8.
Fonblanque, J.R. de. *Letter*, 25 September 1990.
Fry, Michael Graham, Erik Goldstein, and Richard Langhorne. *Guide to International Relations and Diplomacy*. New York: Continuum, 2002.
Fuller, Joseph Vincent. *Bismarck's Diplomacy at Its Zenith*. Cambridge: Harvard University Press, 1922.
Galloway, David. *The Treaty of Nice and Beyond: Realities and Illusions of Power in the EU*, edited by Jackie Gower. Vol. 10, *Contemporary European Studies*. Sheffield, UK: Sheffield Academic Press Ltd, 2001.
Galtung, Johan, and Mari Holmboe Ruge. "Patterns of Diplomacy: A Study of Recruitment and Career Patterns in Norwegian Diplomacy." *Journal of Peace Research* 2, no. 2 (1965): 101–35.
Geertz, Clifford. *The Interpretation of Cultures*. London: Fontana Press, 1993.
George, Alexander L. "Case Studies and Theory Development: The Method of Structured, Focused Comparison." In *Diplomacy: New Approaches in History, Theory, and Policy*, edited by Paul Gordon Lauren. New York: The Free Press, 1979.
George, Alexander L., and Andrew Bennett. "Process Tracing and Historical Explanation." In *Case Studies and Theory Development in the Social Sciences*, Chapter 10. Cambridge: MIT Press, 2004.
George, Alexander L., and Timothy McKeown. "Case Studies and Theories of Organizational Decision Making." In *Advances in Information Processing in Organizations*. Greenwich, CT: JAI Press, 1985, pp. 21–58.
George, Stephen, and Ian Bache. *Politics in the European Union*. Oxford: Oxford University Press, 2001.
Glarbo, Kenneth. "Wide-Awake Diplomacy: Reconstructing the Common Foreign and Security Policy of the European Union." *Journal of European Public Policy* 6, no. 4 (1999): 634–51.
Gnesotto, Nicole. "Introduction ESDP: Results and Prospects." In *EU Security and Defence Policy: The First Five Years (1999–2004)*, edited by Nicole Gnesotto. Paris: EU Institute for Security Studies, 2004.
Goertz, Gary. *Social Science Concepts: A User's Guide*. Princeton, NJ: Princeton University Press, 2005.
Great Britain Foreign Office. *History of the Eastern Question*. Vol. 15, *Handbooks Prepared under the Direction of the Historical Section of the Foreign Office*. London: H.M. Stationery Office, 1920.
Grotius, Hugo. *The Law of War and Peace*. Translated by Johan Blaeu and Francis W. Kelsey. Birmingham, AL: Gryphon, 1984.
H.H.J. "Breakers Ahead! Or the Doomed Ship, the Determined Captain, and the Docile Crew: A Review of Lord Beaconsfield's Policy." In *Tracts on the Eastern Question 1863–79 (British Library)*. London: G.J. Palmer, 1878.
Haas, Ernst B. "Is There a Hole in the Whole? Knowledge, Technology, Interdependence, and the Construction of International Regimes." *International Organization* 29, no. 3 (1975): 827–76.
———. *The Uniting of Europe. Political, Social and Economic Forces 1950–57*. Stanford, CA: Stanford University Press, 1958.
Haas, Peter M. "Introduction: Epistemic Communities and International Policy Coordination." *International Organization* 46, no. 1 (1992): 1–35.

Hamilton, Keith, and Richard Langhorne. *The Practice of Diplomacy: Its Evolution, Theory and Administration.* London: Routledge, 1995.
Hannay, Sir David. *The Growth of Multilateral Diplomacy, FCO Historians Occasional Papers No. 13.* London: FCO Historians, 1996.
Hansard's Parliamentary Debates. Vol. 240, 16 May–20 June, 1878. London: Cornelius Buck, 1878.
Hansard's Parliamentary Debates. Vol. 241, 21 June–22 July, 1878, *Parliamentary Debates, Third Series.* London: Cornelius Buck, 1878.
Harding, Christopher, and C.L. Lim. *Renegotiating Westphalia: Essays and Commentary on the European and Conceptual Foundations of Modern International Law.* Vol. 34, *Developments in International Law.* The Hague: Martinus Nijhoff Publishers, 1999.
Harris, David. *Britain and the Bulgarian Horrors of 1876.* Chicago: University of Chicago Press, 1939.
——. *A Diplomatic History of the Balkan Crisis of 1875–1878: The First Year,* Hoover War Library Publications – No. 11. Stanford, CA: Stanford University Press, 1936.
Hayes-Renshaw, Fiona. "The Role of the Committee of Permanent Representatives in the Decision-Making Process of the European Community." Ph.D. diss., University of London, 1990.
Hayes-Renshaw, Fiona, and Helen Wallace. *The Council of Ministers.* London: Macmillan Press Ltd, 1997.
——. "Executive Power in the European Union: The Functions and Limits of the Council of Ministers." *Journal of European Public Policy* 2, no. 4 (1995): 565.
Hayes-Renshaw, Fiona, C. Lequesne, and P.M. Lopez. "The Permanent Representations of the Member States to the European Communities." *Journal of Common Market Studies* 38, no. 2 (1989): 119–37.
Headlam-Morley, James. *A Memoir of the Paris Peace Conference 1919.* London: Methuen, 1972.
Heatley, D.P. *Diplomacy and the Study of International Relations.* Oxford: Clarendon Press, 1919.
Helm, Sarah. "The 15 Men Who Run Europe on Our Behalf; EU/The Real Decision-Makers." *The Independent,* 18 June 1995, 17.
Henig, Ruth. *Versailles and after 1919–1933.* Second ed. London: Routledge, 1984.
Heukels, Ton, and Jaap de Zwaan, "The Configuration of the European Union." In *Institutional Dynamics of European Integration: Essays in Honour of Henry G. Schermers.* Vol. 2, edited by Dierdre Curtin and Ton Heukels. Boston: Martinus Nijhoff, 1994, pp. 195–228.
Hill, David J. *A History of European Diplomacy.* Vol. 2. London: Longmans, 1906.
Historical Section of the Foreign Office. *The Congress of Berlin.* Vol. 167, *Foreign Office Historical Handbooks.* London: HM Stationery Office, February 1919.
——. *Foreign Policy of Austria-Hungary.* Vol. 1, *Foreign Office Historical Handbooks.* London: HM Stationery Office, 1920.
Hocking, Brian. "Catalytic Diplomacy: Beyond 'Newness' and 'Decline.'" In *Innovation in Diplomatic Practice,* edited by Jan Melissen, 21–42. New York: St. Martin's Press, 1999.
——. *Foreign Ministries: Change and Adaptation.* New York: St. Martin's Press, 1999.
Hocking, Brian and David Spence, eds. *Foreign Ministries of the European Union: Integrating Diplomats.* Houndmills, UK: Palgrave, 2002.
Holborn, Hajo. "World War, World Settlement and the Aftermath." In *The Versailles Settlement: Was It Foredoomed to Failure?* edited by Lederer, Ivo J.; *Problems in European Civilization,* edited by Ralph W. Greenlaw, Boston: D.C. Heath and Company, 1960.

Hooghe, Liesbet. *The European Commission and the Integration of Europe: Images of Governance.* Cambridge: Cambridge University Press, 2001.
Hosli, Madeleine O., Adrian van Deemen, and Mika Widgrén. *Institutional Challenges in the European Union, Routledge Advances in European Politics.* London and New York: Routledge, 2002.
House, Edward Mandell, and Charles Seymour, eds. *What Really Happened at Paris: The Story of the Peace Conference, 1918–1919.* New York: Charles Scribner's Sons, 1921.
"Ideas, Discourse, and European Integration." Harvard University, 11–12 May 2001.
"Intergovernmental Conference on the Future of the European Union." *EU info* 9 (2000).
Jacobsson, Bengt, Per Laegreid, and Ove K. Pedersen. *Europeanization and Transnational States: Comparing Nordic Central Governments.* New York: Routledge, 2004.
Jervis, Robert. *Perception and Misperception in International Politics.* Princeton, NJ: Princeton University Press, 1976.
Jones, Raymond A. *The British Diplomatic Service 1815–1914.* Waterloo, Ontario: Wilfrid Laurier University Press, 1983.
Kahn, Robert L., and Zald Mayer N. *Organizations and Nation-States: New Perspectives on Conflict and Cooperation.* San Francisco: Jossey-Bass Publishers, 1990.
Kapstein, Ethan Barnaby. "Between Power and Purpose: Central Bankers and the Politics of Regulatory Convergence." *International Organization* 46, no. 1 (1992): 265–87.
Kassim, Hussein, and Anand Menon. "The Principal–Agent Approach and the Study of the European Union: Promise Unfulfilled?" *Journal of European Public Policy* 10, no. 1 (2003): 121–39.
Katz, Richard and Bernhard Wessels. *The European Parliament, the National Parliaments, and European Integration.* London: Oxford University Press, 1999.
Katzenstein, Peter J. *Between Power and Plenty.* Madison: University of Wisconsin Press, 1978.
Keck, Margaret, and Kathryn Sikkink. *Activists Beyond Borders.* Ithaca, NY: Cornell University Press, 1998.
Kee, Robert. *Munich: The Eleventh Hour.* London: Hamish Hamilton, 1988.
Kennedy, Paul. *The Rise and Fall of the Great Powers.* New York: Random House, 1987.
Keohane, Robert O. *After Hegemony.* Princeton, NJ: Princeton University Press, 1984.
Keohane, Robert O., Andrew Moravcsik, and Anne-Marie Slaughter. "Legalized Dispute Resolution: Interstate and Transnational." *International Organization* 54, no. 3 (2000): 457–88.
Keohane, Robert O., and Joseph S. Nye. *Power and Interdependence: World Politics in Transition.* Second ed. Boston: Little, Brown & Co., 1989.
———. *Transnational Relations and World Politics.* Cambridge: Cambridge University Press, 1971.
Keylor, William R. "Versailles and International Diplomacy." In *The Treaty of Versailles: A Reassessment after 75 Years,* edited by Manfred F. Boemeke, Gerald D. Feldman, and Elisabeth Glaser. German Historical Institute, Washington DC: Cambridge University Press, 1998.
King, Gary, Robert Keohane, and Sidney Verba. *Designing Social Inquiry: Scientific Inference in Qualitative Research.* Princeton, NJ: Princeton University Press, 1994.
King, Toby. "Human Rights in European Foreign Policy: Success or Failure for Post-Modern Diplomacy?" *EJIL* 10, no. 2 (1999): 313–37.
Kirchner, Emil J. *Decision-Making in the European Community: The Council Presidency and European Integration.* Manchester: Manchester University Press, 1992.
Kissinger, Henry. *Diplomacy.* New York: Simon & Schuster, 1994.

Kleine-Ahlbrandt, William Laird. *The Burden of Victory: France, Britain and the Enforcement of the Versailles Peace, 1919–1925*. London: University Press of America, Inc., 1995.
Knill, Christoph. *The Europeanisation of National Administrations: Patterns of Institutional Change and Persistence*. Cambridge: Cambridge University Press, 2001.
Knutsen, Torbjørn L. *A History of International Relations Theory*. Manchester: Manchester University Press, 1997.
Kupchan, Charles A. "After Pax Americana: Benign Power, Regional Integration and the Sources of Stable Multipolarity." *International Security* 23, no. 2 (1998): 40–79.
Kurbalija, Jovan. "Diplomacy in the Age of Information Technology." In *Innovation in Diplomatic Practice*, edited by Jan Melissen. New York: St. Martin's Press, 1999, pp. 171–91.
Lang, John Temple, and Eamonn Gallagher. *The Role of the Commission and Qualified Majority Voting*. Vol. Occasional Paper 7, Institute of European Affairs. Dublin: Brunswick Press Limited, 1995.
Lansing, Robert. *The Peace Negotiations: A Personal Narrative*. Boston: Houghton Mifflin Company, 1921.
Lauren, Paul Gordon. *Diplomats and Bureaucrats: The First Institutional Responses to Twentieth-Century Diplomacy in France and Germany*. Stanford, CA: Hoover Institution Press, 1976.
Laursen, Finn. "The Lessons of Maastricht." In *The Politics of European Treaty Reform*, edited by G. Edwards and A. Pijpers. London: Pinter, 1997, pp. 59–73.
Laursen, Finn, and Sophie Vanhoonacker, eds. *The Intergovernmental Conference on Political Union: Institutional Reforms, New Policies and International Identity of the European Community, European Institute of Public Administration*. Leiden, The Netherlands: Martinus Nijhoff Publishers, 1992.
———, eds. *The Ratification of the Maastricht Treaty: Issues Debates and Future Implications, European Institute of Public Administration*. Dordrecht, The Netherlands: Martinus Nijhoff Publishers, 1994.
Layard, A.H. "Confidential Print. Russo-Turkish War Part II." In *Layard Papers, British Library*, 1876–78.
———. "Confidential Print. Turkey. Apr.–June 1877. MSS 39144." In *Layard Papers, British Library*, 1877.
———. "Confidential Print. Turkey. 31 July–August 1877. MSS 39145." In *Layard Papers, British Library*, 1877.
———. "Confidential Print. Turkey. 31 Aug 1877–19 January 1878. MSS 39146." In *Layard Papers, British Library*, 1877.
———. "Confidential Print. Turkey. 19 Jan–20 Mar, 1878. MSS 39147." In *Layard Papers, British Library*, 1878.
———. "Confidential Print. Turkey 17 March–5 June 1878. MSS 39148." In *Layard Papers, British Library*, 1878.
———. "Confidential Print. Turkey. 20 April–15 Aug 1878. MSS 39149." In *Layard Papers, British Library*, 1878.
Leech, Beth L. "Asking Questions: Techniques for Semistructured Interviews." *Political Science and Politics* 35, no. 4 (2002): 665–8.
Lentin, Anthony. *Lloyd George and the Lost Peace: From Versailles to Hitler, 1919–1940*. New York: Palgrave, 2001.
Lewis, Jeffrey. "Constructing Interests: The Committee of Permanent Representatives and Decision-Making in the European Union." Ph.D. diss. University of Wisconsin-Madison, 1998.

———. "Is the 'Hard Bargaining' Image of the Council Misleading? The Committee of Permanent Representatives and the Local Elections Directive." *Journal of Common Market Studies* 36, no. 4 (1998): 479–504.

———. "The Methods of Community in EU Decision-Making and Administrative Rivalry in the Council's Infrastructure." *Journal of European Public Policy* 7, no. 2 (2000): 261–89.

Lhuillery, Jacques. "'Federal' Row Revives Doubts over Dutch Tenure of EC Presidency." *Agence France Presse*, 4 December 1991.

Lovin, Clifford R. *A School for Diplomats: The Paris Peace Conference of 1919*. Lanham, MD: University Press of America, 1997.

Luard, Evan. *The Balance of Power: The System of International Relations, 1648–1815*. London: Macmillan, 1992.

Luckau, Alma Maria. *The German Delegation at the Paris Peace Conference: A Documentary Study of Germany's Acceptance of the Treaty of Versailles*. New York: Columbia University Press, 1941.

Macfie, A.L. *The Eastern Question 1774–1923*, Seminar Studies in History, edited by Roger Lockyer. London: Longman, 1989.

Magalhaes, José Calvet De. *The Pure Concept of Diplomacy*. Translated by Bernardo Futscher Pereira, *Global Perspectives in History and Politics*. Westport, CT: Greenwood Press, 1988.

Mahoney, James, and Richard Snyder. "Rethinking Agency and Structure in the Study of Regime Change." *Studies in Comparative International Development* 34, no. 2 (1999): 3–32.

Maisel, Ephraim. *The Foreign Office and Foreign Policy, 1919–1926*. Brighton, UK: Sussex Academic Press, 1994.

Mangone, Gerard J. *A Short History of International Organization*. New York: McGraw-Hill Book Company, Inc., 1954.

Mantoux, Paul. *The Deliberations of the Council of Four (March 24–June 28, 1919)*. Vol. 1. Translated by Arthur S. Link. Princeton, NJ: Princeton University Press, 1992.

March, James G., and Johan P. Olsen. "The Institutional Dynamics of International Political Order." *International Organization* 52, no. 4 (1998): 943–69.

———. *Rediscovering Institutions*. New York: Free Press, 1989.

Marshall, Peter. *Positive Diplomacy*. London: Macmillan Press, 1997.

Marston, F.S. *The Peace Conference of 1919: Organization and Procedure*. London: Oxford University Press, 1944.

Mason, John W. *The Dissolution of the Austro-Hungarian Empire 1867–1918*. Second ed. Seminar Studies in History. London: Longman, 1997.

Mattingly, Garrett. *Renaissance Diplomacy*. London: Butler & Tanner Ltd, 1955.

Mayer, Arno J. *Politics and Diplomacy of Peacemaking: Containment and Counterrevolution at Versailles, 1918–1919*. New York: Alfred A. Knopf, 1967.

Mazzucelli, Colette. *France and Germany at Maastricht: Politics and Negotiations to Create the European Union*. New York: Garland Publishing Inc., 1997.

McClanahan, Grant V. *Diplomatic Immunity: Principles, Practices, and Problems*. London: Hurst & Company, 1989.

McGrew, Anthony. "Democratising Global Institutions: Possibilities, Limits, and Normative Foundations." In *Transnational Democracy: Political Spaces and Border Crossings*, edited by James Anderson, 149–69. London: Routledge, 2002.

McHugh, James T., and James S. Pacy. *Diplomats without a Country: Baltic Diplomacy, International Law, and the Cold War*. Vol. 86, *Study of World History*. Westport: Greenwood Press, 2001.

McNamara, Kathleen R. *The Currency of Ideas*. Ithaca, NY: Cornell University Press, 1998.
Meade, Geoff. "Hurd Set to Resist Federal Plans for EC." *Press Association*. 29 September 1991, Home News in Brussels.
Mearsheimer, John. "Back to the Future: Instability after the Cold War." *International Security* 15, no. 4 (1990): 5–56.
Mee Jr., Charles L. *The End of Order: Versailles 1919*. New York: Elsevier-Dutton Publishing Co., Inc., 1980.
Melissen, Jan. "Introduction." In *Innovation in Diplomatic Practice*, edited by Jan Melissen. London: Palgrave, 1999, p. 1.
Mendl, Wolf. "Strategic Thinking in Diplomacy: A Legacy of the Cold War." In *New Perspectives on Security*, edited by Michael Clarke. London: The Centre for Defence Studies, Brassey's, 1993.
Mendlicott, W.N. *The Congress of Berlin and After: A Diplomatic History of the near Eastern Settlement 1878–1880*. London: Frank Cass & Co. Ltd, 1963.
Meyer, Henry R. *After the War: The Changes and Changes That Will Come with Peace*. London: Simpkin, Marshall, Hamilton, Kent & Co., Ltd, 1915.
Meyer, John W., and Brian Rowan. "Institutionalized Organizations: Formal Structure as Myth and Ceremony." In *The New Institutionalism in Organizational Analysis*, edited by Walter W. Powell and Paul J. DiMaggio. Chicago: University of Chicago Press, 1991.
Michelmann, Hans J. *Organisational Effectiveness in a Multinational Bureaucracy*. Westmean, UK: Saxon House, 1978.
Michelmann, Hans J., and Panayotis Soldatos, eds. *European Integration: Theories and Approaches*. New York: University Press of America, 1994.
Millman, Richard. *Britain and the Eastern Question 1875–1878*. Oxford: Clarendon Press, 1979.
Milojkovic-Djuric, Jelena. *The Eastern Question and the Voices of Reason: Austria-Hungary, Russia, and the Balkan States 1875–1908*. Vol. 213, East European Monographs, Boulder. New York: Columbia University Press, 2002.
Moncrieff, Chris and Geoff Meade. *The Press Association*. July 1, 1992, Home News.
Moore, Sara. *Peace without Victory for the Allies 1918–1932*. Oxford/Providence: Berg, 1994.
Moravcsik, Andrew. *Choice for Europe: Social Purpose and State Power from Messina to Maastricht*. Ithaca, NY: Cornell University Press, 1998.
———. "'Is Something Rotten in the State of Denmark?' Constructivism and European Integration." *Journal of European Public Policy* 6, no. 4 (1999): 669–81.
———. "Negotiating the Single European Act: National Interests and Conventional Statecraft in the European Community." *International Organization* 45, no. 1 (1991): 19–56.
———. "Preferences and Power in the European Community: A Liberal Intergovernmental Approach." *Journal of Common Market Studies* 31, no. 4 (1993): 473–524.
Moravcsik, Andrew, and Kalypso Nicolaïdis. "Explaining the Treaty of Amsterdam: Interests, Influence, Institutions." *Journal of Common Market Studies* 37, no. 1 (1999): 59–85.
Morgenthau, Hans. *Politics among Nations: The Struggle for Power and Peace*. New York: Knopf, 1978.
Morth, Ulrika. "Competing Frames in the European Commission – The Case of the Defence Industry and Equipment Issue." *Journal of European Public Policy* 7, no. 2 (2000): 173–89.
Mortimer, Edward. "European Union Advocated." *Financial Times*, 16 January 1989, 3.

Mun, Thomas. *England's Treasure by Foreign Trade*. London, 1664.
Navari, Cornelia. *Internationalism and the State in the 20th Century*. London: Routledge, 2000.
Neilson, Francis. *How Diplomats Make War*. New York: B.W. Huebsch, 1916.
Nevill, Barry St-John. *Life at the Court of Queen Victoria, 1861–1901*. Exeter, UK: Webb & Bower, 1984.
Nicolson, Harold. *Diplomacy*. Third ed., London: Oxford University Press, 1969.
———. *The Evolution of Diplomatic Method, Being the Chichele Lectures Delivered at the University of Oxford in November 1953*. London: Constable & Co Ltd, 1953.
———. *Peacemaking*. London: Oxford University Press, 1933.
———. *Peacemaking*. Vol. 4, *Montague Burton Lecture on International Relations*. Leeds, UK: University of Leeds, 1946.
Nierop, Tom. *Systems and Regions in Global Politics: An Empirical Study of Diplomacy, International Organization and Trade 1950–1991*. New York: John Wiley & Sons, 1994.
Nugent, Neill, ed. *At the Heart of the Union: Studies of the European Commission*. Second ed. London: Macmillan Press Ltd, 1997.
———. "Decision-Making." In *Developments in the European Union*, edited by Laura Cram, Desmond Dinan, and Neill Nugent. London: St. Martin's Press, 1999, pp. 130–50.
Nuttall, Simon. "The Commission: Protagonists of Inter-Regional Cooperation." In *Europe's Global Links: The European Community and Inter-Regional Cooperation*, edited by Geoffrey Edwards and Elfriede Regelsberger. London: Pinter Publishers, 1990, pp. 143–60.
———. "Where the European Commission Comes In." In *European Political Cooperation in the 1980s*, edited by Alfred Pijpers, Elfriede Regelsberger and Wolfgang Wessels. Dordrecht: Martinus Nijhoff Publishers, 1988.
Nye, Joseph S. Jr. *Soft Power: The Means to Success in World Politics*. New York: Public Affairs, 2004.
Osiander, Andreas. *The States System of Europe, 1640–1990: Peacemaking and the Conditions of International Stability*. Oxford: Clarendon Press, 1994.
Page, Edward C. *People Who Run Europe*. Oxford: Clarendon Press, 1997.
Palmer, John. "Federalists Set to Leave Britain in Cold." *The Guardian*, 19 November 1991.
———. "The Road to Maastricht: The Dapper Scot with a Firm Hand on the Minister's Elbow – Key Player: Sir John Kerr." *The Guardian*, 2 December 1991.
Papadopoulos, Andrestinos N. *Multilateral Diplomacy within the Commonwealth: A Decade of Expansion*. The Hague: Martinus Nijhoff Publishers, 1982.
Peaple, Simon. *European Diplomacy 1870–1939*, Heinemann Advanced History, edited by Martin Collier and Erica Lewis. Oxford: Heinemann Educational Publishers, 2002.
Pearson, Hesketh. *Dizzy: A Life of Benjamin Disraeli*. London: Penguin Books, 2001.
Penson, Dame Lillian. *Foreign Affairs under the Third Marquis of Salisbury, The Creighton Lecture in History 1960*. London: The Athlone Press, 1962.
Peters, B. Guy. "The Problem of Bureaucratic Government." *The Journal of Politics* 43, no. 1 (1981): 56–82.
Peterson, M.J. "Transnational Activity, International Society, and World Politics." *Millennium* 21, no. 3 (1992): 375–6.
Pevehouse, Jon C. "With a Little Help from My Friends? Regional Organizations and the Consolidation of Democracy." *American Journal of Political Science* 46, no. 3 (2002): 611–26.
Pierson, Paul. *Politics in Time: History, Institutions, and Social Analysis*. Princeton, NJ: Princeton University Press, 2004.

Pijpers, Alfred, Elfriede Regelsberger, and Wolfgang Wessels, eds. *European Political Cooperation in the 1980s*. London: Martinus Nijhoff Publishers, 1988.
Pim, Captain Bedford. "The Eastern Question, Past, Present and Future: With Map, and Official Documents." In *Tracts on the Eastern Question 1877–78*. London, 1877.
Platt, D.C.M. *The Cinderella Service: British Consuls since 1825*. London: Longman, 1971.
The Political Correspondence of Mr. Gladstone and Lord Granville 1876–1886. Vol. 1, *Gladstone and Granville*. Oxford University Press, 1962.
"Political Union: A Week before Maastricht, Compromise Begins to Emerge." *European Information Service*, 30 November 1991, 4.
"Political Union: Ministers Move Ahead Inch by Inch." *Europe Information Service*, 26 November 1991.
"Political Union: UK Proposes Taking Foreign Policy Decisions on a Case-by-Case Basis." *Europe Information Service*, 20 July 1991, 2.
Pollack, Mark A. "Delegation, Agency, and Agenda Setting in the European Community." *International Organization* 51, no. 1 (1997): 99–134.
———. *The Engines of European Integration: Delegation, Agency, and Agenda Setting in the EU*. Oxford: Oxford University Press, 2003.
Pond, Elizabeth. *The Rebirth of Europe*. Washington, DC: Brookings Institution Press, 1999.
"The Power-House." *The Economist*, 8 March 1997, 62.
Pudney, J., and Lord Sudley, trans. "Further Letters of Queen Victoria from the Archives of the House of Brandenburg-Prussia." London, 1938.
Putnam, Robert D. "Diplomacy and Domestic Politics: The Logic of Two-Level Games." *International Organization* 42, no. 3 (1988): 427–60.
Radaelli, Claudio M. "The Public Policy of the European Union: Whither Politics of Expertise?" *Journal of European Public Policy* 6, no. 5 (1999): 757–74.
Ragin, Charles. *Fuzzy Set Social Science*. Chicago: University of Chicago, 2000.
Ragsdale, Hugh. *The Soviets, the Munich Crisis, and the Coming of World War II*. Cambridge: Cambridge University Press, 2004.
"Ratification of the Treaty on European Union." In *Travaux préparatoires – United Kingdom*, 1996.
Rawnsley, Gary. "Monitored Broadcasts and Diplomacy." In *Innovation in Diplomatic Practice*, edited by Jan Melissen. New York: St. Martin's Press, 1999, pp. 135–50.
Reeves, Jesse S. "International Society and International Law." *American Journal of International Law* 15, no. 3 (1921): 361–74.
Repgen, Konrad. "Negotiating the Peace of Westphalia." In *1648: War and Peace in Europe*, edited by Klaus Bussmann and Heinz Schilling. Münster, Germany: S.N., 1999, pp. 357–9.
"Revelations from the Seat of War: Russians, Turks, Bulgarians, and Mr. Gladstone." In *Tracts on the Eastern Question, 1877–78*. London, 1877.
Rice, Robert, and David Owen. "Maastricht Ratified as Rees-Mogg Bows Out." *Financial Times*, 3 August 1993, 6.
Richelieu, Armand du Plessis. *Testament Politique*, Amsterdam, The Netherlands: chez Henry Desbordes, 1688.
Risse, Thomas. "Is Transnational Deliberation Possible in Europe." Paper presented at the Ideas, Discourse, and European Integration, Harvard University, 11–12 May 2001.
———. " 'Let's Argue!': Communicative Action in World Politics." *International Organization* 54, no. 1 (2000): 1–39.
———. "Nationalism and Collective Identities: Europe Versus the Nation-State?" Draft (2000).

Risse-Kappen, Thomas. "Did 'Peace through Strength' End the Cold War? Lessons from INF." *International Security* 16, no. 1 (1991): 162–88.

———. "Ideas Do Not Float Freely: Transnational Coalitions, Domestic Structures, and the End of the Cold War." *International Organization* 48, no. 2 (1994): 185–214.

———. "Introduction." In *Bringing Transnational Relations Back In: Non-State Actors, Domestic Structures, and International Institutions*. Cambridge: Cambridge University Press, 1995.

R.L. (An American Gentleman of Matured Experience). "American View of the Eastern Question." In *Tracts on the Eastern Question 1863–79*. British Library, 1878.

Robbins, Keith. *Britishness and British Foreign Policy: A Lecture Delivered at the Foreign and Commonwealth Office 14 May 1997, FCO Historians Occasional Papers No. 14*. London: Foreign and Commonwealth Office, September 1997.

———. *Munich 1938*. London: Cassell & Company Ltd, 1968.

Roosen, William James. *The Age of Louis XIV: The Rise of Modern Diplomacy*. Cambridge: Schenkman Publishing Co., 1976.

———. "Early Modern Diplomatic Ceremonial: A Systems Approach." *The Journal of Modern History* 52, no. 3 (1980): 452–76.

Rosamond, Ben. *Theories of European Integration*. New York: Palgrave, 2000.

Rose, Gideon. "Neoclassical Realism and Theories of Foreign Policy." *World Politics* 51, no. 1 (1998): 144–72.

Rosenau, James N. "The Relocation of Authority in a Shrinking World," *Comparative Politics* 24, No. 3 (April 1992), 253–72.

Ross, George. *Jacques Delores and European Integration*. Oxford: Blackwell Publishers, 1995.

Ruggie, John Gerard. "What Makes the World Hang Together? Neo-Utilitarianism and the Social Constructivist Challenge." *International Organization* 52, no. 4 (1998): 855–85.

Rupp, George Hoover. *A Wavering Friendship: Russia and Austria 1876–1878*. Philadelphia: Porcupine Press, 1976.

Sandholtz, Wayne. "Choosing Union: Monetary Politics and Maastricht." *International Organization* 47, no. 1 (1993): 1–39.

Schwarzenberger, Georg. "The Rule of Law and the Disintegration of International Society." *American Journal of International Law* 33, no. 1 (1939): 56–77.

Scobie, H.M. *Enlargement of the EU and the Treaty of Nice*. London: Pearson Education Publications, 2002.

Sebenius, James K. "Challenging Conventional Explanations of International Cooperation: Negotiation Analysis and the Case of Epistemic Communities." *International Organization* 46, no. 1 (1992): 323–65.

Sen, B. *A Diplomat's Handbook of International Law and Practice*. Third ed. Dordrecht, The Netherlands: Martinus Nijhoff Publishers, 1988.

Seton-Watson, R.W. *Disraeli, Gladstone and the Eastern Question: A Study in Diplomacy and Party Politics*. London: Macmillan and Co., Limited, 1935.

Seymour, Charles. *Letters from the Paris Peace Conference*. New Haven, CT: Yale University Press, 1965.

Shannon, R.T. *Gladstone and the Bulgarian Agitation 1876*. Second ed. Sussex, UK: The Harvester Press, 1975.

Sharp, Alan. "Lord Curzon and the Foreign Office." In *The Foreign Office 1782–1982*, edited by Roger Bullen. Frederick, MD: University Publications of America, Inc., 1982.

Sharp, Walter. *French Civil Service: Bureaucracy in Transition*. New York: Macmillan 1931.

Shepsle, K. *Perspectives on Positive Political Economy*. Cambridge: Cambridge University Press, 1990.

Sherrington, Philippa. *The Council of Ministers: Political Authority in the European Union.* London: Pinter, 2000.

Simon, Sheldon W. "The Great Powers and Southeast Asia: Cautious Minuet or Dangerous Tango?" *Asian Survey* 25, no. 9 (1985): 918–42.

Slaughter, Anne-Marie. *A New World Order.* Princeton, NJ: Princeton University Press, 2004.

Snowden, Philip. "Democracy and Publicity in Foreign Affairs." In *Towards a Lasting Settlement,* edited by Charles Roden Buxton. London: George Allen & Unwin Ltd, 1915.

Snyder, Glenn, and Paul Diesing. *Conflict among Nations.* Princeton, NJ: Princeton University Press, 1977.

Snyder, Jack. "Anarchy and Culture: Insights from the Anthropology of War." *International Organization* 56, no. 1 (2002): 7–45.

Solana, Javier. "Preface." In *EU Security and Defence Policy: The First Five Years,* edited by Nicole Gnesotto. Paris: EU Institute for Security Studies, 2004.

Speeckaert, G.P. "Un siècle d'Expositions Universelles, leur influences sur les congres internationaux." *Bulletin NGO-ONG* 3, no. 10 (1951): 265–70.

Spence, David. "Foreign ministries in National and European context." In *Foreign Ministries: Change and Adaptation,* edited by Brian Hocking. New York: St. Martin's Press, 1999, pp. 247–68.

"Spies, Secrets and Diplomacy: Negotiations with the Russians." Paper presented at the FCO Historians Occasional Papers No. 15, London, January 1999.

Steele, David. *Lord Salisbury: A Political Biography.* London: UCL Press, 1999.

Steiner, Zara S. *The Foreign Office and Foreign Policy, 1898–1914.* London: The Ashfield Press, 1969.

Stephens, Waldo E. *Revisions of the Treaty of Versailles.* New York: Columbia University Press, 1939.

Stevens, Anne, and Handley Stevens. *Brussels Bureaucrats? The Administration of the European Union.* The European Union Series, edited by Neill Nugent, William E. Paterson, and Vincent Wright. New York: Palgrave, 2001.

Strang, Lord. *The Foreign Office.* London: George Allen & Unwin Ltd, 1957.

Suleiman, Ezra. *Dismantling Democratic States.* Princeton, NJ: Princeton University Press, 2003.

Sumner, B.H. *Russia and the Balkans 1870–80.* London: Archon Books, 1962.

Sverdrup, Ulf. "An Institutional Perspective on Treaty Reform: Contextualizing the Amsterdam and Nice Treaties." *Journal of European Public Policy* 9, no. 1 (2002): 120–40.

Sweet, Alec Stone, Wayne Sandholtz, and Neil Fligstein, eds. *The Institutionalization of Europe.* New York: Oxford University Press, 2001.

Tardieu, André. *The Truth about the Treaty.* London: Hodder and Stoughton, 1921.

Taylor, A.J.P. *How Wars End.* London: Hamish Hamilton, 1985.

——. *The Last of Old Europe.* London: Sidgwick & Jackson, 1976.

——. *The Struggle for Mastery in Europe 1848–1918.* Oxford: Clarendon Press, 1954.

Taylor, Robert. *Lord Salisbury.* London: British Political Biography, 1975.

Taylor, Telford. *Munich: The Price of Peace.* New York: Doubleday & Company, Inc., 1979.

Temperley, H.M.V. *A History of the Peace Conference of Paris.* Vol. 1. London: Oxford University Press, 1920.

Temperley, Harold, and Dame Lillian Penson. *A Century of Diplomatic Blue Books 1814–1914.* London: Frank Cass & Co. Ltd, 1966.

———. *Foundations of British Foreign Policy from Pitt (1792) to Salisbury (1902)*. Cambridge: Cambridge University Press, 1938.
Tsebelis, G. *Nested Games*. Berkeley and Los Angeles: University of California Press, 1990.
Tuck, Richard. "Grotius and Seldon." In *The Cambridge History of Political Thought 1450–1700*, edited by J.H. Burns and Mark Goldie. Cambridge: Cambridge University Press, 1991, pp. 499–529.
Ure, John, ed. *Diplomatic Bag*. Cambridge: Cambridge University Press, 1994.
Vahl, Remco. *Leadership in Disguise: The Role of the European Commission in EC Decision-Making on Agriculture in the Uruguay Round, Perspectives on Europe. Contemporary Interdisciplinary Research*. Sydney: Ashgate, 1997.
van der Mandere, H. Ch. G.J. "Grotius and International Society of to-Day." *The American Political Science Review* 19, no. 4 (1925): 800–8.
Wallace, Helen, and William Wallace. *Policy Making in the European Union*. New York: Oxford University Press, 2000.
Walters, H.L. "An Open Letter Addressed to the English Nation from Berlin." In *Tracts on the Eastern Question, 1863–79*. London, 1878.
Waltz, Kenneth. *Theory of International Politics*. Reading, MA: Addison-Wesley Pub. Co., 1979.
Wank, Solomon. *Doves and Diplomats: Foreign Offices and Peace Movements in Europe and America in the Twentieth Century*. Westport, CT: Greenwood Press, 1978.
Warwick, Paul. "Ideology, Culture, and Gamesmanship in French Politics." *The Journal of Modern History* 50, no. 4 (1978): 631–59.
Watson, Adam. *Diplomacy: The Dialogue between States*. London: Eyre Methuen, 1982.
Wendt, Alexander. *Social Theories of International Politics*. Cambridge: Cambridge University Press, 1999.
Westlake, Martin. *The Commission and the Parliament: Partners and Rivals in the European Policy-Making Process*. London: Butterworths, 1994.
———. *The Council of the European Union*. London: Cartermill International Ltd, 1995.
Whitcomb, Edward A. *Napoleon's Diplomatic Service*. Durham: Duke University Press, 1979.
White, John Albert. *Transition to Global Rivalry: Alliance Diplomacy and the Quadruple Entente, 1895–1907*. Cambridge: Cambridge University Press, 1995.
Willis, Virginia. *Britons in Brussels: Officials in the European Commission and Council Secretariat, Studies in European Politics 7*. London: Policy Studies Institute, 1983.
Winkler, G. Michael. "Coalition-Sensitive Voting Power in the Council of Ministers: The Case of Eastern Enlargement." *Journal of Common Market Studies* 36, no. 3 (1998): 391–404.
Worlledge, Heather. *Guide to the European Commission, EIA Guides to EU Institutions Series*. Manchester: European Information Association, 1996.
Wrigley, Chris, ed. *Struggles for Supremacy: Diplomatic Essays by A.J.P. Taylor*. Aldershot, UK: Ashgate, 2000.
Young, Oran R. "Political Leadership and Regime Formation: On the Development of Institutions in International Society." *International Organization* 45, no. 3 (1991): 281–308.
Yue, Chia Siow, and Joseph L.H. Tan. *ASEAN and EU: Forging New Linkages and Strategic Alliances*. Singapore: Institute of Southeast Asian Studies, 1997.
Zacher, Mark W. "The Territorial Integrity Norm: International Boundaries and the Use of Force." *International Organization* 55, no. 2 (2001): 215–50.
Ziegler, J. Nicholas. "Institutions, Elites, and Technological Change in France and Germany." *World Politics* 47, no. 3 (1995): 341–72.

Zito, Anthony R. "Epistemic Communities, Collective Entrepreneurship and European Integration." *Journal of European Public Policy* 8, no. 4 (2001): 585–603.

Zwaan, Jaap W. de. *The Permanent Representatives Committee: Its Role in European Union Decision-Making*. Amsterdam: Elsevier, 1995.

Zweifel, Thomas D. "Who Is Without Sin Cast the First Stone: The EU's Democratic Deficit in Comparison." *Journal of European Public Policy* 9, no. 6 (2002): 812–40.

Zweig, Stefan. *The World of Yesterday, An Autobiography*. New York: The Viking Press, 1943.

Index

Abdul Hamid, Sultan, 82, 86, 100
absolutism, 35, 62, 64, 80, 92
ad referendum agreement, 153
Adler, Emanuel, 1, 26, 27
agency, 65, 136–7, 180, 183–6, 187
   autonomy and, 2, 7, 17, 21, 28–9, 33, 70, 183–4
   bureaucratization and, 70–1
   at Congress of Berlin, 100–1, 103
   in Congress of Westphalia, 48, 54, 61–2, 63
   consensus and, 22
   diplomatic theories and, 7, 16, 17, 19, 21
   epistemic community and, 2, 4, 5–6
   European Union and, 33–4, 153–4
   of French diplomats, 52, 54
   Maastricht Treaty and, 174–5
   networks and, 23, 24–5
   persuasion and, 189
   against state instructions, 185–6
   vs. structure, 28–31
   Treaty of Versailles and, 33, 107
Aix-la-Chapelle, Congress of (1821), 76
Alexander II, Tsar of Russia, 82, 86
alliances, 68, 82, 88, 95, 202n3
   Treaty of Westphalia and, 48, 64, 66
   World War I, 105, 118, 119–20, 121
ambassadorship, 27, 146
   see also diplomats
Amsterdam, Treaty of, 20
Anderson, Anne, 146, 147, 154
Anderson, M. S., 39, 41, 73, 116, 117–18
   on professionalization, 71, 108–9
Andrássy, Julius, 86, 88, 91–4, 102, 103, 186
   Andrássy Note, 81, 83, 93
Anglo-Austrian Treaty (1878), 83
Anne of Austria (regent), 51–2
Antici group (Coreper), 143
Antoniades, Andreas, 25
appointments, 37, 115, 116
April 1st Circular (Salisbury), 90

aristocracy, 75, 92, 113–14, 117, 118
Asolo list, 156, 172
Austria-Hungary, 70, 83, 102, 111, 119–20, 129
   Bosnia and Herzegovina and, 95, 99
   Congress of Berlin and, 86, 91–4, 186
   Eastern Crisis and, 81–2
autonomy, 5, 10, 190, 207n31
   vs. agency, 2, 7, 17, 21, 28–9, 33, 183–4
   bureaucratization and, 70
   at Congress of Westphalia, 48, 49, 51, 56, 61, 202n95
   of European Union diplomats, 152
   of French diplomats, 54, 113
   structure and, 28–30
   telegraph and, 107

balance of power, 76, 108, 119, 126, 137
   at Congress of Berlin, 101–2
   at Congress of Westphalia, 62, 63, 64
   Eastern Crisis and, 82–3
   Thirty Years' War and, 35, 45–6
Balfour, Arthur J., 120, 121, 125, 131
Balkan crisis, 33, 98, 102, 119–20
   Austria-Hungary and, 91–2
   Congress of Berlin and, 69, 80–1, 88, 90
   nationalism in, 93
bankers, central, 2, 28
bargaining theory, 7–8, 11, 13, 19–22, 137
   Congress of Berlin and, 20, 102–3
   Maastricht Treaty and, 20, 141, 142, 148, 175, 176, 180
   Treaty of Westphalia and, 65
Bavaria, 45–6, 55, 185
Belgium, 120, 173, 175
   European Union and, 159, 162, 163, 164, 166, 167
Berlin, Congress of (1878), 68–105, 108, 139, 182, 186
   aftermath of, 103–4
   agency in, 100–1, 103

alliances and treaties affecting, 82–4
Austria-Hungary at, 91–4
bargaining theory and, 20, 102–3
Britain at, 88–91
bureaucratization prior to, 69–71
Eastern Crisis and, 80–4
epistemic community at, 97–100
evolution of diplomacy and, 33
France at, 96–7
Germany at, 87–8
international society in, 79–80
map of Europe after, 84
nationalism and, 68–9
negotiations of, 84–6
professionalism in, 71–2, 73–4
realism at, 101–2
Russia at, 94–6
society of diplomats in, 69–71, 73
technology and, 68, 77–9
unofficial diplomacy at, 98, 100
Berlin Memorandum (1876), 81, 83
Berlin, Treaty of (1878), 99, 123, 171
Bernstorff, Johann, 131
Berthelot, Philippe, 113, 121, 127–8, 129
Big Four, at Paris Peace Conference, 17, 122, 130, 137, 138, 183
ad hoc agenda and, 123
commissions and, 135–6
German delegation and, 132, 134
see also Clemenceau, Georges; Lloyd George, David; Orlando, Vittorio Emanuele; Wilson, Woodrow
bilateralism, 39, 48, 65, 139, 140, 182
Bismarck, Otto von, 115, 117, 119, 202nn2–3, 203n31
Andrássy and, 88, 92, 93–4, 102
at Congress of Berlin, 75–6, 81, 84–5, 86, 87–8, 104
Disraeli and, 87, 91
as mediator, 88, 98
professionalization and, 109–10
"Black Monday" (September 30, 1991), 167
Board of Selection (Great Britain), 115
Bohemia, 45–6, 58
Bolshevism, fear of, 129, 137
Bosnia, 81, 83, 88, 95, 99
bribery, 41–2, 54, 77
British Foreign Service, 72, 108, 112, 118
see also Great Britain

British Navy, 90, 126, 137
Brockdorff-Rantzau, Ulrich, 121, 126, 131–4
Budapest Conventions, 83
Bulgaria, 85, 88, 103
atrocities in, 78, 79, 81–2, 89, 91, 102, 103
Bull, Hedley, 16
bureaucracy and bureaucratization, 34, 74, 100, 175, 184
centralization and, 66, 69
democracy and, 186–7
institutionalization and, 30
in modern Europe, 140, 142, 143, 146, 154, 178
in nineteenth century, 33, 69–71
professionalism and, 70, 71–2, 104, 109–13
supranationalism and, 188
Burley, Anne-Marie, 148
Burton, J. W., 14
Bush, George W., 4, 190
Buzan, Barry, 16

Cairoli, Benedetto, 86
Callières, François de, 38–9, 64, 73, 109, 148
Cambon, Jules, 121, 129
Cambridge University, 114, 147
Carpenter, Rhys, 136
Catalonia, 55, 185
Catholicism, in Thirty Years' War, 45–7, 53
causality, 10, 25, 30
Cecil, Lamar, 110, 114, 115, 117
central bankers, 2, 28
centralization, 66, 69
CFSP, *see* Common Foreign and Security Policy (CFSP, European Union)
Chamber of Deputies (France), 113
Checkel, Jeffrey T., 17, 27, 28
Chigi, Fabio, 48, 61
China, 138
Chinda of Japan, 120, 121
Christians, in Balkans, 69, 81
Christoffersen, Poul, 142–3, 152, 153, 161, 178, 211n27
citizenship, European, 161, 162
class, 32, 33, 39
Clausewitz, Carl von, 9, 52

Clemenceau, Georges, 120, 121, 122, 124, 134, 183
  conference procedure and, 123
  French delegation and, 127–9
  German delegation and, 132, 133
  Lloyd George and, 125, 126
  realism of, 128, 137
  Wilson compared, 130
coded communications, 42
cognition, 23–4
Cold War, 26–7
collective action, 100
collective security arrangement, 66, 67
  see also Common Foreign and Security Policy (CFSP, European Union)
College of Commissioners, 14–15
collegiality, 45, 60, 72, 73, 74
  in Council of Europe, 143, 150
Committee of Permanent Representatives, *see* Coreper (Committee of Permanent Representatives)
Common Foreign and Security Policy (CFSP, European Union), 25, 158, 161–70, 173, 186
  Coreper and, 143, 145, 155, 164
  Dutch Presidency and, 166–7
  Euro-skepticism and, 179–80
  Luxembourg Presidency and, 165–6
  main controversy over, 156–7
  moving closer to, 162–3
  NATO and, 156, 159, 160, 164, 165, 166, 168–70
  points of agreement on, 163–5
  working out details of, 167–70
common good, 15, 27, 36, 79, 97
  as diplomatic goal, 31–2
  realism and, 101–2
  at Treaty of Westphalia, 61–2
commoners, as diplomats, 113, 115
communications, 16, 33, 99, 182
  nineteenth century, 32, 68–9
  seventeenth century, 36, 42–3
  telegraph, 32, 69, 70, 77, 78–9, 107
  see also correspondence; information sharing
Commynes, Philippe de, 108
competitiveness, 49–50
Conference on Security and Cooperation in Europe, 173
conference system, 36, 80, 104
Congress (US), 19, 120, 129
Conseil d'en Haut, 52
consensus, 5, 27, 103, 184, 211n27
  agency and, 22
  at Congress of Westphalia, 56–7
  in European Union, 143, 161
  within Holy Roman Empire, 58
Constantinople, 74, 78, 84, 89, 186
  Russian troops in, 98, 103
Constantinople Conference (1877), 82, 90
Constitution (EU), 180, 190
constructivism, 8, 13, 15, 25–6
Contarini, Alvise, 59, 61
cooperation, *see* international cooperation
Coreper (Committee of Permanent Representatives), 14–15, 33, 180, 190, 210n16, 212n65
  autonomy and agency in, 152–4
  CFSP and, 143, 145, 155, 164
  decision-making powers of, 142–3, 155
  diplomat social background and training, 145–8
  Maastricht Treaty and, 141–60, 174, 178, 183
  meeting frequency, 148–9
  professionalism in, 149–50
  secrecy in, 144, 176
  status of diplomats in, 151
  structure of, 143–5
  technology and, 152
correspondence, 69, 78, 89, 93
  at Congress of Berlin, 99
  at Congress of Westphalia, 54–5, 56, 60
  in seventeenth century, 35, 42–3
Council of Electors (Holy Roman Empire), 45, 58
Council of European Union, 30, 148, 157, 164, 172, 180
  collegiality in, 143, 150
  organizational chart of, 144
  policy decisions in, 143–5
  Presidency of, 162–3
Council of Four, 122, 126, 135
  see also Big Four, at Paris Peace conference

Council of Ministers (EU), 141, 143, 145, 153, 154, 176
  European Defense Concept, 156
Council of Ministers of Foreign Affairs, 135
Council of Ten, 105, 121, 122, 131, 135
Craig, Gordon A., 31, 108
Crimean coalition, 80–1
Crimean War, 32, 68
Croxton, Derek, 52
Cyprus Convention (1878), 83

d'Avaux, Count, Claude de Mesmes, 52–5
Day, Clive, 135, 136
decision-making, 34, 55, 131, 188
  ad hoc, 106, 121, 123–4
  in European Union, 142–3, 144–5, 155
  see also consensus
Delors, Jacques, 142, 155, 177
democratic deficit, 141, 162, 176, 188, 208n50, 210n6
democratic selection, 113, 115
democratization, 27, 68, 107, 138, 142, 182
  bureaucracy and, 186–7
  of decision-making, 124
  supranationalism and, 188–9
Denmark, 110, 147, 159, 162, 170
  federalism in EU and, 172, 173, 175, 188
Derby, Lord, 81, 89
dialogue, diplomacy and, 3–4
  see also communications
Dillon, E.J., 136
DiMaggio, Paul, 24
diplomacy, 31–7
  coercive, 20–1
  defined, 3–4
  evolution of, 31–4
  as foreign policy, 3–5, 13–14
  globalization and, 12
  informal, 36, 60
  modernization of, 36–7, 67, 71–3, 80
  new, 31–3, 106, 124, 138, 182
  old, 106, 124, 131
  open, 119
  process of, 3–5, 11
  see also secret diplomacy

diplomatic society
  European Union treaty and, 142–3
  Treaty of Versailles and, 107–9
  see also social culture
diplomats
  as actors, 8, 25
  as collective, 17
  cooperation and, 4
  defined, 1
  disadvantages to, 37–8
  goals of, 17, 27, 31
  ideal qualities of, 38–9
  motivations of, 43
  in nineteenth century, 32–3
  persuasion of statesmen by, 29
  as plenipotentiaries, 10, 24, 39, 66
  political theories and, 7–8
  ranking of, 76
  rise of resident, 39–40
  selection of, 33, 37
  in seventeenth century, 32
  statesmen and, 19, 22, 24, 33
  structural constraints on, 28–31
  as transmission belts, 14
  as transnational network, 28
  in twentieth century, 33–4
  see also agency
Disraeli, Benjamin, 76, 78, 79, 81, 85–6
  Bismarck and, 87, 91
  at Congress of Berlin, 90–1, 103
  Gorchakov compared to, 96
  Queen Victoria and, 89, 103, 205n65
Dobbin, Frank, 23
domestic factors, 14–15, 18, 27
Dublin, European Council in (1990), 155
Dulles, Alan, 136
Durkheim, Emile, 24, 28
Dutasta, Henri, 127–8, 129
Dutasta, Paul, 122
Dutch Presidency, 159, 166–7
  see also Maastricht Treaty (1992); Netherlands (Dutch, Holland)

Eastern Crisis (1875–1878), 69, 75, 77, 78, 80–4, 89
  alliances and treaties of, 82–4
  Russia and, 80–2, 94, 102
Ebert, Frederich, 126
École Libre des Sciences Politiques, 114

École Nationale d'Administration
    (ENA), 147
Edict of Restitution (1629), 46
education, 39, 114–15, 118, 146–7
    see also training
elites, nineteenth century, 68–9, 75
    see also aristocracy
Ellemann-Jensen, Uffe, 173, 177
Elliott, Lord, 78
Elster, Jon, 30
English language, 76–7, 86, 151
English school, 15–17
Entente alliance, 83
    see also Triple Entente (France, Great
        Britain, Russia)
epistemic community, 1–12, 13, 180,
    182–8, 190
    comparison, 181
    at Congress of Berlin, 97–100
    constituents of, 10
    constructivism and, 25–6
    diplomatic agency and, 183–6
    in European Union, 150, 152–4, 157,
        170–1, 176, 178
    historical trends, 186–8
    networks and, 23–5, 27–8
    norms and, 29–30
    in seventeenth century, 36, 37, 45
    strength of, 2, 5–6, 9, 10–12, 22
    structural constraints and, 28–30
    theory of, 1–3, 5–8, 11
    Treaty of Versailles and, 129,
        134–6, 137
    Treaty of Westphalia and, 48, 60–1
Ersbøll, Niels, 161, 162, 166, 177
Erzberger, Matthias, 121, 131–2
European Commission, 154, 165,
    166, 177
European Council of Rome (1990), 156
European Court of Judges, 148
European Defense Concept, 156
    see also Common Foreign and Security
        Policy (CFSP, European Union)
European Economic Community, 161
European Parliament, 151, 154, 157,
    167, 172
    CFSP and, 158, 164, 165, 166, 170
European Political Cooperation (EPC),
    157, 158, 163
European Union (EU), 25, 72, 140–1, 187

allegiances within, 59
Council of Ministers, 141, 143–5, 153,
    154, 156, 162–3, 176
democracy and supranationalism in,
    14–15, 188–9
diplomat social background and
    training, 145–8
epistemic communities and, 7–8
Euro-skepticism and, 179–80
evolution of diplomacy and, 33–4
institutional structure of, 30
international relations and, 190
languages of, 151
location of institutions of, 41
power and, 17
Presidency, 162–3
research and, 8
Security and Defense Policy, 179–80
worldview of, 5
    see also Coreper (Committee of
        Permanent Representatives);
        Maastricht Treaty (1992)
"EU-speak", 151
examinations, 72, 114–15, 118, 146, 147
exclusivity, 73, 74
expertise, 1, 74
    see also professionalization
Eyskens, Mark, 173, 177

family-resemblance concepts, 9, 10
family ties, in diplomatic corps, 114–15
federalism, in European Union, 160–1,
    166, 167, 170, 172, 175, 189
Ferdinand III (Holy Roman Emperor),
    45, 48, 58–9, 64
financial compensation, 54, 71–2,
    111–12
    in seventeenth century, 37–8, 41–2
Finnemore, Martha, 30
Fligstein, Neil, 24
Fonblanque, J.R. de, 161, 162
Foreign Minister (France), 115
*Foreign Ministries of the European Union:
    Integrating Diplomats* (Hocking and
    Spence), 142
foreign policy, 3–5, 13–14, 106
Fouchet Plan, 156
Fourteen Points (Wilson), 120, 123, 126,
    129, 130, 133
France, 110, 113, 116, 122, 175, 188

aristocracy in, 114
at Congress of Berlin, 86, 96–7
diplomatic decline in, 141
diplomatic social life in, 75
diplomatic staff, 53–4
European Union and, 155, 159, 161, 165–6, 167, 169, 170
Maastricht Treaty and, 171–2
Napoleon's reforms in, 71–2
at Paris Peace Conference, 127–9, 137
professionalism in, 115–16, 147
Thirty Years' War and, 46–7
Treaty of Westphalia and, 17, 48–9, 51–5, 59–60, 62, 63–4, 65, 185
in Triple Entente, 119, 120
war with Germany, 96, 101, 102
Francis Ferdinand, assassination of, 119
Francis Joseph, Emperor of Austria-Hungary, 86, 91, 92, 103, 186
Franco-Prussian War, 96, 101, 102
Frederick William of Brandenburg, 57, 185
French language, 76, 151
functionalism, 15–16, 19, 194n8

garbage-can theory, 20
General Affairs Council (EU), 151, 164
geopolitical approach, 20
Germany, 68, 96, 117, 122, 141, 188–9
at Congress of Berlin, 75–6, 86, 87–8
diplomatic families in, 114–15
diplomatic professionalization in, 109–10, 111, 115
European Union and, 155, 159, 161, 165–6, 167
foreign service reform in, 72–3
Maastricht Treaty and, 171–2, 174, 175
at Paris Peace Conference, 124, 131–4, 137, 138
in Triple Alliance, 119, 120
war reparations from, 123, 126, 128, 129, 130–1
war with France, 96, 101, 102
gift giving, 41–2, 77
Gladstone, William, 77, 89, 91, 205n66
Glarbo, Kenneth, 15, 25
globalization, 12, 16, 139
Gnesotto, Nicole, 180

Gondomar, Count of, Diego Sarmiento de Acuña, 38
Gonzalez, Felipe, 173, 177
Gorbachev, Mikhail, 26
Gorchakov, Alexander, 81, 85–6, 88, 92, 102
Andrássy and, 83, 93–4
Bismarck and, 203n31
Shuvalov and, 94–6
Grandes Écoles, Les, 147
Granville, Lord, 70, 85, 89
Great Britain, 68, 78, 116, 119, 149
at Congress of Berlin, 85, 86, 88–91, 99, 102, 103
diplomatic decline in, 140–1
Eastern Crisis and, 81–2
European Union and, 159, 161, 162, 167, 170
Foreign Service, 72, 108, 112, 118
Maastricht Treaty and, 172, 173, 174, 175
at Paris Peace Conference, 120, 121, 122, 125–7, 136–7
professionalization in, 110, 111–13, 115
see also British Foreign Service
Great Powers of Europe, 68, 69, 81, 88
Congress of Berlin and, 80, 82
Great War, 17, 117
see also Supreme War Council (World War I)
Greece, 159, 173
Grotius, Hugo, 38, 44
group dynamics, 22, 23
Gunning, Peter, 150, 151
Gustavus Adolphus, King of Sweden, 46, 55, 56

Haas, Ernst B., 25–6
Haas, Peter M., 1, 26, 27
Habsburg dynasty, 46–7, 57, 64
see also Austria-Hungary
Hamburg, Treaty of, 47, 200n40
Hamilton, Keith, 31, 79, 106, 116, 139
Hankey, Maurice, 122, 128
Hardinge, Lord Charles, 121, 125, 207n30
Haro, Don Luis de, 41
Hayes-Renshaw, Fiona, 147, 176
Haymerle, Baron, Heinrich Karl von, 93

Headlam-Morley, James, 121, 127
Herzegovina, 81, 83, 88, 95
Hill, David J., 63
historical sociology, 8–9
Hitler, Adolf, 116
Hocking, Brian, 142, 145
Holy Roman Empire, 41, 47, 48–9, 50, 54, 58–60, 66, 199n38
  Electors of, 45, 58, 200n39
  military power of, 63, 64
  Thirty Years' War and, 45–7, 66
House, Edward M., 121, 130
Hungary, 92, 93

idealism, 79, 91–2
identity
  diplomatic, 31–2
  European, 79
  formation of, 73–5
  transnational, 16
IGC, *see* intergovernmental conference (IGC)
Ignatiev, Nicholas, 82, 94–5, 103
Ikenberry, G. John, 1
immunity, ambassadorial, 44–5
imperialism, 68–9
informal diplomacy, 36, 60
information sharing, 3, 33, 41, 78, 98
  in seventeenth century, 36, 39, 42, 43
  see also communications
institutionalization, 23–4, 25, 28, 30
instructions to diplomats, 6, 22, 27, 60
  at Congress of Westphalia, 42, 44, 49, 54–5
  French delegation and, 51, 52, 62
interdependence theory, 18, 20
intergovernmental conference (IGC), 155, 156, 165, 187, 212n65
intergovernmentalism, 14–15
international cooperation, 6, 31–2, 33, 75
  amelioration bias and, 34
  constructivism and, 25
  diplomatic process and, 4–5
  epistemic community and, 1–2
  foreign policy and, 3
  norm of, 27, 80
  power and, 4, 17
  realist diplomacy and, 13–17
  two-level game model and, 18

international–domestic nexus, 18
International Labor Organization, 134
international law, 44, 80
International Organization (journal), 1–2
international organizations, 12, 16, 30–1, 34, 104, 139–40
  see also specific organizations
international relations, 26, 43–4, 163, 190
international society, 14, 117–18, 140, 182
  at Congress of Berlin, 79–80, 101
  at Congress of Westphalia, 61–2
  emergence of, 16, 33, 35–6
  in seventeenth century, 37, 38, 40, 42, 44
  transnational groups and, 12
interpretivism, 9
Iraq war, 4
Ireland, 159, 167, 170, 173, 175
Italy, 37, 55, 86, 111, 119, 141
  European Union and, 159, 163, 165, 167–8
  Maastricht Treaty and, 172, 175

Jervis, Robert, 26
Jones, Raymond A., 112

Kapstein, Ethan Barnaby, 2
Károlyi, Count, 93
Kassim, Hussein, 21
Katz, Richard, 18
Katzenstein, Peter J., 18
Keck, Margaret, 27
Keohane, Robert O., 18, 26
Kerr, John, 173, 176, 177
Kerr, Philip, 121, 127
Keylor, William R., 124
Kleinman, Ruth, 52
Kohl, Helmut, 167, 171, 175, 177
Krane, Johannes, 59
Kristina, Queen of Sweden, 55–7, 62, 64, 79
  Oxenstierna and, 55–6, 65, 185

Labor Party (Britain), 126
Lamberg, Johann Maximilian, 59
Langhorne, Richard, 31, 79, 106, 116, 139
language, 53, 76–7, 86, 151, 210n16
  facility with, 114, 115, 117

Lansdowne, Lord (Henry Charles Keith Petty-Fitzmaurice), 115
Lansing, Robert, 120, 121, 129–30, 131
Lauren, Paul Gordon, 74–5
Layard, A.H., 70, 74, 99, 101
Layard Papers, 69
League of Nations, 123, 126, 127, 134, 137, 138
  Wilson and, 129, 130
Leeper, Allen, 136
Légion d'Honneur, 71
Lentin, Antony, 125
Lersner, Kurt von, 121, 131, 132, 133, 134
letter writing, *see* correspondence
Lewis, Jeffrey, 144, 150
Lichnowsky, Karl Max von, 115
Lloyd George, David, 122, 124, 133
  British delegation and, 120, 121, 125–6, 137
  moderation of, 126, 129, 130
Longueville, Duke de (Henri II d'Orleans), 40, 48, 52–5, 60
Lossky, Andrew, 51
Louis XIV, King of France, 51, 54, 66
Lovin, Clifford R., 122, 133, 138
loyalty (allegiance), 58–9
Luard, Evan, 62–3
Luxembourg Presidency, 159, 165–6
Lybyer, Dr, 136

Maastricht Treaty (1992), 139–78, 183, 186, 188
  alternative explanations, 175–6
  bargaining theory and, 20, 141, 142, 148, 175, 176, 180
  Common Foreign and Security Policy, 143, 145, 155, 156–7, 161–70, 179
  Coreper and, 141–60, 174, 178, 183
  diplomatic actions in, 157–71
  diplomatic agency in, 174–5
  Dutch Presidency, 159, 166–7
  federalism and, 160–1, 166, 167, 170, 172, 175, 189
  listing of statesmen and diplomats in, 177
  Luxembourg Presidency, 159, 165–6
  negotiations, 156–7
  negotiations leading up to, 154–6
  ratification process for, 174

society of diplomats, 142–3
statesmen at, 171–3
twentieth-century diplomacy, 139–42
see also Coreper (Committee of Permanent Representatives)
MacDonnell Commission, 112–13
McNamara, Kathleen, 27–8, 30
Major, John, 171, 172, 173, 175–6, 177
Makino of Japan, 120, 121
Mangone, Gerald J., 31, 32, 104
Marshall, Peter, 140
Marston, F.S., 121
Martens, Wilfried, 173, 177
Masset, Jean-Pierre, 147, 149–51, 154
Mattingly, Garrett, 31, 43
Mattli, Walter, 148
Mayer, Arno J., 133
Mazarin, Cardinal Jules, 41, 48, 50, 51–5, 64, 185
media, 77–8
mediator, 61, 75
  Bismarck as, 88, 98
meetings
  agency and, 6
  bilateral, 48
  face-to-face, 36, 106, 116–17
  frequency of, 5, 36, 39–40, 43, 116–17, 148–9
  see also summitry
Menon, Anand, 21
mercantilism, 35, 43
meritocracy, 33, 108, 109, 118, 146
  in modern Europe, 182, 183, 187
  professionalism and, 71, 73
Mertens group (Coreper), 143
methodology, 8–12
  of bargaining theory, 21
Middle Ages, diplomacy in, 35, 66
military power, 62–4
Ministers for Foreign Affairs (EU), 162
Mitterrand, François, 167, 172, 175, 177
modernization, 36–7, 67, 71–3, 80
monarchy, 43
  see also absolutism; *specific monarchs*
Montenegro, 81
Moravcsik, Andrew, 15, 20, 176
multilateralism, 8, 50, 65, 182, 183

Napoleon, 71–2, 110
nationalism, 68–9, 81, 82, 91, 103

nationalism – *continued*
  in Balkans, 93
  supranationalism, 14–15, 180, 188–9
navette (shuttle service), 144
Neilson, Francis, 82
neofunctionalism, 19
neoliberal institutionalists, 3, 14
neorealism, 7–8, 11, 13, 62, 180
  see also realism
Netherlands (Dutch, Holland), 46–7, 110, 175
  European Union and, 159, 160, 163, 164, 166–7, 170
  Spain and, 46, 48, 64
networks, 23–5, 36
  constructivism and, 25
  European Union and, 7
  norms and, 30
  transnational, 12, 27–8
new diplomacy, 31–3, 106, 124, 138, 182
Nicolaïdis, Kalypso, 20
Nicolson, Harold, 3, 130, 136–7
nongovernmental organizations, 68
norm entrepreneurs, 8, 23, 30
norms, 5–6, 39, 44, 74
  protocol as, 17, 29, 40–2, 75
  shared among diplomats, 5, 29–30, 37, 65
  violation of, 43
North Atlantic Treaty Organization (NATO), 156, 159, 160, 164, 165, 168–70, 173
  United States and, 166, 170, 172, 190
null hypothesis, 11, 13, 62, 65
  see also realism
Nye, Joseph S., Jr., 18

old diplomacy, 106, 124, 131
On the Manner of Negotiating with Princes (Callières), 38–9, 148
open diplomacy, 106, 119
  see also secret diplomacy
organizational theory, 13, 24
Orlando, Vittorio Emanuele, 120, 121, 122, 130, 133, 183
Orthodox Christianity, 69, 81
Osiander, Andreas, 58–9
Ottoman Empire, 69, 82, 84, 98
outcomes, 3
  agency and, 6
  efficient, 17
  minimalism and, 15
  negative, 27
  political theories and, 7
  predetermined, 14
  prediction of, 11, 20
Oxenstierna, Axel, 55–6, 57, 65, 185
Oxenstierna, Johan, 56–8
Oxford University, 114, 147

Page, Edward, 147
Pan-Slavism, 68–9, 82, 94–5, 102, 103
  Serbia and, 81, 84
Pareto optimum, 2, 11, 18, 21, 25
Paris Peace Conferences, 33, 146
  see also Versailles, Treaty of
Paris, Treaty of (1856), 68, 80–1, 83, 85, 96
Parliament (Britain), 174
Parliament (EU), *see* European Parliament
Pasha, Carathéodory, 88
peace, 31–2, 36, 79, 101
persuasion, 4, 22, 24, 29, 38, 60
Philip IV, King of Spain, 46, 49, 64
Philippsburg, 55, 65, 185
Pichon, Stephen, 120, 121
Pierson, Paul, 11
plenipotentiaries, 10, 24, 39, 66
  at Congress of Berlin, 85, 86
  see also autonomy
Political Committee (EU), 159, 160
political science, 1–2, 4–5, 7–9
Pollack, Mark A., 21
Pomerania, 65, 185
Portugal, 160, 170, 173, 175
Powell, Colin, 4
Powell, Walter, 24
power, 15, 66, 68, 94
  absolutism and, 35, 62
  cooperation and, 4, 17
  international society and, 16
  networks and, 23–4
  outcomes and, 3
  perceptions of, 16–17
  realism and, 13–17, 62–3
Practice of Diplomacy, The (Hamilton and Langhorne), 139
precedence, 23, 67, 76
  at Congress of Westphalia, 53, 56

in seventeenth century, 17, 37, 40–1, 48
preferences, 20, 22, 25
prestige, 74, 75
  see also status
Princip, Gavrilo, 119
principal–agent theory, 19
procedure, 23, 37, 60–1, 75, 123–4
  see also protocol
process tracing, 10, 20
professionalization, 67, 73–5, 118, 138, 146, 190
  bureaucratization and, 70, 71–2, 104, 108–13
  defined, 198n3
  epistemic community and, 5, 9, 182–3, 187–8
  identity-formation and, 79
  in modern Europe, 142, 149–50, 178
  in nineteenth century, 33
  organizational fields and, 24
  in seventeenth century, 35–8, 43, 44, 45
propaganda, 118, 119
property qualification, 112
Protestantism, 45–7, 59
protocol, 48, 54, 184
  as norm, 17, 29, 40–2, 75
  see also procedure
public opinion, 69
  on Bulgarian atrocities, 81–2, 89, 91, 102, 103
  Congress of Westphalia and, 52
  Coreper and, 144
  domestic pressures on, 27
  media and, 78
  Paris Peace Conference and, 33, 118–19, 122, 124–5, 126, 128, 132, 134, 138
Putnam, Robert, 18, 22, 26

Quai d'Orsay, 75, 97, 113, 116, 127

ratification process, 18, 174
rational-choice theory, 8, 19, 20
realism, 3, 13–17, 26, 52, 80, 179
  allegiances and, 59
  of Clemenceau, 128, 137
  at Congress of Berlin, 91, 101–2
  critique of, 16–17
  neorealism, 7–8, 11, 13, 62, 180
  null hypothesis of, 11, 13, 62, 65
  socially constructed, 9, 25
  structural, 15–16
  subjective, 28
  in Treaty of Westphalia, 62–5
reasoned request, 153
Redesdale, Earl of (John Thomas Freeman-Mitford), 79–80
reform, 108–9, 110–12, 118, 183
  in Germany, 72–3
  in modern Europe, 142, 146
Reichstadt Agreement, 83, 84, 85
religion, 32
  in Thirty Years' War, 45–7, 50–1, 58, 59–60, 66
Repgen, Konrad, 50
Republican Party (US), 129, 130
research, design of, 8–12
reservation, 153
resident ambassadors, 74, 75, 76, 85, 96, 100
  establishment of, 32, 37
Richelieu, Cardinal Armand Jean, 38, 51, 62, 66
Risse, Thomas, 20–1, 26–7, 28, 148
Rome, Treaty of (1957), 141, 179–80
Rosenau, James N., 18
Rosenhane, Schering, 48, 57
Rubens, Peter Paul, 38
Russell, Lord John, 70
Russell, Lord Odo, 93, 96, 116
Russia, 33, 79, 83, 92, 111, 186
  "Big Bulgaria" and, 84, 85, 91
  at Congress of Berlin, 94–6, 103
  Constantinople and, 98, 103
  Eastern Crisis and, 80–2, 94, 102
  in Triple Entente, 119, 120
Rytter, Jakob, 161

Saburi, Sadao, 122
St. Vallier, M. de, 96–7
salaries, 111–12
  see also financial compensation
Salisbury, Lord, 72, 85, 90–1, 98, 103
  Layard and, 100
  Shuvalov and, 83
Salvius, Johan Adler, 56–8, 185
San Stefano, Treaty of (1878), 79, 82, 83, 85, 90, 94, 95

Schwarz, Albert, 133
scrutiny reservation, 153
Sebenius, James K., 26
second-image theory, 18
secrecy, lack of, 96, 121, 138
secret diplomacy, 50, 74, 106, 124, 139
  in Congress of Berlin, 76, 82, 83, 92
  in Coreper, 144, 176
Secretary General (France), 113
self-interest, 17, 31
  at Congress of Westphalia, 64, 65
  intergovernmentalism and, 15
  neorealism and, 14
  vs. norms, 30
  principal–agent diplomacy and, 19
Serbia, 81, 84, 92, 93, 119–20
Servien, Abel, 52–5
Seton-Watson, R.W., 91
Seymour, Charles, 121, 128, 130–1, 136
Shuvalov, Peter I., 83, 94–6, 103
Sikkink, Kathryn, 27–8, 30
Slaughter, Anne-Marie, 27–8
Slavs, *see* Pan-Slavism
Smith, Adam, 28
Smuts, General Jan, 126–7
social background, 5, 23, 24, 37–9
  see also aristocracy
social culture, 75, 77, 115, 117–18
  see also status
sociology, 13
  agency and, 29
  historical, 9
  networks and, 23–5
  structures and, 28
Solana, Javier, 179–80
Sonnino, Giorgio Sidney, 120, 121
Soviet Union, 26
  see also Russia
Spain, 53, 60, 160, 163–4, 167
  Dutch and, 46, 48, 64
  Maastricht Treaty and, 172, 173, 175
  Thirty Years' War and, 46–7
  Treaty of Westphalia and, 17, 48–9, 63–4
Spence, David, 142
state, 66
  defined, 51, 69
  see also nationalism
statesmen, 19, 33, 44, 106
  at Congress of Berlin, 85–6

networks and, 28
persuasion of, 4, 22, 24, 29, 38, 60
power-sharing by, 68–9
predominant role of, 107
  see also specific statesmen
status, 5, 66–7, 73–4
  power and, 24
  in seventeenth century, 37–8, 40, 42
  Treaty of Versailles and, 12
Stendevad, Ejner, 153–4
structural constraints, on diplomacy, 28–31
structuralists, 5, 16
  see also under realism
subsidiarity rule, 144–5, 171
sufficiency minimum, 10
summitry, 33, 106–7, 138, 139, 183
Sumner, B.H., 96
supranationalism, 14–15, 180, 188–9
Supreme Peace Council, 105
  see also Council of Ten
Supreme War Council (World War I), 105, 121, 124, 127, 128, 183
Sverdrup, Ulf, 22
Sweden, 37, 46–7, 106–7, 110
  Pomerania and, 65, 185
  Treaty of Westphalia and, 17, 48, 55–8, 62, 63–4
Switzerland, 50, 110, 176

Tardieu, André, 121, 123, 130, 135
  procedural planning by, 127, 128–9
Taylor, A.J.P., 82, 101
technocracy, 34
technology, 12, 32–3, 152, 182
  Congress of Berlin and, 68, 77–9
  diplomatic autonomy and, 106, 107
  international society and, 16
  meeting frequency and, 116–17
  typewriters, 72
  see also communications
telegraph, 32, 69, 70, 77, 78–9, 107
Testament Politique (Richelieu), 38
theories of diplomacy, 13–19
  constructivism, 8, 13, 15, 25–6
  English School, 15–17
  epistemic community and, 1–3, 5–8, 11
  intergovernmentalism, 14–15
  principal–agent theory, 19

realism and, 13–14
two-level game diplomacy, 17–18
see also bargaining theory
Thirty Years' War (1618–1648), 35, 45–7, 58
see also Westphalia, Treaty of (1648)
Three Emperors' League, 83, 88, 95
Tit-for-Tat strategy, 20
training, 5, 32
  in nineteen century, 71–3
  old school, 95
  in seventeenth century, 36, 39, 48
  see also education
Tranholm-Mikkelsen, Jeppe, 147, 148–9, 154, 157, 210n16
transaction costs, 2, 3, 7, 16, 17, 19, 21
transnationalism, 12, 25–8, 75
  epistemic community and, 6, 11, 25–6, 97
  power of, 31
  professionalism and, 109
  in seventeenth century, 37, 39, 44–5
transparency, 33
  see also secrecy, lack of
Trauttmansdorff, Maximilian von, 57, 59
travel and transportation, 33, 38, 68, 76, 144
Treasury Department (Great Britain), 112, 118
triangle (procedural) model, 61
Tripartite Treaty (Britain, France Austria), 80, 83
Triple Alliance (Austria-Hungary, Germany, Italy), 119–20
Triple Entente (France, Great Britain, Russia), 113, 119–20, 133
trust, 38, 43, 74
Turkey, 74, 79, 83, 88, 186
  autonomy of, 89, 90, 102, 103
  at Congress of Berlin, 86
  Eastern Crisis and, 80–2
  two-level game diplomacy, 17–18
Tyrrell, William, 121, 126

unilateralism, 33, 190
United Nations (UN), 4, 165
  Security Council, 162, 163, 169
United States, 17, 114, 122, 127, 176
  Congress, 19, 120, 129
  European integration and, 164, 166, 170, 172
  at Paris Peace Conference, 121, 129–31, 132, 136–7
  unilateralism of, 190
  in World War I, 105
university education, 114–15, 146–7

Venice, 37
Versailles, Treaty of, 33, 105–38, 171
  agency in, 136–7
  causes of World War I and, 119–20
  and climate of times, 105–7
  epistemic community and commissions of, 134–6, 137
  failures of, 17
  France and, 127–9
  Great Britain and, 125–7
  negotiations, 120–2
  procedural and organizational failures at, 123–5
  professionalization in, 108–13, 138
  public opinion and, 118–19, 122, 124–5, 126, 128, 132, 134, 138
  social background and training, 113–16
  society of diplomats and, 107–9
  status and, 12
  status of diplomats prior to, 117–18
  technology and meeting frequency, 116–17
  United States and, 129–31
Victoria, Queen of Britain, 86, 89, 103, 205n65
Vienna, Congress of (1815), 31, 76, 124, 139
Vienna, Treaty of, 123, 188
Von Baden, Max, 120

Waddington, William Henry, 78, 95, 96–7
Walewski, Alexandre Joseph, Comte de, 72
war, 21, 32–3
  see also peace; *specific war*
Warburg, Max, 132
Watson, Adam, 3–4, 16, 38, 39, 61
wealth requirement, 113–14, 115
Weber, Max, 72
Western European Union (WEU), 172, 173

Westlake, Martin, 144, 150
Westphalia, Treaty of (1648), 17, 35–67, 118, 123, 171, 182
   aftermath, 65–7
   agency in, 48, 54, 61–2, 63
   communication technology in, 42–3
   Congress of Westphalia and, 29, 48–65, 79
   diplomatic agency in, 185
   diplomatic professionalization prior to, 35–8
   epistemic community, 60–1
   evolution of diplomacy, 32
   France in, 51–5
   Holy Roman Empire and, 48, 50, 54, 58–60
   international society prior to, 35–6
   lead up to, 45–7
   meeting frequency in, 36, 39–40, 43
   negotiations, 48–51
   professional status and norms, 40–2
   realism in, 62–5
   Sweden in, 17, 48, 55–8, 62, 63–4
Wilhelm I, Kaiser of Germany, 86, 88
Wilhelm II, Kaiser of Germany, 109, 123
Wilson, Woodrow, 119, 122, 124, 133, 137, 183
   on concessions to Germany, 131
   Fourteen Points of, 120, 123, 126, 129, 130, 133
   on Lloyd George, 125
   on open diplomatic process, 107–8
win-sets, 18, 22
women, diplomatic work of, 111, 146, 187
World War I, 105–9, 119–20
   see also Versailles, Treaty of
worldviews, 5–6, 65, 101

zero-sum gain, 17, 35, 62, 64, 80
Zito, Anthony R., 22
Zweifel, Thomas D., 176